THE OXFORD
UNIVERSITY PRESS

'University Printing House', an engraving from a sepia drawing by F. Mackenzie, c. 1832

THE
OXFORD
UNIVERSITY
PRESS

AN INFORMAL HISTORY

PETER SUTCLIFFE

1978

OXFORD
AT THE CLARENDON PRESS

Oxford University Press, Walton Street, Oxford OX2 6DP

OXFORD LONDON GLASGOW
NEW YORK TORONTO MELBOURNE WELLINGTON
IBADAN NAIROBI DAR ES SALAAM LUSAKA CAPE TOWN
KUALA LUMPUR SINGAPORE JAKARTA HONG KONG TOKYO
DELHI BOMBAY CALCUTTA MADRAS KARACHI

© *Peter Sutcliffe 1978*

British Library Cataloguing in Publication Data
Sutcliffe, P. H.
    The Oxford University Press
    1. Oxford University Press—History
    I. Title
    338.7′6′107050942574   Z232.098   77–30690
    ISBN 0-19-951084-9

*Printed in Great Britain
at the University Press, Oxford
by Vivian Ridler
Printer to the University*

PREFACE

THIS book deals for the most part with the period after 1860, when the Delegates of the Oxford University Press conceded that as a deliberative body they were ill-equipped to administer directly a growing publishing business, and appointed first a London publisher and then an executive officer in Oxford to conduct their affairs for them. The Delegates, under the Chairmanship of the Vice-Chancellor of the day, remain in charge now as then, and since 1867 their Finance Committee has acted as a committee of general management. They are responsible to the University, of which the Press is a department. But during this period not only the day-to-day running of the Press but also, except in broad terms, its publishing policy devolved gradually but increasingly on the Secretary and the senior officers in Oxford and London. The Oxford University Press in London and in New York came to enjoy considerable tactical independence of the parent body. By 1860 the Press already had a long history, chiefly as a Bible house, and prolonged survival of large institutions is abnormal. This one has often appeared a little ramshackle. Yet not only did it survive: for over a century it has been in a state of continuous growth both at home and overseas, in what might be regarded as its old age. The process continues.

Many great works published by the Press receive no mention here. Lists of book titles can make tedious reading; and the names of many of the scholars who wrote these books are now forgotten by all except their direct heirs working in the same field. They made their contribution, broke new ground, and have been absorbed into one tradition or another. Nevertheless it was upon them that the reputation of the Clarendon Press depended, once the skills of the University Printers and their learned readers had come to be taken for granted. After 1900, books published by the London Business under the Frowde, Milford, and Cumberlege imprints reached out beyond the academic world. They were intended for the more general reader, for the 'incurious lover of literature'. They were also intended to be profitable, so that together with the Bible they could help to subsidize the publication in Oxford of learned books unlikely to be remunerative.

It has been remarked that great epochs of literature came and went, that a scientific revolution transformed the intellect of the civilized world, and that all these momentous events passed Oxford by. There is some truth in the charge. Sir Thomas Bodley did not allow the works of Shakespeare in his Library. Marx, Darwin, and Freud fitted into no curriculum. The University, and in consequence its Press, has not until recent times regarded itself as closely associated with the world outside its walls. It is a relatively new concept that contemporary literature has anything to teach. The primary object of scholarship was—and basically still is—to cherish and nurture the ancient heritage. Mark Pattison, no philistine, wrote in 1855, 'We do not want to turn out poets or philosophers. If such persons are of any use, nature will provide them.' Nature has provided an abundance of scholars to do justice to the neglected giants of the past, and no major writer has escaped the attention of the modern Press: to minor and often neglected writers it has been more than generous.

The history of the Press before 1860 has in this book been compressed as far as is compatible with intelligibility. No doubt distortion has occurred in consequence, and some generalizations may appear sweeping. The earlier period has been well covered elsewhere. The first volume (to the year 1780) of Harry Carter's *A History of the Oxford University Press* (1975) is indispensable for a full understanding of the complex origins of the modern Press, but as the author wastes no words it largely defies abridgement. John Johnson and Strickland Gibson wrote with relish of the tribulations of the Press in the seventeenth century in *Print and Privilege at Oxford to the Year 1700* (1946). Percy Simpson's *Proof-Reading in the Sixteenth, Seventeenth and Eighteenth Centuries* (1935) is another work of original scholarship in which the Press figures prominently. Falconer Madan's three volumes of *Oxford Books* list virtually everything printed in Oxford up to 1680. The only previous attempt at a general history was made by R. W. Chapman, Secretary to the Delegates from 1920 to 1942, in *Some Account of the Oxford University Press 1468–1921* (second edition 1926). But Chapman had a habit of secretiveness and was giving nothing away: his book was a piece of elegant publicity. The *Report of the Committee on the University Press*, known as the 'Waldock Report', published in 1970, furnished a comprehensive account of the functions and workings of the business as a whole.

On nineteenth-century Oxford there is a large literature, though references to the Press are few. It appears as a foreign body, impossible to assimilate into a history of the University or of its colleges, an alien institution which does not properly belong. The books from which the present author pleads most guilty of pilfering are V. H. H. Green's *Oxford Common Room* (1957), W. R. Ward's *Victorian Oxford* (1965), E. G. W. Bill's *University Reform in Nineteenth-Century Oxford* (1973), and John Sparrow's *Mark Pattison and the Idea of a University* (1967). The Revd. W. Tuckwell, M.A., drops into the narrative from time to time like an old friend who needs no introduction. His *Reminiscences of Oxford* (1900), rejected by the Delegates, abounds in anecdote, gossip, and half-remembered rumours, and provides a colourful background to the period which would have seemed drabber without him.

The idea of this book originated with D. M. Davin, the Oxford Academic Publisher. A 'short, popular' history of the Press, it was thought, might make an appropriate contribution to the Quincentenary celebrations planned for 1978. It has turned out to be neither short nor, it is to be feared, popular—except in the rather technical sense of having no footnotes. Their absence requires a word of explanation. The bulk of the material is taken from Press files, letter-books dating back to the 1860s, miscellaneous heaps of paper, stray notes of predecessors who once toyed with the idea of a similar book, and the Delegates' minutes. No useful or comprehensible system of references could be devised.

A special word of thanks is due to Mrs. Philip Gell, however, who generously made available the papers of Philip Lyttelton Gell at Hopton Hall in Derbyshire, and to Miss K. M. Elisabeth Murray, an early draft of whose *Caught in the Web of Words: James A. H. Murray and the 'Oxford English Dictionary'* (1977), the author was permitted to see. Dr. Francis Price kindly lent the family album which outlines the life of his eminent grandfather, Bartholomew. The *Periodical* since 1896 was naturally an invaluable source. The Press records on the Fowlers have been supplemented by G. G. Coulton's memoir, *H. W. Fowler* (1934).

Harry Carter was invariably helpful and considerate, even when his own researches were being hindered by the naïve inquisitions of a novice. Not only the conception but the completion of the book owes much to Dan Davin: his encouragement, kindness, and resolution, his refusal to concede defeat when the author would have been glad to see the sponge thrown in, made it possible. The long memories of veterans of the Press yielded more insights and information than could be gleaned from many files. Miss Elizabeth Withycombe, Mr. Geoffrey Cumberlege, Sir Arthur Norrington, Mr. E. C. Parnwell re-created an image of the Press in the inter-war years, just as May Wedderburn Cannan in *Grey Ghosts and Voices* (1977) evoked the atmosphere of the office in Walton Street during the First World War.

Many of the young men who joined the Press after 1918 remained with it to complete fifty or more years of service, and have lived to tell their tales. Messrs. G. E. Durham, M. H. Westell, and L. Lardner recall the old days with amusement, affection, and something approaching wonder. Mr. G. W. G. Laitt joined the Clarendon Press at the age of 13 during a school holiday in 1915, liked the place, and decided to stay. In 1947 he succeeded A. E. Durham as accountant. Durham himself, who left a brief record of his experiences, had succeeded W. J. Jeeves in 1900. Today, when accountants tend to be numerous, it may seem remarkable that between 1866 and 1966 the Clarendon Press employed three, and between 1900 and 1971 the Oxford University Press in London employed two. In the inter-war years the total publishing staff in Oxford never exceeded thirty: in 1975 the old Clarendon Press (now the Academic Division) alone employed 250. 'No man is irreplaceable' is a truism: but there are some men with good memories and long experience who can be adequately replaced only by departments. To the individuals who contributed so much to the individuality of the Press in the past the author is indebted.

Miss Phœbe Allen scrutinized the typescript with enthusiasm, sacrificed her leisure, and almost turned into an Architypographus (see p. xviii). Miss Audrey Bayley read the proofs and offered valuable advice. Miss Irene Kurtz typed the appalling manuscript, sympathetically endured the vexing symptoms of morose self-pity induced by writer's block and impending deadlines, and treated both the book and its author with unflagging and tender concern.

CONTENTS

LIST OF ILLUSTRATIONS

PROLOGUE

I T is a regrettable paradox of history that when the Oxford University Press became really entitled to that name it went almost immediately into a decline. In 1690 the University inherited a 'learned *imprimerie*' from Dr. Fell, and its affairs were entrusted to a board of Delegates, under the chairmanship of the Vice-Chancellor. Before long the Delegacy was appropriated by the Heads of Houses—those Masters, Presidents, Provosts, Principals, Rectors, Wardens, and Deans of Colleges who in the early eighteenth century were notoriously indifferent to scholarship and literature. They met on average once a year, and on average published a new book every three years. This was the Press that the illustrious young lawyer William Blackstone found in 1757 'languishing in a lazy obscurity, and barely reminding us of its existence, by now and then slowly bringing forth a programma, a sermon printed by request, or at best a *Bodleian* catalogue'. Blackstone took it upon himself to recall the Press to its duties. He recommended no innovations, but only that the Delegates should accept the trust invested in them by their ancestors. He looked to the past, to the old charters and statutes, and to the men whom he regarded as founders of the Learned Press, Archbishop Laud and Dr. Fell.

The idea of a university press had a long history, one more glorious than the reality that Blackstone faced. In the year that it came of age and began the infirm administration of its estate, John Wallis, a great mathematician and controversialist and a veteran warrior on behalf of the privileges of the University, wrote: 'The Art of printing was first brought into England by the University, and at their Charges; and here practiced many years before there was any printing in London, and we have been in the continual possession of it ever since: and long before there was any restraint put upon printing; which was not at all till Queen Elizabeths time.' For Wallis a university press had existed since 1468. He was wrong in every historical particular, but sound in his convictions.

The first book printed in Oxford, probably by Theodoric Rood from Cologne, purporting to be an exposition of the Apostles' Creed by St. Jerome, had been dated 1468—some nine years before Caxton began printing in London. Bibliographers, with one notable exception, were subsequently to conclude that the date was a mistake for 1478, an x having dropped out of the roman numeral. The exception was the indefatigable chronicler of Oxford printing, Falconer Madan, who preferred to be called a bibliographist to distinguish himself from the more acidic members of his fraternity. In the first volume of *Oxford Books* published in 1895, he conceded that the critical spirit of the age might soon expose the Oxford 'Jerome' as an impostor. In the third volume of *Oxford Books* published in 1931, the spirit of the age had as far as he was concerned done no such thing, and the burden of proof still rested with the disputers. Nobody had successfully explained why the first book printed in a place of learning by men presumably trained in exactitude should carry such a blatant error. But, date apart, it was not in any case by Jerome. It was by Rufinus, a fourth-century contemporary of the Saint.

Seventeen books were printed in Oxford between 1478 and 1486. After that, apart from a brief and mysterious interlude in 1517-18, when eight books are recorded, there was no printing for nearly a century. But the antiquity of Oxford printing could when necessary be stressed, and there came a time when it appeared to be the only justification the University had for printing at all. It had no charter, and the nearest it came to legitimacy was through a Decree of Star Chamber of 1586 primarily concerned with confining printing to the City of London. Exceptions were made for one press each at Cambridge and Oxford. Cambridge had received a charter from Henry VIII in 1534 entitling them to print 'all manner of books' (*omnimodos libros*), on an assurance that it was in the interest of 'suppression of error'. Oxford had no such privilege.

The Tudors were only too aware of the novel and curious authority of the printed word and took every precaution to ensure that it was not abused. As in the early days of broadcasting, a need for charters, licences, codes, and statutes was felt. The 'art or mystery of printing' could spread sedition and heresy more perturbingly than word of mouth. By confining the privilege to the Royal Printer and to the Company of Stationers the necessary checks and restraints could be more easily imposed. Cambridge did not venture to use its privilege until 1583, when it incurred the wrath of the Stationers, and also apparently the envy of Oxford. For the following year, Convocation, the ruling body of the University, approved a loan of £100 to a local bookseller, Joseph Barnes, to set up a press. At the same time a supplication was addressed to the Chancellor of the University, Robert Dudley, first Earl of Leicester. It was a kind of formal application for the Queen's permission to print, and it is likely that Leicester himself was familiar enough with the arguments and that Barnes already enjoyed his patronage.

The supplicants had less confidence in their history than Wallis, and could only recall that fifty years before, more or less, there had been a man in Oxford who printed books. 'If at that time, in a ruder age, the University had its printer, how much more is he needed in the present abundance of learning?' And they added, rather as if by coincidence, that Joseph Barnes was available and willing. They went on to formulate most of the reasons for setting up a university press that have ever been adduced. Leaving aside the peculiar question of Cambridge, they could present the basic argument on which many subsequent claims were based: other universities had them. As 'no university, however small, in Germany and France is without its press, foreigners find it as good as a marvel that in the whole realm of England printers are to be met with only in one city, and that, having no university, prints in virtually nothing but English'. Oxford, it was pointed out, surpassed all the universities of Europe in the grandeur and wealth of its colleges, yet was 'behindhand of every one of them in having no press'. The supplicants presented their case with some cogency:

First of all: hidden away in the libraries of the University there are many very important manuscripts foully beset by dust and rubbish, and these could by means of a press set up in this city be rescued from vanishing for ever and spread over all Europe doing credit to our nation.

Second. Besides that, there are men in the place extremely skilled in all manner of languages and liberal arts, who as things are now are prevented by the slenderness of their means from staying in London while their works are being printed; consequently these men are overlooked and unknown among foreigners and barely known to their own countrymen, but given the convenience of this press they could very easily and swiftly refute and blot out the charge of laziness daily brought against them by foreigners.

Third: Foreigners have always thought it self-evident that where there is a settlement of scholars, there should be printers, so that books can be printed most correctly and texts most carefully collated. A university cannot be deprived of printers without loss to literature.[1]

The first book printed by Barnes, on Aristotle's *Ethics* by John Case, carried a long dedicatory epistle to Leicester, dwelling on the benefits to the University that his benefaction had brought. Over the next thirty-three years Barnes produced some three hundred books, mostly tracts or sermons. Some, however, are still highly prized, notably Captain John Smith's *Map of Virginia* (1612), Charles Butler's *Feminine Monarchie* (1609), and the first Bodleian Catalogue of 1605. He was succeeded as 'Printer to the University' in 1617 by John Lichfield, whose family continued to print in Oxford until the middle of the eighteenth century. Among his books was *The Anatomy of Melancholy, What it is. With all the kindes, causes . . . and several cures of it* by Robert Burton of Christ Church. Five editions appeared between 1621 and 1638. The author, who 'lived a silent, sedentary, solitary, private life . . . penned up most part in my study', constantly elaborated and refined this unique monument to himself.

Barnes, Lichfield, and later William Turner printed books of their own choice. As private business men they would be unlikely to refuse any book if the author or a bookseller could afford to pay for the printing. Calvinistic tendencies were evident in a number of the titles they put out. In 1629 Archbishop Laud, once President of St. John's, became Chancellor of the University. His vision was of a society free from all dissent and of impeccable High Anglican orthodoxy. That dissent itself was becoming an orthodoxy escaped him for too long, but in Oxford at least he built an enduring stronghold of Anglo-Catholic principles. His first task was to collect and codify the Statutes of the University, 'which had lain in a confused Heap some Hundreds of Years'. His reforms were intended to restore Oxford as a clerical seminary, governed by the Heads of Houses whose appointments could be manipulated by the Court in London. They were to meet once a week in term as the Hebdomadal Board. He personally

---

[1] The translation from the Latin is by Harry Carter.

regulated every detail of university life, from attendance at sermons to the dress, behaviour, and hair-styles of undergraduates, whom he found crying out for a stricter discipline. By the end of his chancellorship virtually all the Oxford colleges had capitulated to those Laudian precepts of Royal Supremacy and pre-Reformation ritual, that made him so calamitously unpopular in the world outside.

Laud's passion for scholarship expressed itself in the collection of manuscripts, some 1,300 of which he gave to the Bodleian Library, the majority in Hebrew or Arabic. Towards printing his attitude was traditional, or old-fashioned. This was its proper function, the multiplication of the manuscripts of antiquity, and it was to this end that he sought to create a university press. The art or mystery was too often wasted on contemporary literature which, if it did not consist of frivolous trifles, was likely to be 'libellous, seditious, and mutinous'. A Star Chamber Decree of 1637 added thirty-three new censorship clauses to those that already existed, imposing more severe restraints than ever before. One way of countering Calvinistic and Presbyterian distortions of the truth was by printing the truth itself in the form of the writings of the Early Fathers of the Church. They could teach not only purity of doctrine but the political virtues of obedience to the State, for the Fathers themselves recognized an element of divine right in the Christian emperors under whom they lived. That the first book printed in Oxford had been a patristic text was extremely apt. The Fathers were often to prove a godsend to Oxford men in times of doubt and controversy.

Oxford had first to be put on the same footing with Cambridge. By Letters Patent of Charles I in 1632 the Chancellor, Masters, and Scholars of the University were granted the right to appoint three printers. By the 'Great Charter' of 1636 the University's right to print all manner of books was at last plainly established. Oxford was in a position to challenge the King's Printer and the Stationers' Company in London: over the years through royal prerogative they had acquired exclusive patents to print Bibles and Prayer Books, almanacs and grammars, and indeed all books for which there was a sure and steady demand. But Laud advised caution: 'Let your Privilege settle a while.' So the first of a series of 'Covenants of Forbearance' was signed, by which the University agreed not to trespass on the Company's patents in return for an annual payment or bribe of £200. 'I shall require this of you and your successors,' Laud wrote to the Vice-Chancellor, 'that this money which you yearly receive may be kept safe, as a stock apart; *and put to no other use than the settling of a learned press.*' The italics are those of Blackstone, quoting Laud in 1757 in denunciation of the University's deplorable failure to make use of the funds available. In 1637 the money was spent on the purchase of new types from Holland, mostly of Hebrew and Arabic.

Whilst Laud was setting Oxford firmly on the course it was to follow for over two hundred years, Lichfield printed in 1633 a third edition of Francis Bacon's *Advancement of Learning*, first published in 1605. Bacon was the most powerful advocate of secular learning before John Locke. 'There is no hope,' he wrote, 'except in a new birth of science.' He appealed for 'a fresh examination of particulars', for experiment, for a true physics that would make metaphysics superfluous. Through what became known as the Wadham Group, or 'The Philosophical Society of Oxford' which met in John Wilkins's rooms in Wadham during the Interregnum, and through Robert Boyle, Bacon's 'new philosophy' was assimilated and handed on. After the Restoration it was practised at Gresham College in London, and by the newly created Royal Society.

Bacon's concept of the advancement of learning was the reverse of that of Laud. He did not accept the authority of antiquity. Even the humanists of the previous century had made but a small contribution to knowledge, allowing themselves to become obsessed by the classical texts that had come to light, devoting their time to textual studies and commentaries on the classical authors. Far worse were the medieval schoolmen, or scholastics, with whom for the purposes of his argument Bacon was inclined to associate the Early Fathers of the Church. 'This kind of degenerate learning', he wrote, 'did chiefly reign amongst the schoolmen: who having sharp and strong wits, and abundance of leisure, and small variety of reading, but their wits being shut up in the cells of a few authors (chiefly Aristotle their dictator)... did out of no great quantity of matter and infinite agitation of wit spin out unto us those laborious webs of learning which are extant in their books.' These 'cobwebs of learning' were admirable for the fineness of their thread, but 'of no substance or profit'.

Bacon's modernism, and his concern for a more practical curriculum, gained little ground in Oxford. 'Which of the Nobility or Gentry', it was asked by Seth Ward, Professor of Geometry, would wish to 'send their sons hither that they should be set to Chymistry or Agriculture or Mechanicks?' Oxford maintained faith with the ancients, and its role in society as the breeding ground of Anglican clergymen. Until the middle of the nineteenth century two-thirds of its graduates took holy orders—in Cambridge it was about half.

In 1633 a committee or Delegacy of eleven men was appointed by the two University Proctors. Its purpose was to make an annual choice of a manuscript in the Bodleian Library to be printed, according to Laud's wishes. The Delegacy, which met only once, selected the chronicle in Greek of John Malalas of Antioch, a history of the world since the birth of Adam written some time between A.D. 600 and 1000. The work was to be printed by William Turner, a man described as 'extremelie needie of witt and wealth'. Malalas cannot have been to his taste, and what might have been the first book to result from Laud's initiative was not printed because of his 'extraordinarie peevishness or extreme sottishness, hard to say which'— as the Vice-Chancellor reported to him. The local printers were only interested in cheap and profitable books, 'caring not at all for beauty of letters or good and seemly workmanship'. Laud saw that a university press needed three things: money, a building, and a man of authority and diverse talents to control it. He did not have time to see his design unfold, but some money, if not a home, had become available. The man in whom he placed most faith was a mythical creature he chose to call an Architypographus.

'He shall be a man thoroughly acquainted with Greek and Latin literature and deeply learned in philological studies,' Laud wrote into the Statute. He was also to be possessed of considerable technical skill: 'In all work that comes from the University's public printing office he shall determine size of type, quality of paper, and width of margins, correct correctors' mistakes, and take unremitting care of the good appearance and fine workmanship of the product.' It might well be asked where such a man could be found, but with the confidence of a great bureaucrat Laud had an immediate if absurd answer: he was to be found in the person of the Superior Bedel of Civil Law, who was thought to be less busy than other bedels. As soon as it next fell vacant the office was to 'be for ever annexed'.

Only once was the post satisfactorily filled, though it remained in the Statute until 1856. Occasionally in the eighteenth century a Superior Bedel going innocently about his largely ceremonial tasks might be recalled to his statutory duties: as late as 1783 one was startled by a request to correct proofs of an edition of Polybius. But the Platonic idea of the Architypographus was one of Laud's bequests to the modern University Press. Thomas Hearne, scholar and antiquary, had held the post briefly in 1715, before his political and religious views and quarrelsome temper made him unacceptable. It was he who really defined the role, or confined it within reasonable limits. The Architypographus was the man who passed the proofs for press, after the compositor had made his corrections, the author had made his, and another proof-reader—perhaps an outsider—his. This was clearly less than Laud had intended. But it was the learned 'correctors' of the Press who in modern times were most conscious of the responsibility that Laud had imposed upon them, although with time the meaning of the word 'corrector' changed. It had once referred to the person who prepared the copy. So in current parlance the Architypographus would be editor, copy-editor, and 'learned reader' all in one.

A second Delegacy was appointed in 1636 to take charge of the £200 forbearance from the Stationers and to render accounts. Again it appears to have met only once. With the outbreak of war the Oxford printers were fully occupied printing Royalist pamphlets, and in due course those from the other side. During the Interregnum, in 1652, a Delegacy of fifteen was appointed 'to supervise the University Press', a curious expression for it still did not exist. This was a powerful committee, which included Jonathan Goddard, Gresham Professor of Physics; John Wilkins of Wadham, and later Master of Trinity College, Cambridge; Ralph Bathurst, a physician, theologian, and former Royalist; and the Vice-Chancellor, John Owen, who though a staunch Independent found Laudian Oxford in many ways congenial and preserved the traditions of the place. In the five years of its existence this Delegacy showed no signs of life. It was supposed to report to Convocation, but there is no evidence that it did, or even that it ever met.

After the Restoration an entirely new Delegacy was appointed by the Proctors 'to deliberate and act with regard to publishing and printing and to report to Convocation'. It was proving uncommonly difficult to translate Laud's words into action. One of the Delegates was John Fell, who was to become the most powerful man in Oxford, and another was the great Orientalist Edward Pococke, Laudian Professor of Arabic and Regius Professor of Hebrew. But again there is no evidence that for the first six years of its existence the Delegacy ever did anything. One difficulty undoubtedly was the want of a suitable building. The Oxford printers worked in their own hired premises, accepting odd jobs from the University but not in these years producing any major work. The appointment of Anne Lichfield, widow of Leonard, as Printer to the University was, as Madan sadly recorded, a serious set-back to the development of good printing in Oxford: she 'was inaccurate and unbusinesslike, and knew no more Latin than a cat'. She did much damage to Oxford's self-esteem.

It was the gift to the University of a 'Structure' designed for the advancement of learning, as well as for the performance of 'Publique acts', that at last activated this Delegacy. The Sheldonian Theatre was formally opened in 1669, designed by Christopher Wren at the request of Gilbert Sheldon, formerly Warden of All Souls and since 1663 Archbishop of Canterbury. In a letter of endowment to the Vice-Chancellor read out at the opening ceremony, he expressed the hope that the building would not need much in the way of repairs: but 'time and Weather will prevaile against it, and Decayes will come. I never meant, that what I intended for a Benefitt should lye as a Burden upon the University; And therefore, to take you off from that Care, I doe hereby desire you to acquaint the University, That I have lay'd by for you Two Thousand Pounds.... What shall every year be remaining . . . over and above the Charge of Repayres, I desire may be imployed for the best advantage and encouragement of the Learned Presse . . . which I pray God prosper.'

This blessing was not unconnected with the Dean of Christ Church, Dr. Fell, who as Vice-Chancellor had intimated to the Archbishop that his Theatre might admirably serve the purpose of a printing house, even if not built with any such purpose in mind. Indeed it could hardly have been less suitable, for the presses were in a cellar where no light penetrated, and the compositors who worked in the passages upstairs had to move out whenever the Theatre was needed for public functions. However, the 'Theatre' money was in effect the first modest endowment that the Press received.

The earliest minute of a meeting of the Delegates of the University Press is dated September 1668. It records a decision to print the synodical canons of the Eastern Church. It was characteristic of Fell, who was said to have 'set his heart' on this book, to undertake as a first venture a work far beyond the resources of the existing press. William Beveridge's edition of the *Synodicon*, as the collection was called, made two folio volumes of 1,588 pages of Greek, Latin, and Arabic. It was a notable work of scholarship, precisely what Laud had had in mind, but for poor Anne Lichfield and her associates it was clearly too much. It could only be done with the help of Robert Scott, reputed to be the greatest bookseller in Europe, and although the University made available all the types and printing materials it had in its possession he himself had to provide large quantities of Greek, Roman, and Italic type, and also to supply the paper. Moreover he had to bring over compositors from France experienced in setting Greek. Not surprisingly the enterprise nearly ruined him. But this was the first great work of scholarship to be manufactured on the initiative and under the supervision of the Delegates. It was also the last for some years. For by the time it appeared in 1672 the University had leased the privilege of printing to a private company, of which Fell was in effect chairman and managing director.

It had the appearance of a *coup d'état*. Fell feared the meddlesomeness of Convocation, rather than the dilatoriness of committees. 'It is certain that while the charge of the Presse lyes at large in the hands of the University, it can never be lookt after, or managd to advantage', he had written to his friend Sir Leoline Jenkins, Judge of Admiralty, Principal of Jesus, and Delegate of the Press, in July 1671. The Delegates were persuaded not to renew the covenant of forbearance with the Stationers, and to lease the privilege of printing instead to Fell, Jenkins, Thomas Yate, and Joseph Williamson at the same rent of £200. Yate, Principal of Brasenose, was known to be an astute business man; Williamson was a politician, who in 1674 became Secretary of State. Fell was to need all the help he could get from lawyers, business men, and politicians in the long and tortuous struggles that lay ahead.

His assumption of power did not go uncontested. Thomas Barlow, himself a Delegate, thought it 'an unreasonable bargain' that Fell and his friends 'should have their Priviledge, room and furniture for two hundred pounds per annum' when the Stationers paid the same amount for 'the bare priviledge'. Moreover in the past Fell's attempt to get his own man appointed Architypographus had been rebuffed by a rebellious Convocation, which elected instead a nonentity called Norton Bold. Fell was so incensed that he appealed directly to the Crown to have the appointment set aside. 'Our Angry men', as Fell called Convocation, then appointed Christopher Wase, who was not only a Cambridge man but 'crazed in his head, and void of all manage'. Fell made do without an Architypographus. These inept appointments were not forgotten when Blackstone rendered his account of violations done to Laud's memory and intentions.

Fell was an awesome figure, fanatical in diligence, celibacy, and learning, determined to exterminate all traces of the hiatus in civilization that occurred between the martyrdom of Laud and Charles I and his own coming, traces that might be found in, for instance, Thomas Hobbes whom he relentlessly maligned, or even possibly in John Locke, an intelligent student of his own college not above suspicion, whom he was eventually obliged to expel. Fell glowed or glowered with a fine Tory arrogance.

He and his three colleagues, known as the 'undertakers' or 'farmers' of the privilege, did, however, create what would on their relinquishing control become the University Press. They invested substantial amounts of their own money in the business—both Fell and Yate were wealthy men—and established what was recognizably a publishing house. They drew up ideal lists, prospectuses, and sought out authors; calculated costs, prices, and profits; even sent out a traveller, Yate's nephew, to make a survey of the country trade. The one thing always lacking, however, was a way of selling the books produced. They were not only by their nature likely to be of limited appeal, but the channels of distribution to the trade in London were controlled by the Stationers with whom Fell was soon in conflict.

Fell's publishing programme drawn up in 1672 listed sixteen works that 'We purpose to Print, if we may be encouraged'. This was just a start, but it was an astonishing document, calculated it would seem to keep the Press busy until the end of time. Beginning with the Greek Bible in a royal folio, it went on to envisage whole series of works which have indeed in one form and another engaged the attention of the Press ever since: the 'Greek and Latin fathers in their order'; the 'Classical authors both Greek and Latin; Historians, Philosophers, Orators, and Poets'; the 'ancient Mathematicians Greek and latin in one and twenty volumes'; the 'authors of the Middle age from our Sauiours birth'. All were to be based on fresh collations of the manuscripts, and 'illustrated with Annotations'. He proposed to publish contemporary works by learned men in Latin and English too. On another list appear the portentous words 'A dictionary'. He did not advertise the possibility of a Bible in English.

Not only time but large sums of money and a constant flow of it would be needed to carry through so magnificent a scheme. The Theatre money would not go far, nor was Yate's purse inexhaustible. Bibles and school-books might provide the necessary revenue. Though these were still largely controlled by the London monopolists, there was no longer a covenant of forbearance and Oxford had the privilege. It only took a sanguine and fiery amateur of Fell's calibre to invite disaster by directly challenging the Stationers' Company and the King's Printer.

The autocratic Dean was at a disadvantage when faced with men of greater business experience. Neither the lash of his tongue nor the fearsome silences that cowed undergraduates made much impression on the hard men who trafficked in the precincts of St. Paul's. Business was also a distraction: he himself was primarily concerned with 'Letters' in the strictest sense, as pieces of type. An attempt to produce school-books was made fruitless by competition and lack of access to the market. Fell's Bible of 1675 was the first to be printed in Oxford. It was a Crown quarto, not a popular size, but one specifically allowed to the Universities by an Order in Council of 1636. Fell had the law on his side, but nothing else. The Stationers immediately cut their prices and drove it out of the market, compensating themselves by raising the prices on Bibles in other formats.

It cannot have been easy for Fell to swallow his pride, and to form an alliance with a group of London booksellers themselves ready to defy the King's Printer. Two of them, Peter Parker and Thomas Guy, stood him in good stead. They became sub-lessees in 1678, paying a rent to the undertakers of £200 a year. According to Wallis they were chosen by Fell on the principle of setting a thief to catch a thief: they have been described as freebooters, freetraders, freelances, and interlopers. To comply with the privilege, printing had to be done within the precincts of the University, so the Londoners moved into the Sheldonian bearing with them their own type. Fell had created a hybrid. Driven out of the Theatre by the interlopers, his printers occupied an adjoining house, and until the twentieth century the Bible side and the Learned or Classical side were separate departments of the Press.

To carry out his programme Fell needed new types, including Syriac and Coptic. Not trusting the British type-founders, he sought new matrices on the Continent, and in 1676 succeeded in bringing to Oxford a Dutch type-founder of German descent, Peter de Walpergen. He was given a workroom in the Dean's lodgings in Christ Church, where he cut punches and made matrices and acquired a reputation for dissolute living. He remained at work until his death in 1703, and is credited with sixteen complete type-faces, including a type for music not at the time used. By importing founts of Dutch type Fell introduced another anomaly, for the Dutch type was higher than the English type used by the Bible printers. So the Press was divided not only because of the nature of the work on which it was engaged, but because of the different heights of type used. When the two sides finally merged in 1906 it was 'Learned' height that was adopted as standard, though it is peculiar to the University Press and all machines when installed have to be specially adjusted. The famous Fell types were gradually put aside and forgotten. They were brought out again towards the end of the nineteenth century as a beguiling novelty and used to great effect in an age of aestheticism.

It was Parker and Guy who had to bear the brunt of ten years of remorseless and squalid litigation with the King's Printer, in league with the Stationers. This focused mostly on the sizes of Bibles that Oxford was allowed in law to print, on the printing of the Psalms to bind up with them, on the number of presses the printers were allowed to own, and on the status of these sub-lessees—it could be argued that, by reaching them, the privilege granted to the University had become too attenuated and frail to withstand contention. From the King in Council, through interminable Chancery suits, through the King's Bench, to *Quo Warranto* proceedings in 1688, the Stationers and the agglomeration of Oxford interests battled it out. The result was a stalemate, brought about at great cost, shared in Oxford between the University, Fell, Parker, and Guy. But at least Oxford had not lost. What had in the end been accomplished by free if hazardous enterprise was a vast proliferation of Bibles, which brought prices down by half. The ancient business of Bible-running from Holland ceased to be profitable. Wallis noted that it was now possible to supply all the Plantations with Bibles printed in England.

Fell died in 1686. Though he had plunged the University into a tumult by his association with the interlopers, he bequeathed to it a press technically as well equipped as any in Europe. All the punches, matrices, and moulds he had collected were handed over by his executors to the University four years after his death, when as stipulated in his will they had satisfied themselves that 'the interests of learning and printing were encouraged in the said University'. In little more than fifteen years Fell had published 150 books under the imprint of the Sheldonian Theatre. Among the more remarkable were Pitt's *English Atlas,* Spelman's *Life of King Alfred,* the Bodleian Catalogue of printed books of 1674, his own edition of St. Cyprian and his Greek Testament, George Hickes's Anglo-Saxon grammar, a number of titles in Welsh, and the collection of David Loggan's engravings in *Oxonia Illustrata.* Yet it was an ambiguous legacy. Fell had employed mercenaries to build up a large manufacture of Bibles, but he insisted that his own press should be 'freed from mercenary artifices'. Making profits for booksellers was emphatically no part of its functions: it existed, like Richelieu's royal printing-press at the Louvre, for 'the interests and convenience of scholars'. As far as the booksellers were concerned, it was a frame of mind 'as unwise as it was ungenerous', Harry Carter wrote—'and handed down to later generations of Delegates did more than anything else to hinder the progress of the University Press'.

At the same time Fell did more than anybody else to bring Oxford books to the attention of the learned world. For Blackstone in 1757, 'This was the period of the greatest glory that our *Oxford* press ever knew; and which established that fund of reputation upon which it has principally subsisted ever since.' Thomas Hearne wrote, 'Hence it was that our Press became so noted beyond seas, where . . . those that are curious esteem such Books as have been printed at the Theatre far beyond any that were printed by old Elzevir, looking upon them as more correct and . . . more neat and more creditable Editions.' Perhaps most impressive is a tribute from one of Fell's most famous authors, Anthony Wood, who had reason to hate him. His *Historia et Antiquitates Universitatis Oxoniensis* had been ruthlessly handled by Fell, with the gross want of tact for which he was notorious. Yet Wood, in his published work at least, wrote without rancour: 'He was a great encourager and promoter of learning in the university . . . He likewise advanced the learned press, and improv'd the manufacture of printing in Oxford . . . He was a bold and resolute man, and did not value what the generality said or thought of him so that he could accomplish his just and generous designs.'

With the appointment of a new Board of Delegates in 1691, the continuous history of the Learned Press begins, and Fell's losing battle was finally lost. The Bible Press was up for sale. At the same time the Delegates were at a loss to know what to do with a superfluity of books now left in their care. Though Parker and Guy bid for a renewal of the lease, a powerful faction in the University resented their presence and no gratitude was to be wasted on them. Instead it went to three men acting secretly on behalf of the Stationers' Company—Isted, Mortlock, and Bellinger. Wittingly or not, the University had thrown itself to the wolves. Parker and Guy, whom John Wallis at least trusted—they were the 'mastiffs'—were forcibly evicted. Wallis feared the worst. The argument of those who had conspired against them seemed to him to be that 'if the Sheep will be persuaded to part with their Maistifs, the Wolves can as well defend them; who have no ill-will to the Sheep but to the Maistifs onely; it is so thin a Pretense that none but scholars could be caught by it.' But he exaggerated. The sheep were to be allowed to graze in peace.

Guy made a fortune and endowed the hospital bearing his name in spite of having engaged in Bible printing, an occupation that brought few rewards before the nineteenth century, however fiercely coveted the privilege might be. Competition from the former sub-lessees had forced the Stationers into an agreement far from satisfactory to themselves. A similar arrangement with Cambridge was workable because there was still no learned press there: in Oxford they had to grapple with the consequences of Fell's extravagance. There was no economic way of coping with the output of his press or of disposing of its stock, though several quite illusory methods of doing so were guaranteed and had a sedating effect.

The University and the Delegates could now look forward to a more restful period. A drowsiness descended. With the Stationers within the gates, and no longer competitors, there would be no need for so furious a manufacture of books. The Press had already become too commercialized. As Harry Carter put it, 'To look back on the number of Bibles and psalms that "those mercenary fellows", Parker and Guy, had been allowed to bring out in the University's name prompted a feeling that on such a scale printing was not proper work for an academy, and to abet it meant undermining an old order.'

The three volumes of Clarendon's *History of the Great Rebellion*, on which towards the end of his life Wallis worked as a corrector, were published between 1703 and 1707. This was the first big success of the Press, and to discover money pouring in at last was a novel experience. Unfortunately the money was not pouring into the University Chest but into the pockets of the Vice-Chancellor, William Delaune, President of St. John's, who embezzled the proceeds of the first two editions. His successor as Vice-Chancellor, William Lancaster, charged him with owing the Press £2,280. 3s. 9d. This appears to have been about right. Delaune lost the presidency of his college, his rectory was sequestered, and eventually much of the money was recovered. It is assumed that Delaune was a gambler, but as there is no proof of addiction the possibility that he had other ways of disposing of large sums of money cannot be ruled out. Thomas Hearne recorded that he was 'a good Companion and one who understood Eating and Drinking very nicely'. Indeed he was generally popular, and his sermons were eloquent. In that permissive age it was sympathetically understood that he was a man who needed money. To relieve him of distress he was elected Lady Margaret Professor of Divinity in 1715. In 1721 he again became a Delegate, and a Delegate of Accounts.

With what could be salvaged from the profits of the *History*, and with a contribution of £2,000 from John Baskett—bookseller, paper supplier, publisher, and printer—the University built a new printing house and named it the Clarendon Building. The Sheldonian had been badly damaged by the Bible printers, and by the time the Stationers arrived in 1692 it was thought to be too dangerous to continue printing there. They had to find premises in St. Aldate's. The architect of the new printing house, Nicholas Hawksmoor, chose to adorn the city and to provide the craftsmen of the Press with a small palace of their own. Although it was designed in two halves to accommodate the two businesses, few other concessions were made to the needs of compositors and pressmen. It did include, however, a splendid room for the meeting of Delegacies. The Clarendon Press imprint was first used in 1713 for a selection of verses in honour of Queen Anne, but 'At the Sheldonian Theatre' continued to be more common for many years.

It was with the opening of its magnificent new printing establishment that the Press fell into its torpor. Between 1713 and 1755 only fourteen new books were published. The dominant figure was John Baskett, 'the greatest monopolist of Bibles who ever lived', who had leased the Bible privilege in 1713. His 'Vinegar Bible', so called because of a misprint in the Parable of the Vineyard, was printed in 1717. It has been described as 'magnificent in its press work, but sadly deficient in textual accuracy'. John Baskett was also the King's Printer, as were his sons, and they held the Oxford lease between them until 1765, paying the University increasingly high rents. They were succeeded by the London Stationers Wright and Gill, who were prepared to pay £850 for the privilege.

But by 1780 when the leasehold again fell vacant the Oxford privilege could attract no bidders. War with the American colonists had badly damaged the market overseas, and there was a chronic disposition to believe that the privilege itself would not endure. The Delegates reported that there were only two choices: either they must make no use of their privilege, or they must 'take the exercise of it wholly upon themselves'. At the same time they admitted that neither choice was acceptable. The former would not be to 'the honour of the University', and the latter was 'manifestly impracticable' in view of 'the reduced state of the Finances of the Clarendon Press'. An alternative was found. It was agreed to admit master printers into partnership who could take upon themselves 'the care and trouble of managing the trade for our mutual advantage'. It was to be in the form of a joint-stock company, with 48 shares of which the University as 'owner partner' held half. Expenses were to be shared equally with the partners and profits equally divided. The first two partners, assuming the title of 'Printer to the University', were William Jackson of Oxford and Archibald Hamilton of London who both held twelve shares.

The partnership system lasted for a hundred years, with the University gradually increasing its share in the business. It was commended to Cambridge by the University Commissioners in their report of 1852: 'We are satisfied that no Syndicate, however active and well chosen, can replace the intelligent and vigilant superintendence of those whose fortune in life is dependent upon its success.' At the time the Delegates in Oxford were beginning to doubt the truth of this, and within a few years it was almost a matter of deliberate policy to prove the Commissioners wrong. But the partnership system on the whole had served them well, and the prosperity they then enjoyed and the confidence that went with it owed much to such men as Thomas Bensley and Edward Gardner of London, and Samuel Collingwood and Joseph Parker of Oxford. Parker had been apprenticed to the Warehouseman of the Learned Press in the 1780s before founding the family printing and bookselling business in Oxford, with which the University was associated for many years. The Press in 1780 stood in need of those whose fortune in life was dependent upon its success. It needed too its full share of the Bible profits, and the first partners were eager to build up the trade. The Bible privilege, which concerned no more than the Authorized Version of James I without notes, had not been challenged in a court of law since 1758, but it had to be jealously guarded. There were always those bent on infringing it. The worst offenders were the Scottish Bible printers, whose patent allowed them to sell only in Scotland. But Scottish Bibles with forged Oxford title-pages were common, often on sale from pawnbrokers. 'Annotated' editions with a few spurious notes at the bottom of the page which could easily be trimmed away by the binders were another mischief. In all it was estimated that fifty-five cases were successfully brought against the pirates and invaders of the privilege.

There was one further vestige of a privilege to be enjoyed. The two Universities and the Stationers' Company had held the exclusive right to print almanacs. In 1779 this was taken away by Act of Parliament, but compensation was subsequently negotiated. Each university was to receive an annual payment of £500 from the government. This made ample amends for the loss of the privilege, and did much to sustain the Learned Press in the lean years to come. The Oxford Almanacks themselves, introduced by Dr. Fell, continued to appear: from 1676 until the present day the sequence has been unbroken.

In the eighteenth century there was a danger as time passed that the neglect of the Learned Press might go unnoticed, as memories of what it had once been faded. Blackstone's partial rescue was made possible by a spirited Senior Proctor who wished to assert the right of the Proctors to make an appointment without the Vice-Chancellor's consent. In the midst of heated controversy, Blackstone was made a Delegate in 1755. He was no Head of a House, only a Fellow of All Souls, and he was a mere 32 years of age. But he was already a man of influence. With his appointment as Vinerian Professor of English Law in 1758 his reputation increased, and his legal and political contacts in London made him powerful enough to threaten the Vice-Chancellor of the day, Dr. Randolph. If the Delegates did not reform their Press, he warned, they would be called upon to justify their conduct 'before another less indulgent Tribunal'.

In an open letter to the Vice-Chancellor he dwelt at length on the Press's failure to fulfil its responsibilities, and sought to revive 'the spirit of our ancestors'. The first cause of inactivity was the 'want of a regular *time* and *place* for the meeting of the delegates to deliberate on business'. Secondly, no proper record was kept, despite Laud's advice 'that some handsome registerbook were bought'. Thirdly, the Delegates should be permitted to audit and examine the accounts of the workmen employed. Fourthly, they should have copies of the charters for printing, of the lease to Baskett, and of all relevant Acts of Parliament, so that they knew where they stood. Fifthly, they must find an industrious and skilful overseer: the Superior Bedel of the day was as usual quite unqualified, and the overseer of the Learned Press was no better than William Turner, combining peevishness with extreme old age. And so he went on. The Oxford Press was more expensive than any printing house in London, and characterized by incivility and negligence. He estimated that over the past forty years the accumulated income from the Theatre money, Baskett's rent, and other sources had reached £20,000: it was 'slumbering in the public chest, and ready to be employed in the service of learning whenever the Delegates of the Press shall think that service worth attending to'.

Blackstone succeeded in reforming the Delegacy. Appointments were subsequently not confined to Heads of colleges. Professors were invited to attend meetings to recommend books which in their opinion would be 'most acceptable to the Public, and most for the Honour of the University'. The Delegates were to meet at least four times a year, keep a full record of their proceedings, and keep accounts. His 'almost oppressive spirit of orderliness' communicated itself, at least for a time, to the custodians of the Learned Press.

It was also necessary to impress not only upon them but on all in the University who would listen the importance of initiating scholarly works. Like Fell before him and several who followed, Blackstone suggested a 'great Plan for publishing an intire edition of all the Classics in an elegant Manner and at a very cheap Rate for the benefit of Students'. He intended to begin with Cicero, and the Delegates accepted his proposal for a 'cheap, simple expeditious Edition' in 1760. Blackstone's ruthless energies were not sufficient to bring anything of that sort about. The first editors determined that a collation of all the manuscripts of Cicero in England was necessary for a start. After three years they became disheartened and the project lapsed, to be revived again some ten years later. A Clarendon Press edition of Cicero did eventually appear in 1783. It was in ten volumes and by no means cheap.

Blackstone administered a severe jolt to the Press and to the University, but too many of his schemes went awry after he left Oxford in 1766. His reforms were short-lived. One man could not change a society, and it was the society—intellectually isolated and estranged from the world—that was at fault.

PART I

1800–1860

1. The Want of Vent

THE Press, the Bodleian Library, the Old Ashmolean, the Divinity School with Apodyterium, and the Church of St. Mary the Virgin were about the only physical manifestations of the University in the first half of the nineteenth century. It owned these institutions but could scarcely be said to be in possession of itself. It was not so much governed as supplanted by a gerontocracy of Heads of Houses, the Hebdomadal Board, representing college interests and a fervent concern for the *status quo*. The colleges were rich, the University poor. The Laudian Statutes of 1636 had 'laid the foundation of that fatal divorce between the Universities and the national mind, which has lasted ever since', Mark Pattison wrote in the early 1850s. The Press could no longer be accused of languishing in a lazy obscurity, for it was busy printing Bibles, but until the University was restored to the nation it would remain isolated from the mainstreams of learning and literature.

Oxford was much abused. It was no mere backwater but a stagnant, sullen, scurfy pond, breeding strange disorders—'the sick fatigue, the languid doubt'—and inhabited by some very queer fish. The *Edinburgh Review* published a series of articles between 1808 and 1810 on the backwardness of classical scholarship in the University generally. The Clarendon Press came into the reviewer's line of fire as a result of an edition of Strabo's *Geography* in 1807—as well it might, for at £8 on large paper and £6 on small paper it was far and away the most expensive book the Press had published within living memory. Having dismissed it as 'a ponderous monument of operose ignorance and vain expense', the reviewer observed that 'though this learned Body' had occasionally availed itself of the sagacity and erudition of Ruhnken, Wyttenbach, Heyne 'and other *foreign* professors, they have, of late, added nothing of their own, except what they derived from the superior skill of British manufacturers, and the superior wealth of their establishment; namely, whiter paper, blacker ink, and neater types'. No distinction was being made between the University and the Press, which might otherwise appear to have emerged with some credit. To have attached to itself three such eminent European scholars was no small achievement, and it is probable that its standing then was rather higher on the Continent than at home.

There was undeniably a dearth of local talent. Before the theological pandemonium of the 1830s, perhaps only M. R. Routh and Thomas Gaisford, both of them Delegates, could lay claim to an international reputation, and that of the former was curiously confused by his longevity. He lived to be ninety-nine, dying in 1854 through chagrin, it was said, at the collapse of Russian securities during the Crimean War. The only changes in Oxford may have been of persons and outward fashion, but Routh defied even these. He was the last man in Oxford to wear a wig. He had known Dr. Johnson, and witnessed the hanging of two undergraduates for highway robbery. One of his aunts had known a lady who had seen Charles I in Oxford. He was President of Magdalen for sixty-three years, a myth in his own lifetime.

In 1784 the Press published his editions of the *Euthydemus* and *Gorgias* of Plato. In 1788 he issued a prospectus for a major edition of pre-Nicene patristic texts, which first appeared in four volumes as *Reliquiae Sacrae* in 1814-18, and in a revised edition in five volumes in 1846-8. He edited Burnet's *History of My Own Time* in 1823 (a devout Tory, Routh wrote 'I knew the man was a liar, and was determined to prove him so'), and *Scriptorum Ecclesiasticorum Opuscula* in 1832. His patristic studies endeared him to the Tractarians, and Newman dedicated a volume of his lectures to him, saying that he had 'been reserved to report to a forgetful generation the theology of their fathers'.

Routh was a Delegate from 1795 until 1819. Thomas Gaisford was appointed in 1807 and continued until his death in 1855, when the Delegates recorded in their minutes an appreciation of his 'unwearied attention to the interests of the University Press', which had 'contributed so much to the prosperity of the concern, and the promotion of Classical literature'. He had in fact created by his industry much of the work that the Delegates then inherited, so bringing to their attention a discontinuity in their publishing arrangements which sooner or later would have to be remedied.

Gaisford was Regius Professor of Greek and Dean of Christ Church. Of humble origins, he was not popular among the Christ Church aristocrats of his day, but he returned their scorn in good measure and became widely disliked, the more so as he got older. Ruskin dreaded him: 'scornful at once, and vindictive, thunderous always, more sullen and threatening as the day went on'. But, together with Edward Cardwell, a church historian who took a keen business interest in the Press between 1827 and 1861, he prepared the way for a greater involvement by the Delegates than had been contemplated since Blackstone's day. It is unfortunate that he is best remembered for the autobiographical sermon in which he said: 'Nor can I do better, in conclusion, than impress upon you the study of Greek literature, which not only elevates above the vulgar herd, but leads not infrequently to positions of considerable emolument.'

Among his few admirers was the prolific W. Dindorf of Leipzig, who in effect used him as publisher of his editions of the Greek dramatists and other classical texts. Gaisford, following Ruhnken, studied the Greek lexicographers. He was an indefatigable collator of manuscripts, but it was said that he preferred to copy out the notes of others than to write his own: he was dismissed in his own day as he has been since as an industrious pedant. Through Joseph Parker he published classical texts for schools, specifically Westminster School where Henry Liddell, his pupil and eventual successor as Dean of Christ Church, was headmaster. These presumably were not unprofitable. His more scholarly works, like those of Routh, represented a considerable investment by the Delegates: editions of Eusebius, 'the Father of Church History', and of the *Suda*, the medieval Greek lexicon, reflected 'the superior wealth of their establishment'. The latter cost £3,685 to produce and sales rarely climbed above ten copies a year. It was not by his own books that he contributed to the prosperity of the Press.

Wyttenbach's *Plutarch* was another massive undertaking, not at the time of the *Edinburgh Review* article complete. Indeed it had just been seriously interrupted by a barge exploding on a canal in Leyden and setting fire to Wyttenbach's house. The work had been 'commissioned' by the Delegates in 1788, the first volume published in 1795, and copy for the seventh and last volume of his commentary reached Oxford in 1820, shortly before his death. It was one of many monumental Oxford productions that are a mystery to anybody brought up to associate publishing with the sale of books. Wyttenbach's *Moralia* remained in the Oxford Catalogue until 1956. In the last fifty years of the nineteenth century it did not sell a single copy.

The staying power of Oxford books became a matter of pride, proof of continuity and an enduring concern for scholarship, in striking contrast to the shabby habits of commercial publishers who put books out of print as soon as there appeared to be no further demand for them. The record for endurance is held by Wilkins's *Coptic Gospels*, published in an edition of 500 copies in 1716. 'The book was hard to sell,' Carter records in his *History*. 'The first hundred had gone by 1760, and the Delegates never gave up hope of disposing of the rest.' R. W. Chapman in his *Account* was less matter of fact, recalling with a touch of wonder how from the dark vaults of the old Delegates' warehouse 'was drawn into the upper air, in 1907, the last copy of Wilkins's *Coptic New Testament* . . . the paper hardly discoloured and the impression still black and brilliant.' Moreover it was sold at 12*s*. 6*d*., the price to which it had been reduced some time in the nineteenth century. It had cost a guinea originally. It was not uncommon in the twentieth century to find in the catalogues of second-hand booksellers old Oxford books offered as 'rare' at high prices when in fact they were still in print and available from the publisher as technically new. Nobody without intimate acquaintance with the Oxford lists could possibly be expected to know.

The output of the Learned Press in the first half of the century varied between five and sixteen titles a year. These books were not strictly speaking 'published'. They were printed for the University at the University Press and could be purchased in sheets from Joseph Parker in Oxford, 'Bookseller to the University', and after 1832 from the Bible Partners' warehouse in Paternoster Row. But they were given no publicity, there were no travellers, no review copies, no basic library or bookshop sale. Matters in this respect had not improved since the seventeenth century, when the sale of learned books had been entrusted to the Stationers' Company in London. The controllers of the Press then complained bitterly of the failure to advertise the books, to offer attractive credit terms, to exploit the export market. The Stationers 'always stifled them up in Stationers Hall (or, their Oxford Warehouse, as they call it), so that except they were enquir'd after, they were never exposed for sale'. Later, in 1718, the Delegate Arthur Charlett wrote, 'The vending of books we never could compasse.' He added that 'the want of vent broke Bp. Fell's body, public spirit, courage, purse and presse'. The Delegates of the early nineteenth century were less worldly and less vulnerable than their predecessors. They had no wish to be thought of as mere business men, and the 'want of vent' would not break them as long as the Bible Press continued to prosper.

2. The Bible Press

THE relative importance of the two sides of the Press can be seen from the bills for paper in 1814: the Learned Press paid £1,003, the Bible Press £19,073. The profitability of Bible printing always seemed a little too good to last. In the 1770s the end of the Bible privilege was thought to be imminent, and in any event the difficulty of selling in America and the influx of Scottish and pirated Bibles into the home market spelt ruin for the trade. Such fears continued to be expressed and continued to be unfounded. Costly litigation was felt to be necessary at the beginning of the nineteenth century to fend off the vendors of Scottish Bibles and to counter other inroads on the privilege. At the same time the Delegates and partners were building up the capacity of the Bible Press to meet the ever increasing demands upon it, and in consequence running into debt to the University. Stereotyping was introduced in 1805, a major step towards the elimination of those errors for which earlier Bible printers were best remembered, and a major economy in that it did away with composition costs. By 1815 the Bible Press was paying good dividends, and for the next forty years it enjoyed a period of unparalleled prosperity.

Having outgrown the Clarendon Building the Press was in need of new premises. In 1825 the Delegates bought land in the water meadows north of Worcester College in an area known as Jericho. Building began there the following year from a design by Daniel Robertson, and by 1827 the entire front overlooking Walton Street and the south wing were finished. They were to house the Bible Press. The north wing in due course accommodated the Learned Press, and on the west side were houses for the superintendents. The cost was about £30,000. Built on the quadrangular plan it was thought to be more like a college than a factory. But it was curiously unlike either, an imposing and ambiguous structure on the outskirts of town that had more in common with the great railway termini. Within, the industrial revolution steamed and roared: an outward front of dignified piety advertised its evangelizing mission, a Bible in every home in Christendom.

After 1830 the output of the Learned Press increased. For the first time since the Civil War it reached a hundred items a year. But this meant no increased activity in the Delegates' publishing business. Much of the work was still being done for private customers, the Delegates only insisting that it should never be allowed to interrupt work on their own books, and that it would not be done without their cognizance. For sermons and short pieces, however, it was sufficient to get leave from the Vice-Chancellor, and it was sufficient too for any books printed during the Long Vacation, between June and October. The partners, competent men of business, went about the maximization of their profits, to the University's benefit as well as their own.

No provision was made for a publishing office in Walton Street, nor could anybody foresee at the time that the next generation would need one. The Delegates continued to meet in the Clarendon Building, as they still do. The University Registrar attended the meetings and kept the minutes. Transactions with authors and editors, often very informal, were in the hands of the Vice-Chancellor or individual Delegates, though on occasion one of the partners might be asked to conduct the actual correspondence. In 1834 Samuel Collingwood was desired to convey to Professor Dindorf the regret of the Delegates that they could not pay him the fee agreed to for his notes on Sophocles because they failed in every way to come up to their expectations. Presumably on this occasion Gaisford, who normally dealt with Dindorf, flinched from the task.

Edward Cardwell was chairman of the Bible Committee which represented the University in its dealings with the partners. It was appealed to from time to time on literary matters, such as the placing of a disputed comma or the lay-out of a verse. It was Cardwell who in 1856 came to some sort of agreement with Benjamin Jowett for a translation of Plato's dialogues. Years later, after his death, the Delegates tried to discover its precise nature, but the minutes were obscure and Jowett would not enlighten them. Older Delegates recalled vaguely that it had been for a limited number of dialogues with a limited amount of commentary. Jowett was abiding by no limits, and the work was eventually published in four large volumes in 1871. By then it had been resolved that under no circumstances should individual Delegates enter into agreements with authors.

In 1838 Samuel Collingwood resigned his post as Printer to the University and superintendent of the Clarendon Press after thirty-six years

C

and was succeeded by Thomas Combe. The Press had advertised for a man who was 'not much above 40 years of age', Church of England, proficient in Latin and French, and 'a regularly bred printer'. Combe, son of a Leicester bookseller and printer, was forty-one and employed at the time by Joseph Parker. He remained at the Press until his death in 1872, and during those years he was the main influence on Oxford printing. In 1841 he was admitted as a partner, and in 1851 he became the senior partner, holding eight shares. The Bible Press had never known nor would it know better days. Combe became rich, also a benefactor and patron of the arts, particularly of the Pre-Raphaelites. Millais and Holman Hunt stayed at his house in the quad: his important collection of their paintings and drawings was bequeathed to the Ashmolean Museum. Combe founded and paid for the Church of St. Barnabas in Jericho, intended primarily for his employees, to ensure that they did not drift into dissent. It became a fashionable haunt of the High-Church party in the University. On first arriving in Oxford Combe had stayed with his sister, who let lodgings to Newman and Pusey; their influence upon him was lasting. He also started a Sunday school for the boys at the Press and taught there regularly for twenty years, as well as giving evening classes in secular subjects. Equally solicitous in this respect was Edward Pickard Hall, who became a partner in 1853 and remained one until the final dissolution of the partnership in 1884, when he faced poverty in old age. Combe amassed a fortune of £80,000. But a later Printer to the University, Charles Batey, recorded in 1967 that, 'unfortunately, I can find no evidence that he had any interest in good typography, nor have I discovered any specimen of his work which has the least merit'.

The University was receiving its share of Bible profits, though it was not always certain what to do with money it was unaccustomed to possessing. Vice-Chancellors vacillated, unable to decide whether one cause was worthier than another, whether in fact to spend the money at all was not to squander it. The Delegates themselves allocated sums for specific purposes. At the end of 1830 Joseph Parker and Samuel Collingwood had to report that the Clarendon Building, recently vacated, was in a 'very ruinous condition'. The Press contributed £1,000 towards repairs, and later in 1831 paid £2,000 towards its conversion into University offices. In 1836 the Delegates, finding that they had more money available than was needed for the immediate purposes of printing, offered to 'resign to the general purposes of the University the annual sum of £1,050'. In 1841 they voted £10,000 towards the building of the University Galleries; in 1843 and 1844 two further contributions of £10,000 were made; in 1845 a sum of £3,000 was placed at the Vice-Chancellor's disposal for their completion. In the end the Press had spent more on the Ashmolean Museum (as it was eventually called) than on its own building in Walton Street.

The *embarras de richesses* culminated in 1850 when surplus profits of £60,000 were handed over to the Hebdomadal Board. The Vice-Chancellor proposed that a substantial part should go to the building of a museum, with laboratories and other amenities, for the new School of Natural

Science. There was violent opposition from the High-Church party. To spend the profits from sacred books on sciences which were not only profane but attracted no students would be both blasphemous and futile. It was better that it should go to supporting poor scholars than to 'building a receptacle for dried insects'. E. B. Pusey warned Convocation that, 'having parted with the education of most of those who are to serve God in secular professions, we are now ceasing to educate enough men for the supply of clergy'. Throughout the 1850s payments to the University remained substantial, rarely falling below £10,000 a year.

In 1855 Combe bought the paper-mill by the river at Wolvercote, and had it completely rebuilt and equipped. It was to be run as a separate business by the partners, the purchase having been approved by the Delegates. A single Fourdrinier machine began to produce paper for the Bible Press in 1857: it went on turning it out until 1940, when its last gasp could be heard in Walton Street. In 1898 further building was needed to house a second machine to double the output. That endured until 1966, by when an entirely new mill of advanced design had been built on the site.

The Delegates on the whole had reason to be grateful for Combe's foresight, particularly in wartime. But the Mill was apt to fall victim to unpredictable market forces that did not apply, in the same way or at the same time, to other parts of the business. Then a cloud of misgiving would descend, and it would be asked why the Press needed its own paper-mill when other publishers did not, any more than they did a printing-press, and by what foolishness had the Delegates allowed it to come into their possession, as eventually it did.

Moreover during the nineteenth century it created appalling problems of pollution. It was feared that it would have to be closed down because no answer could be found that would satisfy the Thames Conservancy Board. The effluent was said to be equivalent to the sewage of a town of 6,000 inhabitants. Much of it passed into the river. The manager of the Mill in the late 1860s, John Stacey, wrote: 'The materials which have been found most advantageous in making paper for the Oxford Press are canvas sails and cotton rags.... The principal impurities in the former are the tarred thread with which the sails are sewn and the particles of pitch from the ships' deck and rigging. The bulk of the cotton rags are generally of a lower character, and ... contain a perceptible quantity of animal matter, the nature of which may be imagined, when it is stated that they are the cast-off garments of the lowest class of society.... The animal matter is very perceptible to the smell.'

The abominable rags were eventually superseded by wood-pulp, and the problem of the effluent was overcome.

3. The Press and the Tractarians

THE aim of the Press as publisher has been defined as the advancement of knowledge and religion, 'though excluding religious controversy'. In the 1830s what Gladstone called 'a spirit of dementation' afflicted Oxford. It went by the names of Tractarianism, Puseyism, or the Oxford Movement, and it broke out in earnest in 1833 when John Keble declared in a sermon a state of national apostasy and aroused the enthusiasm of John Henry Newman. The religious controversy that ensued was prolonged, intemperate, and debilitating. The Press did its best to stand aside, and succeeded to the extent that it remained discreetly behind the times. The Tractarians were in their way making contributions to scholarship, not by advancing knowledge but by retreating two hundred years to do again the work of their martyred ancestors.

'Liberalism' in theology was the greatest threat to the Anglican church, but political developments precipitated the crisis. The repeal of the Test and Corporations Acts in 1828, the Catholic Emancipation Bill of 1829, the Reform Bill of 1832, finally an act abolishing two archbishoprics and ten bishoprics in Ireland, persuaded Keble and his friends that the Church of England as a divine institution was in peril from the secular state. In the name of Charles the Martyr, Laud, and everything that Oxford held dear, they embarked on a crusade of heroic insularity, the object of which was to prove that the Anglican church was the one true catholic church, the Church of Christ as it had existed before the schism between east and west, and before the emergence of Roman error. The seventeenth-century Anglican divines, and through them the Fathers of the Church, were the safest guides to truth in this grave moral and spiritual dilemma. The Bible, written before the church existed, was 'from the nature of the case', as Newman put it, 'inferior as an instrument of proof, in directness and breadth, to Councils, to the Schola, and to the Fathers, doctors, theologians, and devotional writers of the Church'.

The University Press, having been founded very much for the purpose, had a strong back-list of patristic and theological texts and was ready enough to add to it. Newman in his spare time collated manuscripts for an edition of Dionysius of Alexandria, an occupation he found relaxing. But he had little spare time. The Tractarians were in a hurry and in pursuit of converts. The *Tracts for the Times*, edited by Newman, began to appear in leaflet form in 1833. They were distributed free at first but as they grew in size and substance it was necessary to find a publisher. Parker was unable (or according to Newman unwilling) to sell them. In 1835 they were transferred to Rivington, who did no better until he issued a collected edition which was an unexpected success. From then on the Tracts sold in large quantities. E. B. Pusey became Newman's most powerful and influential contributor. His Tract XVIII, *Thoughts on the Benefits of the System of Fasting*, had little appeal, for unknown to him fasting had generally gone out of fashion, but subsequent works on baptism transformed the Tracts from pamphlets into learned treatises. Pusey applied himself wholeheartedly to a cause which experience in Germany had convinced him was desperate: there he had felt 'the deadly breath of infidel thought' upon his soul. He sold his carriage and horses, and his wife sold her jewellery, to help finance 'A Library of the Fathers', published by John Henry Parker. Parker also launched a 'Library of Anglo-Catholic Theology', publishing six volumes of some 400 pages each year. Rivington started a 'Theological Library', concentrating on the Councils of the Church. The Tractarians also produced a series of 'Lives of the English Saints'.

The Press was not equipped to take part in a race of this kind. The Tracts, being controversial, did not fall within its province, and the 'Library of the Fathers' consisted of translations for which the Delegates saw no need, though they were willing to print the texts in Latin. In 1839 they exercised their veto when Pusey applied for leave to print at the Press a letter from the Bishop of Oxford on imputed tendencies to Romanism in Tractarian doctrine: the Vice-Chancellor was asked to inform him that the Delegates, 'while they wish to be understood as expressing no opinion in the controversy of which this Letter will form a part decline undertaking it at the University Press; in as much as their so doing would involve the obligation of printing any reply to it that might be offered to them'. An attitude of stern neutrality was consciously adopted. But Oxford's long obsession was bound to leave its mark. In 1833 the list was still predominantly classical: by 1860 it was predominantly theological. The scholars who edited the works of the seventeenth-century theologians for the Press would have been suspect if they had shown symptoms of the fanatical zeal that gripped Newman and Pusey. They were certainly not inspired by the urgency of the cause to work as they did sixteen hours a day. The massive theological tomes they eventually produced came too late, when the bottom had dropped out of the market.

In 1841 Newman published his Tract XC on the Thirty-nine Articles, minimizing or obscuring their Protestant content. It was attacked by a group of tutors, and by the Hebdomadal Board, and the Bishop of Oxford imposed silence on its author. Newman withdrew from Oxford and into the Church of Rome. Under Pusey's leadership the movement continued for a few years more. But in 1843 Pusey himself was suspended from preaching, on grounds too complex to be understood by the layman. People in Oxford were becoming either totally bewildered by the intricacies of theological debate, or nervously disgusted by the intolerance and acrimony that accompanied it. An amiable obsession with King Charles's head, after the manner of Mr. Dick in *David Copperfield*, who regrettably never finished his Tract, was one thing: the furious self-righteousness of the heresy-hunter another. Timorous dons lowered their voices, for there was no sure way between Rome, dissent, scepticism, and perjury. Oxford was so very different, from London obviously, but from Cambridge too. Elsewhere not only dissenters but agnostics and radicals were freely walking the streets. But, within the University, to question the Thirty-nine Articles meant expulsion and disgrace, if it did not lead to a cardinal's hat. For a time it seemed that Oxford could only be reached through a kind of underground radical press, in which gentlemen sought others of a similar persuasion who wished to engage in uninhibited discussion of the historicity of the Bible, and other delicate matters. But the inevitable reaction came.

The Fathers of the Church went out of favour. Even Gaisford dismissed them as 'sad rubbish'. Voltaire had done more good than all the Fathers of the Church put together, Jowett could say when the storm had passed. In his *Memoirs*, written at the end of his life, Mark Pattison recalled that in 1839 'fanaticism was laying its deadly grip around me'. Under Newman's spell he too had squandered his time on those 'degenerate and semi-barbarous Christian writers of the Fourth Century'. But by 1850, he claimed, theology had been banished, free opinions were rife. The repercussions of the Oxford Movement were felt throughout the country and for the rest of the century, chiefly in the forms of worship, but the theological debate subsided.

Many of the Clarendon Press editions of the English divines had yet to come, however, and they were of frightening proportions. The works of Thomas Jackson (1579-1640) ran to 12 volumes. Those of Sanderson (1587-1663) appeared in 6 volumes in 1854; of Waterland (1683-1740) in 6 volumes in 1857; of Patrick (1625-1707) in 9 volumes in 1859; of Hall (1574-1656) in 10 volumes, the third collected edition of the century, as late as 1863. It took a long time for these and similar books to work their way out of the system. Until well into the twentieth century there were many who associated the Press with Bibles and these large, unread, unwanted, densely printed tomes of religious polemic bound in a dull chocolate brown.

Some were edited by reputable scholars. But considerations of scholarship as of profitability were not always uppermost in the minds of the Delegates in this period. There was chronic unemployment in the University as Fellows waited for a college living to fall vacant, and the Delegates were not unwilling at times to mitigate the hardship it caused. Blanco White, a man of Irish extraction from Andalusia who voyaged through the fringes of Oxford life from Roman Catholicism into Unitarianism, complained in 1828 that he was not eligible for relief. 'Had I had supporters among the leading members of the University, it would have been easy to employ me in *editing* for the Clarendon Press, which is frequently the *secondary* employment of young men not particularly distinguished for their knowledge.' It was natural to put such men to work on whatever books were being talked about at the time. For a decade or so it seemed that nothing was being talked about that did not stem in one way or another from the Tractarian movement.

Alexander Macmillan, who became Publisher to the University, gave his account of what had happened in a letter to Gladstone in 1865. Gladstone had asked about the sales of Oxford books, which Macmillan had to admit were small. He attributed this to 'the very remarkable and somewhat sudden change that has taken place in theological study and reading of late years. Perhaps I should rather say the *fashion* in theological book-buying—for to be honest . . . I have my doubts whether much that could be called *reading* went on, still less *study*. . . . But it was the *purchase* arising from interest in seventeenth-century divinity that justified numerous reprints that were made at the University Press some fifteen or twelve years since. This was owing to the Oxford movement, and the praise bestowed by the leaders of that movement on these divines. The works of Jackson, Patrick, and others of that class were in high demand. . . . Dr. Newman and others seemed convinced that the mind that was in them, if reproduced in our time, would redeem us from liberalism and other deleterious influences in religious and political regions. . . . What wonder if the delegates of the Press, used to the *stable* and delighted to find that the most active minds were maintaining that the stable was also the advanced, went in for the reproduction of the great advocates of *order* in Church and State.'

Macmillan was wrong about the demand. It had scarcely ever existed, and in the six years since Patrick's works had been printed only eight copies had been sold. Some volumes of the Works of the English Divines, the first 'Series' to appear from the Press, served a useful purpose and sold relatively well: for Hooker, Butler, Pearson, and Barrow there was a steady demand. But their descent cannot be traced to the Tractarian movement.

4. A Society of Shy Hypochondriacs

DURING the 1840s the Press acquired two valuable properties, Liddell & Scott's *Greek-English Lexicon* and Charles Wordsworth's *Greek Grammar*. The former was originally a translation and revision of Passow's *Greek-German Lexicon*. Robert Scott had been urged by the Oxford publisher and bookseller, David Talboys, to undertake it shortly after the German lexicographer's early death in 1834. Scott agreed on condition that his friend and contemporary Henry Liddell would collaborate. They were both tutors at Christ Church, still in their early twenties. Tallboys died in 1840, and it was then that the Press assumed responsibility. The first edition of 3,000 copies was published in 1843: an abridged version for schools had been prepared simultaneously. Passow's name remained on the title-page until the fourth edition in 1854. Thereafter Liddell and Scott went hand in hand into eternity. The seventh edition of 1883, for which he received £1,650, was by Liddell alone, the eighth of 1893 the last of his lifetime. But the pair were still inseparable on the title-page of the revised and augmented 'Liddell & Scott', which began to appear in fascicles in 1925.

Liddell, Dean of Christ Church after 1855, was an important and imposing figure in nineteenth-century Oxford. The Radical Goldwin Smith compared him to Leonardo da Vinci, and Tuckwell remembered him in the

1830s as 'already magnificent in presence, less superbly Olympian than he afterwards became'. Despite strong liberal sympathies his orthodoxy went unchallenged: he was prominent on the Oxford Commission of 1850 and subsequently on the Hebdomadal Council until his death in 1898. Scott was elected Master of Balliol in 1854, a triumph for which he was never fully forgiven. In a rancorous contest he defeated Jowett, whose views both on religion and education were heterodox. Jowett finally became Master in 1870, when Scott was appointed Dean of Rochester.

Charles Wordsworth, nephew of the poet, belonged to the same fine breed of Christ Church students as Liddell and Scott, as well as Gladstone and Canning and various other luminaries. He glittered more than any of them, appearing in his youth like a Greek god returned to earth to teach his native tongue. He offered his Grammar to the Delegates in 1844: acceptance was on condition that he would receive £20 for each 1,000 copies printed. Printing numbers increased from 3,000 to 12,000, as all the public schools except Eton came to depend upon it. In 1863 sales reached 5,000 copies, and it escaped any serious competition for some forty years. The abridged Greek Lexicon had a record sale of over 11,000 copies in 1880. These two books transformed the business of the Learned Press, reluctant though it was at first to draw any conclusions from their great success.

To understand the slow gestation of the modern Press it is necessary to take into account the society from which it sprang: its parochialism, its isolation, its fears of the world beyond its gates. It was a society of shy hypochondriacs. There were men of formidable talents concentrating most of their intellectual energies on matters peculiar to Oxford. Exposure to the outside world was seen as a positive danger. Pusey had learned German the better to understand the nature of the foe, but it was said that there were only two other men in Oxford at the time who knew the language. Pusey himself manned the Oxford defences. Throughout his life he cared passionately for the purity of youth, the intensity of his own feelings of sinfulness releasing an appalling image of the perils to which the young were exposed. When it was suggested that students might be allowed to live in halls of residence or even lodging-houses—a move intended to allow Nonconformists an Oxford education without subscribing to collegiate oaths—Pusey saw his defences crumbling. 'Lodging-houses are the worst form of temptation', he declared, a vision of servant maids opening the doors at all times coruscating through his mind. The railways, the great symbol of progress and of all the powerful energies of the age, were to the morbid isolationists of Oxford an even greater threat to morality than lodging-houses, exposing young men to London, even perhaps to a malign contagion from Germany where learning and licentiousness went hand in hand. The London to Bristol line was successfully diverted at Didcot in 1835. It was of course a lost cause, and the first trains from Paddington eventually reached Oxford in 1844. They were found to be carrying neither harlots nor atheists but quantities of country parsons ready to vote down measures for reform in Convocation in support of the clerical party.

Only in such a context can the two Yorkshiremen, Mark Pattison and Benjamin Jowett, be seen to stand for principles of enlightened rationalism. They lent symmetry to nineteenth-century Oxford as archetypal opposites, but at least they shared a desire to return the University to the nation in one form or another. Pattison sought no disciples but by his very existence epitomized the concept of the pursuit of knowledge as an end sublime and complete in itself. It should have led to an inner fulfilment, but it left Pattison morose, repelled by events that he himself had helped to bring about. His failure to get the Rectorship of Lincoln in 1851 spelt the end of all his earthly hopes, it seemed at the time, and as the years passed he did become a more and more unearthly figure. In many ways he answered to Nietzsche's description of the well-read man, who cannot think unless he has a book in his hand. 'The scholar is a decadent', Nietzsche wrote. 'With my own eyes I have seen gifted, richly-endowed, free-spirited natures "read to pieces" at thirty—nothing but matches that have to be struck before they can emit any sparks—or "thoughts".' But Pattison went through too many manifestations for generalization to be possible. There is a lingering suspicion that he may have been a great man. The German scholar Max Müller once said that anywhere but in Oxford he would have grown into a Lessing. In Oxford it was a matter of some relief that he did not.

In 1850 he had been fascinated by one of the latest publications of the Press, the diary of the classical scholar Isaac Casaubon (1559–1614). His life's work, he resolved, was to be a history of European learning since the Renaissance: his life of Casaubon, published by Longmans in 1875, was a small part of the great work never completed. It was as Casaubon that he stepped into George Eliot's *Middlemarch*, as an ageing, thin-lipped pedant, with perpetually cold and clammy hands.

'Little, white-haired, cherub-faced Jowett', as Tuckwell called him, was a natural predator. He stalked generations of undergraduates in search of prey, and was rewarded by a loyal and domesticated following of able, practical, active men. 'In some of us', he wrote, 'Liberalism soon took the practical shape of an effort to reform and emancipate the University, to strike off the fetters of medieval statutes . . . set it free from the pre-dominance of ecclesiasticism, recall it to its proper work, and restore it to the nation.' Its proper work was to teach and send out into the world men who would administer and govern it.

A habit of nervousness lingered on, an understandable reluctance to speak one's mind unless in a spirit of deadly righteousness. At a meeting of the British Association in Oxford in 1860 on the origin of species, T. H. Huxley, a little heatedly but without any fear of reprisal, told the Bishop of Oxford, Samuel Wilberforce, that he 'would rather be descended from an ape than from a divine who employs authority to stifle truth'. In the same year *Essays and Reviews* was published in London, a book to which both Jowett and Pattison contributed. It was an appeal by a group of academic liberal Anglicans for free criticism in religious matters. The Bishop of Oxford denounced it intemperately; two contributors were actually tried for heresy in the Court of Arches; Jowett was summoned to appear in the Vice-Chancellor's court in Oxford; and a mass protest of clergy ensured that the book was synodically condemned. There were still two worlds, and Oxford still belonged to the other one in which eternal punishment had to be taken seriously into account.

An impression of Oxford in the first half of the century as a rather frightened adolescent, nervous of the extremes to which it felt itself impelled, is enhanced by the prevalence of an excruciating shyness that afflicted some of its leading figures, often with unfortunate consequences to the future development of their personalities. The two men who could always fill churches and hold congregations rapt were both victims: Pusey was described as 'shy beyond conception', and Newman never quite overcame or forgot the memory of tongue-tied gaucherie in his early years, when he and his contemporaries appeared as twitching mutes in common-room. Even Jowett, in a letter to Tennyson, wrote of 'the devil of shyness' within him. Pattison as an old man recalled the blushing and trembling, the acute self-consciousness, that afflicted him as a 'physical nervousness' in his early years at Oxford. 'This sheepishness, and wondering what others were think-ing of me, was a source of unspeakable misery.' Terrifyingly prolonged silences had been a feature of Oxford life since Dr. Fell's day at least, and were to frighten later generations too. But the most usual way of calling attention to shyness was to point to an attribute that concealed it. Tuckwell's description of the suave and superb Liddell is a replica of many an Oxford obituary: 'beneath the stern, reserved, austere outside lay a man humble, reverent, tender-hearted; his severity straight-forwardness, his *hauteur* shyness. . . .' It was almost a test of sensibility, and perhaps shyness has always lurked in the academic psyche. But it had to be strenuously repressed and transmuted as Oxford men generally found a part to play in the world. Overcome, it provided the nervous energy behind that supposedly effortless superiority claimed by later generations.

In 1850 Lord John Russell set up a Royal Commission to investigate the two ancient Universities. To the Hebdomadal Board in Oxford it was an outrageous and unnecessary invasion of privacy. The University's statutes had been revised by Laud as recently as 1636, 'at a time when not only the nature and faculties of the human mind were exactly what they are still, and must of course remain, but the principles also of sound and enlarged intellectual culture were far from being imperfectly understood'. The Oxford Act of 1854 abolished the Board, replacing it by a Hebdomadal Council consisting of the Vice-Chancellor and Proctors, seven heads of Houses, eight professors, and six members elected by Congregation. Revision of the statutes created two new faculties: the Schools of Natural Science and of Law and Modern History came into being. The classi-cal curriculum became less literary and philological, more historical and philosophical. The first steps were taken towards opening the University to all according to merit.

The constitution of the Press Delegacy was changed as well. It had consisted of the Vice-Chancellor and two Proctors *ex officio*, and of eight 'perpetual' Delegates appointed by them. In 1856 it was divided into five perpetual and five junior appointments, vacancies among the former being filled by the Delegates themselves, among the latter by the Vice-Chancellor and Proctors as before. The Proctors, however, ceased to be Delegates *ex officio* and were not restored to the Delegacy until 1921. The University, it was finally asserted, belonged to the nation and could not be regarded 'as a mere aggregation of private interests', or colleges. Hazily the principle was emerging that, just as the University's interests were not local, so it was proper for the Delegates to be concerned with all manner of books: in particular with education, at home and eventually abroad, at a variety of levels. The Press could no longer be content with the mere printing of books. It had to publish them.

PART II

1860–1884
'VIGILANT SUPERINTENDENCE'

---

1. The Call of the Metropolis

IN the early 1860s the long connection with the Parker family began to break down. Joseph Parker, a Bible printer since 1790 and a partner since 1810, had contributed much to the recovery of the Bible business. On his death in 1850 he held eight and a half shares. His nephew John Henry Parker succeeded him in the family business, but was not admitted to the Bible partnership. He continued as Warehouse keeper, responsible for the printed sheets stacked in the cellar of the Sheldonian and for those stored in Walton Street, until 1862, when he was told that his services were no longer needed. The Delegates had decided to be their own 'Warehouseman'. The handing-over of the key to the cellar by Parker was a more or less symbolic gesture. But the next year it was decided that his son James should cease to be the sole agent and distributor of Clarendon Press books. No loss of confidence was implied, the Delegates were at pains to insist, and the services of the family to the University were duly acknowledged.

Some such assurance was necessary to advertise an amicable parting of the ways. The Parkers had, as it happened, recently offended the Delegates and the partners by issuing a 'paragraph' Bible which though novel in arrangement was essentially the Authorized Version: accused of having 'invaded' the privilege of the University they had been forced to withdraw the book. They had also taken over a series of cheap classical texts and other books for schools, no crime in itself but unfortunate at a time when the Press was planning to enter the educational field too. The break with the Parkers, however, signified a more radical change in the mood of the Delegates. Concern about the future of Bible sales and profits, and a realization that it was not a little absurd that the Learned Press should have on its list only two really saleable books—Wordsworth's Grammar and the Liddell & Scott Lexicons—had persuaded some younger Delegates that the Press's achievements in secular publishing had lagged sadly behind the times. There was a new and pressing demand for new books. A deeply rooted preference in Oxford for old books could obscure it for a while—German professors, it had been noted with aversion, seemed to have hardly any books in their libraries over thirty years old—but the reforms of the 1850s and the cautious welcome to new studies made new books essential.

In 1861 Bartholomew Price became a Delegate. By the end of the century he had been accorded the place of fourth great man in the history of the Press—after Laud, Fell, and Blackstone. At the same time his friend Henry Liddell was appointed. Robert Scott had been made a Delegate six years earlier, on becoming Master of Balliol. John Griffiths, Keeper of the Archives, a mild retiring uncontroversial man, who had nevertheless been one of the four tutors to attack Tract XC in 1841, was also active. Walter Shirley, Professor of Ecclesiastical History and one of the most promising young historians in Oxford, was made a Delegate in 1862 but died four years later at the age of 38. Henry Mansel was the most outspoken of the High-Church and Tory faction. Committees and subcommittees were formed, and a revitalized and inquisitive Board of Delegates thoughtfully reviewed its procedures.

The Delegates were conscious of their power and resources. But they lacked experience, and a part of the business—the executive part—seemed to be missing. In London there were great publishers guiding the cultural destiny of the nation, possessed of an expertise that seemed to run in families and make them prosperous. Owing, perhaps, to their example, the later history of the Press is remarkable for the way in which a few Oxford dons eliminated distinctions between amateur and professional, leaving their studies to become executives of a great business. For a time Robert Scott by reason of assiduity and some seniority slid almost inadvertently into the executive role, keeping a 'Press drawer' at Balliol into which papers sometimes disappeared, and conducting the Delegates' business during vacation.

It was Scott who addressed the first appeal for help to John Murray III in London in April 1863. He told Murray of the break with Parkers, and of the need for a successor: 'We want more energy in our publishing department,' he wrote. 'We want an Agent who could be a more satisfactory and able Confidential adviser. We want one who would also assist the other department of the University Press, by bringing printing business to it. And we are inclined to think, though this perhaps is open to doubt, that our Agent should have a retail-business in Oxford in combination with a London House.' In short they wanted somebody to show them how to publish new books, and they realized that this meant once again entrusting a part of their business to professionals in London.

John Murray was not tempted. He was eminent enough and lived to be the only publisher in London to intimidate Bernard Shaw. Alexander Macmillan, however, recently arrived in London from Cambridge and already a distinguished publisher, found the further distinction of being Publisher to the University of Oxford irresistible. He was second on the Delegates' list, and Scott, Griffiths, and Price were appointed a committee to confer with him about terms. Agreement having been reached he was appointed publisher of 'all books issued by the University from the Learned side of the Press' in 1863. The arrangement lasted until 1880. He was not a partner in the old sense but an agent.

A new partner, Henry Latham, had made his appearance in 1862. He acquired four shares, and was responsible, under the general superintendency of Combe, for the printing works and for the Paper-Mill. Edward Pickard Hall was responsible for discipline—or labour relations—and the London partners, Gardner & Son, for the Bound Book Business, the selling of Bibles and Prayer Books. Latham spent an uncomfortable eight years with the Press. Little is known about him, except that he had been called to the Bar, but presumably failed to find a practice, and considered his work compatible with residence in London, or even overseas, a view not shared by the Delegates. He suffered too from their new assumption of authority, as a result of which he appeared not to know his place. Price disliked him and resented his interference in matters of policy. A strong suspicion was gaining ground that the interests of the partners and those of the Delegates were not necessarily identical. Moreover Latham had a grievance. He had come too late to enjoy a share of the booty that Bible sales brought in during the 1850s. He blamed the decline in profits on Gardner, whom he fiercely denounced to the Delegates as incompetent and idle. 'Mr. Gardner was all very well in the days when the U.P. was like the Pagoda-tree and those who sat under it had only to hold their pockets open. But matters are very different now. . . . Notwithstanding . . . I believe that under proper management there are few better trades in England than the Bible trade.'

But Mr. Gardner could not properly be blamed for the decline in Bible profits. Combe had bought the Paper-Mill partly because he too was afraid that the privilege might soon be taken away. Paper constituted two-thirds of the total cost of producing Bibles, so in any price war the saving had to be made there. The privilege survived, but the competition was intense. The very cheapest paper had to be bought abroad, in Belgium or France: 'third-quality' paper, as it was called, was the principal product of the Mill as the demand for fine paper diminished. By 1865 the output of the Bible Press reached a million books a year. Two-thirds were being sold to the British and Foreign Bible Society, and its demand was for the cheapest possible product. In 1864 an extremely small Bible (24mo) was being sold for 4*d*. Sales increased but the profits dwindled and by the 1860s the Bible Press had ceased to be particularly lucrative. Dividends to the University and partners fell by more than half in a decade.

This in itself might have been enough to prompt an energetic Board of Delegates into action. As a start, a Warehouse Committee was appointed in 1862 and its first report made depressing reading: 'books of slow sale have remained for many years as they were stacked; some, it is thought, from the very opening of the new Printing office. . . . Dust and dirt have gathered about.' One stack at least, of Archbishop Sharp's work in five volumes, had been irrecoverably damaged by mildew. The Committee was authorized to waste superfluous stock: 768 sets of sheets of the Archbishop's works were so disposed of, and eight sets were salvaged—enough to meet the demand for the next eight years. The same committee, consisting of Griffiths, Scott, and Price, but calling itself the Learned Press Committee, recommended that the Delegates should consider the question of issuing books already bound. Oxford was one of the last publishers in the country to sell its books in sheets. But the Board of Delegates as a whole found it difficult to take decisive action: it could only refer the matter back to the Committee, which in its turn could not act without the consent of the full Board. With vacations inevitably intervening, the implementation of decisions could be protracted, and it was not until 1870 that the Press acquired its own bindery in London. In the meantime Macmillan arranged for the binding of learned books as he required them.

2. The Clarendon Press Series

In May 1863 Bartholomew Price read to the Delegates an important proposal for a series of educational books. It was referred to the Warehouse or Learned Press Committee, which recommended setting up a School-book Commitee. The Delegates concurred, and the three members of the former committee were converted into the latter, with further assistance from Henry Mansel, Liddell, and Shirley. It was instructed 'to take all necessary measures for the speedy publication' of elementary classical works, delectuses, and exercises; elementary French books; and treatises on heat, light, electricity, and magnetism. Macmillan promised to advise, and did so enthusiastically. Even before he had officially taken up his appointment he was recommending new editions of Chaucer, Locke, Berkeley, and Butler: the Delegates had also authorized him to spend up to £600 in negotiating with Joseph Bosworth, Rawlinson Professor of Anglo-Saxon, the copyright in his Anglo-Saxon Dictionary. The School-book Committee members said that they would prefer 'to undertake such works as they find to be wanted rather than a systematic series'. A very large number of books were found to be wanted, and in the end there was certainly nothing systematic about them except that they belonged to the 'Clarendon Press Series'.

By February 1864 the Committee had completed its preliminary investigations, and presented a substantial report. It had been particularly concerned 'to give an interest, pecuniary as well as other, to all parties concerned in the work—Authors, Editors, Publishers, and Delegates of the Press'. The Committee was determined to be generous, believing that financial inducements would improve the quality of the books. Eminent academics and school-teachers were to be enlisted, and books of the kind required could not be done on the cheap. There was to be no more hack work for poor scholars. 'The truth is', wrote Mark Pattison to Price some years later, 'that to write really valuable notes on an English classic requires an amount of previous knowledge, and present labour, which can not be paid for by any publisher; hence the job necessarily falls into the hands of young and raw beginners.' But to begin with it was proper to aim high, and it was up to Pattison and his fellow Delegates to ensure that standards were maintained.

In its report the School-book Committee wrote: 'The Delegates can, it is presumed, by means of the Clarendon Press and their relation to Oxford, give a certain authority to a book: but they are bound to take all possible care that the character of the book merits their "Imprimatur"; and a distribution of pecuniary interest appears well calculated to secure this object so far as may be possible.' The reasoning is not easy to follow, nor was it followed. But the Committee, altogether too sanguine in its assessment of pecuniary interests, had asserted a portentous principle, one which expressed a new conception of the Delegates' functions and responsibilities. It had not escaped Henry Latham, for one, that the first half of the proposition applied. The Oxford imprint on a Bible was a commercial advantage he understood well, and there was no reason why secular books should not also enjoy it. The reciprocal obligation was a different matter. To fulfil it would take time. It also meant entering into competition with other publishers trying to meet the demand for better school-books. At an earlier period their efforts might have been seen to justify inactivity: now it was a challenge to the Press to do better. A complete form of agreement was drawn up in a businesslike fashion, with many blanks left to allow for various permutations of royalty and profit-sharing arrangements. Basically payment would be at a generous rate per sheet of 16 pages. Taking a book of 500 pages and 2,000 copies as the norm, it was proposed to pay £100 on publication and 2s. a copy on all copies sold. The writer should eventually receive £300, a rate of £9. 12s. per sheet—'a very liberal remuneration', as the Committee realized. To Macmillan it seemed a lot for a school textbook: a lump sum of £30 would have been nearer the mark.

The Committee had gleaned from the eminent schoolmasters they had consulted, and from professors and teachers in Oxford, that good English editions of almost all the Greek and Latin classics read in the higher forms of the public schools were urgently needed, as well as good grammars and exercises: there was 'a great and urgent want of Delectuses, Analecta, and generally of books of Selections from Authors, for use in Schools'. It had also been discovered that history books were far below current require-ments, and that in the physical sciences good books suitably adapted for schools did not exist. The venture into secular publishing quickly assumed the nature of a crusade. Naturally enough the classical void was the easiest to fill. With the help of the Professor of Latin, Conington, the Committee had been offered ten substantial editions, and with the help of Professor Jowett Greek would be adequately covered. But history books could not so

Thomas Combe, Printer to the University, 1838–72

Alexander Macmillan, Publisher to the University, 1863-80

easily be gathered in. The Delegates had already accepted a History of England from the earliest times to the death of Henry VII by Professor Goldwin Smith. The Committee could find nothing else to recommend. Professor Brodie advised acceptance of an Elementary Chemistry by Professor Williamson of University College, London, and was willing to allow his own name to appear on the title-page to indicate his approval of the work. One of Macmillan's authors, Balfour Stewart, promised an elementary treatise on heat. But, apart from a possible book on laboratory practice, that was all the Committee had to offer for the advancement of science. A textbook on law by William Markby promised well.

In October 1865, though no books had yet been published in the series, it was acknowledged that the work of the School-book Committee had become so complicated that somebody would have to be appointed to look after its affairs. The man chosen was G. W. Kitchin, later Dean of Winchester and Durham. He had been headmaster of a preparatory school, then Censor of Christ Church until he married in 1863. Before becoming Secretary to the School-book Committee he had been lecturing for several Oxford colleges, mostly on history, though he was extremely versatile. Six months later he was appointed Secretary to the Board of Delegates, the first of a distinguished line, on a salary of £220.

Kitchin was a man of strong liberal sympathies throughout his long life—he died in 1912 at the age of 85. He showed skill in dealing both with the Delegates and with Macmillan, behaving as a detached and rather irreverent individual—unlike his successor Bartholomew Price, who was himself an institution. Kitchin was also patient. He endured for two exasperating years the failure of the headmasters of the great public schools—'the awful Nine', as he called them—to decide which grammars were to receive their imprimatur. Upon this the provision of exercises and delectuses depended. Rumour reported that Kennedy's *Latin Grammar* from Longmans was the favourite: would they select Wordsworth's Greek, or perhaps insist on adaptation or revision? The Delegates, Robert Scott in particular, manœuvred, conspired, and brought all influence to bear: they also took the opportunity to send prospectuses of the Clarendon Press Series to headmasters and school-teachers, soliciting advice and support. They were successful in that no decision was ever reached about the Greek grammar, and Wordsworth flourished as before.

The School-book Committee focused its attention initially on the needs of the public schools, assuming that an example set by them would be followed elsewhere. Kitchin took a much more broad-minded view, confident that the real opportunity for expansion lay in the Middle Class schools. The Universities by establishing the Middle Class Examinations had assumed control of a broad section of national education. The Delegacy for Local Examinations prescribed the books to be used in schools throughout the country. The object came to be that they should prescribe Oxford books, but the relationship between the two Delegacies was always delicate. At the same time new universities opening in London

D

and the provinces wanted a substitute for Greek, no longer held to be indispensable, and Kitchin had to look outside Oxford to broaden the scope of the series. He found J. S. Brewer, Professor of English Literature at University College, London, who planned an English series, consisting of selections from the finest authors, with introductions and notes. Before long Kitchin was telling prospective editors that his English list was full. An edition of Chaucer was in hand; Clark and Aldis Wright from Cambridge were to edit Shakespeare's history plays, and Wright was also preparing an edition of Bacon. Brewer himself was doing Dryden, and Kitchin, holding himself in reserve, eventually chose Spenser. Mark Pattison's offer of Pope was accepted on the understanding that 'all words, phrases, or passages unfit to be seen by ladies' should be expurgated. Kitchin had high hopes that his English series would sell well in the ladies' schools. Macmillan suggested that F. D. Maurice might be invited to edit Milton. Maurice, the 'Christian Socialist' and much loved preacher and teacher, was Macmillan's favourite author. He had been dismissed from the Chair of English to which Brewer succeeded at University College for being unsound on eternal damnation, but became in due course Professor of Moral Philosophy in Cambridge. 'I should very much like to see his name,' wrote Kitchin, 'but the Delegates are a timid folk.' It would be safer to try somebody else. The quest for safety proved unfortunate, for the Milton volume by R. C. Browne, M.A. was unsatisfactory and later exposed the Delegates to a savage attack by a young man called Churton Collins.

Macmillan, however, was not happy about the English series and confided in Latham that he was aggrieved because his views had not been properly taken into account: for once Oxford had moved too fast for him. Kitchin explained that the Delegates knew well that he was not in favour, because he did not regard it as commercially sound. It seemed prudent for Macmillan to adopt this view in an attempt to curb the generosity of the Committee. Many of the books were unlikely to be profitable, he insisted, and the higher the remuneration the less profitable they would be. As he had generously agreed to forgo his normal commission until the Delegates' costs were covered, that was a further powerful inducement to keep them down. But Kitchin had changed his tune: pecuniary advantage was no longer a major consideration. The Delegates had to do what they could for English education. 'Their conviction that they can influence Middle Class Schools for good', he told Macmillan, 'has overborne their fear of an unfavourable commercial result.'

But there was more to it than that. Oxford was too conspicuously duplicating Macmillan's own publications. He already had an edition by Aldis Wright of Bacon's *Essays* in his Golden Treasury series, and as for Shakespeare he had plans for an edition, edited by Wright and Clark, which would be 'the most perfect text and most perfect set of readings that has ever been done'. A Clarendon Bunyan was also in direct competition with a Golden Treasury Bunyan. This was a problem never resolved. 'He always has his own Publishing interests to consider,' Kitchin wrote to Brewer, 'and one is not sure of a quite fair opinion from him; though he behaves very well towards us—Scotchman, though.' Eventually Oxford took possession of Aldis Wright, whose editions of Shakespeare's plays stood beside the Greek grammars and lexicons as the staple commodities of the Press, and for generations battled it out with Cambridge's rival product, Verity's *Shakespeare*. They grew old and old-fashioned together, until a time in the twentieth century when it seemed that they had not only lost their freshness but had been unsuitable for use in schools from the start.

Macmillan in fact was extraordinarily tolerant, even magnanimous. He diverted some of his own books into the Clarendon Press Series. His enthusiasm and energy may have waned over the years, but at the start he hardly discriminated between his own and Oxford books, regarding both as being on 'our list'. Gladstone he regarded as one of 'our' most esteemed authors, almost as a son of 'our' University. Robert Scott once retaliated by rejecting a book proposed by Macmillan as unsuitable for 'our Clients, the school-boys'.

Kitchin also acted upon the Delegates' original instruction that there should be a French series, a matter overlooked in the report of the School-book Committee, and began a series of French classics edited by G. Masson. A series of German classics was added by the indefatigable C. A. Buchheim, of whom Tuckwell could only say that he had once failed to meet George Sand despite an introduction from Liszt. And Kitchin ranged further into elementary education too. As a result the Clarendon Press Series became the most heterogeneous series imaginable, divisible eventually into twelve sections, ranging from the reading books of Miss Clough and Miss Roberts at 4*d*. through the editions of the classics to Mr. Veitch's *Irregular Greek Verbs* at 10*w*. Veitch's habit of picking holes in Liddell & Scott, exhibiting the editors as 'culprits' wherever he could, was attended to by Scott himself, who edited these passages out, on behalf of his 'brother Delegates', explaining that they would not wish to see one of their own books so pilloried.

For several years there was little to show for all the activity. The books had still to be written. The Delegates gave guarded approval to the various proposals, but a decision on publication was deferred until one, or even two, sheets of a book had been set up. On the basis of the first sixteen or thirty-two pages they would decide whether to accept it or not. Henry Latham fretted, dreaming of lost profits. He had studied the lists of books prescribed for the Oxford Examinations, and those mentioned in the Report of the Public Schools Commission, and apart from Wordsworth's Grammar and Liddell & Scott not one of them was from the University Press. The opportunities were unlimited for starting a 'great manufacture' of educational books, but at the beginning of his fourth year in Oxford the last proof of the first school-book of the Clarendon Press Series was still not returned for press.

Macmillan too wondered that more rapid progress was not made, in spite of the many resolutions passed by the School-book Committee and the Delegates. 'You must have patience,' Kitchin told him. 'We deal with a large and slow going body here, as you know: and then this body has further hampered itself by attaching to itself the two Professors; who object in principle to quick movements.' One of the professors was Goldwin Smith. The other was Mark Pattison, not a professor but perhaps the equivalent in Kitchin's eyes. But the real reason for slowness, he went on, was that authors did not approach Oxford with their books already written, as they did London publishers. They offered to write books, and 'your Oxford Don is worked hard in Term time, and has Switzerland before him in Vacation'.

Even so the first titles in the series began to appear early in 1866. Among them was Williamson's *Chemistry*, 250 copies of which went out with flyleaves at the end advertising Macmillan's 'private books'. These were cancelled in the remaining copies, and Macmillan was told that it must not happen again. In 1867 the Delegates ordered that all the Clarendon Press Series so far published, and all books published in 1866, should be shown at the Great Exhibition in Paris. They made a modest display, but the entry into the market-place was itself significant. Once thoroughly launched, the series gathered momentum. In the two years 1868 and 1869 some forty new titles were published, whereas outside the Clarendon Press Series only twelve new books appeared, and of these only two were original works written in English— *Vesuvius* by the Professor of Geology, John Phillips, and the first volume of *A History of the Norman Conquest of England* by E. A. Freeman. By 1870 fifty titles had been published. The Pitt Press series of school-books from Cambridge started to appear in 1875, but some of those first in the field, like Longmans and Rivingtons, began to think of dropping out. Looking through the syllabus for the Oxford Examinations in 1878, C. J. Longman was disheartened to find that although his firm published editions of many of the books set, not one of them was listed. 'Although the absence of competition on our part no doubt promotes the pecuniary interests of the Clarendon Press,' he wrote to Price, 'it cannot be good in the long run for education.' In the same year a spokesman from Rivingtons was expressing what was perhaps mock surprise: 'We were not aware that the Clarendon Press do not recommend books for the Local Examinations, since they set the subjects and issue books on them at the same time.' They were exaggerating. The market for textbooks was growing steadily. In 1878, referring to the various series of English classics, Macmillan observed that none of them were 'really jostling each other'.

3. Alexander Macmillan

IN so far as the long association between Macmillan and Oxford was harmonious it was largely a triumph of good manners. The Clarendon Press still carried too much slow-selling stock, and continued to add to it, for the publisher to be able to regard it as a commercial asset. He had no part in the Bible business. There was much to irritate both parties to the arrangement, and Macmillan was a stubborn and irritable man. He once wrote to his elder brother Daniel, 'You must make some allowance for a man with chronic dyspepsia. You can hardly realise . . . the utter unreasonableness of a man whose acid stomach is always getting into his brain and clouding his heart.' Towards the Press he was always reasonable, patient, and in his early dealings with the Delegates fatherly, even though the man with whom he had most often to deal, Bartholomew Price, was himself patriarchal. To Macmillan the ancient University Press was still an infant, and it needed his guidance.

His own success began early and continued without interruption. Mr. Macmillan's 'private books' had glittering qualities denied to Clarendon Press books. Macmillan had no university education himself, but once he and his brother Daniel had established themselves in Cambridge they quickly became a centre of university life. Macmillan's authors were his friends. Kingsley brought him *Westward Ho!* and *The Water Babies*; Tom Hughes brought him *Tom Brown's Schooldays*; F. T. Palgrave made his *Golden Treasury*; F. D. Maurice brought him his immensely popular sermons and lectures, and Macmillan once said that he was proud to be publisher to Oxford University but prouder still to be Maurice's publisher. His Thursday evening gatherings, first in Cambridge and later at 23 Henrietta Street in London, were celebrated intellectual occasions. The 'Tobacco Parliaments' were attended by Tennyson, Thomas Huxley, Tom Hughes, F. D. Maurice, David Masson, Palgrave, Coventry Patmore, Kingsley. They represented the Broad Church, anti-Oxford Movement, with tendencies towards free-thinking on one side and towards the inbred Scottish puritanism of Macmillan himself on the other. From these meetings emerged *Macmillan's Magazine*, edited by David Masson, which was soon selling 15,000 copies a month. After moving to London Macmillan published Bryce's *Holy Roman Empire* and, whilst Oxford was looking vainly about for some history books for schools, he published J. R. Green's *Short History of the English People*, a runaway best seller. The one-volume Globe Shakespeare edited by Clark and Wright was also a great commercial success. Wright thought that the title was 'claptrappy': Macmillan delighted in it because it referred not only to Shakespeare's theatre but to his own territorial ambitions as a publisher. He had a flourishing agency in India in the 1860s, and by the end of the decade he had opened a branch in New York. The Delegates had contributed £50 towards the expenses of a visit to America in 1867, during which he had been deeply impressed by the courtesy and refinement he found there. It was a great continent throbbing with gentle humanity and new ideas. In the wild west he met farmers who had read Carlyle, Mill, Ruskin, and Lecky. And the money spent on educational endowments made the country even more attractive to an enterprising publisher. Macmillan was always headily in advance of anything that Oxford aspired to at the time.

But Macmillan had been extraordinarily quick to detect the newer breed of Oxford men, who in the latter part of the century dominated politics and administration and helped to build the Empire. The difference from Cambridge he recorded among his first impressions. Cambridge people seemed to him more open, more manly: or, putting it another way, rougher and less gentlemanly. 'The Oxford manner', he noted, 'has more what might be called fine gentlemanliness—everyone almost has it—a certain softness and repression of manner.' Together with this went 'a habit of mind in the place that they are bound to take action in some way on the world without. . . . And it is rather curious as joined to the very quiet, almost finikin manner.'

There were others in Oxford who were still preoccupied with the world within, however, and the religious controversies of previous decades had not vanished without trace. Macmillan's own publishing could not take into account all the niceties of Oxford feeling in this respect. Many of his friends, like Maurice or T. H. Huxley, remained unacceptable. He was scrupulous enough early on to consult the Delegates about some of the theological works he had in preparation. To a letter written in the Long Vacation he got a reply from Robert Scott. He could not commit the Delegates, but Scott ventured the opinion that if Macmillan were to publish a work of Presbyterian theology on his own account it would not be actually wrong. It was, however, a very difficult question. There were many people who would be annoyed—'as I should be myself,' Scott added, 'if you were to go into the Colenso line'.

Macmillan already was 'in the Colenso line'. J. W. Colenso had been bishop of Natal, a controversial figure controversially excommunicated for having questioned the veracity of Scripture and the doctrine of eternal punishment. As a missionary he was reluctant to accept the belief that all heathen souls were burning in hell—though some missionaries found it an incentive. Macmillan had published Colenso, whose first book had been dedicated to F. D. Maurice. He was on highly treacherous ground. Among his new masters was the Delegate Henry Mansel, a gladiator of the old school, who struck out against the pernicious doctrines of J. S. Mill and engaged in a long public controversy with Maurice. Whatever his personal opinions it was politic for Macmillan to establish as far as possible friendly relations. Chided by Maurice for being too much 'a man of the world', Macmillan justified consorting with his foe by appealing to his own doctrines: even Mr. Mansel, he supposed, was not excluded from God's love and keeping. That serious trouble was averted was partly due to Macmillan's tact, and partly to Bartholomew Price, who allowed that responsibility for books published over Macmillan's imprint was un-doubtedly his, just as responsibility for books published with the Clarendon Press imprint belonged exclusively to the Delegates. So far as the Delegates were concerned he was 'the salesman', and all questions of publishing were firmly in their hands.

4. The Secretary: Bartholomew Price

IN 1865 Macmillan had told Gladstone that changes were on their way at the Press. The obsession with reprinting the works of seventeenth-century divines had passed. 'Numerically large bodies move naturally and inevitably very slowly,' he had to admit. 'There may be wisdom in the multitude of counsellors, but certainly there is not much speed. Still, since they did me the honour to appoint me their publisher, I have found the greatest possible readiness to listen to any suggestion I might make, and I am sure that in a very few years you will see a considerably different class of books issue from the Press of your University.'

In that year the Press published seven books, and one was a reprint of Keble's 1836 edition of Hooker's *Works*, another was P. E. Pusey's edition of St. Cyril's commentary on the minor prophets in 250 copies. Printing numbers were decided by the Warehouse Committee, also responsible for putting in new boilers, improving the ventilation in the printing works, and authorizing a new fire grate for Mr. Combe's kitchen. But despite the meagre output, the Delegates and the partners shared Macmillan's belief that they were in the midst of change. The business as a whole was growing, and particularly the publishing business, not only as a result of all the Clarendon Press Series titles in preparation but also slowly by accretion as the decades passed and no books ever went out of print. There was a danger that it might get out of control. 'A vigilant superintendence' was needed, therefore, and proper profit and loss accounts of the whole concern must be kept, 'as also of each book, and also of the books in the warehouse and in the hands of the Selling Agent Mr. Macmillan'. So the Delegates decreed in 1867, when these responsibilities were entrusted to a Finance Committee, consisting of the Vice-Chancellor and four Delegates. The Delegates nominated were the Warehouse Committee members, Price, Scott, Griffiths, and Mountague Bernard. The Warehouse Committee therefore became Finance Committee, which has remained as a committee of general management ever since.

Mountague Bernard was Professor of International Law and Diplomacy, a man active on many commissions and committees, not all connected with the University. He had been involved in the case against Jowett in the Vice-Chancellor's court. Meticulous and methodical, he prepared a memorandum on 'the business of the "Press" and the means for transacting the same'. It was followed by one from Bartholomew Price on 'The Duties of the Secretary'. The main conclusion was that a deliberative body like that of the Delegates could no longer be expected to discharge all the work required. A responsible executive officer was essential. Kitchin was a pioneer in educational publishing, but would have been the last to claim that he was a man of business. He worked at home, did not attend Delegates' meetings, and when asked to keep a profit and loss account was thoroughly disconcerted. 'Easier said than done!', he wrote to Macmillan, not knowing where to begin. For the kind of responsibilities envisaged by Bernard and Price he had no appetite at all.

The publishing business was conducted by the Delegates alone and the partners had no share in it. On the other hand the Delegates had a considerable share in the four businesses—the Bible Press, the Learned Press, the Paper-Mill, the Bound Book Business in London—conducted by the partners, and the partners were not above suspicion. There was too little incentive for them to modernize and invest in new machinery. It was in their interest to keep the trading capital high because on the termination of a partnership, or the death of a partner, the University was obliged to purchase his shares at whatever figure the capital was fixed. It was in their interest to depreciate as little as possible. The executive officer would have to watch closely over their affairs, and gradually in fact displace them. There was also Macmillan, technically above suspicion, whose accounts nevertheless were in need of 'strict examination'. There was a mysterious 5 per cent discount to certain booksellers on top of the normal 25 per cent, and Bernard noted that in the previous year the bill for advertising had been no less than £450. 14s. 7d. Macmillan might easily spend that amount on two or three of his 'private books', and he handled over 300 Oxford titles, but to Bernard and Price it appeared extortionate. It was clear that the man appointed to run the business would be dealing with matters of 'a very delicate kind': he must be ready, and have the necessary stature, to 'expostulate' with the partners and even with Macmillan.

Bartholomew Price was appointed Secretary in 1868. As he had explained in his memorandum, he was to be no mere 'Clerk of a Board' but its agent and executive officer. He would prepare the agenda and attend the meetings of the Delegates and Finance Committee, would transact 'the mechanical part' of the publishing business in which his services were most needed, and he would be the 'Secretary of Accounts'. Above all he would exercise that 'vigilant superintendence' of the business that the 1852 University commission had said could never be expected from a committee of dons. An eminently practical man, he stated his requirements: an office, a fire-proof safe, a copying press, convenient cupboards, and a clerk. He was to be paid £500 a year, and Kitchin continued to be paid as Secretary to the School-book Committee until 1874.

The presence of 'Bat' Price was felt in Oxford for over fifty years. In life span he was close to Queen Victoria, comparable with her too in the way his personality quietly suffused the society in which he lived. He achieved nothing spectacular, but his dogged ubiquity is recorded in countless footnotes to the histories of nineteenth-century Oxford. His *Treatise on the Differential Calculus* had been published in 1848, when he was thirty. Between 1852 and 1860 his *Treatise on the Infinitesimal Calculus* was issued in four volumes, the second edition being reverentially kept in print until 1928 when R. W. Chapman, one of Price's successors, scribbled a memorandum—'Let us be men and waste the quires'. In 1855 he became Sedleian Professor of Natural Philosophy, and in the same year he was elected in the face of strong High-Church opposition to a place on the Hebdomadal Council. There were few boards, commissions, or committees of inquiry that did not feel the need for his advice. He associated with the reforming radical party in the University, but was above controversy, at least of the acrimonious sort. To disagree with Price was to court a reputation for instability or extremism. It was said that a few plain words from him settled many a debate in Congregation. In a scarifying period, when almost every Oxford figure of repute could expect to be called a humbug or worse by somebody sooner or later, Price passed on his way unscathed.

He soon discovered that being Secretary of the Press was a full-time occupation, but he could not escape the many calls for his counsel. He was almost immediately appointed one of a committee to look into the delicate question of permitting undergraduates to live in lodgings, despite Pusey's warnings: a result of the committee's work was that Kitchin became 'Censor' of Non-collegiate students. In 1870 he was busy with the commission investigating the 'Past and Present Conditions of Scientific Instruction in Oxford', and in 1871 Gladstone invited him to become a member of the Cleveland Commission inquiring into the financial relations of the two Universities and their colleges. In 1876, when another executive commission was appointed by Disraeli to implement the report of the Cleveland Commission, Price was not included because of his liberal views; a motion in the House of Commons that his name should be added was defeated by eleven votes.

Tuckwell, who thrived on eccentricity and malicious report, could find nothing to say in his *Reminiscences* about 'Bat' Price, so devoid was he of idiosyncrasy. He did note that Mrs. Price 'painted her St. Giles' drawing room in no Philistine taste', apparently under the influence of Morris and Burne-Jones, a matter worth recording perhaps if it were widely known that her husband, as the family recalled, had no aesthetic sense. C. L. Dodgson, his pupil and friend, recorded evenings of dancing and amateur theatricals at 11 St. Giles', with the Prices and their five daughters, one of whom was called Alice. He enjoyed their hospitality after Henry Liddell, father of the other 'Alice', had withdrawn his. Bat Price, as he flitted from one committee to another, may have come to seem an increasingly remote figure, but Lewis Carroll's lines 'Twinkle, twinkle little bat, How I wonder what you're at' raise him from the footnotes of history into a different sphere.

A strong personality, combined with a rare gift for submerging where necessary his own individuality, made him ideally suitable as Secretary to the Delegates. Henceforth he always spoke with the voice of the majority, and no differences of opinion between himself and the Board could by definition occur. Henry Liddell, Bishop Stubbs, and Mark Pattison were Delegates throughout the sixteen years he held office, and with them all he got on admirably. Liddell was an old friend, dependent on Price for making up his mind for him. In August 1870, when on holiday in Llandudno, he had to decide whether to accept the Vice-Chancellorship from Lord Salisbury.

He begged Price to take an excursion ticket and hasten to North Wales to advise him, for he was greatly worried by the prospect of routine work and public meetings, at which he was certain he would be a failure. Price was able to reassure him without making the journey. Bishop Stubbs was a High-Church conservative, but he was also a great historian, an author, and Bishop of Oxford, and his presence on the Board in the early days of the History School was invaluable. Mark Pattison had a notable distaste for committees and for the men who served on them, but he did not complain of the Press. He attended Delegates' meetings conscientiously and advised on many manuscripts. If he approved, his verdict was often laconic: 'I think it will do' would suffice. But he took pains when he could see his way to help. All other University business he appeared to detest. He deplored those men of middle age who are 'struck with an intellectual palsy, and betake themselves, no longer to port, but to the frippery work of attending boards', and those men of business who dine together 'with the comfortable assurance that they have earned their evening relaxation by the fatigues of the morning's committee'. Price might be thought to answer to the description. But he had important work to do and deserved more help than the University could give him. He had supported Pattison in the past in the campaign to strengthen the professoriate, and to promote research. In 1868 Pattison was writing, 'The fact that so few books of profound research emanate from the University of Oxford materially impairs its character as a seat of learning, and consequently its hold on the respect of the nation'.

The relationship between Price and Macmillan was marked by great delicacy on both sides. They met regularly, either in Oxford when Macmillan attended Delegates' meetings, or in London for lunch at the Athenaeum, and Macmillan numbered Price, with Liddell, Jowett, and Thomas Combe, among the Oxford men whose friendship he valued most. They were of the same age, fifty in 1868: what perhaps they had most in common was the belief in hard work and in the family life that was a man's only legitimate solace from it. Like many another great Victorian family man Macmillan was rarely at home, and when he was he read until two o'clock in the morning and was up again at six. The roles that the two men played, however, were not quite what had been foreseen. Macmillan as the man of business with more than twenty years' publishing experience behind him was to advise a board of unworldly dons, guiding them through the thickets of London commerce. But Macmillan's real interest was in books and authors. He was an excitable Scot, with an unappeasable intellectual curiosity. He much preferred to leave the administration of his growing business to somebody else. 'I feel overwhelmed at times', he wrote after accepting Oxford's offer, 'with all that is on my head and hands, but feel clear and plucky on the whole.' Two years later he was feeling desperately in need of a partner or agent himself. Price, on the other hand, of dour Welsh stock, insisted that his work was 'chiefly "Business" and finance'. He wrote with a strict impersonality to his authors, as indeed he did to Macmillan, beginning 'I am instructed by the Delegates' and rarely venturing again into the first person. It might have appeared that he had no mind of his own. Macmillan cajoled, hectored, and offered advice. His enthusiasms show a mind uninhibited by academic discipline, and he still avidly read books, even those sent to him by the Clarendon Press. Publishing remained an intellectual adventure. Price needed and created routines.

It was also a reversal of the expected order of things when it came to appear that the University Press with its great funds was struggling to make ends meet whilst Macmillan grew richer and richer. The strict examination of his charges to Oxford proved painful and dispiriting for Price. Having established a relationship of friendliness and goodwill in his first year in office, he was appalled at the end of it to find that the financial arrangements the Delegates had entered into were proving disastrous, and he had at once to expostulate with Macmillan. In 1868-9, £13,000 had been spent on book making, and the profit was nil. 'We cannot go on,' he wrote with deep feeling. 'The first element in a concern like ours must be commercial success.'

Macmillan had agreed to spend less on advertising, and to stop the extra 5 per cent discount to the trade. But he constantly made exceptions. Indeed he had failed to abide by his earlier undertaking, and in the course of the year there had also been a 10 per cent increase in his binding charges. Macmillan took his regular commission of 10 per cent, 30 per cent discount might be allowed to the trade—or even more when allowance was made for the 'odd' book (selling 25 for 24)—so when advertising, binding, and miscellaneous expenses were added to the bill for paper and printing there was little left to be divided between the Delegates and their authors. Price had to express the 'great dissatisfaction felt here about the heavy deductions made in your accounts'. A mockery was being made, it seemed to him, of the whole notion of employing a London agent to promote the sale of Oxford books. Moreover the Press was losing authors, who could get better terms elsewhere. 'We and the Authors of our new books are copartners, and they have a share in the profits; they ask for our accounts, of cost, allowance, advertising etc. How can we refuse them? . . . How do you reply to this?' Macmillan's reply was to have nothing to do with authors who asked to see the account: he did not regard his authors as co-partners with him. He preferred paying an outright sum or a royalty. But most of the Oxford agreements were on a profit-sharing basis, and Price had to explain to authors that half the returns were being swallowed up by the London publisher. He demanded that he should see a statement of the amount spent on advertising for each book, and that the 5 per cent discount should be stopped once and for all. 'And what is this £50 for postage?' irritability led him to add.

The next morning he was almost contrite, inclined to appease Macmillan. 'I was very sorry to have to write to you such a letter as I wrote yesterday; but the Finance Committee of the Delegates instructed me.' As he went on, however, some of the previous day's wrath welled up again, and he found himself repeating that the situation was grave and that they could not go on.

It was particularly disappointing to find books in the Clarendon Press Series hardly able to pay their way because of the exceptional overheads. The return to the Press and to the editors turned out to be much as Macmillan had foreseen when the Committee was setting so much store on pecuniary interests. If the agreement were based on actual rather than notional profits the editor might find himself out of pocket.

The high discounts to the trade were in fact greatly deplored by Macmillan himself: they led to underselling and had driven many good booksellers out of business. In a famous letter to Gladstone, written in 1868, he had stated his misgivings about the effects of price competition: 'whereas in former days there used to be many booksellers who kept good stocks of solid standard books, one or more in every important town in England . . . the case is now that in country towns few live by bookselling, the trade has become so profitless that it is generally the appendage to a toy shop, or a Berlin wool warehouse.' He was convinced that an intelligent bookseller in every town of importance would be almost as valuable as an intelligent schoolmaster or parson. It was his nephew Frederick who pioneered the 'net' book—offering a smaller discount but a fixed retail price.

In dealing with Scott or Kitchin, Macmillan had never had to undergo such vigilant superintendence. Mutual respect nevertheless sustained the connection for eighteen years. In due course he was prevailed upon to reduce his commission, and to conduct his Oxford affairs as thriftily as he decently could. Faced by the most unsaleable of Clarendon Press books he was always stoical, though there was often little he could do except advise putting up the price. Having sampled a work on passerine birds, a translation from the German of Müller's *Certain Variations in the Vocal Organs of the Passeres* (*that have hitherto escaped notice*), he wrote to Price: 'If there are musicians who add physiological considerations to their studies they will certainly value such a book, or on the other hand physiologists who care about the musical result of voice organs. Even your own mathematical science is probably involved. How many people in each quarter are likely to buy such a book? Are they poor men to whom the difference of 5/- or 7/6 would be of importance? My own feeling is that the price should be 7/6.' On this occasion Price accepted his advice, although it was a book of only 82 pages. It did not require any great flair to recognize that Müller's *Passerine Birds* was going to be a slow seller. Not even the author's best friends or worst enemies would necessarily buy the English translation. Nevertheless its sales record was remarkable: 784 copies were printed, and in the first year seven copies were sold (and forty given away); in 1880 one copy was sold, and 1881 two copies. Another copy was sold in 1884, and three more went in the 1890s. After twenty-five years it had sold twenty-one copies. The book had been warmly recommended to the Delegates by Charles Darwin.

5. The Oxford History School

THE development of the Oxford History School was hampered by eccentric or dilatory professors, and by a dearth both of tutors and of books, the latter being perhaps the most deeply felt. The study of the Classics had always been based on set books, which at the same time were the basic texts. The basic texts in history were hard to find. Moreover what history there was tended to be controversial, especially when it reached the sixteenth and seventeenth centuries. The recommended authority was Lingard, whose eight-volume history of England up to 1688 had been completed in 1831. A subsequent edition ran to fourteen volumes. Lingard had been a Roman Catholic, and the student needed to be on his guard, but at least he was dull and voluminous. Too many historians outside the academic world, like Carlyle, Froude, Macaulay, Grote, and J. R. Green, had written in a style designed to please, making history appear 'an easy School for rich men', as E. A. Freeman, who was working in the opposite camp, put it. *The Annals of England*, published by Messrs. Parker & Co. and advertised as 'recommended by the Examiners', provided three volumes of source material that professors and tutors could use as their texts if they could think of any coherent way of doing so.

The Regius Professor of Modern History when the School of History and Jurisprudence was created was Henry Halford Vaughan, Earl Russell's choice. His eloquence attracted large audiences to his lectures, but he did not write, or at least not history, and his contribution to the discipline was slight. He contemplated a great work on the origins of morality, and retired early to a remote castle in Pembrokeshire to work on it. When he died he left £300 in his will for a competent person to edit it for publication, but what survived, according to Leslie Stephen, appeared to be numerous versions of the first chapter. Vaughan had often complained that large parts of the manuscript disappeared overnight, largely due to the malevolence of maidservants. Some believed that he disposed of them himself in his sleep. He never lost the variant readings of Shakespeare he collected throughout his life, and eventually produced *New Readings and Renderings of Shakespeare's Tragedies*, which was published by Kegan Paul. His biographer, E. G. W. Bill, records that the first volume sold four copies, the second three, and the third fourteen—a record even Müller's *Passerine Birds* could hardly match. He had refused to live in Oxford largely because of the climate, and the twenty lectures he was obliged to give a year were packed into the summer term. In the end he declined even to deliver those. He also resisted appeals to publish them, and in his retirement accused Freeman, Hallam, and Stubbs of having connived at their theft. He was 'barely sane in one direction', Leslie Stephen said.

Vaughan was succeeded by Goldwin Smith in 1858, an appointment of Lord Derby. 'We all saw in him the coming man,' wrote Tuckwell, 'but he married, settled in America, and never came.' He stayed in Oxford until

1868, long enough to impress other observers as one of the most influential radical thinkers of his day, but not as a historian. He had been trained in the law, was an accomplished essayist and journalist, and had no taste for research. Macmillan regarded him as a 'man of might' and never lost the conviction that he had it in him to write a great book. Of the several books he did not write, one was the history of England for the Clarendon Press Series, another the volume on Wordsworth for Macmillan's English Men of Letters series, and a third the anonymous *Ecce Homo*, attributed to him until the identity of the author, J. R. Seeley, was established. His energies were mostly consumed by liberal causes, in Oxford and in the world at large. Disraeli called him 'the wild man of the cloister', and 'an itinerant spouter of stale sedition'. He was further pilloried as an unnamed Oxford professor in *Lothair*, which according to his biographer in the *Dictionary of National Biography*, Sidney Lee, finally drove him to anti-Semitism. But racialism was not uncommon among the more rabidly romantic liberals of the time: not only Jews, but Celts, Negroes, and Latins dangerously threatened the purity of the Anglo-Saxon race. E. A. Freeman once wrote of the United States that it 'would be a great land if only every Irishman would kill a negro and be hanged for it'. Goldwin Smith maintained that Vaughan had resigned his Chair because of hypochondria. He himself accepted an offer from Cornell because he feared his health, both mental and physical, was too precarious for him to endure the stresses of Oxford and London life. He survived until 1910, however, and by his journalism and regular forays into his mother country remained a force to be reckoned with. He was a Delegate from 1865 to 1868.

In its first seventeen years the School had achieved little, though the numbers of students increased. In 1867 William Stubbs was summoned from his country parsonage in Essex, invited by Lord Derby to become Regius Professor. He had not applied. He had been a candidate for the Chichele professorship of modern history in 1862, when he had lost to a naval commander called Montagu Burrows, who occupied the Chair unobtrusively for the rest of the century. Having also been defeated in a bid for the Chair of Ecclesiastical History, Stubbs had decided to compete no more. But he was already renowned among the few for his extraordinary knowledge of the sources of medieval history. In 1858 the Press had published his first book, *Registrum Sacrum Anglicanum*, tracing the course of episcopal succession in England, a work that made a minute impact at the time. But it was Stubbs who established the study of history as a reputable academic discipline. In 1867 J. R. Green wrote that 'history was struggling out of that condition in which it was looked on as no special or definitive study, but as part of that general mass of things, which every gentleman should know'. Delving in early deeds and charters, with all the dust and drudgery involved, was an occupation for Germans rather than gentlemen, and Stubbs found himself lecturing to depressingly small audiences. When he left Oxford to become Bishop of Chester in 1884, he was far from satisfied by his achievement. The English historical school he had tried to establish still lagged far behind the great 'think tanks' of Germany, and not nearly enough original research was being done. But at least it was no longer 'an easy school'. Stubbs's *Select Charters*, which went through many editions, was the most used history book for generations, and his mighty three-volume *Constitutional History of England* could leave nobody in any doubt about the difficulty of the subject. Both books appeared in the increasingly heterogeneous Clarendon Press Series. While Professor, Stubbs also produced fifteen substantial volumes for the Rolls Series, the 'Chronicles and Memorials of Great Britain and Ireland from the Invasion of the Romans to the Reign of Henry VIII'. Although he disliked committees almost as much as Mark Pattison did, he was a Delegate from 1868 until 1884, and again on his return as Bishop of Oxford from 1891 to 1901. Tractarianism had made him into a High-Churchman and a Tory, but he belonged to the generation that had no taste for controversy and, like Bat Price of the opposite persuasion, was reluctant to express an opinion on any subject whatsoever.

His *Constitutional History* took the subject only up to the Tudors. In 1871 the Modern History Board of Studies approached Price, explaining that there was a difficulty about the later period. Lingard's history was unsatisfactory and there was no other eligible book in English. Leopold von Ranke's *History of England*, principally in the seventeenth century, would suit exactly. They asked Price to lay the proposal for a translation before the Delegates. It could be done in a year, and would be a service to the History School: payment to the translators was of no consequence. The Delegates agreed and appointed Max Müller to act as intermediary. The great German historian accepted £100 and gave his consent. The translation, supervised by G. W. Kitchin among others, took a little longer than expected, but the six volumes were ready for publication in the Clarendon Press Series in 1875. It was the first occasion on which the Delegates accepted a book specifically at the request of one of the new faculties. That it had to be a translation from the German was irksome but inevitable.

With the help of Kitchin's own three-volume *History of France*, the first volumes of Thomas Hodgkin's *Italy and Her Invaders*, Finlay's *History of Greece*, and the endless outpourings of E. A. Freeman, the Oxford history list began to fill out. Freeman succeeded Stubbs as Regius Professor. Regarded as a man of the left, he was rancorous and bigoted, and managed to stay on reasonable terms with Stubbs only because of a common concern for the History School. His *History of the Norman Conquest of England* in six volumes including an index volume was published between 1868 and 1879, and *A Short History* for the Clarendon Press Series appeared in 1880. They were followed by two volumes on William Rufus, and a four-volume history of Sicily. 'Freeman's death must have delivered the Delegates from a heavy obligation,' Liddell wrote privately to Price in 1892. 'One regrets that a man possessed of such qualifications for a historian should not have had some power of selecting his materials, and should have insisted on pouring

over the world the *whole* contents of his accumulated stores.' Once
described by Freeman as a 'blockhead and blunderer', as living proof of
'the hollowness of Oxford liberalism that they cannot see through such a
humbug', Liddell was having the last word. James Anthony Froude,
hounded from Oxford in 1849, and persecuted mercilessly throughout his
life by Freeman for alleged inaccuracies in his work, succeeded him in the
Chair as a further insult to his memory.

6. Towards the End of Partnership

THE Press records are quiet about the printing of *Alice in Wonderland* in
1865. Dodgson was publishing it at his own expense through Macmillan:
2,000 copies were printed, and 48 were bound for distribution to friends.
One went to the illustrator, John Tenniel, who objected to the printing of
his drawings. Dodgson agreed with him that the quality of the work was
poor and decided to scrap the entire edition. The remaining 1,952 sheets
were sold to Messrs. Appleton in New York, and the author recovered 34 of
the original 48 bound copies. He kept 2 for himself, and sent the rest to
hospitals, where chances of survival were small. The remaining 14 copies
became in the wonderland world of bibliolatry some of the rarest and most
coveted of all rare books.

Bartholomew Price must have been embarrassed by the failure of the
Press to satisfy his friend, although Dodgson was perversely fastidious.
Some twenty years later he had the same experience with *The Game of
Logic*, printed by Baxter in Oxford. This time it was an edition of 500. Again
Dodgson told Macmillan that they must be sold off in sheets in America
and the book had to be reprinted: 'just what happened in '65 with Alice', he
noted in his diary, with a touch of self-satisfaction. But if Price were seeking
anyone to blame it would undoubtedly have been Henry Latham, whom he
frequently had occasion to rebuke. As far as Price was concerned Latham
was solely responsible for the efficient running of the printing business.
Angry over a delay in reprinting a volume of the *Norman Conquest*, he once
told him, 'It creates a *substantial* grievance, which Mr. Freeman will take
advantage of. Our Press has already a bad character for punctuality and
despatch; let us not give more ground for the report.'

A prolonged dispute about apprentice money had not endeared Latham
to Thomas Combe either. Apprentices paid the Masters for learning their
trade by deduction from their wages: if they earned 15s. a week they were
paid only 5s., and the balance was paid into a fund and eventually divided
between the partners. Latham like Pickard Hall owned four shares: Combe
owned eight. The apprentice money was divided on that basis, which
seemed to Latham unjust. It was not being suggested that Combe gave
twice as much instruction to the apprentices as the other two partners; it

Benjamin Jowett

'Bat' Price, by C. L. Dodgson

The Revd. Dr. Price, *c.* 1890

was quite wrong therefore that the money should not be divided equally between them. No sympathetic ear was lent by Price to Latham's complaints. His advice and suggestions about publishing policy also went unheeded, but not his restlessness, nor a spirit of independence that caused the Delegates to fear at times having an absentee partner on their hands. Grudgingly he was granted four months' leave in 1866 to visit America. The Delegates took the precaution, in case he did not come back, of telling him that they could not contemplate the possibility of one of the partners being resident in a foreign country. Latham's absences in London could not in the end be tolerated. In 1869, when he was in fact ill, the Delegates decided that he must 'reside continuously in Oxford'. Soon afterwards his partnership was terminated, and the Delegates purchased his four shares. At the same time they at last bought a binding business in London, making the fifth business of the Press. As a result of these and other impending depletions of capital it was quietly resolved that the loss on books issued in the promotion of learning and science should not exceed £750 a year.

In 1872 Thomas Combe died, ten days after having adroitly sold the Delegates the Paper-Mill for the price he had paid for it in 1855 plus compound interest at 3 per cent. The Press was dipping deeply into its reserves: £25,000 had to be raised to purchase Combe's eight shares. The following year E. Bensley Gardner of the London Bound Book Business retired and his five shares were ingurgitated by the Delegates, to give them forty-three in all. Pickard Hall retained four shares, and the manager of the Paper-Mill, John H. Stacey, had acquired one. They were all that was left of the partnership. In 1874 Henry Frowde, a young man of twenty-three with some experience in book-selling, was employed as manager of the Bible warehouse in London.

These changes affected the position of the Secretary. In 1873 it was resolved that he should take an active part in the management of all the businesses, 'exercising vigilance and efficient control over all departments'. The measure of his increased responsibilities was an increase in salary from £500 to £1,250 a year, to be charged annually in the accounts of the five partnership businesses, and not as formerly in the Publishing business accounts of the Delegates. Combe had enjoyed Price's full confidence: his letters to him had been addressed 'My Dear Combe', as opposed to a chilly 'Dear Sir' to Latham. The Secretary now assumed Combe's general responsibilities as senior partner, whilst continuing to conduct the 'mechanical part' of the publishing business as before.

John Stacey had been running the Paper-Mill with great efficiency since 1855. Following the death of Combe he was called upon to undertake the duties of Superintendent of the Clarendon Press as well, and these proved less congenial. Price, he discovered, was a hard man to work with at close range. He campaigned bravely on behalf of the employees, first recommending an incentive and then a pension scheme. In 1872 he estimated that the wages paid at the five businesses equalled £25,125 a year. A small bonus relating to annual profits, say $\frac{1}{2}$ per cent, might work out at

E

£6. 4s. 10d. a year for a £2 a week man. For Price's benefit he justified such an arrangement by saying, 'My experience of workmen is, that as a class, they are grossly extravagant, not perhaps from a want of moral perception of its wrong so much as a feeling that in the midst of plenty, and with all the signs of wealth around them, carefulness in small matters cannot be needed'. An incentive scheme, such as he proposed, would help to instil in the minds of the workers that the general welfare of the business affected them all. The bonus would be forfeited for bad behaviour. His proposal was not taken up.

Nor was the pension scheme, which he thought might be on the basis of £1 for each year of service: a tradesman retiring at the age of 65 after forty years should be able to get by on a pension of £40 a year. Pensions for all did not at that time seem a practicable proposition. The Delegates might vote in favour of a pension in special cases: in the mid 1860s a compositor retiring after fifty years was granted 10s. a week in recognition of his services. As the Delegates were under no legal, and possibly under no moral obligation, it need not appear ungenerous even in comparison with the £37 voted for Combe's kitchen grate, or the £500 a year paid to both Liddell and Scott throughout the decade. Appeals to the Delegates for help from their old servants were compassionately heard. 'I entered your employment as a compositor in the year 1840,' wrote a certain Mr. Woods in 1878, whose failing eyesight had obliged him to leave work; 'I am now in my 76th year; I have a wife and one child at home—a boy of 13—earning 4/- per week—the rest of my children are getting their own living—some are married and have young families, and in the third week of Sept. next I shall become superannuated on my Benefits Club (the Oxford Friendly Institution) when I shall on my own part be in receipt of only 4/- per week ... Under the above circumstances I earnestly and humbly solicit your assistance.' He was awarded 5s. a week, for which he returned his most sincere thanks, 'trusting that I may ever feel grateful for, and continue to deserve it'.

To Stacey, partnership in the Press, which he had coveted for many years, brought disillusionment. Allowed no voice on any matter of policy he felt himself superfluous. He objected too that the capital he had invested in the business was fixed, and that both at Wolvercote and at the Clarendon Press the inability to increase the capital on which his income was based meant a continuing drain on his resources: the partner with fixed capital must inevitably fare worse each year, 'until he is swamped altogether'. Altercations with the Delegates eventually led to arbitration, and the opinion going against him he withdrew from the Press and confined himself to the Mill for the rest of his life. In 1876 he wrote to Price:

Under the present system I am not allowed to exercise either my duties or my rights;—vexatious interference on your part in practical matters and a contemptuous disregard of any right of mine to give an opinion on the conduct of ordinary business, have resulted in a state of affairs at the Press, which destroys all authority and position, and neutralizes every effort of mine as a managing partner.

I do not wish to recapitulate the many occasions during the past year when I have suffered under a tyranny which could only be borne with equanimity by one devoid of all manly feeling or by one conscious of deserving blame—to me, faithful, industrious and self-sacrificing as I have ever been, such treatment has made my present life miserable and my future (if in connection with yourself) hopeless . . .

The fourth great man in its history, the architect and founder of the modern Press, enjoyed relations with his peers that were always unruffled: over his subordinates he could ride roughshod. He had after all been employed to expostulate.

7. Oxford India Paper

IN 1875 an exceedingly small Oxford Bible on exceedingly thin paper was published and within a few weeks sold a quarter of a million copies. The use of Oxford India paper, first for Bibles and Prayer Books and later for other books, was of incalculable importance in the growth of the Press up to 1914, but its manufacture was surrounded by so much secrecy that it has become almost impossible to distinguish legend from fact. It was reported in the *Publisher's Circular* in 1896 that the secret was known to only three living beings. Henry Frowde, who himself helped to perpetuate the not altogether reliable oral tradition, may not have been one of them, but it was he who was responsible for the 1875 Bible. He had stumbled upon one of the twenty-four copies of a tiny Bible printed by Thomas Combe in 1842. The paper was extraordinarily thin, tough, and opaque, and nothing quite like it had ever been achieved since. Frowde, making his first dramatic appearance on the scene of Oxford publishing, asked for more.

The story was that in 1841 an Oxford graduate had brought back from China a small fold of this unique paper and presented it to Combe, enough only for the twenty-four copies. Unable to trace the paper to its source or analyse its structure, Combe made extensive inquiries, even appealing to Gladstone, who recommended a search in Japan. Papers found there were equally thin but not opaque enough, so that it was impossible to print on both sides. Experiments at Wolvercote were unsuccessful, yielding a paper far too yellow to be acceptable. The original 'India paper' that had been used for years, often mounted on ordinary paper and designed to receive fine impressions of copperplate or steel engravings, was indeed made in China, and yellow in colour. Whatever had come into Combe's possession was something different, though in time the matter was forgotten.

In 1874, however, on receiving Frowde's request, Stacey seemed to know that paper similar to that used for the 1842 Bible and made of rope had once been manufactured in Staffordshire under the name of 'Pottery Tissue'. He wrote to Thomas Brittain & Sons of Hanley and was successful. They undertook to match the paper, and the samples they supplied were satisfactory. With their help Wolvercote also started to produce Oxford India paper and, although it still tended to be too yellow, the bulk of the paper for Frowde's Bible was supplied from there. But as Brittains' product was superior, Wolvercote ceased to compete and some ten years later the secret of its manufacture had again been forgotten. By 1887 Brittains monopolized the supply, Oxford the demand, and the latter was so great that Brittains could no longer single-handedly meet it. It was agreed that they would lend Oxford the only man who fully understood the process, a Mr. Haigh. After his visit to Wolvercote it was realized that the manufacture of India paper involved so much lime that the effluent would kill all fish in the river for miles around. Mr. Haigh could find no answer to the problem. Eventually Brittains opened a new mill of their own which could supply all the needs of its only customer. Oxford also had the right to market the paper abroad. Having secured the monopoly, the Press was anxious to warn the public against imitations. There was only one 'Oxford India paper'. Until the 1890s its use was confined largely to Bibles and Prayer Books, but it could be put to sensational effect at international exhibitions, where it won the Press many Grands Prix. Volumes of 1,500 pages could be suspended from heights by a single leaf. Indeed a short strip of this tissue-thin paper only three inches wide could support a load of a quarter of a hundredweight. When rubbed severely it assumed a texture resembling chamois leather and could be used for cleaning windows. The saving in shelf-space, an increasingly important factor, was prodigious, and Henry Frowde delighted in it as if he had invented it himself.

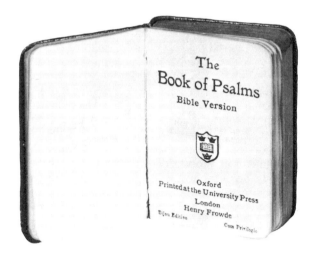

The
Book of Psalms
Bible Version

Oxford
Printed at the University Press
London
Henry Frowde
Bijou Edition
Cum Privilegio

8. Teaching and Research

IT was always improbable that the University would disencumber itself of undergraduates altogether, but there were moments in the nineteenth century when anything seemed possible. Teaching could seriously interfere with research: it was very much more taxing since the reform of the examination system. A country living might have attractions not hitherto attached to it—the opportunity to write. Mandell Creighton, for some years the most successful history tutor in Oxford, succumbed to the temptation of a living at Embleton and devoted the next ten years of his life to his books and a less exacting flock. By 1870 Mark Pattison was of the opinion that all Oxford colleges and fellowships should be abolished and their endowments pass to the University. Nine of the colleges should be turned into the headquarters of nine faculties: the rest, it was allowed, could be halls of residence. The power of the professors would be supreme.

Whether the University existed to promote learning and research or to teach and prepare young men for the world had become a sterile preoccupation of the times. It had been a popular topic in the first era of reform, when the basic question of what a university was for was being asked again. But a conviction that the two functions were totally incompatible seemed almost to be a part of the ageing process. Pattison and Benjamin Jowett came to epitomize the two extremes, caricaturing each other's points of view with extravagant relish. Pattison concocted the crude slogan 'Science and Learning *v.* School-keeping', and complained that he was surrounded by 'an arid waste of shop-dons'. It was easier and more traditional to dismiss the diffusion of useful knowledge as being outside the scope of the most ancient university: an explicit rejection of the higher scholarship was more difficult. But Jowett would scoff at 'useless learning', and deplore the want of utility in Oxford studies.

This should perhaps have been the least of the Press's problems, and the grave authority that lay behind the Secretary's benignly wrinkled countenance did much to keep it in its place. Price as usual was in an advantageous position, being on both sides, as indeed common sense dictated: he believed in principle in the endowment of research and all that that involved in terms of unremunerative books; in practice he promoted the Clarendon Press Series, and even in his own field of mathematics preferred to accept manuals and textbooks rather than seek out original work, which could safely be left to Cambridge. His immediate concern had to be with business and commerce. But those more fervently attached to the cause of research could look askance at commerce and find in history some shadowy ground for scruple in publishing anything that smacked of it. The right to print money by printing Bibles could not be questioned for it had come from on high. That the Press was first and foremost a printing house, however, and that its privileges were all related to printing, was a consideration that might induce in a sensitive Delegate the uneasy feeling that somebody from the Stationers' Company was looking over his shoulder. He might even suspect that the Delegates had no right to be publishing anything at all. Mountague Bernard, in the memorandum on the Press written five years after Price had proposed the series of educational books, still thought it necessary to tell the Delegates that publishing was not entirely 'beside their function, for the North Wing of the Printing House was built for the purpose of the Learned Press, and it is quite proper for an University to publish Educational and Learned books'.

Ten years later, in 1878, the Delegate Max Müller, whose commitment to research matched that of Mark Pattison, addressed himself weightily to the problem. There was to his mind something wrong already with the new arrangements, and to trace the trouble to its source it might be advisable, if not to question, then at least to mention the part played by the executive officer. A clear distinction should be drawn, he wrote, between the books 'which we publish as booksellers, and those that we publish as Delegates of the University Press'. The former could safely be left 'in the hands of our experienced Secretary'. The latter required the setting-up of what he proposed to call a 'Learned Fund'. A quarter of a century later some such distinction emerged with the appearance of the London business, but nobody could say that it was clearly drawn.

Max Müller is remembered as the man whose wife received the Imperial Order of Chastity, Third Class, after entertaining an Oriental potentate for lunch. He was very illustrious in his day, the equivalent of the twentieth-century 'television don'. He lectured to packed halls up and down the country on Aryan roots and the origins of religion, once giving a royal command performance before Queen Victoria on the Isle of Wight. He had come to England from Germany in 1846 at the age of 23, seeking his fortune in Sanskrit rather than in the over-worked field of the European classics. He moved to Oxford and took rooms in Walton Street for the time-honoured purpose of being close to his printer when his text of the *Rig Veda* was going through the Press. The first volume was published in 1849, the sixth and last in 1874. By then he was famous as a pioneer in England of the science of comparative philology. Like so many of his eminent contemporaries he had suffered as a kind of bereavement the failure to be appointed to a Chair, as Boden Professor of Sanskrit in 1860. The founder, Colonel Boden of the East India Company, had intended it for the training of Christian missionaries, and as Müller had a vested interest in the survival of Hinduism it was not too scandalous that the election went against him, after a bitter campaign in which he found Robert Scott of Balliol organizing the opposition. Monier-Williams won and occupied the chair until 1899: in 1872 he published his *Sanskrit-English Dictionary*, which has remained in print with remarkably little revision ever since. Max Müller achieved in the end, however, a position that ideally represented the aim of those scholars committed to research. A Chair of Comparative Philology specially created for him by the University in 1868 was not precisely what he wanted: he fell into a melancholy—exacerbated by the award of an honorary D.C.L. to

Monier-Williams—and talked of going back to Germany. Council chose therefore to relieve him of all his responsibilities, made him Professor Emeritus on £600 a year, and appointed a deputy to do his work on half the salary. At the age of 52 he was able to devote all his attention to the promotion of learning.

In his memorandum to the Delegates in 1878 about the 'Learned Fund' he agreed that it was well known that the University had ample means for fulfilling equally well the two duties incumbent upon it—'that of teaching or handing down the stock of knowledge already acquired, and that of carefully sifting it and constantly adding to it new material'. The first duty it performed better than any other university: neglect of the second was causing comment both in England and on the Continent. 'We are told again and again', Müller wrote,

that no critical editions, no original treatises, nor great collective works useful to the student, are issued from Oxford, and that even the excellent series of schoolbooks published by the Clarendon Press is a commercial speculation, that might have been left to private enterprise. . . .

Without admitting the truth of the last assertion, it certainly strikes me that as Delegates of the Clarendon Press we might try to foster not only educational works, and works that are likely to pay their own expenses or prove remunerative, but that we ought to encourage publications of high scientific or literary value, without any consideration of their remunerative character.

Only at this period in the history of the Press would it have been thought necessary to make such an apparently obvious statement. Müller's memorandum was complicated, however, by the existence of the Royal Commission investigating University and college funds, of which Price himself had formerly been a member. Müller's argument was that some of these funds should be diverted to the Press, which in view of the injunction that no more than £750 a year should be spent on unremunerative books was clearly in need of it. Heavy existing commitments, such as the Revised Version of the Bible which Müller did not expect to be profitable, further prevented the Press from assuming some of the responsibilities the University was claiming for itself. 'There is much talent lying fallow among the younger members of the University,' he wrote, 'which might be evoked and properly guided, if the Clarendon Press would undertake some of the duties performed in Continental Universities either by the Government or by the *Sanctus Academicus*, or by Academies, viz. to suggest literary works of real utility, to engage the services of young scholars for carrying them out, and to superintend through properly qualified Commissioners their proper execution.' In other words college money would be better spent in this way than by endowing University fellowships for young men without attaching to them any definite duties.

The £750 set aside for learned publishing came from the almanac money and the interest on bequests. To make their proper contribution to research the Delegates reckoned that another £1,000 a year was needed. It was resolved to write a begging letter to the University Commissioners, on the basis of Max Müller's statement, and a curious document it was. Bartholomew Price signed it, but some rebarbative insertions, serving to remind the Commissioners that the voice of Laud was not yet silent in Oxford, are unlikely to have been composed by him. He had a slight impediment in his speech, which encouraged him to brevity in both the spoken and the written word. Money had been laid out and expended, the Commissioners were told, in promoting different branches of literature and science, 'to the great increase of religion and learning and the general benefit and advantage of these realms'. In return for £1,000 a year, works would be produced 'which, although not remunerative in the proceeds of their sale, would add lustre to the University and justify, in the eyes of all men, the existence of a great Academical Press'.

The response of the Commissioners was negative; it could hardly have been otherwise, for they presumably thought that the Delegates could make their own arrangements with their own University, and that these could be straightforward enough. For apart from the Learned Fund, which would be kept separate, the other funds derived from the sale of ordinary books, the Bible and Prayer Book business, and the Paper-Mill would after allowing for overheads all be transferred to the general fund of the University. That, the Commissioners must have thought, was where the money should come from, if it were needed at all.

A suggestion recorded in the minutes that the disposal of certain fellowships should be left to the Delegates was overlooked in the letter, which also had little to say about the Press's future commitments. Understandably no mention was made of the Revised Version of the New Testament, which contrary to Müller's expectations was within three years so enormously to swell the funds, nor surprisingly to the new English dictionary already under contract, which for fifty years was constantly to deplete them. Instead the emphasis was on the heavy losses incurred by publishing the five folio volumes of the Septuagint in 1798, and the many other great works of learning that had followed, including The Sacred Books of the East under the editorship of Max Müller, Dean Payne Smith's *Syriac Lexicon* which was thirty-three years in the press and the death of thirty-one compositors, Professor Bosworth's *Anglo-Saxon Dictionary*, and Dr. Neubauer's *Hebrew-Arabic Lexicon*. These, it might be said, were directly sanctioned by Archbishop Laud. It was no more than hinted that financial considerations might force the Delegates to hesitate before accepting further laudable proposals of this nature, and the Commissioners remained unimpressed.

9. Commissioners and Custodians

ACCORDING to his biographer, Nirad Chaudhuri, Max Müller was surprised to find errors queried by the Press in the proofs of his *Rig Veda*. He was told that the queries came from the compositor himself, who knew no word of the language. 'Well, sir,' the man told him, 'my arm gets into a regular swing from one compartment of types to another, and there are certain movements that never occur. So, if I suddenly have to take up types which entail a new movement I feel it, and I put a query.' No doubt the compositor did have occasional inklings of error, but the proofs of all six volumes of the *Rig Veda* were read by J. C. Pembrey, the most extraordinary of all the correctors of the Learned Press. Bound apprentice to Thomas Combe in 1846 at the age of 14, he was within a year proof-reading H. H. Wilson's *Sanskrit Grammar*. Seventy years later he was having difficulty walking to and from the Press, but proofs were still sent to him at his home. Many authors expressed gratitude to him in their prefaces. Canon Driver acknowledged his debt in the 1913 edition of *Notes on the Hebrew Text of the Book of Samuel*: 'Nearly every Oriental work that has been published by the Press during the last fifty years, including, for instance, Max Müller's *Rigveda*, Payne Smith's *Thesaurus Syriacus*, and Neubauer's *Catalogue of Hebrew MSS in the Bodleian Library*, has had the benefit of Mr. Pembrey's watchful supervision: but, notwithstanding his years, his eye, as I can testify from experience, is still undimmed, and he is still as able as ever to bestow upon a book passing through his hands this interest, and more than conscientious care, which so many Orientalists have learnt to appreciate.' He died in 1918: how he retained his health and sanity through so many years of awful labours is not recorded, nor the extent to which he acquired some working knowledge of the languages he read, eyes moving unerringly from manuscript copy to proof sheets, back and forth, in quest of an error the discovery of which was perhaps its own reward.

Max Müller's grand design for the Sacred Books of the East in twenty-four volumes was approved by the Delegates in 1875, after he had enlisted the help of Lord Salisbury, at one time Secretary of State for India, Sir Henry Maine, and perhaps most importantly Dean Liddell, to whom he had confided his intention of going to Vienna and publishing the books there if Oxford were not interested. The expenses of production were to be shared equally between the Press and the Government of India. Müller had discovered James Legge, a former missionary in China, who had retired to a corner of Scotland to translate the Confucian and Taoist texts. It took all Müller's diplomacy, and a great deal of Price's time, to persuade the Government of India that these fell within its province. Müller was possessed by the grandiose spirit of the age. With the first series almost complete he proposed a second, to consist of another twenty-four volumes, and the Delegates agreed, subject to satisfactory negotiations with the India

Office. The second series ran in the end to twenty-five volumes, and with the addition of an index volume the library was finally completed in fifty volumes in 1910—twenty-one devoted to Hinduism, twelve to Jainism and Buddhism, eight to Zoroastrianism, six to the Chinese classics, and two —E. H. Palmer's translation of the Koran—to Islam. It was a massive, even startling achievement, and by no means as unprofitable in the end as had once been feared. Forty years after the inception of the series sales were still going up.

Almost from the time he became a Delegate in 1870 Max Müller had been urging that one of the prime responsibilities of the Press was the publication of unpublished manuscripts in Oxford libraries. There were many reasons for feeling that the time was not ripe, that it was a retrograde step, that improved communications since Laud's day had reduced the necessity. He raised the matter again in 1878 during the debate about the Learned Fund and the University Commissioners, reminding the Delegates that it was work that corresponded 'to the intentions with which certain privileges were originally granted to the Clarendon Press'. It was not until 1881, however, that any concerted action was taken. An Anecdota Committee was then set up consisting of Max Müller, Bishop Stubbs, Mark Pattison, and his protégé Ingram Bywater. This was all that came of the original proposal to distinguish between the Press as booksellers, and as a department more directly responsible to the University. The Committee was to keep its own separate accounts, and the Delegates were to place £600 a year at its disposal. No fees or royalties were to be paid to contributors, who would instead receive 200 copies, and if these proved an embarrassment they could be sold on the contributor's behalf by the Delegates and the contributor would get half the retail price on each copy sold. Few of the titles published sold even that many. There were four series: Aryan, Classical, Semitic, Medieval and Modern. The standards of editing were a little higher than those of the Early English Text Society, which was at the time scouring the country for unpublished manuscripts and rushing them into print as a matter of urgency. Much painstaking work was done, by both young and mature scholars, on the Oxford series. Old manuscripts were dusted off, transcribed, and printed: some rare printed books were reprinted. It was allowed that manuscripts not in Bodley or in other Oxford libraries might yet be entitled to disinterment; in that case the editors must at least be members of the University. Anecdota Oxoniensia, the first paperback series issued by the Press, proved that the Delegates had not forgotten their ancient legacy, and satisfied the purists to whom Bartholomew Price's stubborn commercialism was suspect. The series spluttered defiantly on from 1882 until 1914, and was never formally put to rest. A volume appeared out of the blue in 1929.

Anybody as popular in the world at large as Max Müller was likely to come under some suspicion in Oxford. His good looks, charm, and engaging manners could not be expected always to stand him in good stead. Mark Pattison in fact attributed his failure to get the Boden Chair largely to his 'unpopular manners', as well as to 'the experience his own friends (including myself among the number) have had of his inability for real attachment. We all knew that he only valued us so far as we could be of use to him.' It was also recorded that the great German historian Mommsen had once said on a visit to Oxford: 'Do you breed no humbugs in your country, that you must import them from mine?' A man who could describe India as the country in the whole world 'most richly endowed with all the wealth, power and beauty that nature can bestow—in some parts a very paradise on earth' without ever visiting it might well be suspected of either charlatanism or romanticism. But his sweeping idealism accomplished more than the arid acerbities of many of his contemporaries and he kept the printers busy. Apart from his work on Eastern religions, mythology, and comparative philology, he edited two large volumes of German Classics from the fourth to the nineteenth century, and a translation of Scherer's *History of German Literature*, and helped many other scholars with their work. He had solemnly considered the duties of a Delegate, and for getting on for thirty years he sought to fulfil his own prescription—'to suggest literary works of real utility, to engage the services of young scholars for carrying them out, and to superintend through properly qualified Commissioners their proper execution'.

Mark Pattison had also accepted the role of 'Commissioner', but he made his contribution by attending to what was put before him rather than by seeking out new works, none of which could be expected to reach the standard he himself aspired to. By 1880 he had entered into his final manifestation, and become the 'dim, remote figure, passing his days . . . in Lama-like seclusion', whom Henry Asquith observed as an undergraduate. His disenchantment was complete, the clear streams of reform had all been muddied by Jowett and his henchmen, the University turned into a 'cramming shop' cravenly devoted to worldly advancement, teaching to perfection the art of writing 'leading articles'. He had yet to suffer the mortification of seeing Jowett as Vice-Chancellor and Chairman of the Delegates. There was only one man who seemed to him to hold out hope for the future, the Greek scholar Ingram Bywater, a bibliophile after his own heart. To him the torch could be handed on.

From 1879 until his death in 1914 Bywater was the most active of the Delegates in his concern for pure scholarship. To a select few he seemed as close to perfection as human kind could get. The only reproach openly levelled against him was that he devoted too much of his time to the Clarendon Press. The obituarists in the end could not conceal a feeling that, like Pattison, he had in his own work insufficiently rewarded the world. 'I will not say with the newspapers,' wrote H. W. Garrod, 'in the cant phrase which condones so much of the literary inertia of Oxford, that Bywater was "greater than his books." I do not think so.' But he did, or at least it depended on what was meant by 'his' books. 'There are at any rate', Garrod went on, 'a great many books in the world which would never have come there save for Bywater . . . I doubt if any man was ever so generous in the assistance which he gave to young and untried scholars. . . . His learn-ing, which seemed infinite, and his judgement, which was, perhaps, as near faultless as the nature of human frailty permits, was at their disposal. . . . Indeed, he spent more time and pains . . . over other people's books than most men spend on their own.'

Bywater drawled and lisped, and was extremely reserved except with a few intimate friends, amongst whom were Charles Cannan and, later, R. W. Chapman. As a young man he had been friendly with Walter Pater before he lapsed into pagan hedonism; he had exhibited certain liberal tendencies, and argued rationally that learning and education should be seen as complementary and not incompatible. It was not a view he was able to sustain into middle age. The perfection of learning, the pursuit of the Pattisonian ideal, took possession of him and disseminating knowledge came to seem a shameful waste of a great scholar's time. A genuine scholar could afford no distractions: popularizers like Jowett were indifferent to true scholarship, propagating the heresy that a knowledge of Greek thought might be more useful in modern life than a knowledge of the Greek language and a firm grounding in textual criticism. Bywater's first published work was an edition of the fragments of Heraclitus in 1877, which was admired in Germany and earned him an international reputation. He also worked on the text of Priscianus Lydus, the sixth-century Latin grammarian, for the Berlin Academy of Sciences. But it was on Aristotle that he laboured for most of his life. His edition of the *Ethics* was the model on which the Oxford Classical Texts came to be based. His love-affair with Greece, like Max Müller's with India, was never to be spoilt by a visit to the country, though he travelled much in the Mediterranean—and 'never spoke of Switzerland except as a natural obstacle', no doubt to tease the numerous Alpinists of his day. He tried hard to maintain the narrowness of his interests but, persuaded to read some manuscript for the Press, enthusiasm sometimes took him unawares. He complained once that one such work had given him 'a horrible interest in medieval geography, and there is no subject so remote from my proper studies'. An overriding horror of shoddiness made him keeper of the Press's conscience for thirty-seven years.

10. The Revised Version

THE publication of the Revised Version of the New Testament and the ending of the liaison with Alexander Macmillan were not unconnected, though no overt suggestion of cause and effect was ever made. By 1880 in any case Macmillan's ambition was almost spent and he was dreaming of retirement in the Scottish Highlands: meanwhile Henry Frowde's business in London had so far developed for it to seem natural that the University should wish to assume full control over all its publications.

Macmillan was awarded an honorary M.A. on 25 March 1881, a token of gratitude and esteem. 'The cap and gown of an Oxford M.A. were given after seventeen years' examination in certain not easy lines', he wrote. 'All my then Masters remain my valued friends.'

Six years earlier, in 1875, Price had written to Macmillan to convey the Delegates' wish to amend the clause in their agreement by which they were precluded from selling books except through him and his agents. They wished to be free to sell particular books on special terms without necessarily consulting him. Macmillan did not care for the suggestion. Later in the year he was more firmly informed that the time had come for reconsidering the terms of his employment, and by February 1876 a new agreement had been drawn up. Macmillan had to accept a cut in his commission to $7\frac{1}{2}$ per cent. But again he jibbed at the clause that would enable the Delegates to sell their books through other channels and pay no commission to him. A compromise was reached. The Delegates insisted upon their liberty to sell books wholesale to persons other than Macmillan, and he retained the option of purchasing those books on the same terms as anybody else.

The Revised Version was described by R. C. K. Ensor as the 'culminating phase in the Victorian cult of the Bible'. Since the mid century the Authorized Version had been coming under fire: in 1855 the *Edinburgh Review* was campaigning for revision because of changes in the language and the great advances in Biblical scholarship. In 1870 the Convocation of Canterbury agreed in principle, and appointed a revision committee. This appointed two 'companies' of revisers for the Old and New Testaments, who were to proceed along the most conservative lines possible. Any alteration to the Authorized Version had to be approved by a two-thirds majority of the revisers. In 1873 an agreement was made for publication of the Revised Version by the two Universities, which were to contribute £20,000 to the expenses: they would hold the copyright, to the exclusion of the Queen's Printer. The Queen's Printer at the time was John Spottis-woode, distinguished mathematician, President of the Royal Society, former pupil and lifelong friend of Bartholomew Price. It was a useful connection, postponing at least the possibility of friction.

Among the more active members of the New Testament revision company were F. J. A. Hort, B. F. Westcott, and J. B. Lightfoot, all of them at one time and another Professors of Divinity at Cambridge. Closely associated in their early days with F. D. Maurice, Kingsley, and Tom Hughes, they formed part of Macmillan's circle and remained on affectionate terms with him despite a dilatoriness he found hard to understand. In 1852 Hort and Westcott had dedicated their considerable energies to establishing a revised Greek text of the New Testament, which Macmillan intended to publish. By 1878 he was becoming impatient. He begged Westcott to persuade Hort 'to let the text come out'. By that time Hort had written two introductions to it. 'Does he think it needful that the last hair in all our beards should be actually blanched before recognizing the fact that we are getting up in years?', Macmillan asked. To the perfectionist Hort he wrote, 'You have had your way now for several years, to our serious loss, and deference to your judgement has been already carried beyond due limits. I therefore am ordering paper ... and mean to publish the book in time for the opening of the public schools in August.' Hort, for the thousandth time, made his excuses, and Macmillan dismissed them with feigned amazement. 'Twenty-four years is a long slice out of any man's life', he wrote. 'We will begin to print on August 1.'

It made no difference and the Greek Testament was not published until 1881, one week before the Revised Version itself. Oxford and Cambridge had every intention of publishing the Greek Testament too, however, with the readings adopted by the revisers as a whole. Such hectoring familiarity with members of the New Testament company and so selfish a pre-occupation with his own concerns were not altogether consistent with Macmillan's responsibilities as Publisher to the University. But as his own business continued to proliferate with the accession of his son George, and his nephews, Frederick and Maurice, the role of University publisher became increasingly anomalous. In a letter to Liddell referring to Oxford he admitted that the 'modest part he had played in tending the twig which is now a prosperous and fruitful tree' afforded him a special pleasure. From Oxford the perspective was different, and Macmillan could appear to be patronizing. In every direction his list ramified and the Oxford list seemed to grow in its shade. Cherished Oxford authors like the non-performing Goldwin Smith, and Mark Pattison, even Gladstone himself, were recruited to write for his English Men of Letters series. Only the Bible gave Oxford a clear advantage. The new agreement of 1876 was to last for five years. By the time it lapsed, production of the Revised Version had already begun, and it was not renewed. The generally unsatisfactory nature of an agreement that would have given him $7\frac{1}{2}$ per cent commission on sales of the New Testament had been seen well in advance.

For Price and Frowde publication of the Revised Version portended an era of massive prosperity. A vast and nearly hysterical public awaited it. Not even Dickens had held so many in suspense as this staid committee of theologians that refused to be rushed. Preparations at the Press were altogether exceptional. Production of a million copies a year of the Authorized Version was taken for granted, a routine operation perfected over the years and falling outside the Delegates' province. But the Revised Version was a Delegates' book, and had to be treated accordingly. Their minutes begin to make strange reading, everyday business being punctuated by items of an altogether different order of magnitude. E. A. Freeman's request for permission to include thirteen maps in his book on William Rufus was not granted lightly: the Secretary was 'instructed to ask for specimens of the maps, and to obtain an estimate of the cost of re-producing the same'. At the same time Frowde's order for another half-million copies of the New Testament in a variety of formats was passed without question.

Since his appointment in 1874 Frowde had become increasingly the agent of the Delegates in practical matters such as the purchase and development of premises in London. The binding-house in Garter Court, Barbican, soon fell victim to the Artisans and Labourers Dwelling Improvement Act of 1875 and had to be moved to superior new premises in Aldersgate Street, purchased for £9,750. Frowde bought out the machinery and stock of a book-binder who had gone into liquidation to help furnish it. He renewed the lease on 7 Paternoster Row, acquired the lease on adjoining premises, and began to give the London publishing business an air of dignity and permanence at 'Amen Corner'. He was setting a pattern of expansive behaviour that became increasingly noticeable over the years. The day chosen for him on which to make publishing history was 17 May 1881. On that day one million copies of the Revised New Testament were sold.

It is truer to say that they were distributed, for Frowde had already received orders for a million copies by the middle of March and announced that he could accept no more for delivery on publication day. Copies to the colonies and the United States had been shipped by 9 May. In Britain special arrangements were made with the railway companies for early delivery on the morning of the 17th in all towns and villages throughout the kingdom. As the clock of St. Paul's struck midnight the doors of the two University Press warehouses were opened and delivery to the London trade began. Extra police were called in to control the traffic, and before noon there was not a bookseller in the land without the Revised New Testament.

A contemporary report in the *Leisure Hour* told the story.

The excitement in the forenoon in Paternoster Row was intense, and the public were literally scrambling for copies. The shilling size was being sold at the Underground bookstalls as rapidly at one-and-sixpence per copy as by the discount booksellers at ninepence. One City bookseller alone sold during the day 15,000 in single copies ranging in price from a shilling to a guinea. In every omnibus, in every railway compartment, and even while walking along the public thoroughfare, people were to be seen reading the New Testament. It was the universal subject of conversation throughout the land. On the evening of that memorable day the newspapers were full of it. The whole nation seemed to be reading or discussing the revision. Mr. Frowde and his staff then enjoyed the almost forgotten luxury of going to bed!

Despite what amounted to extensive industrial espionage the secrets of the Revised Version remained intact until publication day. A foreman in Oxford was said to have been offered £2,000 for an advance copy by an American agent, but as Frowde reported to the newspapers, 'The honour of the Oxford Press was as dear to every workman engaged on it as it was to the Delegates themselves'. Another enterprising American tried to sub-stitute a dummy copy for the real thing in the home of one of the revisers in Scotland, and was thwarted by the reviser's daughter. On board the steamer carrying Frowde's consignment to America, however, were representatives of Messrs. Appleton of New York: they had the entire New

Testament set up in type and stereotyped during the crossing, and two days after the boat arrived thousands of these printed copies were on sale. On 22 May the *Chicago Times* printed the text of the Gospels, the Acts, and the Epistles to the Romans—some 118,000 words, which had been cabled from New York. This scoop was said to have cost the paper $10,000.

The revisers had followed their instructions conscientiously. The Authorized Version had been altered just enough to enrage those indissolubly wedded to the familiar text, but for those who had most eagerly awaited it the timorous conservatism of the revisers was almost an affront. It found favour scarcely anywhere. The Anglican Church was unsure of its legality and not until 1899 did the Convocation of Canterbury pronounce it acceptable. Even so it was little used in cathedrals or parish churches, and for private reading the Authorized Version was almost universally preferred. The novelties of the Revised Version quickly wore off, and publication of the Old Testament in 1885, though an immense publishing success in any ordinary sense, was a much less spectacular event.

The two University Presses, however, were understandably overwhelmed by the magnitude of their achievement. A million people had been fortunate enough to get copies on publication day, millions more had yet to be supplied. There was to be no respite. When the Delegates met again on 3 June they put through further printing orders: Nonpareil, 300,000; Brevier, 150,000; Long Primer (old face), 50,000; Long Primer (new face), 100,000; Pica Demy 8vo, 10,000; Pica Royal 8vo, 5,000. At the next meeting on 17 June deep gratitude was expressed for the efforts of the Managers and Superintendents in all departments, for their great zeal and efficiency: 'each person principally concerned' was requested to accept a bound copy 'in recognition of his services and as a token of the high value placed upon them by the Delegates'. They followed this act of unworldly generosity by ordering another 200,000 copies of the Nonpareil, and then dispersed for the Long Vacation.

The inevitable happened. The Revised Version was grossly over-printed, and in time Frowde's triumph came to be regarded as his one great blunder. Stocks began to pile up in the warehouses, whilst the machines continued inexorably to turn out more copies. If sales of one style dropped, copies in a possibly more popular format were ordered: eighteen months after publication Cambridge University Press printed 250,000 copies of a Small Pearl Bible, and Oxford printed half a million. The combined resources of the two Presses were at one time so stretched that Nelsons of Edinburgh had to be entrusted with some of the machining. As a result there occurred what came to be known as the 'quire famine'—there were no more quires of the Authorized Version, for work on it had virtually been suspended to make way for the Revised Version. This was a serious set-back, from which the Queen's Printer benefited. Unhappily there was not time to learn from the mistakes of 1881 before the Old Testament was ready, when the same mistake was made again. A heroic depreciation was ordered in 1888, amounting to £9,000 on the stock at the Bible Press and £5,900 at the

London warehouse—which in effect was 31 per cent of the profit declared in the first Revised Bible year. The profit was still substantial, but it was a source of complacent grief to Bartholomew Price's successor to contemplate how much greater it might have been if so much had not been wasted on the manufacture of superfluous stock. Frowde's mistake was, he would also point out, directly sanctioned by the Delegates.

11. The New English Dictionary

ONE author whom Macmillan shared with the Clarendon Press was a largely self-taught elementary school teacher, a philologist, named Richard Morris. In collaboration with W. W. Skeat he produced an edition of Chaucer for the Clarendon Press Series, and his *Historical Outlines of English Accidence* for Macmillan was an immensely successful school-book that went through many editions. Before Macmillan could fully exploit this lucrative author Morris turned his attention to the study of Pali, and the rest of his life's work was published by Henry Frowde for the Pali Text Society.

In 1876 Morris was President of the Philological Society. He mentioned to Macmillan the new English dictionary the Society hoped one day to produce, and also James Murray, who might well edit it. He added that Harpers of New York were also interested. There had been few dictionaries published in recent years, indeed only one in England since Dr. Johnson, and Macmillan wrote at once to Murray, plunging into a situation of much greater complexity than he had imagined. Although he got specimens from Murray, and produced nine different sets of proofs of them, he was soon in difficulties.

The Philological Society had been sporadically engaged on 'a completely new English Dictionary' for nearly twenty years. The first advocate had been Richard Chenevix Trench, Dean of Westminster and later Archbishop of Dublin, an active member of the New Testament revision company. The date of the dictionary's inception was recorded as 7 January 1858; on 5 January 1928 the last sheets were passed for press in Walton Street, and it was still uncertain whether its correct name was A New English Dictionary, or The Oxford English Dictionary, or just the Oxford Dictionary.

The first editor, appointed in 1859, was Herbert Coleridge, grandson of the poet, who estimated that 'in about two years we shall be able to give our first number to the world'. He added that 'were it not for the dilatoriness of many contributors, I should not hesitate to name an earlier period'. To contain the materials on which the dictionary was to be based he had built a set of pigeon-holes which could contain some 60,000 slips. Within two years Coleridge was dead of consumption at the age of 31, leaving to his successors his pigeon-holes and gift for false prophecy. His task was taken

F

over by Frederick Furnivall, a man of turbulent character, part clown, part scholar, a charlatan of fanatical integrity. For the next fifty years he was living proof of the mad foolhardiness of the whole enterprise. Teetotal, non-smoking, vegetarian, over-exercised, he was also an agnostic and an anti-sabbatarian, who married a lady's-maid and compounded the offence by leaving her.

His approach to the dictionary was the reverse of that of Herbert Coleridge. They were not yet at the beginning: an immense amount had to be done before a start could even be made. Many more voluntary contributors or sub-editors must be recruited, and most important of all, as the dictionary was to record the history of every word in the language, the earliest literature in English, contained in innumerable unpublished manuscripts scattered about the country, had to be put into print. Furnivall was an insatiate founder of societies: the Chaucer Society, the Ballad Society, the New Shakespeare Society, the Wycliff Society, and most productive of all the Early English Text Society which went to work with messianic fervour to reclaim the national inheritance. He himself produced a dozen texts in seven years, and Richard Morris and Walter Skeat almost as many. One of the most scrupulous and knowledgeable of Furnivall's team was the Scotsman James Murray, formerly a bank clerk and now a master at Mill Hill School. He was already known as the author of a pioneer study in philology, *The Dialects of the Southern Counties of Scotland* (1873), and of the *Encyclopaedia Britannica* article on the English language.

During Furnivall's nominal editorship the dictionary itself disappeared from the agenda of the Philological Society. In 1874 the President suggested that a society was better fitted to collect the materials than actually to compile a dictionary, and intimated that the man most clearly marked out by his scholarship to edit the work was the Oxford philologist and phonetician Henry Sweet, later known to the world as Bernard Shaw's Professor Higgins in *Pygmalion*. However, Murray himself had begun to take a close interest in the materials already collected, and it was with him that Macmillan believed he had to deal. He did not make due allowance for Furnivall, who in the end proved fatal to the project as far as he was concerned. He squabbled over the length, and over the name—it was not to be Macmillan's Dictionary, he insisted, but The Philological Society Dictionary. An ultimatum declaring that unless Macmillan agreed to a half share of the profits with the Society Furnivall would go elsewhere finally persuaded Macmillan that it was impossible to do business with him. It was upsetting at the time. Later his son George wrote, with quiet understatement, 'I do not think we had any reason to regret that the enterprise passed out of our hands into those of the Clarendon Press.'

Immediately after this failure Furnivall urged Skeat to approach the Cambridge University Press, but it soon became apparent that the Syndics would have nothing to do with any project in which Furnivall was involved. So it was Henry Sweet, author in his time of twenty books published by the Press, who eventually approached Bartholomew Price. On 20 April 1877 he dangled before him the fruits of nineteen years' work—'half of it sub-edited and ready for publication'. It would be wonderfully remunerative, with vast sales: Littré's French dictionary in four large volumes of 1,000 pages each sold 40,000 copies, effortlessly. Furnivall intervening prodded Price further: would Macmillans—'such a keen set'—have proposed to take it up if they had not seen their way clear to a certain success? On 1 June the proposal appeared on the Delegates' agenda and was deferred for further consideration.

Subsequently Price was instructed to ask for specimens, and Max Müller was asked to report. He recognized that everything would depend on the editing of the contributions of the voluntary workers, and was unimpressed by Sweet's claim that half was ready for publication. But the idea of Max Müller advising the dictionary editors on etymologies, as he proceeded to do, was hair-raising even then: his own etymologies tended to justify his mythological theories and, despite his reputation, did not conform to the scientific principles of the new philology. Asked to provide further specimens, Murray found himself involved in dispiriting etymological arguments. He received Price's report on the Delegates' deliberations so far in December 1877, and felt inclined, as he was often to do, to drop the matter. More information was wanted on the methods of research of the voluntary readers. Not even Furnivall could supply that, for he had never been explicit about method: Murray had seen only a part of what had been done and knew it to be erratic in quality, some of it worthless. The phonetic and etymological parts, it was suggested in view of Max Müller's misgivings, should be omitted altogether. The Delegates had just accepted Skeat's *Etymological Dictionary*. To Murray it seemed that they might be under the illusion that this was a definitive rather than a preliminary work, and might even decide against the new dictionary in consequence. Skeat, who had gone ahead on the assumption that the Society's dictionary would never get done, could argue that his own work would save Murray much trouble later on.

Finding Murray disheartened, Furnivall took up the negotiations and visited Henry Liddell, showing him a list of the 393 readers who had so far supplied slips, a list that he then lost. He was determined to employ tact, which his unusual versatility enabled him to do over short periods. He assured Murray that if he humoured the Delegates now he would be allowed a free hand later on. As negotiations proceeded, Murray was told just the opposite by Henry Sweet, a great scholar but of a rather murky and sour disposition: it was clear to him that Price and the Delegates were only being agreeable until they had got control of the Society's materials. Then Murray would be fired, and 'some Oxford swell, who will draw a good salary for doing nothing' would take his place. 'I know something of Oxford,' he told him, 'and of its low state of morality as regards jobbery and personal interest.'

The situation was complicated by the fact that Murray had still not finally made up his mind. Could he sacrifice ten years of his life to editing the dictionary? He might be better off as a headmaster in Huddersfield. But in April 1878 he was invited for the first time to Oxford to meet the Delegates in person. By then they had more or less made up their minds, subject only to Murray proving amenable and sane. Had he turned out to be another Furnivall or Sweet, the outcome might have been different. As it was he appeared docile if dogged. Once again Max Müller was asked to report. The principles adopted by the voluntary contributors were still largely unfathomable. A very wide range of books had been consulted, but some seemed to be unworthy: his own *Lectures on the Science of Language*, he modestly submitted, hardly deserved to be quoted as an authority on the English language. He said nothing about the use of newspaper quotations, one of Furnivall's favourite sources: it was said that if the Dictionary at one period quoted the *Daily News* and at another the *Daily Chronicle* it was because Furnivall had changed his paper in the meantime. The materials, such as they were, did however form a nucleus of sorts. 'But in an undertaking of such magnitude,' Müller went on, 'in which one might almost say the national honour of England is engaged, no effort should be spared to make the work as perfect as possible.' Perfectionism came to be synonymous with tardiness and expense, and to be dreaded above all things. But fortunately Max Müller was prepared to compromise on etymologies. The etymology of every word should be given but it should not go beyond the 'immediate feeders of the English language'—Early English and Anglo-Saxon antecedents for Saxon words, Norman French and Latin for Romance words, etc. Everything else, the 'ultimate etymologies' that he himself hankered after, belonged in an etymological, not in a historical dictionary. Finally, Max Müller felt able to assure the Delegates that from a commercial point of view they had nothing to fear.

Murray was satisfied by Müller's report, and so too were the Delegates. After a year's deliberation the work was accepted in principle; it just required another year to negotiate a contract between the Vice-Chancellor, Murray, and Furnivall on behalf of the Philological Society. Murray really needed to be protected from himself. He thought it his duty to do some of the work without remuneration as his own contribution to English literature. His first estimate of costs was £6,500 for the first three years, to cover salaries and all other expenses. After that the editor would be paid by results: £1 for each page completed for press. With Furnivall the bargaining was necessarily hard and long. Price was a great stonewaller, not to be flurried by Furnivall's erratic attacks. The Society's share of the profits was to be 40 per cent, out of which 20 per cent would be paid to the editor. Agreement seemed imminent when Murray, having had more time to examine the materials—some two million slips, it turned out, in all sorts of condition—increased his estimate for editorial expenses to £9,000. In that case, said Price, the Press would take 65 per cent of the profits, the editor 20 per cent, and the Society 15 per cent. Furnivall exploded. 'It's that mean old skunk rat Bart. Price, damn him,' he wrote to Murray. 'Tell Price at once that all this means putting off work.'

In December 1878 Furnivall and Murray together met the Delegates, and Furnivall voiced his opinion of their shiftiness and cupidity. It was an embarrassing occasion that left much ill-feeling. Murray even offered to share his profit with the Society, making it 17½ per cent each, but Price objected: Murray and his heirs would deserve every penny he could make. The Delegates would not yield, but with great circumlocution declared that although they could not bind their successors they would venture to express a confident expectation that if the profits proved higher than expected their successors would entertain favourably any application put to them by the Society. There were never to be any profits, but Furnivall was unforgiving. Many years later in an unsigned but characteristic article in the *Oxford Review* headed 'How *not* to treat a Man of Letters', he was writing of the 'miserable parsimony and sharp practice' of the Delegates. On 1 March 1879 the agreement was eventually signed, and Murray formally began work on the Dictionary at the age of 42. The target was 7,000 pages in ten years.

The materials by which the Society set such great store were often an encumbrance to Murray. Quite apart from the fact that one letter appeared to be missing from the bundles of slips, and another had been nearly burnt by the widow of the compiler, and Furnivall had lost his list of workers which he claimed Price had, it became clear that there was both too much and too little. It would always be the case.

In April 1879 the Philological Society sent out 2,000 copies of an *Appeal to the English-speaking and English-reading Public*, seeking 1,000 new readers over the next three years. Before long Murray was receiving at the Scriptorium he had had built in the grounds at Mill Hill some thousand slips a day. From the start, therefore, the Dictionary was inflationary, and estimates of length had constantly to be revised. The tendency of the volunteers, many of whom were cranks, was to collect unusual words, and to ignore those in common use, the words which inevitably caused the editor most trouble in the end. But they produced nevertheless a constant accession of fresh quotations all of which had to be carefully sifted and pigeon-holed. In 1880 and 1881 Murray presented his annual reports to the Delegates. They were received without comment. After two years of painful negotiations, he was being left to carry on quietly by himself. At his own request, a subcommittee was appointed of Henry Liddell, Max Müller, and Mark Pattison, which he could consult if necessary on literary matters. But he rarely did so.

Murray was sustained for the rest of his life by an illusion that time, however quickly it ran out, was on his side. For a moment in history the language had paused and come to rest. It could be seized and captured for ever. Murray and his successors did not dwell on the romantic aspects of lexicography, on the mystery of language and the beckoning enticements of etymology, that lured them on. Lexicography had mostly to do with slips of paper measuring, preferably, six inches by four. Nor for that matter was Bishop Stubbs much aware of the passion that sustained him as he groped through the mists of history for the primeval sources of the institutions of Britain. Like Antarctic explorers and other agents of an unworldly colonialism, hard work and drudgery were all such men immediately had to offer themselves. The moment for such endeavours had come: they would seize it, and perhaps in some scarcely foreseeable future they or their successors would reap a transcendent reward.

Walter Skeat, who was in at the beginning, once said to Sir William Craigie, who was in at the end, that it would have been impossible to produce the Dictionary very much earlier. He meant that the materials did not exist, the sources had not been opened. To Craigie it was equally clear that it could not have been started very much later. The language was soon manifestly on the move again, with new technical terms emerging, and above all Americanisms, which remained an abomination to lexicographers long after they had been welcomed as an enrichment of the language by those who used rather than enshrined it. Murray was too close to the Dictionary to be able to rationalize. But whenever he was moved to give up, by some disagreement with the Press or sheer fatigue, or by well-meaning assurances that what remained to be done could well be left to the next generation, he rallied himself with the conviction that the work had to be done then and could never be done again. In that he was right. It could only be supplemented.

12. Benjamin Jowett, Vice-Chancellor

BENJAMIN JOWETT became Vice-Chancellor in 1882 when he was already sixty-five. He had every intention of making his presence felt in the next four years, and drew up a list of things he wished in that time to change and reform. On it was the Clarendon Press, which for too long had been able to elude his attention. At the end of Michaelmas term 1882, having surveyed the scene, Jowett gave notice of intent to the Delegates that he proposed to superintend a series of Greek texts, with the Homeric scholar D. B. Monro and Evelyn Abbott as his collaborators. Moreover he there and then moved that a return should be laid before the Board of all the unprofitable books published by the Press between 1860 and 1880. Price was left to perform this unwholesome task during the Christmas vacation.

Fifty-one titles fell within the category, a substantial number considering how few had been published annually before the Clarendon Press Series began to change the appearance of the list. The record of Müller's *Passerine Birds* was perhaps too painful to be contemplated by whoever helped Price to compile his report: a sales figure of 49 concealed 40 copies given away. The most expensive aberration during the period, however, had been Burnet's *History of the Reformation*, published in 1865. It had been edited by the Revd. N. Pocock of Clifton who before devoting himself to historical research had been a distinguished mathematician and Bartholomew Price's tutor. He had been informed in 1864 that the Delegates, 'having ventured to print 2000 copies', were in a mood to be generous and wished him to accept £700 rather than the £100 originally offered. It was indeed a monumental work in seven volumes, but few editors were so handsomely rewarded. In 1872, 1,310 sets were wasted, yet when Price drew up his list ten years later there were still 524 remaining and the debit balance against the book was £2,434.

The list of unprofitable books naturally contained many titles of which the Press had reason to feel proud, but it was not a heartening statement to have to lay before the new Vice-Chancellor. The losses incurred were estimated at £26,304, out of production charges of £31,657. Though stocks had been wasted in 1863 and again in 1872, only very rarely had books been actually put out of print, and Jowett might have found a list of those that continued to be kept in stock but had ceased to sell of some interest. It was ten years, for instance, since a copy of Bishop Smalridge's *Sermons* had been sold, and it was not until 1885 that the next customer came along; in 1895 there was another, the last. The only recorded response of the Delegates to the Secretary's post-mortem was to instruct him to take steps to improve the advertising of Oxford books. Henceforth Jowett adopted the maxim that to make money rather than to advance learning was the primary policy of the University Press. He did, however, introduce to Oxford and to the Press the great Johnsonian scholar, G. Birkbeck Hill, who in turn introduced the eighteenth century as a legitimate field of study.

Jowett's proposal for a series of Greek texts was presented in the form of a printed prospectus and considered by the Delegates in February 1863 at a meeting at which both Pattison and Bywater were present. A proposal from Pattison for an edition of Schiller's minor poems by one of his students, Theodore Althaus, was unfortunately also on the agenda. It was rejected and Jowett's scheme was approved. 'The conversation which ensued', Pattison recalled, 'showed that you may be Regius Professor of Greek without knowing the most elementary conditions of the formation of the Greek text.' The prospectus was, in his view, a most unscholarly document, and the whole undertaking entirely repugnant.

Jowett casually stated that the texts should be based on the best German texts, 'with some original work on MSS where needed'. That matter disposed of he could get down to business. From two to four volumes were to be published each year, beginning in January 1885. They were 'to be printed on the best paper and in the best manner; in a larger size for Libraries; and in a smaller size from the same types, or reduced by photography from the printed page, for Schools'. He listed the first ten authors and the names of possible editors, who were to be rewarded by a fee of £100 and a royalty of 1s. on every copy sold. As the books were intended to be cheap, this was as unrealistic as any of the lavish proposals put forward by the School-book Committee at the start of the Clarendon Press Series. The only editor on his initial list who eventually produced a text was

S. H. Butcher, whose *Demosthenes* ran to 1,480 pages: he was paid £125 on publication, and 2*d.* a copy after 3,000 copies had been sold. But that was not until the twentieth century.

A year later Jowett came up with a revised and slightly more refined prospectus. The texts were 'to be based on the best critical apparatus already in print, with some original work on MSS where needed'. He had dropped the idea of photographically reduced editions, but still in the interest of cheapness proposed that the books should be split up into parts, bound in paper, and sold at 1*s.* 3*d.* for 100 pages—the student thereby being required to buy only the parts he needed. The name of Bywater appears against Aristotle's *Poetics* and that of Monro against Homer, and the two of them together with Jowett, Professor Goodwin of Harvard, Professors Jebb and Butcher, and Dr. Evelyn Abbott were to act as general editors.

But not even Jowett could impose his will upon Delegates so deeply suspicious as Pattison and Bywater. Although the project had been accepted in principle, a great deal could be done to impede its realization. Jowett knew that if based on fresh collations of the manuscripts the work would take too long and cost too much. But nothing less would be worthy of the Clarendon Press, the collective conscience of the Delegates protested, and scholars of the highest repute would not countenance Jowett's short cuts. Reproducing the German texts would have done no credit to British scholarship and might indeed have been thought to serve no useful purpose at all. The plan hardly differed from that of Kitchin twenty years before, which was in fact still maturing. But Jowett was only interested in cheapness, availability, and profit. 'How he hated learning!' as York Powell, a Delegate who had the privilege of being briefed by him in his new duties, used to say. In time Jowett's Greek Texts were transmuted by Bywater and his colleagues into the Oxford Classical Texts, but as Jowett had guessed many years passed, and subcommittees came and went, and the century itself elapsed before the first books appeared.

Jowett was the first person from Oxford in an official capacity to visit James Murray in his Scriptorium at Mill Hill. He found him hostile and suspicious. A sense of being neglected combined with a fear that a watchful and critical eye was being kept on him prohibited any peace of mind. He had already realized the magnitude of his initial miscalculations both of the time needed and of the ultimate length of the Dictionary. He was measuring himself against Webster, and his instructions were to maintain a proportion of 4 to 1. Yet at times he found himself exceeding Webster by 10 to 1, which meant that he was creating a monster. On the other hand to stick to the original length would be disastrously to impoverish the work. In · his relations with Oxford he had found a mediator, however, who could be trusted to state his case with less provocation than was to be expected from Furnivall. Henry Hucks Gibbs, later Baron Aldenham, had been a member of the Philological Society for many years, and had worked on the Dictionary as a sub-editor. In 1882, after having been for a time Governor of the Bank of England, he resumed the work and struck up a friendship with Bartholomew Price. An attempt to persuade the Delegates to improve the equation to 6 × Webster (or 10,000 pages) was partially successful: they granted the possibility of six volumes of 1,400 pages each.

In 1883 a new Dictionary subcommittee was appointed under Jowett consisting of Liddell, Max Müller, Bywater, and Sir William Markby, Reader in Indian Law at Balliol, who had recently been appointed a Delegate. Part I of the Dictionary was already in proof. Jowett found the proofs, possibly the most heavily corrected proofs ever known, particularly fascinating. It seemed to him that the illustrative quotations should always be from the work in which a word was used in a particular sense for the first time. Many other ideas occurred to him too, and he was able to compose for Murray's benefit detailed 'Suggestions for guidance in preparing copy for the Press'. No instances of the use of words were to be given later than 1875, the use of newspapers as sources should be curtailed, and scientific and slang words were to be included only if they were 'to be found in literature'. Appended to the 'Suggestions' were some notes from an unnamed Delegate who wished to see the omission of 'Aardvark' and 'Aardwolf', the very first words that any lexicographer has to contend with and without which the language has no beginning.

It was by this time difficult though not impossible to raise questions about the Dictionary that had not already been raised in the past twenty years. But this had not occurred to Jowett. Murray was thrown into despondency. How could this recently appointed committee expect to understand all the problems? And nothing could be more unwise than to suggest to a perfectionist that he should carry his researches a little further. Hucks Gibbs assured Murray that it was 'ignorant misapprehension' on Jowett's part and not 'gratuitous impertinence'. Jowett, who was genuinely enthusiastic, hardly knew what he had done. He had simply made some suggestions.

But Jowett and the Dictionary subcommittee had equal difficulty keeping their hands off Murray's introduction to Part I. On receiving proofs Murray found that it had been partially rewritten, though no explanation was offered. He reacted with such piteous indignation, threatening to resign, that Jowett felt something approaching remorse. Nothing had finally been decided, he explained. It was to be hoped that the changes were for the better, but they were only suggestions. Murray visited Oxford, Hucks Gibbs and Price calmed feelings, and with an assurance that Murray would be allowed to write his own introduction the crisis passed. In January 1884 Part I, A–Ant, was eventually published in an edition of 5,000 copies. The first 352 pages of the Dictionary had taken five years to produce. Any satisfaction at seeing something in print at last was quenched by that dismaying reality, for it had been supposed and was still supposed that the Dictionary would pour from the press at the rate of 704 pages a year, every year. In view of the expenses so far incurred, the return on the sales of Part I was derisory. The Delegates appealed to the First Lord of the

Treasury for a Civil List grant for Murray, and Jowett insisted that he be brought to Oxford, and supplied either with a co-editor or a larger permanent staff.

In the summer of 1884 Murray agreed to leave Mill Hill. Furnivall had once hinted that if he moved, Price would be able to acquire for him one of the new professorships created by the High Commission, and Jowett certainly allowed him to believe that a University appointment, possibly a research fellowship, would be his reward. It was something he coveted. He had received an honorary LL.D. at Edinburgh ten years earlier, which entitled him to wear a cap and gown. The former became an essential part of his working gear: he donned it on entering the Scriptorium and wore it for all dictionary work. Admission to the University of Oxford would have been an even higher distinction. But the Government granted him a Civil List Pension of £250 for life, and it was no longer necessary, in the view of those who knew nothing of Murray's inner longings, to obtain for him an academic post.

Murray and his eight assistants were more than ever committed to achieving the impossible. The negotiation of new terms meant further anguish, for the Delegates wished to make them dependent on an absolute guarantee that 704 pages would be published each year. Murray was troubled too by Jowett's growing insistence that he should look for a second editor. Publication of Part I had prompted a long and discerning review in the *Academy* by Henry Bradley, a cutler's clerk from Sheffield recently made redundant. Somehow he had acquired an extraordinary understanding of lexicography. But Murray was not sure that there was room for two experts. In any case the suggestion implied the Delegates' displeasure, and that always saddened him.

In the garden of his new home at Sunnyside, 78 Banbury Road, Murray began to build a new Scriptorium. His next-door neighbour was a raving lunatic called Dicey—or so it must have seemed to Murray as the freakish figure, the absent-minded professor incarnate, gibbered and stared at him across the garden wall. Letters of furious complaint were received by Price, and the Scriptorium had to be dug more deeply and damply into the ground so as not to spoil the great lawyer's view. Oxford was strange territory, backward beyond belief in English studies. E. A. Freeman advised Murray to expect 'an aggressive contempt for all wise learning', and Henry Sweet was always on hand to remind him of impending perfidy. But there was one consolation. Jowett welcomed him into Balliol, and from being an insufferable meddler became a dear friend. Murray had been in the habit of giving his children such names as Rosfrith, Ethelwyn, Aelfric, and Ethelbert. The tenth he chose to call Benjamin. But Jowett told him that he had never himself liked the name, and would have called any son of his after his old friends Arthur Stanley and Arthur Hugh Clough, so the tenth and penultimate Murray was christened Arthur Hugh Jowett.

With Stacey's sullen withdrawal to Wolvercote after his disagreements with Price in 1876, the Bible Press, and the printing works generally, were controlled by Edward Pickard Hall. When Jowett decided that it was time to advertise for a suitable person 'to take the management of the Press at Oxford', Pickard Hall had completed thirty years of diligent service. His working hours were 6 a.m. to 6 p.m. and he was never known to fail. It was outside working hours, however, that he gave most of himself. The physical, moral, and spiritual welfare of several hundred men and boys was his responsibility, particularly after Thomas Combe's death in 1872. Four nights a week during the winter months up to eighty boys voluntarily—or so it was said—attended night school and were instructed by him. He also gave readings and lectures. At weekends he organized games on the Saturday half-holiday, Sunday school on Sunday afternoons, and singing classes for the compositors at his home in the evenings. He took pride in the brass band that he rehearsed and conducted, and in the drum and fife band for the boys. He started a provident club for medical aid and a clothing club—the boys deposited their tuppences each Sunday morning, a contribution was made by the firm, and the aggregate was dispensed in the form of useful garments at Christmas.

As a printer he had his limitations. A managing partnership in the Bible Press was, in his view, the 'blue ribbon' of the profession, and it was essentially as a Bible printer that he regarded himself. The object was to maintain the quality and improve the quantity, which the regular purchase of new machines enabled him to do. By 1880 he was proud to record that the Pearl Bible could be produced at the rate of eight perfect books a minute, or 6,000 copies a day. He also recorded that the amount of paper used for printing Bibles in the course of a year would form a band $8\frac{2}{3}$ inches wide which would stretch round the whole world, taking its diameter as 25,000 miles. The Caxton Memorial Bible of 1877 might be regarded as one of his achievements. An edition of 100 copies was printed and bound within twelve hours, just to show how far the art and mystery had advanced since Caxton's time. Printing began at two o'clock in the morning from movable types which had not been used for several years. The sheets were artificially dried and put on the nine o'clock express to London. There they were bound, in turkey morocco, with gold lettering and the arms of the University on the side, and a parcel of ten copies was delivered at the Caxton exhibition in South Kensington at two o'clock in the afternoon when Gladstone was due to open it. Gladstone considered that this feat might be fittingly called 'the climax and consummation of printing'. But Falconer Madan, in awarding credit for it, made no mention of Pickard Hall: that was to be divided between Mr. Henry Stevens of Vermont who suggested the scheme, Mr. Henry Frowde, on whom the burden of the special arrangements fell, and Professor Bartholomew Price, who decided that the idea could be carried out.

Jowett was interested in printing, particularly the printing of his own books with which he was never satisfied—partly because he could not reconcile a taste for good clear margins with his predilection for marginal notes. He could recognize a lack of typographical distinction, but was not knowledgeable enough to advise the printer. It is doubtful whether even if he had been a younger man Pickard Hall would have been acceptable to Jowett as Manager of the Press. He had never been an innovator. When he was summarily dismissed in 1884 he was seventy-six years of age. The decision of the Delegates, however, was unexpected. 'The blow to me and to my family is unspeakably painful', he wrote to Price. The suddenness of the decision suggested to him some grave dereliction of duty, for which he was to be punished by poverty in old age. He appealed to the Delegates to improve on his compensation. 'It would be but for a *very short-time*, and would make my closing years content and tranquil and ever inspired with a recollection of your generous consideration of an old servant.'

His departure and the death of Stacey in the same year brought about the end of the partnership. The Delegates were in possession of the forty-eight shares. A committee headed by Jowett had interviewed the candidates for the post of 'Comptroller', or Manager of the Printing business, and appointed Horace Hart, a man of forty-three. He had started work at the age of 14 as a 'reading boy' for the printers Woodfall & Kinder in London. He had been in turn compositor, 'literary editor', book-keeper, and, at the age of 26, Manager. When he joined the Oxford University Press he had for two years been in charge of Messrs. Clowes & Son's principal London business. He was well qualified to take over a large and expanding business which by the nature of its growth was so peculiar. He found many of its resources inadequate and out of date, and began to make plans for improvement. He proposed with Max Müller's enthusiastic support to establish 'a department for the facsimile reproduction of rare books and MSS', recommended the purchase of a fount of Chinese, and obtained approval for buying a Gills Hot Rolling Press, nine new printing machines, a 16 horsepower gas engine, and for building an annexe to hold the new machinery. He was interrupted in 1886 by Jowett forcing the appointment of a subcommittee to 'investigate the alleged deterioration in the quality of printing at the University Press'. As Bartholomew Price's successor recalled to Hart with affection many years later, it was Jowett who 'first stirred the fire and set us all running'. It took a great deal out of all concerned, he added.

Some help had been provided for Price by the appointment of an assistant secretary. The need for one had been recognized in 1873 when he took over the management of all the businesses, but it was not until 1879 that the post was satisfactorily filled. C. E. Doble, a shy, self-effacing scholar, graduate of Worcester College, was appointed 'to exercise a general superintendence over the printing of all Delegates books', and to correspond with authors. He was also to attend meetings of the School-book Committee, for which he would act as secretary. Doble remained at the Press, in sickness and in health, for thirty years, and as the duties of the Secretaries became increasingly administrative he represented for much of that time the entire editorial and production staff.

It might seem from Jowett's behaviour that Price's management had left here and there something to be desired, but Price enjoyed an immunity from explicit criticism. He was a great administrator. There were those ready to say that he created a legend in his own lifetime. In 1898 the vigour of his constitution still astonished Oxford. But in 1884 he was exhausted and became seriously ill. Whether or not Jowett was proving too much for him he decided to retire. 'The selection of the person to fill the post of Secretary', it was written in the Waldock Report of 1970, 'is . . . a matter of the highest consequence to the University. . . . Indeed, it may perhaps be considered the most important of all the functions performed by the Delegates.' In 1884 that function was usurped by Benjamin Jowett.

PART III

THE MYSTERIOUS AFFAIR OF LYTTELTON GELL

1. Over Pattison's Dead Body

ETWEEN 1884 and 1897 the Secretary to the Delegates was Philip Lyttelton Gell, a man whose name has been written out of the history books by a malign censor. He saw to the running of the Press during a period of rapid growth and mounting tensions, not all of them created by himself. In the scanty but enduring oral tradition he is remembered as idle, quarrelsome, and incompetent. A man who joined the office staff in 1897, A. E. Durham, later Chief Accountant, recalled on retirement fifty years later that Gell arrived at the office each morning promptly at ten o'clock in a coach and pair—bringing with him a luncheon hamper to which in due course legend added a bottle of champagne. He left again promptly at four. But by 1897 the doctors had diagnosed an acute case of over-work and ordered Gell to rest. The tradition that he was a serious and prolonged disaster descends from Bywater, through Charles Cannan and R. W. Chapman, and may be largely attributed to the fact that he was Jowett's man. It may also be assumed that Bartholomew Price had a low opinion of him, for in the Price family album he is accused of having lacked 'application' and 'ability', and of having hastened Bat Price's death at the age of 80 when his long absence from Oxford imposed upon the old man many extra burdens. In the Murray family tradition too he is a figure of ill-repute. Years later R. W. Chapman wrote, 'It is difficult now to make out just what was wrong with Gell.' That something had been wrong he had no doubt. He was convinced that the natural growth of the nineties, 'to be expected with a strong delegacy and great literary activity in the University and outside, was undoubtedly retarded by the attitude of the Delegates' secretary'. Chapman might have been better able to substantiate this view if he could have persuaded Gell's successor, Charles Cannan, to be a little more communicative. But 'Cannan was very reserved and we dared not ask questions.' His one recorded utterance on the subject was: 'Gell was always here, but I cannot make out what he did.' It was a curious observation. He knew what he did, much the same as he was himself doing. On the other hand he was not always there. It was his long absences through ill health brought on by over-work that eventually proved his undoing, and gave Cannan his opportunity. Chapman did not raise the matter again. He accepted the implication of idleness, formed his own opinion that Gell was not interested in learned books and hated committees, and passed on the tradition of a dark age in the modern history of the Press. Sir Humphrey Milford too had the impression that when he joined the Press in 1900 it was only just beginning to recover from a fearful malaise.

If a mistake was made in the appointment of Gell it was not one the Delegates ever repeated. He is the only outsider to have held the post. All other incumbents have either been Delegates themselves or had long experience within the Press. Nor did they ever again appoint one so young—he was thirty-three. And they took steps to ensure that no decisions of such magnitude should in future be taken in the month of August, and without a full meeting.

Finding a successor to Bartholomew Price would under normal circumstances have been a lengthy and intricate procedure, the Delegates' responsibility being made more onerous by the weight of the man to be replaced. Jowett, however, was not sympathetic towards democratic procedures in committee and saw no need for a multitude of candidates when he had one of his own. At a meeting of the Delegates on 20 June 1884 Finance Committee and the Secretary were authorized to make inquiries for a suitable person: whether he should be a 'purely literary man' or one with experience in publishing was a question left unsettled. It was agreed that he should be a graduate of the University. Without more ado Jowett wrote to Gell, determined to move fast during the vacation. Price must have assumed that no appointment would actually be made before October. Within a few weeks Jowett had overcome Gell's initial misgivings about a possible drop in salary and was intimating the possibility of better terms than he could possibly guarantee.

A Balliol man, with a good first in history, Lyttelton Gell was making a name for himself with the publishing house of Cassell & Gilpin. It was no doubt in Jowett's mind that somebody with experience in commercial publishing in London was very much what the Press needed. He had known Gell's father, a friend of Clough and Matthew Arnold, and he had every reason to remember Gell himself from his Balliol days, when Jowett had had his covetous eye on a young man called Arnold Toynbee (uncle of the historian), who already as an undergraduate was exerting a powerful influence. His promise was irresistible. Although he had matriculated as a commoner at Pembroke in 1873, Jowett was determined to lure him away. He urged him to compete for the Brackenbury history scholarship at Balliol, confident that he would win it. Gell won it instead. An unseemly fracas with the Master of Pembroke ensued, and as Price was Senior Fellow of the college he was involved too. Jowett was prepared to offer Toynbee rooms in Balliol. It was an offer he was unwilling to refuse, for it was the college of the men he most admired—T. H. Green and Henry Nettleship, as well as Jowett himself. The Pembroke Convention Book records that

Toynbee, 'without the privity of the Master or the Tutors, made a private arrangement . . . with the Master of Balliol to migrate thither as a commoner'. The arrangement was deplored and vetoed, with the result that for a couple of years Toynbee ceased to be a member of the University altogether, though he remained in Oxford. He was one of the men whom Gell most admired.

Gell's closest friend was and remained Alfred Milner. They had both been at King's College, London, with Arnold Toynbee, before coming up to Oxford. They had toyed with the law subsequently, and then with journalism, in an unsettled period when they looked for a cause rather than a career. Milner's decision to abandon a promising career at the Bar had to be justified to Jowett. 'If I live,' Milner wrote to him reassuringly, 'I mean to do you some credit yet.' And it was because of Milner that Gell renewed his old association with the Master of Balliol in 1882. He composed a long letter on behalf of his 'oldest and nearest friend'—'a subject upon which I know well you are just now as anxious as myself'. He solicited Jowett's help in finding a suitable post for Milner. Had it been two years later the history of both the Oxford University Press and the British Empire might have been changed.

Gell had been building up the educational list at Cassells, which he claimed to have found in a rudimentary condition, and he had had one stroke of luck. He had been responsible for the publication of *Treasure Island* in 1883. The manuscript had been on his desk one afternoon when Milner called to take him on the river. Milner read parts of it, was 'greatly struck', and Gell had discovered a best seller. In three years his income had risen from £400 to £1,200, and he confidently expected it to increase annually until it had rather more than doubled. About £300 a year represented interest on his own capital invested in the business, the loss of which on his move to Oxford was to haunt him for the next fourteen years. When Jowett made his first soundings Gell confided his misgivings on that score, even though he was prepared to make sacrifices: 'I should not ask to be paid for serving the University as highly as when I am earning dividends for idle capitalists', he told him.

Jowett misled Gell into believing that everything could be satisfactorily worked out once his appointment had been confirmed, and in doing so gravely diminished his chances of success. 'If, as you suggested,' wrote Gell, 'the Delegates would be prepared to assign to the Director of the Press an adequate share of the profits he might earn for the University, I should be ready to take the risk of a possible diminution of income, trusting to my own powers to recover it. And I should be quite willing to invest capital myself if they would accept me on the basis of partnership.' Gell had been misled, but he blamed the Delegates rather than Jowett for the misunderstandings that inevitably followed.

In the middle of the vacation, the opposition safely dispersed, Jowett called a series of extraordinary meetings of the Delegates, though at no time could more than five be mustered. They met first on Friday, 31 July, and

Mark Pattison

Lyttelton Gell, Secretary to the Delegates, 1884–98

again the next day when only Jowett and Max Müller attended. Gell was in Oxford over the weekend, dined with Jowett, and gave him a copy of *Treasure Island*. Finally on 6 August he was offered and accepted the post. On the last occasion there were only three Delegates to keep Jowett company, Max Müller and two staunch Balliol men, Edwin Palmer and Sir William Markby. Bartholomew Price had gone on holiday as usual at the end of July, and Bywater was absent. Years later R. W. Chapman recalled that Bywater had told him that 'private business—someone had died— made it impossible for him to be there, though Price wrote "imploring" him to attend'. Somebody had indeed died, the sad old sage Mark Pattison, at Harrogate, on Thursday, 30 July. With masterly timing Jowett had contrived a triumph of bad taste, the appointment of his own candidate all too literally over Pattison's dead body. So Gell, young and relatively innocent, found himself at once in a situation of some complexity. He had become a sort of local reverberation of the controversy that had dislocated Oxford for a generation.

It is impossible to say how much Price knew of what was going on, though he was accustomed to knowing everything. It is hard to think of him being unprepared or overpowered, even by Jowett, but on this occasion he appears to have been confounded by the speed at which he worked and disarmed by the impudence of it all. Even so he must have counted on Bywater to obtain a deferment for further consideration by the full Delegacy. An ingenuous letter from Jowett to Price dated 14 August was an appeal for help of which he had not hitherto been assured. 'What I have seen of Gell', he wrote, 'impresses me greatly in his favour: I think altogether, if we have the advantage of your help and of finance committee we have made excellent arrangements.' It was an odd way of referring to a man he had known for twelve years and whose cause he had just successfully promoted. But if Price's support could not be counted on all might be far from well, for he had already been appointed Chairman of Finance Committee.

In a postscript Jowett admitted to further qualms. He would go down to the Press that day, he said, and 'have a talk with Mr. Dobell [*sic*] whom we must keep, if possible'. Doble was clearly unhappy. On 6 August he was complaining of the intense heat—another possible reason for the poor turn-out of Delegates—and his letters express uncertainty about the future. Devoted to Price he appears to have been deeply pessimistic about working with his successor, and although he had no plans he doubted whether he would remain at the Press. If he had any other reason than fear of the unknown for suspecting the wisdom of the appointment he can hardly have welcomed a visit from Jowett. Moreover on the day that the Master trotted round from Balliol he was much harassed by a manuscript he had been reading, of which he could make little sense. 'The style is ridiculously affected,' he had written to Frowde the previous day, 'and is curiously like a translation from an unknown tongue.' Certain references to the Old Testament were totally unacceptable and the book could not possibly

G

appear under the Oxford imprint. Now he was reconsidering the matter. If the author were prepared to remove objectionable passages, he told Frowde, 'I will gladly, if I am at the Press, make another examination of it'—but 'nothing short of absolute excision would be of the least use'. Whether because of the heat, or the shock of Gell's appointment, or even of Jowett's visit, Doble was making an unfortunate error of judgement, for the work was Charles Doughty's 'Travels in Arabia Deserta'. After many vicissitudes, and the intervention of T. E. Lawrence, it was recognized as a work of genius and years later came safely to rest with Jonathan Cape. But Doble was not to know that the style was deliberate, an endeavour 'to continue the older tradition of Chaucer and Spenser', as the author later explained, 'resisting to my power the decadence of the English language'.

Doble's uncertainty persisted throughout the summer, and even after Price had persuaded him to take a belated holiday he insisted on his return that he was back only for a time, ready to do any trifling service for the Dictionary again. Gell was free from his commitments at Cassells by the end of October. Once he was installed in Oxford and present daily in the flesh, Doble's misgivings receded and life returned to normal for him. He continued as Assistant Secretary for many years, suffering appallingly from ill health. He and Gell had that much at least in common, and it may have been some consolation for Doble to be assured that such bodily suffering was a result of over-work, which Gell always assumed in his own case. There is no record of any friction between them, and Gell more than once called the attention of the Delegates to the position of his 'loyal and invaluable Colleague, Mr. Doble—than whom they have no more faithful officer', hoping to secure for him an annual bonus based on the sales of the publishing business. One of the answers to the problem posed by Chapman as to what was wrong with Gell is unfortunately that neither he nor Doble had the necessary stamina. When Gell began to suffer the breakdowns that eventually led to his dismissal Doble struggled on, but in such poor shape that the memory of his condition could well have led people to believe that the fortunes of the Press in general were at that period at a very low ebb. Birkbeck Hill reported a meeting with him in February 1896 in a letter to Price: 'In what a sad state he is poor fellow—with his great bodily sufferings—for they are very great—and now added to them the death of his wife's mother to whom he was much attached.' After his death in 1914, Henry Bradley wrote to Robert Bridges: 'Did you by chance know C. E. Doble, who was for thirty years Assistant Secretary of the Press? He died on Sep. 19—his brain gave way three years ago. A good man if there ever was one, and a good scholar.'

There were not many among the Delegates whom Gell served who would immediately recognize the merits of a man not tested in the school of *literae humaniores*. To the older generation his background was strange. The ideas he and Milner had absorbed as undergraduates and which they had continued to promote since were far removed from any Pattisonian ideal of learning. The 1870s in Oxford saw the emergence of a new and radical philosophy of social change. This major shift in advanced liberal thinking has been attributed, as far as Oxford is concerned, to the work of the idealist philosophers, Edward Caird and T. H. Green, Gell's tutor, and of Green's other young disciple, Arnold Toynbee. Almost all those involved, as Henry Asquith recalled, were nurtured at Balliol in the days of Jowett's ascendancy. He had in the end captured Toynbee and appointed him tutor in economics, not a popular subject in Oxford. But Toynbee was a man who could make converts, of immense personal charm by all reports, handsome, gracious, and passionately sincere. Gell and Milner were captivated by his precocious philanthropy. He was also always young, for in 1883 he died of meningitis at the age of 31.

T. H. Green's faith in history, in evolution as an ultimately benign process through which the idea of good would inevitably prevail, gave new confidence to an age not far from despair. The spectre of *laissez-faire* banished, it might after all be possible to do something at the practical level to improve the state of society. The warm glow of Green's philosophy suffused Toynbee's study of economic history and persuaded him too that the worst of the industrial revolution was over. The struggle between capital and labour belonged to the feudal age of industrialism which was already giving way to the era of co-operation. 'Not only has the law given to workmen and employer equality of rights,' he wrote, 'but education bids fair to give them equality of culture. We are all now, workmen as well as employers, inhabitants of a larger world.' He envisaged a social contract based on class harmony, and co-operation, and in practical terms he joined with his friend Canon Barnett and his wife to help the poor in Whitechapel. There too Milner and Gell were drawn on leaving Oxford, to take part in the new University Extension Society. As Milner put it, those who listened to Toynbee 'were deeply impressed with their individual duty as citizens and filled with enthusiasm for social equality which led them to bridge the gulf between the educated and the wage-earning class'. The extent to which they did so has been much disputed. But a year after his death, Toynbee Hall was opened in Whitechapel, a residential college for working men, and Gell became the first chairman.

These ideas were held by a minority, but the views of the new liberals have been described as the strongest intellectual force originating in the 1870s. The ideas had in fact lost none of their novelty a century later, when workers' participation and 'Industrial Democracy' still seemed the inevitable outcome of improved education and higher standards of living. At the time there were inevitably those who regarded it as too anodyne to serve any useful social purpose. It was the next generation of more systematic socialists, like R. H. Tawney and William Beveridge, who worked at Toynbee Hall, that recognized that the true cause of poverty was low wages, and that free school meals might be more edifying than the best efforts of distinguished academics to improve the minds of the poor. There were others too who found the enthusiasm itself distasteful, and the ideas shallow. In a history of Pembroke College written by Douglas Macleane in

1897, the 'school of moral and social fervour' of the 1870s was recalled with some aversion: the old and philosophical liberalism had given way to a new and emotional kind that attracted 'many intense and able young men'. With this movement Pembroke 'had a passing connexion in the person of Arnold Toynbee'. His transience was all that could be said in his favour, and although he did not delay long on this earth young men of his kind were better left to Balliol. Gell inevitably was tarred with the same brush. Social fervour and the higher scholarship were of doubtful compatibility, and it might be asked whether he could be entirely trusted to uphold the old traditions of the academic institution to which he now belonged. Price, Fellow of Pembroke for over fifty years and eventually Master of the college, was not on his side.

Within a few weeks of coming to Oxford, Lyttelton Gell was attending a meeting of the Protective and Provident Society of Women working in Trades, at which the recently widowed Mrs. Pattison gave the opening address. The cause was not one that her husband had espoused, though to women working outside trades he had given much kindly attention. Gell spoke up about experiments at Cassells for taking workers into partnership, and about the Cooperative Shirtmaking Company organized by Edith Simcox, George Eliot's infatuated friend. The time would come, he inescapably concluded, when men and women workers would be so trained by their unions that they would be able to manage their own affairs, and the distinction between capital and labour would disappear. The mind of Ingram Bywater could not be brought to bear on such issues: he inevitably had doubts about any man who raised them. But seven years later Gell had not altogether lost heart or conviction. 'Possibly the day may come', he wrote to the Vice-Chancellor, 'when the Delegates will decide to authorize the introduction of some measure of cooperation, to the elaboration of which I would very gladly devote my best abilities.' He was never invited to elaborate.

In 1884 Milner became Private Secretary to Toynbee's old friend Henry Goschen at the Treasury and at last entered the world of politics, therein to do his duty as a citizen on a wider stage, and to fulfil his promise to Jowett to do him credit yet. He ended his life as chancellor elect of the University. Gell meanwhile began to pave his way to oblivion. With his youthful idealism not yet extinguished, rather with it fanned by the recent death of his friend and his own responsibility for perpetuating his name, he found himself face to face with the ancient Board of Delegates, with an old world to conquer if he could. His first surprise was to discover how close an interest the Delegates took in the day-to-day business of the Press. Powerful men, disconcertingly different from one another in character, they all appeared to be busily engaged doing the job that he had supposed that he had been employed to do. This was the way it had always been in Bartholomew Price's time, and Gell was to find that Price's time outlasted his.

Price was now a Perpetual Delegate by special vote of Convocation, and paid Chairman of Finance Committee during all Gell's years at the Press, a stern and unyielding presence never behind the scenes. No man can serve twelve masters, Gell lamented, 'especially when he has found by experience, that personally, they often hold different opinions'. Yet he had no other function but to serve: it was said only 'That he be expected to perform such duties as the Delegates may require of him'. In so far as there was anything in the nature of a general will emanating from the Delegates it was likely to be incarnate in Price. It must be admitted that Gell showed little respect for his seniors, and there was a certain peremptoriness in his early exchanges with the Reverend Professor, whom he maladroitly began by addressing as 'Dear Mr. Price'. The awful incompatibility between his role as managing director, appointed by Jowett to plan 'the active development' of a large and expanding business, and as the Delegates' humble clerk, is reflected in the tone of his letters, which lurch between servility and truculence in a manner apt to displease in either direction. Price himself at times might have been reminded of Clarendon's words on his Stuart master. He did not love the conversation of men of more years than himself, 'and thought age not only troublesome but impertinent'.

His first difference with Price concerned the negotiation of his salary, a business made unsavoury by Jowett's initial presumption. Gell had been offered £1,000 a year, rising by annual increments of £50 to £1,250. He was thus a poorer man, the more so as he understood it to be the wish of Finance Committee that he should withdraw his capital from Cassells. He wanted to invest £12,000 in the Press, and a share of the profits if the publishing business increased. Finance Committee considered his requests, but deferred a decision until 'a more opportune season'. Gell uneasily acquiesced, asking only that if it were finally decided against his investing in the Press he should receive an extra £175 a year 'in compensation'.

A more opportune season did not occur until mid December. A draft agreement was drawn up by Finance Committee and referred to solicitors, who could see no sufficient reason for calling upon Gell to withdraw his investment in Cassells. The possibility that he might invest £12,000 in the Press, however, suggested that he might become in effect a partner, which would be inconsistent with his role as Secretary, and the solicitors advised that the provision should be struck out. Finance Committee acted on this advice, and on being informed by Price, Gell wrote back bitterly. The conclusion of Finance Committee, he need scarcely point out, 'extinguished far more peremptorily than I was led to anticipate the original proposal that I should receive a direct interest in the results of the business'. He had been relying on a very different decision when he resigned from Cassells, and he had already, in obedience to what he took to be instructions the previous August, begun to liquidate his interest in the firm. He must now accept his £175 a year in compensation.

Even then the matter was not settled. In March 1885 two Delegates, Sir William Markby and Alfred Robinson, again went through the draft agreement. They too saw no reason why Gell should withdraw his money from Cassells immediately. It would be enough to claim the right to call upon him to withdraw at any time. But waiving the right to call upon him to withdraw his money immediately undoubtedly gave the Delegates the right to reconsider the question of the £175 to be paid in compensation. Furthermore, the clause concerning Gell's claim for an increase in salary if the profits of the publishing business increased, which Finance Committee had agreed to reconsider the previous August, should be either omitted or amended to read the profits of the business as a whole. 'I suppose that Gell will be secretary for the whole business,' Markby wrote, still uncertain eight months after Gell's appointment, 'and the success of the whole business will depend in a great measure on his exertions. On the other hand he ought to have no motive for making one part of the business more profitable than another.' He was in the end never permitted to invest in the business or to enjoy any share of the profits.

This was Gell's first and most dire experience of committee rule, and he never fully trusted the Delegates again either to reach the right decision or to abide by it if they did. However liberal his beliefs and sincere his philanthropy, he had no personal taste at all for egalitarianism. If a gentleman were to do good in the world he needed the necessary means. The sense that he himself deserved a little more than anybody was prepared to pay him rankled throughout his life, even after he left the Press. When the agreement expired in 1891 after seven years there was more hard bargaining over its renewal, and many of the old arguments about a share in the profits were rehearsed. Gell could by that time point to a substantial increase in the profits of the publishing business and of the business as a whole, and to an equivalent increase in his own work and responsibilities. It was agreed then that his salary should be increased to £1,800 a year.

His personal grievance was soon transmuted into a more general dissatisfaction with the way the Delegates went about their business and interfered with his. It was a matter on which he and Price never agreed. As far as Gell was concerned the Delegates themselves should learn to delegate. Once the general outlines of policy were decided, all the responsibility for carrying it out should devolve upon the executive. It was both unreasonable and unsatisfactory to charge members of the Board with the details of administration, 'which could be carried through with far less effort, far less friction, and far more precision through the office'. So he put it to a sympathetic Delegate, wearily, towards the end of his career in Oxford. 'The minutes of the Delegates are now choked with unfinished projects, negotiations, etc., of different sorts, in the hands of various individual Delegates, or—what is worse—Committees. . . . What makes our chariot go so heavily, is the fact that it is always carrying the dead weights of scores and scores of matters which no-one will nerve themselves to finish.'

Gell had another perennial grievance. In one of his first letters to Jowett, he brought up the question of the representation of the Clarendon Press in London. 'I have no knowledge as to the present arrangements,' he wrote, 'but the active development of the business which you hinted at, seems to me impossible unless its *commercial* centre were in London. It needs all the advantages of those distributive agencies which are centred here.' For fourteen years he campaigned unsuccessfully for an efficient publishing outlet in London, the first function of which would be to sell Clarendon Press books. Frowde's main, and at first almost exclusive, concern was Bibles and the Bound Book Business. He ought not to be diverted from pursuing interests which, Gell admitted, were infinitely more vital than those of the publishing side: he 'has a far heavier burden to carry than is wholesome and I should oppose in the general interest of the Press any attempt to put more upon him'. But in any event he was not the right man to be involved in the promotion of learned or educational books, or to advise on strictly publishing matters. He absolutely lacked that kind of experience. A 'publishing Manager' should be appointed, with a salary more or less dependent upon results. But Gell was frustrated until the end. 'It always seems to be impossible', he wrote, 'to make the Delegates realise how big the business is, and what a necessity there is for strengthening what I would call the Sub-Managerial Staff.'

Frowde himself never called for help of this kind and greeted it most warily when years later it arrived. Meanwhile Gell was left with a sense that whilst the Delegates obsessively pursued their own preoccupations he alone was aware that something truly momentous was happening to the business as a whole. Sooner or later they would have to learn to depend on the 'office' for getting things done. The inadequacy of the office as then constituted to bear the demands that ought to have been imposed upon it had also constantly to be stressed.

Gell did not formally assume the position of Secretary until June 1885, having been allowed an academic year to acquaint himself with the business and to learn what he could from Bartholomew Price. By then Jowett's term as Vice-Chancellor had only a year to run. Yet Gell always remembered him as a tumultuous force that precipitated the Press into the modern world. There was an antiquated mustiness about the place as he found it, as indeed there appeared to be to Charles Cannan fourteen years later. But once Jowett had taken command, it seemed to Gell that there occurred what he termed the 'dead-lift' required to modernize the Press—and that was something, he recalled later to Hart, which 'would not have to be faced twice'. There was truth in this, exaggerated though it was with the lapse of time. Jowett's investigation into the 'alleged deterioration in the quality of printing' was undoubtedly overdue. There was dinginess and murky monotony too about many of the books, as Hart readily admitted in the report he submitted to the investigating committee. 'In regard to matrices,' he wrote, 'upon the number and condition of which the beauty of the printed page absolutely depends, there is great weakness. Most of the punch-struck matrices are old and greatly worn by continual casting, and a thick or broken appearance in the face of the type is a consequence.' Hart's report suggested a crisis brought on by years of neglect. The committee ordered five new Wharfedale printing machines, but the real problem was the supply of new types from the type-foundry and for this there was no easy remedy. Ideally the cutting of 'new puncheons' to renew the matrices was required, but this was a very slow process and punch cutters were rare outside the big typefounding houses. To cut a single fount might take a good man a year, and where was he to be found? 'The Press cannot afford to employ an inferior or drunken workman', wrote Hart, 'who might design half a fount for us and leave us in the lurch.'

The Press and William Clowes were probably the only printing houses in the country to possess type-foundries of their own, and it could be argued that they were unnecessary. The fact that the Press had always had one weighed with Hart, but there were other important considerations. The very large number of founts needed to produce books with a great mixture of type sizes and languages, and the special requirements of the Dictionary, made it essential to keep it, and in consequence to seek new matrices. These could not be found in England, because English type-founders had formed a ring: 'they would not part with *strikes* at any price, because strikes are the springs of business.' So Hart turned to the Continent. 'I propose', he wrote, 'to replenish the Oxford Type Foundry with what the type-founder calls "fresh faces", from Germany, the birthplace of the art of printing; and I venture to remind the committee that this is only repeating, 200 years later, what Bishop Fell, the great patron of the Oxford Press, did for its foundry in the year 1675.'

Hart set off for Germany and bought thirty new founts. Some of them as it turned out were never used. It was not long before the first mechanical composing machines began to be heard of. If Hart had been able to make do for another decade or so the urgent quest for 'fresh faces' would not have been necessary. But Jowett demanded action and the remedies proposed by Hart were carried out. On his return from Germany he began to re-equip the type-foundry, and he continued his reorganization of the printing business as a whole. More Wharfedale machines were introduced. In 1890 he was authorized to build and equip a collotype department, a decision of considerable importance to the publishing business, and in 1891 folding and stitching machines were bought, the first steps in the creation of the Oxford bindery. In this flurry of modernization Hart and Gell introduced the telephone, and Gell himself purchased a typewriter. One of the first letters to be typed on it was to the manufacturer, complaining of a lack of elegance in the type-face. To the Telephone Company Gell wrote complaining of the difficulty of making himself heard in London.

It later became the declared policy of the Press that the output of the publishing departments in London and Oxford should always exceed the capacity of the printing works, so that no pressure could be brought to bear on them to publish merely to keep the Printer employed. After Hart's reconstruction such a principle would have been difficult to apply. No new books might be accepted, consciously at least, to provide his compositors with work. But the extraordinary proliferation of reprints at the end of the century reflected not only an increase in public demand but also the massive capacity that Hart had built up.

Jowett's biographers, Abbott and Campbell, recorded confidently their view of the part he had played. 'Under the new management established through his influence, and with the new energy which his sympathy aroused in the staff, the business of the Press rapidly increased; the number of employées was almost doubled; and new buildings were erected.' To Gell he remained 'My Dear Master', a friend and a solace until his death in 1893. 'He sometimes harassed us', Gell told Abbott and Campbell, 'by pressing proposals or changes which seemed to us unfruitful or even unsafe, or by requirements which were not quite practical; but we were all so impressed by his insight and appreciation, and above all by his single-minded public spirit, that no trouble was too great to take at his instance.'

In 1891, when he was seriously ill, he was staying with the Gells at their house in Headington, Langley Lodge. Mrs. Gell reported that 'He met his doctor's prescriptions with quotations from Plato, and would not admit that any substantial advance in medical science had been made since those days. So little did he believe in the efficacy of remedies that at first he altogether omitted to take them, and when he was persuaded to give them a trial, he gravely proposed to take them all before breakfast, "for that would save time".'

2. 'Progress of the Press, 1885–1891'

MILNER and Gell worried about each other with a touching solicitude throughout their lives. They invariably addressed each other in correspondence as 'My Dear Boy'. Not long after Gell joined the Press, Milner was concerned that he was working too hard and worrying too much. Moreover he was allowing work to interfere with his political activities, which Milner was inclined to regard as more important: they did in fact campaign vigorously and effectively for Liberal Unionism, organizing a team of academic spokesmen for the cause which included A. V. Dicey, Goldwin Smith, William Anson, Thomas Raleigh, and Gell's uncle, Charles Brodrick, Warden of Merton. Staying at Langley Lodge during an election campaign in 1886, Milner wrote to Gell's brother, Henry: 'I fear he is always rather overworked in term time. He is not always up here in the evening, and when he does come, it is generally rather late.' As the years passed he became seriously alarmed. 'I saw that you were fretting yourself to death—for what?', he wrote. 'I have long seen no object in your remaining at the Press except to save a certain amount of money.' By then Gell's enemies were closing in, his frustrations mounting, the catalogue of intrigues growing longer in every letter.

Gell's intention to marry in 1887 filled Milner with dismay. He wrote a despairingly flippant letter. 'The captiousness of a discarded mistress is as inevitable, as it is venial', he pleaded in mitigation of his lack of enthusiasm for the match. Gell was considerate enough not to marry until 1889, when Milner was about to leave for his first appointment abroad, as director-general of accounts in Egypt. Gell gave his approval to that venture on condition 'that Langley Lodge stands in your heart and thoughts for *home*'. Truly, he concluded, 'this seems to be our *annus mirabilis*'.

There were two good years yet to come. Business prospered. Books to Gell's taste, such as Thomas Raleigh's *Elementary Politics*, which sold nearly 7,000 copies in the first year after publication, and Edwin Cannan's *Elementary Political Economy*, convinced him that even in spite of the Delegates' incorrigible habit of losing money the publishing business might be made to flourish as a more or less rational concern. The list now occupied fifty-six pages in the *University Calendar*. It included many old works of divinity, as well as many titles initiated by Kitchin for the Clarendon Press Series. But that label had been dropped, after having impressed itself on the minds of a generation of teachers and schoolchildren, and its various parts dispersed. 'A Series of English Classics' included Skeat's five-volume *Chaucer*, G. Birkbeck Hill's works on Johnson which eventually ran to thirteen volumes, the first part of H. C. Beeching's edition of *Paradise Lost*, as well as a dozen Shakespeare plays edited by Aldis Wright. A. C. Bradley edited T. H. Green's *Prolegomena to Ethics*, and there were the beginnings of a list of books on law and political science.

When Gell's first seven-year contract ran out, he was able to present to the Delegates a triumphant report. His memorandum headed 'Progress of the Press, 1885-1891' was an ominously complacent document. These had been years of rapid growth in all departments, he recorded, most notably in the Delegates' publishing business and in that of the Learned Press at the expense of the Bible Press. Although sales of the Bible continued to increase, and the Bible Press was still appreciably the largest single department in terms of trading capital, it was being steadily overtaken. The time was not far off when the Press as a whole could, if necessary, declare its independence of Bibles. 'I have it constantly in mind', wrote Gell, 'that in the steady development of the Commercial side of the Publishing Business, we are building up a future resource upon which we can fall back if days of adversity ever come upon the Bible-trade of the Press. It is already the second, and bids fair to become the first of the Delegates' Businesses in point of Capital, and if necessity should in days to come compel us to conduct it within Commercial limits, as good Dividends could be reaped from it as from the Bible Press.' Of course the Delegates' policy of deliberately courting financial loss in the interests of learning distorted the picture. 'Whilst the present tide of prosperity is flowing, there is fortunately no need to decline the burdens laid upon the finances of the Press by its traditions and quasi-national position.' But if necessary it could be converted almost overnight into an exclusively commercial operation. The Delegates 'need only suspend or restrict their liberality in the production of unprofitable books to secure the desired result—and it is a result which good and enterprising management could increase indefinitely'. Thus Gell showed a flexibility towards the principles of learned publishing which Jowett would have appreciated.

The number of new books published annually had by Gell's reckoning just doubled, from an average of 29 new titles in the period 1880–5 to 58 in 1886–91. Virtually everything else had doubled as well. In 1885 there had been in the Delegates' catalogue about 400 publications, in 1891 there were 800. Moreover there were 100 titles listed as 'New Works in Progress', the existence of which would have proved awkward if the Delegates had decided to suspend their liberality. The amount contributed by the Press to the University Chest over the period was £55,000, double the amount contributed in the years 1879–85. Seven years later it had become £120,000, and as Gell rightly observed, without this, 'in these times of agricultural depression and increasing Academical demands, the University would have been in great straits'.

Gell was able to congratulate himself too on successful labour relations. 'Complicated Trades-Union questions, which with unskilful and unsympathetic handling might have proved disastrous have been settled without impairing the prosperity of the Press.' He was on excellent terms with the men, invited to their dinners, consulted about their clubs and societies. He looked forward to the opening of the Clarendon Press Institute in Walton Street, confident that it would strengthen those links of mutual respect which were 'so essential a supplement to the unstable and uninspiriting "cash nexus" of modern employment'.

The Clarendon Press Institute had been proposed by Horace Hart as a centre for relaxation and further education: there were to be a reading-room, library, gymnasium, and opportunities for learning French, German, Greek, and Latin, as well as mathematics and shorthand. It was warmly supported by Gell as entirely in keeping with his principles. Moreover his wife had been making vigorous efforts to form a boys' club but had been unable to find accommodation. The Misses Liddell and Miss Max Müller were also anxious to start a wood-carving class. In 1883 the Bible and Learned Presses had employed 278 men and boys. When the Clarendon Press Institute opened in 1891 there were 540 employed in five different categories: adult artisans, 216; apprentices and junior artisans, 64; women and girls, 57; adult unskilled labourers, 54; unskilled boys, 149. The Press had become the largest employer of labour in the city. Gell's offer to elaborate for the Delegates' benefit the principle of co-operation having been stonily received, more paternalistic methods had to be adopted. The depraved character of the women employed in the Aldersgate Street binding-house had been commented on by 'secularist lecturers'. Gell enlisted the services of several ladies in London, 'who with the cordial consent of all parties, give especial attention to our binding girls, visiting them once a week in the Dinner Hour'.

At the Paris Exhibition in 1889 the Press had achieved the first of a series of successes in what became rather costly and extravagant publicity stunts. It was the only British printer or publishing house to gain a Grand Prix for books and printing, together with two gold medals. Gell supplemented his catalogue of achievements with a reminder that through his 'entanglement in the cross-decisions of the Board' at his appointment he now found himself a poorer man by at least £3,000. The Board showed its appreciation both of his achievements and of his financial sacrifice by reappointing him for another ten years and increasing his salary to £1,800 a year. For the moment he appears to have been as contented as it was in his nature to be. His salary was three times that of the Regius Professor of Modern History.

But the years of easy prosperity were over. In the economic depression that began to develop in 1892 the Press ran into difficulties. The Managers were summoned by the Delegates to explain the decline in profits during the year ending March 1893. Frowde hardly thought it necessary to do so. The diminished sales, he observed drily, 'call for little comment'. The decline dated from the commencement of the great commercial depression, and was only to be expected though it could have been substantially worse. Asked to account for an increase in wages, advertising, and miscellaneous trading expenses he explained that it cost more and took more effort to sell books in a bad year, and there had been no scope for economies. The eight-hour day had come into force on 1 January 1892 and increased the cost of labour by about 12 per cent. The main cause of the drop in Bible profits was the increasing ferocity of the competition and the public demand for cheaper and inferior goods. Both the Queen's Printer and the Cambridge Press had again reduced their prices to the various Bible societies, and Hart had been compelled to do the same. In America there had been formidable reprints of the Teachers' Bible which forced down Oxford's prices, and Collins of Glasgow had also entered the field. What had become known as the American Department was showing no profit at all.

The days of adversity had arrived sooner than expected and Gell's faith in the capacity of the Press to cope with them was abruptly put to the test — though it was not only the Bible trade that was depressed. The time had obviously come for the Delegates to curb their liberality, and to apply what Gell always capitalized as Commercial Standards to the publishing department.

3. Gell's Twelve Masters

ALTHOUGH Gell could not be expected to see it in historical perspective he had to deal with the most energetic and versatile Board of Delegates in the whole history of the Press. Among them were Max Müller, Ingram Bywater, Stubbs on his return as Bishop of Oxford in 1891, York Powell, Sir William Markby, Henry T. Gerrans, Charles Cannan, Alfred Robinson, and always and for ever Bartholomew Price, who in 1891 became Master of Pembroke. They were all actively involved in the affairs of the Press, some like Bywater and Max Müller devoting themselves to books, others like Markby and Gerrans more generally to business. These were some of the men whom Gell hoped to instruct in the art of self-effacement.

A curious and disturbing presence among them was Frederick York Powell, maverick intellectual and dabbler in all things quaint and arcane, a Delegate since 1885. His appetite for knowledge was ungovernable, and he appeared to be an authority on almost everything. In his early days he had fallen under the influence of the Icelandic scholar Gudbrand Vigfússon, whose Icelandic-English dictionary had been published in 1874. For twelve years they worked in partnership, and there was something in Vigfússon's weird but imposing personality that was able to concentrate York Powell's easily distracted mind. Henry Bradley described Vigfússon as 'a lank man with long hair and a wrinkled lean white face, who never speaks without writhing himself into the oddest snaky convolutions'. York Powell on the other hand resembled a sea captain, according to H. A. L. Fisher: 'he was broad, burly and bearded, brusque in manner, with dark hair and eyes, and a deep rich laugh'. He certainly saw himself as being on a voyage of discovery with Vigfússon as navigator.

In 1879 he was shocked when the Delegates declined to publish the Landnáma-Bók, the Book of the Settlement, the primary source for early Icelandic history. The next year, however, he approached the Press again with a detailed proposal for a complete *Corpus Poeticum* of the old Northern poetry, written in Iceland, Scandinavia, the British Isles, and Greenland, in the dialects of Old Norse. There was 'no body of poetry existing in such an unhappy condition', he explained to the Delegates, and to Vigfússon he wrote, 'they must see that it is the greatest honour to them, in fact their only *raison d'être*, as a University Press, to publish books which won't immediately pay'. The proposal was accepted and three years later the book appeared. They were then ready for their crowning achievement, a translation of all the major classics in the Northern prose, and in 1884 Powell drafted another manifesto for the Delegates calling for an edition in five volumes. It was accepted in part and became eventually *Origines Islandicae*, published in two large volumes in 1905. Vigfússon worked on it until his death in 1889 when much was already in proof. For the next fifteen years Powell exercised to the full his incomparable gift for procrastination, and not until he himself was dead was further progress possible. These books were definitive in that they defied revision. Later scholars found them so idiosyncratic, the notes so littered with York Powell's inspired but deluded guesses, that nothing short of a fresh start would do, and there were no starters.

Powell soon became vastly interested in all aspects of publishing. He never doubted that the University was primarily for research, and as such there were only two requirements: a good library and a good Press. After Vigfússon's death his own researches became increasingly promiscuous and he was unable to write. But he had a special intuition about books, and seemed able to gut and assess their contents without going through the ordinary processes of reading. There thus accumulated in his mind a vast storehouse or debris of knowledge—paralleled in his physical environment by what Robert Bridges described as York Powell's 'heterogeneous knick-knackatory of Japanese carvings, old Psalters, Parisian advertisements etc. etc.'—of little utility to a scholar but of some advantage to a publisher. The Clarendon Press was for him as for Bywater a vocation. He sought out authors, read and reported on their manuscripts, edited them, read the proofs, and busied himself too with all the technicalities of printing, binding, and marketing. 'No point of detail was too small for his attention', wrote Horace Hart. 'Upon all matters of printing or illustration, the justification of an initial letter, the disposition of print upon the page, the degree of success of a chromo-collotype, even the composition of different inks, he was able to give instantly, or after brief inquiry, advice that was useful in practice.' He spoke as one 'professional' to another.

Powell was reticent about his work at the Press, perhaps because he knew that some people disapproved of the lengths to which he was taking it. They blamed the Press for preventing him writing books of his own. He may have been uneasily aware that that was just what he wanted it to do: his greatest talent was for detecting talent in others. For his biographer, Oliver Elton, he had made the right choice. 'The Press was the chief, not the only, means he found for following what I have called his profession in life, the encouragement of the right man in his predestined task.' He had far too many ideas to do justice to them himself. 'His mind teemed with *desiderata*, with a list of "felt wants": he had a continual vision of tasks, in art, in history, in letters, that were waiting for the performer.' Had he not by a whim of Lord Rosebery been made Regius Professor of Modern History in succession to J. A. Froude in 1894, it would have been difficult to define his place within the academic community. He had taught law and political economy at Christ Church because of a vacancy, two subjects in which he was least interested. His career as Regius Professor is remembered mainly for its inception, when the college servant confidently identified the Prime Minister's letter as a tradesman's bill and put it aside, knowing that Mr. Powell preferred not to be troubled with such items. It took special inquiries from the Private Secretary to bring it to light. It was notable also for his Inaugural Lecture, which lasted for twenty minutes and was inaudible. He was successful neither as a teacher nor as a researcher nor as an organizer of research, and his biographer confessed that it would be reasonable to ask in the light of the record what after all he did, and what he was. His answer was brief: 'He was a spirit!'

When he died in 1904 *The Times* obituarist attributed his failure to write in later life to the fact that he was unmethodical, 'and so accessible and good-natured that much time which might otherwise have been spent in historical composition was devoted to helping others or to giving counsel to the Clarendon Press'. There was a feeling too that by setting himself an impossibly high standard he had, like Mark Pattison and Bywater, deprived the world of books which he alone could have written.

Commenting on his kindness to authors and young scholars, a writer in the *Oxford Magazine*, probably Charles Cannan, observed that 'services of this kind can be rendered without the formalities of an office, without even the virtue of punctuality, and at the Press York Powell's reputation for un-businesslike character was wholly unintelligible'.

He had, however, once lost a manuscript—it was found among his papers after his death—for which the Press had to pay the author £100 in compensation. And one man at the Press found his reputation entirely intelligible. To Gell he was a non-performer, a dilettante and an aesthete, an irresponsible Bohemian agnostic, a muddler. More or less a contemporary, he was by the standards of Gell, Milner, and Toynbee irredeemably frivolous. It was much more difficult to understand how he had acquired a reputation for hard work. H. A. L. Fisher was once asked by York Powell to prepare a new edition of Kitchin's three-volume *History of France*: it should take a fortnight, he told him. Fisher was quite prepared to believe that York Powell could have done it in the time. 'But then he knows the subject very much better than I do,' he wrote to Gell, 'and is a giant for work.' Gell could see no evidence of it. The most meddlesome and unpredictable of all the Delegates, Powell was a conspicuous symptom of the sickness that in Gell's diagnosis sometimes afflicted the body as a whole—a fault in the metabolism that prevented a project being carried through to its completion.

In 1888 the Delegates considered once again a proposal for an Oxford history of England. It was a modest enough proposal for a textbook of some 300 pages for use at the Oxford Local Examinations, and it was resolved that York Powell should be entrusted with its preparation. He was allowed £100 to remunerate his contributors. It was to be in four parts, written by four authors. In 1897, Gell reported on progress to the Delegate H. T. Gerrans. He had received the manuscript of three parts, which covered the history from Henry II to 1858. The first part was in the hands of Owen Edwards, one of York Powell's own students. 'During the $9\frac{1}{2}$ years which have elapsed since then,' wrote Gell, 'I have brought up the matter as often as consideration for York Powell's feelings would allow me. . . . There is a hiatus in the scheme at Henry II; and, as you know, we have had a promise from Edwards once a term, for (let us say) the last five years, that his part would be delivered without fail within three months.'

As usual in dealing with Powell the knowledge that he might so easily have done the work himself was an added aggravation. At the age of 24 he had been asked by his own tutor, Mandell Creighton, to contribute to Longmans' 'Epochs of English History' series, and in 1874 *Early England to the Norman Conquest* was published, a substantial school textbook that pleased both Creighton and his publisher. Again in 1885 he had written for Rivingtons, as part of their general History of England for schools, the volume *From Earliest Times to the Death of Henry VII*. Yet here he was making no visible progress as editor of a far less ambitious project. 'Your question as to the future management of the details,' Gell went on, 'goes to the root of that general question of administration, upon which the Master of Pembroke and myself have always taken opposite views. This particular question was one of the first points of divergence. . . . It would have been absolutely inconceivable that this thing should have dragged on in this way, if I had been once instructed to carry it through. It would have become a first charge upon my time and thought instead of being another man's bye-play.'

By 1897 Gell was very weary. 'Personally,' he wrote, 'I am not in the least desirous to have a finger in the Oxford English History pie. At the outset I was greatly interested in it; but, after nearly ten years of perfectly unnecessary delay, the subject has got stale; and I fully anticipate that the result will be a failure.' And so it was.

The giddiness of Powell's intellect, the awful sublimity of Bywater's erudition, the Germanic romanticism of Max Müller, contributed to the harassment of Gell. These were Delegates with a vocation, but they were not men to whom he could talk business or in whom he could confide. With the patriarchal Price he was often in open disagreement. Sir William Markby, on the other hand, was an ordinary human being, with many amiable if unspectacular characteristics. He belonged to the other breed of Delegates who saw themselves as custodians of the University's interests rather than as creative publishers. This seemed to Gell to be their proper function, and there was neither bitterness nor rancour in his dealings with him. Unlike Price, he made Gell feel that he was engaged as an equal on serious business, and he uncomplainingly fed him the data he needed for his numerous investigations and reports on the legal and financial affairs of the Press.

A pupil of Sir Henry Maine, Markby had for twelve years been Calcutta Judge, before returning to Oxford as Reader in Indian Law at Balliol. He was an unquestioning admirer of Jowett. His work as a Delegate from 1881 to 1907 was, as his widow put it in a memoir published by the Press in 1917, 'in every way congenial to him, not only owing to the interesting nature of the work from a literary point of view, but also as constituting him an employer of labour on a considerable scale which brought him into contact with a very intelligent body of workmen'. He became the Delegates' principal adviser on legal matters, on copyright and the privilege, and especially on the setting-up of the American branch: he was active on much business of 'delicacy and importance'. He published *Elements of Law* with the Press and a book on Hindu and Mahommedan law, and was responsible with Anson, Pollock, Holland, and Dicey for founding the *Law Quarterly Review* in 1884. Like Gell, he was a liberal and he took a lively interest in University Extension lectures. He was also a vigorous temperance man. 'It was a constant grief to him', wrote his wife, 'to pass the endless public-houses just at the foot of Headington Hill as he walked down to Oxford through St. Clement's.' This black spot caused much concern to Balliol liberals, and T. H. Green once opened a coffee shop in St. Clement's,

The Secretary's room in 1895, with Gell's new telephone

Max Müller

Frederick York Powell

Ingram Bywater

which might be thought to be carrying idealism too far. Markby's only folly was to entertain for fifteen years the possibility of a new edition of the Year Books, the reports of English common law cases for the period 1292–1534. He aspired to establish the best text, and to provide a translation. The whole enterprise was to make forty volumes of about 600 pages each. He solicited support from the newly founded Selden Society and the Inns of Court, but managed to extract only a niggardly promise of some £20 a year. Eventually the vision faded and incurred no serious loss to the Press.

He was for a time Fellow of All Souls, wherein were gathered many of the leading Oxford lawyers. Sir William Anson, the Warden, had published *Law of Contract* in 1879, and a new edition appeared every two years. 'I never liked the law nor do I now', he wrote in 1881, but he did not relinquish personal responsibility for the book until 1909. The twenty-fifth edition should celebrate its centenary in 1979. He produced his *Law and Custom of the Constitution* in two volumes in 1886 and 1892. A member of Parliament and to all outward appearances a supremely confident man of the world, he was in one curious respect characteristic of his age. As Jowett was to Milner, his old Eton schoolmaster was to Anson. He vowed, if he lived, to do him credit yet. 'I say, "if I lived" advisedly,' he wrote, 'for I was a hypochondriac, and without ever being ill I was never well. I had a misgiving throughout my whole University career that I should soon die, and a desire to leave some record of myself . . . alone enabled me to contend with a nervous depression of almost overwhelming force.' He was regarded as the best teacher of English law of his day.

The Oxford Law School had achieved its independence of the Modern History School only in 1873, and the teaching of law had been determined inevitably by the availability, or non-availability, of good textbooks. There had been nothing at all available on contract. Gradually the Press built up a basic list of introductory or more advanced books—Anson and Markby, Digby on *Real Property*, Hall's *International Law*, Holland's *Jurisprudence*, Moyle's *Justinian*, Thomas Raleigh's *Outline of the Law of Property*. Though Gell successfully canvassed A. V. Dicey's support for the cause of Liberal Unionism, he was unable to enlist him as a Press author. Perhaps Murray's Scriptorium still rankled.

When the depression of 1892 caused a flutter of apprehension throughout the Press, it was Markby who recognized the need for a careful scrutiny of existing and future commitments. He reminded the Delegates of what he himself had only just discovered by accident—that in 1878 they had approved a series of resolutions controlling the expenditure on unremunerative books. Though these resolutions appeared to have been overlooked for many years, he suggested that the Delegates were now bound to carry them out. He took a broad if anxious view of his own legal and moral responsibilities. He fully agreed that expenditure on unremunerative books was one part of the duty of the Delegates. 'But it is a duty of a very delicate kind. We are called upon to expend the money of the University without having received any directive as to how the money is to

H

be expended or having obtained any sanction of our expenditure. This is a responsibility which few men of business would care to undertake. But accepting this responsibility, as we must, it seems to me that at least we ought to be able to show that we have watched very carefully this expenditure, keeping ourselves informed as to its amount, limiting it so as not to interfere with our other duties, and regulating it so as to apply it to the best objects.'

The Delegates decided therefore that in future the Publications Committee, which was responsible for submitting titles for their approval, should clearly state whether the books were expected to be profitable or not, and if not to estimate the probable loss. They were also to prepare a list of all unremunerative works already in progress or undertaken, and to add to it each new book accepted that fell into this category. Forms had to be filled in, always a bad sign.

Books recommended as remunerative had to be 'of educational value' or 'of permanent value and importance' (alternative words to be expunged): unremunerative books had to be entitled by their 'merits or utility to subsidy from the Press Funds', and an estimated ultimate net loss not exceeding a certain figure had to be supplied. These forms endured until Charles Cannan by imperceptible degrees allowed them to become obsolete in more affluent days. The first unremunerative books to be accepted were an edition of Ovid's *Heroides*, D. B. Monro's *Modes of Ancient Greek Music*, and D'Arcy Thompson's *A Glossary of Greek Birds*. These were presumably accepted on grounds of merit rather than utility. Later, in 1893 A. C. Madan's *English–Swahili Dictionary* passed the test. With the help of a grant from the S.P.C.K. it was estimated that the loss would not exceed £50: by 1970 it was handsomely in credit and selling about 1,000 copies a year. The Delegates respectfully declined a far greater proportion of books submitted than they had in the previous five years. C. P. Lucas's *Historical Geography of the British Colonies*, Major Green's *Hindustani Grammar*, and Baden-Powell's *Short Account of the Indian Land Revenue* were accepted as likely to be remunerative. (Some thirty volumes in 'The Rulers of India Series' appeared in the 1890s, as the Press assumed its imperial responsibilities.) In the first five years after Markby's introduction of the new system, roughly 150 remunerative and 40 unremunerative titles were accepted. In 1897 the accounts showed a profit during the year of £3,255 on the former, and of a paradoxical £93 on the latter. As the Dictionary costs that year were put at £2,364, and there were University publications and the Anecdota Oxoniensia to be allowed for, the over-all profit was estimated at £558. Gell's attempt to apply Commercial Standards had been thwarted, or had misfired.

Gell could be frank and uninhibited with Markby. In 1896, when the incorporation of the American Branch as a company was presenting fundamental legal and administrative problems, Gell boldly suggested that the opportunity should be taken to raise the whole question of the general incorporation of the entire business, and felt free to confide some delicate forebodings about the future of the Press. 'We should once for all be relieved from the emergence of these fundamental but time-wasting questions, involved in the fact that the Delegates have no defined powers, no legal entity, no common seal, and I also think, that looking into the far future, it might not be imprudent to take the only step which can legally discriminate the funds of a huge commercial concern from the general funds of the University. Imagine, when we are all dead and gone, some clever scoundrel, or some theoretical Academic amateurs, ruining the whole concern, and thereby bringing the University into Bankruptcy. The temper and prudence of the more experienced Delegates, is of course at present a guarantee against any such contingency within any time which we can foresee, but I am very far from thinking that the contingency is an impossible one.'

In writing to Williams, the solicitor, Gell admitted that the suggestion of incorporation would 'make the hair of some of our Veterans stand on end'. Markby was sixty-seven. It is unlikely that Gell included him among the Veterans, although only the septuagenarians, Price, Müller, and Stubbs, were senior to him. To Gell the threat from 'theoretical Academic amateurs' was more real and less remote than he allowed it to appear in his letter to Markby, and so too was the contingency he envisaged. Gell's vision of his own future at that time was clouded, and his hopes of converting the Press into an efficient modern business based on sound and scientific managerial principles had sadly withered away.

Henry Gerrans, a mathematician, also had his feet on ground which Gell trod with assurance. As well as being a Delegate of the Press he was Secretary to the Delegates of Local Examinations, one of whom was Gell. In time most of the work of this Delegacy came to be done by Gerrans himself. The Vice-Chancellor did not attend its 2 o'clock meetings because he supposed they would overlap with another meeting at 2.30, but often found that the former had dispersed before he arrived for the latter, with such authority and dispatch had the Secretary transacted its business. An important part of Gerrans's work in this capacity was to select the books to be prescribed for the Local Examinations. As a Delegate of the Press he was in a position to acquire or recommend books that would be suitable, and which his own Delegates would then accept without demur. He was therefore a kind of double agent, but one of impeccable integrity. Although prepared to complain that the Press Delegates disregarded the needs of his own, he could not allow himself to intervene. They had had every opportunity of discovering from him what sort of book was set. If they were opposed to issuing such books that was their own affair, and he could only record his dissent. He would on no account recommend to his Delegates an Oxford book if it were not precisely what was required.

It seemed to him, as he explained to Gell, that the issue was perfectly simple. If the Press Delegates chose to publish school-books for the Local Examinations they must realize that their control over them was strictly limited. The contents were predetermined, and if an individual Delegate presumed to interfere he could easily render the whole work unsuitable, and indeed unpublishable. 'If the books are not taken by the Locals Delegates,' he told Gell, 'the Press will be very ill-advised if it publishes them; and the books will not be so taken, unless they are of the required kind.' Gell may have been bewildered, but he could warm to a man with a grievance. Gerrans hoped that the interests of the two Delegacies might coincide and was disappointed when they did not.

Gell, whose first publishing experience had been with educational books, was only too well aware of a lost opportunity. Shortly before his appointment Jowett had disbanded the School-book Committee, replacing it by a Publications Committee. It was a reasonable enough decision, for the former had dominated the publishing policy of the Learned Press for long enough. No drastic change was intended, but the time had come when the Clarendon Press Series induced in some Delegates feelings of satiety. They became indifferent particularly to books at the elementary level, and in black moods Gell might reflect that he had lost a vocation before he had properly entered upon it. 'I have always assumed', he wrote to Gerrans, 'that very elementary school books were liable to be thrown out intermittently, without reference to their sale or merits, by those of the Delegates who think this kind of publication unsuited to the Press.' On occasion he referred to an Education Department, though he can have meant only one aspect of the business rather than an organized branch of it. To Cannan he deplored the want of educational travellers. As a Delegate of Local Examinations he fully agreed with Gerrans that it would be unfitting for the Delegacy to use its influence to force Oxford books upon the public—'as the Cambridge people do'. But short of that 'there is a great deal to be done by the establishment of harmonious and sympathetic relations which, I am confident, has been greatly developed during the last few years. When I first found myself upon the O.L. Delegacy there seemed to be a positive aversion to Clarendon Press Books.'

There may have been an improvement in public relations, but Gell ceased to claim—indeed positively disclaimed—any right to influence the Delegates in the choice of books to be published. In this respect he became increasingly passive, having learned early that alone he could make no impression upon the Board. Gerrans's sturdy neutrality did not help. So although like Henry Latham before him he kept a close watch on the books presented by various examining bodies, he despaired in the end of being able to supply them. He told Gerrans that he had found that 'the delay in deciding upon books at short notice here, and the fastidiousness (very necessary to a University Press), and the absence of any machinery for pushing the books amongst second grade schools, made them rarely successful; and as experience thus showed that we were not adapted to such productions, I have for some time ceased to call the attention of the Delegates to them.' It was another of Gell's 'failures'. Later the attitudes of the Delegates changed, and Gerrans found that his two roles could be happily combined. He became himself, in Gell's sense, the education department.

4. The New York Branch

THE opening of a branch in New York was inevitable sooner or later, but neither Gell nor the Delegates expected it to happen as suddenly as it did. It was Frowde who decided that arrangements with Thomas Nelson & Son were unsatisfactory. He did so rather abruptly and dramatically in the summer of 1895. Nelsons had the exclusive right, frequently infringed, to sell Oxford Bibles and Prayer Books in the United States. Fierce competition and what Nelsons described as an unprecedented depression of trade forced them to ask for better terms. Frowde complained that reduced prices from Oxford had already made the trade largely profitless, and that if any more concessions were made he would be selling at a loss. He took a stern line. He was convinced that under good management good business could be done. The deaths of two of Nelsons' senior partners meant that he had to deal with a less experienced and less energetic management at a time when the profit from Bible sales had dropped from more than £50,000 annually to £27,000.

'Wherever we are face to face with the booksellers, as in England, Scotland, Ireland and Canada, we do the great bulk of the Bible trade and all the fine bindings,' he told Gell. His conviction that the Press was now ill-served in New York reached a climax on 2 August, when he wrote to inform Gell that he proposed to go there to see for himself, and intimated that the time had probably come to end the existing agreement. The letter came 'as a thunderbolt'. August was the month for not making decisions. Gell did not attempt to stop Frowde from going, but he begged him to be careful, and not to commit himself to anything until the Delegates could be reassembled. He agreed that Oxford could not afford to make losses to give Nelsons profits.

On arriving in New York Frowde took only a few days to confirm impressions formed in London. By his own frugal standards Nelsons' business was being extravagantly run from expensive premises. Much that had been said about the depressed state of the trade was evidently true, and the native printers were competing fiercely. But it was a question of holding on, and fighting back. He had no doubt at all that it was time for the Oxford University Press to do the business itself in its own name. On 23 August he wrote to Gell asking for an entirely free hand to terminate the agreement. He would expect within 48 hours of his receiving the letter a cablegram from Gell containing the one word 'Obviate'. In the meantime, as there was nothing more for him to do in New York, he would go to Toronto and visit the Oxford representative there.

Gell had always wanted to strengthen the London side of the business. Now his London Manager was showing resolution and an independence of mind not a little unnerving. He consulted the Vice-Chancellor, Magrath, who agreed that a hastily summoned meeting of the Delegates would be of no avail. He had better go ahead. On 3 September Gell sent the cablegram, and two days later Frowde, on behalf of the Chancellor, Masters and Scholars of the University of Oxford, was obviating the first agreement with Nelsons, which went back to 1883, entitling them to the Authorized Version. Next he disposed of the agreement for the Revised Version. On his return to London he was seriously considering whether to take over Nelsons' American branch in its entirety as a going concern. Frowde had completed the work of demolition. The Delegates, Markby in particular, had now to ponder the legal niceties involved in creating a new department of the University Press in New York.

When the Delegates met again on 25 October, however, negotiations with Nelsons could be said to be continuing. The shrinking profits, the dwindling skill and enterprise of the agents, were explained to them, but for the time being no action was called for. Frowde had held out the possibility of a new agreement. He wanted Nelsons to guarantee that their total purchase each year would amount to £40,000 (Gell thought this unreasonable, as they could not be expected to buy more than they could sell). He insisted too that in any further reductions in prices to meet the competition Nelsons' losses should be equivalent to any losses that the Press might be called upon to bear. There was little likelihood that agreement would be reached, and the twelve months' notice required in the contract to terminate the agency effectively began on 5 September 1895.

One practical problem, that of staffing the new office, settled itself, though not without bitter recrimination from Nelsons' headquarters in Edinburgh. Frowde was accused of having 'induced' several members of their staff in New York to leave, despite promises that they would remain in Nelsons' service. In a letter intended for the Secretary and the Delegates, amazement was expressed that any representative of the Oxford Press could behave so discreditably. Frowde denied all charges. The men concerned had, one by one, approached him of their own accord on his return to London, after negotiations had broken down. John Armstrong, who was to be the first Manager, had had over twenty years' experience with Nelsons. W. W. McIntosh, who was to succeed him in 1915, had been a traveller for twenty-six years: he survived until 1927, making a total of fifty-seven years in the trade. Two other seasoned employees had applied to Frowde: Olver, with twenty-four years' experience, ten of them in charge of the office, and a relatively young traveller called Schepmoes, who had spent sixteen years with Nelsons. What spell had been cast upon them by Frowde is not known: the chance of buying a few shares in the business could not have been much of an incentive. Of the 443 shares with which the company was launched, 408 were in the names of Cannan, Gerrans, and Shadwell. Few people approached Frowde with a view to personal enrichment. But the logic and convenience of the appointments quite outweighed any embarrassment he may have felt about the defections: without apparent effort he had acquired the services of men rich in experience of the American Bible trade.

The Branch was formally opened in September 1896. By then premises had been found at 91 and 93 Fifth Avenue, where a ten-year lease was taken of the entire second floor and half of the loft. They were too big for current needs, but in due course they would be able to house large stocks of Clarendon Press books, most of which in 1896 were still handled by Macmillans. The first floor in the same building was occupied by Longmans.

5. Oxford Classical Texts

THE Scriptorum Classicorum Bibliotheca Oxoniensis or the Oxford Classical Texts represent a major achievement, and probably no series in any subject has ever quite so satisfactorily fulfilled the dual and sometimes discrepant purposes of the University Press. Learning and education were happily united at last. Jowett, had he lived, would have claimed parentage: in the end it was Bywater who reared the bastard. He studied proofs of all the books included, and there were seventy of them by the time of his death. The Oxford texts came to be used as set books in schools. As the early prospectuses for the series always pointed out, they were also used at the Universities themselves, so 'volumes bought at school should serve as the beginning of a small library which will be used by its possessor throughout school and undergraduate life; and be a better stimulus to literary interest than annotated editions of the parts of an author's works which are set for the next examination'. Increasing sales over the years were attributed to the growing recognition of the value of complete and unannotated texts as an instrument of education. Gone was the shade of Jowett the crib-monger, and his marginal glosses. No English was allowed to appear in any parts of the books, not even on the title-pages.

Teubner's German texts remained cheaper and more comprehensive in their coverage until 1914, but there were notable scholarly achievements by British editors. 'In point of scholarship', it was explained, 'the main principle upon which the texts are constructed is now well known. They are intended to be *hübsch objectiv*, to represent the facts of the tradition rather than the emendations of the editors. The principle the Delegates understand has approved itself in practice to some who were at first inclined to plead for the hard places being made plain.' The application of the principle had imposed great and prolonged labours upon many of the editors, as Jowett had feared and hoped to avoid. Bywater's own work, T. W. Allen's extensive collations of the manuscripts of Homer, the work of Clark and Peterson on the history of the manuscripts of Cicero, of Lindsay on Plautus, Burnet on Plato, gave their editions an authority over and above that normally required of school-books. They were internationally recognized, even in Germany, as important contributions to scholarship.

The Classical Texts Committee was excluded by Lyttelton Gell from his

denunciation of committees in general, for it had after all something very
definite to show. But as usual he could have wished that once the principles
had been decided, the texts to be included and the editors responsible
chosen, he might be left to get on with the execution of the scheme. This was
not to be. For most of 1896 the Delegates debated the question of terms,
each case being decided on its own peculiar merits. The idea of paying a
simple royalty to each editor was still not acceptable. Instead there were
again permutations of infinite complexity. The length of the text, the likely
demand for it, the status of the editor, his affluence, neediness, or known
cupidity, all had to be taken into account. Bywater was to get £15 on
publication of the *Poetics*. Robinson Ellis undertook to do Catullus for
nothing. For his *Euripides*, Gilbert Murray was to get £75 on publication,
and 2*d.* a copy after 2,500 copies had been sold. The most common
arrangement was £25 on publication and 1*d.* a copy after 1,000 had been
sold, but every possible variation was tried.

So even this splendid enterprise began to turn sour on Gell after eight
months had passed and he had still not been able to effect a single binding
agreement for any book in the series. He knew that there was competition.
To York Powell he wrote, 'I am afraid that one of our weak points has been
that we have gone so slow that Methuen have had time to form and
complete their plans whilst ours have been maturing'. Years after, Charles
Cannan was still engaged in harassing negotiations and compromises with
Methuens. On 29 January 1897 Gell at last had the satisfaction of sending
off signed agreements to twenty editors, all on the same day. Something had
been attained, he conceded, but at 'the expenditure of an amount of time
and labour, which, if paralleled in the other Departments of the Delegates'
Business, would bring the whole thing to a dead-lock'.

6. The Dictionary: Distrustfully–Doom

MANY years after he had left the Press, Gell recalled those critics who had
always insisted that with 'a little more energy and better organization' the
Dictionary could be finished off in no time. As long as the Delegates
regarded 704 pages a year as a realistic target, the end was always in sight.
But the target was never reached. Years went by and nothing appeared in
print at all. During Gell's period as Secretary there were two major crises
when the abandonment of the project was seriously considered, in 1892 and
1896. Rising costs, tardiness, and gigantism nearly destroyed it.

In Miss Elisabeth Murray's biography of her grandfather Gell appears
as a malign figure, a kind of sadistic headmaster before whom the former
schoolmaster James Murray went in cowed and angry terror. His name was
something to frighten the children with. Murray seemed to assume that Gell
ought to side with him against the Delegates, whereas Gell's task was to

prod or bludgeon Murray according to their temper. He carried a more awkward burden than either Price, who once the agreement had been signed had only the problem of salaries and fees to worry about, or his successor, Cannan, who arrived on the scene after the last serious crisis of 1896, when the dedication of Volume III to Queen Victoria had bestowed upon the work an aura of permanence and sanctity, and made its unfolding as inexorable as progress itself.

The first part only, A–Ant, existed in print when Gell assumed uneasy control. Anta–Battening was published in November 1885, Battenlie–Bozzom in March 1887, Bra–Byzen in June 1888. That completed Volume I, nine years after work on the Dictionary had begun in earnest. The terminal words by which each part was known were themselves unfortunate, confirming suspicions, sometimes expressed, that the editor was enthralled by obsolete or even non-existent words, and progress hindered by his fanatical pedantry. Not only Gell but reviewers and subscribers were beginning to complain. Murray's move to Oxford had made no difference to the output though it had added to the expense, and for Gell the fear of mounting costs and the possibility that the editor and his assistants might eventually come to a complete standstill was more than he cared at times to contemplate. He never visited Murray in his Scriptorium, and little as he liked him Murray was far too sensitive not to be affronted by such neglect. It is clear that for long periods Gell preferred to try to forget about the Dictionary. In his lengthy report to the Delegates in 1891 he made no mention of it. Perhaps for that Murray should have been thankful. It must certainly have been difficult for Gell to feel that he was himself participating in a great act of creation, in the building of a national monument, when his experience was more like that of an incompetent muleteer. Despairing at last of making any impression on Murray he reverted to the idea of a second editor, with a second team of assistants. Battenlie–Bozzom was scheduled for publication in 1886. In March Gell informed the Delegates that only 56 out of 352 pages were in final proof. In April he appointed Henry Bradley to assist in the completion of B.

In his twenty years as a clerk in a cutler's exporting firm in Sheffield, Bradley had perfected his knowledge of Latin and learned most of the modern European languages. As a child he had, according to Robert Bridges, learnt to read upside down, standing before his father at family prayers, and throughout his life he could read either way up with equal facility. In 1883 he moved with his wife and four children to London, where he tried to make a living as a book reviewer. He also became an occasional contributor to the Dictionary. Murray respected his work, but the intervention of Gell was always suspect and Bradley's appointment could only mean a lack of confidence in himself. It was Doble who sought to assure him that the intention of the Delegates was simply to make things easier for the future, so that 'There will be no occasion for these harassing communications.' But Murray was unappeased. 'It is an embittering consideration for me', he wrote to Gell, 'that while trying to do scholarly work in a way which scholars may be expected to appreciate circumstances place me commercially in the position of the *bête noire* of the Clarendon Press, who involves them in ruinous expenditure.' Gell curtly demanded 'a less vexatious discrepancy between expenditure and results'.

The employment of Bradley did not immediately help. The intractability of B had taken everyone by surprise. It had been assumed, even by the experienced Skeat, that A was typical, that forecasts of time and length could be reliably based on it. But this was another illusion. Murray's best assistant, Mr. Mount, worked for three months on 'black' and its derivatives. There was a danger that each letter might prove more difficult than the last, for the slips were accumulating all the time and there was more and more material to be sifted and assessed. But this was too awful a prospect to be faced: it was better to regard B as an almost impenetrable jungle and to believe that once through it the going would become easier. When Part III was finally published in March 1887 the Delegates as usual saw no reason to rejoice. They instructed Gell to call Murray's attention to the increased cost of proof corrections, which was indeed alarming. Murray insisted that only when he saw the words in type could he decide the correct order of meanings, which quotations could be cut, and which definitions shortened. The result was that charges for proof corrections were higher than for the original composition, an intolerable state of affairs.

It was clear to Gell that so long as Murray had the sole responsibility and insisted on doing everything himself, checking and rewriting every line of proof, he would continue to thwart all efforts to force the pace. In 1887, therefore, Bradley was made an independent editor and entrusted with the letter E, and Murray's staff was reduced by half. Each editor was ordered to produce one part a year. But in 1890 nothing appeared at all. York Powell had not helped by persuading Bradley to prepare a new edition of Stratmann's *Middle English Dictionary*, which took up far too much of his time. Murray was in despair and physically ill, and talking of giving up. Bradley's health began to go too, but by a supreme effort the editors managed in 1891, for the first and only year, to produce their allotted parts—Closca–Consigner, and E–Every. If not sufficient to jolt Gell into optimism, at least it may have contributed to the complacency with which that year he was able to face the future.

When the tide turned the following year, however, there was no consolation to be found in that direction. Bradley broke down completely, and was ordered to rest by his doctor, who also recommended a change of scene and sea-trips. The Press granted him three months' leave and he went to recuperate in the Norwegian fiords. The year passed with no visible addition to the Dictionary and Gell wrote to Furnivall, conveying the profound dissatisfaction of the Delegates. In the face of rising costs they were seriously thinking of abandoning the project. Perhaps even Gell was surprised to find that Furnivall and the Philological Society tended to take his side. Furnivall of all people recommended a compromise. He agreed that Murray's perfectionism was a threat to survival, and that he must be persuaded to lower his standards. His son could wait for the second edition, his grandson for the third. But of course Murray lacked faith in posterity in spite of all that he was doing for it.

Compromise was agreed upon by the Delegates. It was to be between 'what is theoretically best and what is practically possible', as all good compromises should be. The interpretation of it, however, was left largely in the hands of the editors. To Murray it was 'a defeat for Mr. Gell'. But Mr. Gell retaliated by introducing a bonus system which in practice was a defeat for Dr. Murray. The bonus was to be paid if the annual target was reached or exceeded. Murray paid his assistants a fixed salary which assumed the bonus payment and was always out of pocket while the arrangement continued.

The making of the Dictionary during this period is a sad saga of over-work, ill health, and frustration. On the completion of the letter C, Walter Skeat published a celebratory verse in *Notes and Queries*, no doubt to cheer Murray up; it may only have caused him to look more dolefully into the immediate future:

> Wherever the English speech is spread
>   And the Union Jack flies free,
> The news will be gratefully, proudly read
>   That you've conquered your A, B, C.
>   But I fear it will come
>   As a shock to some
>   That the sad result will be
> That you're taking to dabble and dawdle and doze,
> To dolour and dumps, and—worse than those—
>   To danger and drink,
>   And—shocking to think—
> To words that begin with d—.

D was safely negotiated, Bradley overcame E, but the Dictionary nearly came to an end with F. In 1896 Bywater discovered that both editors were exceeding Webster by more than 8 to 1. The Dictionary was likely to make 12,800 pages instead of the 8,400 approved in 1882. It was Murray himself who had allowed this alarming fact to come to the attention of the Delegates by pointing out that Bradley was editing F on such a scale that it would be impossible to include his own H in the same volume. The Delegates promptly resolved that Bradley's connection with the Dictionary must end if he did not contain himself, and Bywater and York Powell were appointed a subcommittee to investigate further. It was then found that both men were equally guilty. Incensed, Bywater moved on 21 February 1896 that the scale henceforth should be 6 to 1 of Webster, that Murray and Bradley should undertake to abide by that scale, and that if they declined to do so the Delegates should consider suspending publication, 'for such time as may be thought advisable'.

Bradley responded by throwing out a challenge. If any competent person were to go through a section of F reducing it to the required scale, it would be found that the Dictionary was being almost entirely divested 'of those qualities to which its unique value and reputation are chiefly due'. Murray replied more humbly but to the same effect. Rather than see the crumbling of his ideal of a dictionary on historical principles—for the historical material was most at risk—he would prefer to stop altogether, with a frank admission that the cost was too great, and in the hope that in some future happier age someone else might carry on.

The Philological Society came quickly to the aid of the editors. If the Delegates would agree to accept the 8 × Webster limit, Furnivall would appeal to the Government, the Press, and the public for financial support. The Delegates had no desire for publicity, much as they might have welcomed the money, and so they appointed another committee, which included the Provost of Oriel, D. B. Monro, as well as the two former members, to scrutinize the proofs again and to make any other suggestions for reduction that might be acceptable to Murray and Bradley. News of a possible suspension was, however, leaked to the press, which alerted the public to an impending national calamity: it would be 'an indelible disgrace to the University', the *Saturday Review* warned. In April Gell wrote to the editors, more or less appeasingly. He made no mention of scale, and confined himself to general principles concerning etymologies, the number of quotations, Americanisms, slang, the choice of vocabulary—taking particular exception to the inclusion of 'fooldom', a word coined by Ruskin. He was on safe ground, for it had so often been covered before, the main risk being a deepening of Murray's depression. He enclosed proofs of sections of F with possible omissions marked on them. Monro, Bywater, and Powell had done their utmost, but Gell even so was at pains to state that the Delegates were not insisting on the omissions. They were simply specimens of the kind of reductions which might be made without affecting the general character of the Dictionary.

Bradley acknowledged the ability and fairness of the Delegates only too gladly, for he soon discovered that if all the suggested deletions were made the scale remained 8·72 pages to one of Webster. The point had been made. Murray, 'fagged and weary', was spending a few days in Malvern in the hope that fresh air might revive him. He had several times been on the point of breaking down, he told Gell. His brain would not work, and all the heart had gone out of him. He did not have the proofs with him, and could only say that he would do his best during the next few months. If the Delegates were still dissatisfied, he would retire from the work. 'I am already weary and dispirited with its disappointments.'

In fact this proved to be a turning-point, and the worst was over. In May Gell informed Murray that the Delegates had rescinded their order of 21 February, and that he might continue as before. For the rest of his time Gell was mostly concerned to impress upon the accountant, and those Delegates who had difficulty in grasping the fact, that the Dictionary was not a commercial proposition. By 1896, after seventeen years, he estimated that the expenditure was £50,000, and that only £15,000 had been recovered in sales. It is strange that at so late a date he still felt it necessary to explain that the Dictionary was 'a charge on our resources, not a source of income'. To the accountant he expressed 'a very emphatic personal opinion (which I am quite sure every practical man would endorse) that the *New English Dictionary* is immensely overvalued in our books as a commercial asset'. It was certainly a charge on the Delegates' resources, but it was the baffling extensions of space and time that caused more anxiety than the annual outlay, which was substantially less than that paid to the University Chest. The parts that appeared in Gell's last year again carried direly significant titles, including what may have seemed a direct reference to the stubborn Murray himself—Distrustfully–Doom, Doom–Dziggetai ('It approaches the mule in appearance'). By this time a part might be only 64 pages, and the parts were no longer appearing in alphabetical order.

In 1897 on the advice of the Provost of Oriel and York Powell, the Delegates invited William Craigie, formerly at Oriel and then at St. Andrews, to join the Dictionary team. He was the son of a jobbing gardener and his native language was the Lowland Scots of Angus. Without informing Murray, Gell wrote offering him a post on an experimental basis for three months, at £25 a month. If he eventually attained the position of independent editor he would be paid largely by results, and could expect £500 in a good year. Again Murray took it as a vote of no confidence and threatened briefly to resign. Murray knew his own worth, but had never been fully persuaded that others did. After all this time he still felt insecure. At last it occurred to the Delegates that if they had to continue to humour and reassure him they might as well do so openly and in style. In October 1897 the Vice-Chancellor, John Magrath, gave a dinner in his honour. It marked the completion of Volume III, and its dedication to the Queen— and by the terms of the dedication its formal acceptance by the University. Murray announced that he hoped to finish by 1908. Walter Skeat and others deplored that the Dictionary was not more widely known or used: every man who paid income tax should be obliged to buy a copy. And Sir William Markby, little more than a year after it had been on the brink of foundering altogether, said, 'We have never hesitated in the performance of what we consider to be a great duty which we owe to the University and to the nation, and we have never felt any doubts as to the ultimate completion of the work under the able editorship of Dr. Murray.'

7. Decline and Fall

IN December 1896 the first issue of the *Periodical* appeared, 'with Mr. Henry Frowde's Compliments'. It consisted of sixteen pages of extracts from or comments on Clarendon Press books, an article on India paper, a miscellany of facts and literary gossip later to become a regular feature as

'Obiter Scripta', and advertisements. It marked the beginning of what might be called a 'publicity department' in London, though for forty-five years it was the responsibility of one man, R. M. Leonard, who had previously worked on the *Pall Mall Gazette*. He edited 206 issues of the *Periodical* with unflagging relish, remaining anonymous throughout. In 1936, on the completion of its fortieth year, he let it be known that every number had been compiled by the same person. He could also justly advise future literary historians that they would neglect his record at their peril. By then it had grown into a substantial quarterly, the four issues of that year running to some 400 pages. It was available free to all who asked for it, postage paid. Leonard was a familiar figure over the years at Amen Corner and later at Amen House, though he had other occupations, being a particularly active member of the Anti-Bribery and Corruption League. For the Press he compiled many successful anthologies. He had a special gift for assembling verses suitable for any occasion, Coronations and Jubilees, wars, victories, and declarations of peace, doing on the whole a better job than the poetasters of former times.

In the very first issue of the *Periodical* he came to grips with the problem of promoting what he regarded affectionately as the quintessential Clarendon Press book, one so impenetrably erudite that it was impossible to extract from it any passage likely to entice the non-specialist reader. He met the challenge of A. E. Cowley's *Samaritan Liturgy* by quoting from a review in the *Guardian*. Having noted that the Samaritans had never distinguished themselves by originality in any branch of knowledge, and never succeeded in influencing anybody, the reviewer went on: 'Yet the opinion should not be allowed to prevail that the few students—they may be counted on less than the fingers of one hand—who devote themselves to Samaritan learning are nothing but literary martyrs. The historical, the literary and the linguistic faculties of men, soon discover that there is something to feed upon . . . and humanity at large ought to be grateful to these few specialists.' Here, Leonard was quick to recognize, was a classical justification of the quintessential Clarendon Press book.

Gell conveyed his general approval of the first issue to Frowde, whilst advising him to keep an eye on the new man, whose tongue might be in his cheek. Gell did not immediately appreciate that Leonard was exploiting the 'advantages of those distributive agencies' centred in London and helping to develop the business along lines he had once felt to be essential to its prosperity.

But Gell was in a very disturbed condition. The growing pressure of work in the 'office', which he attributed to the rapid growth of the business and to the special gifts of the Delegates for creating disorder, had begun to prey seriously upon his mind. By 1895 he was already a man at the end of his tether, in failing health, obsessed by the need for a long rest but unable to get away. For a poignant moment, with the appointment of Charles Cannan as a Delegate, he thought that he had found a friend. He wrote a letter which he must subsequently have regretted. Addressing him for the first and last time as 'My Dear Cannan' (it was to be a bleak 'Dear Cannan' in future), he regretted that his doctor's orders prevented him welcoming Cannan on his accession, but looked forward to explaining to him in due course 'the general outlines of our huge and complex machine'.

'We have had uphill work', he wrote,

to reduce it all to system and order in the time of transformation and expansion which has marked the last twelve years and in my own judgement we have still much to do. But you will soon perceive that we have strong Conservative forces to deal with, and at the moment I am weary of the long struggle over questions that have been debated again and again—and always left unsettled.

However I shall be ready enough to begin again the campaign of methodizing upon which I was started by Jowett Markby and Robinson eleven years ago, if I see the Delegates again inclining that way. At present much time and energy is wasted in manœuvring backwards and forwards over questions of deadly familiarity.

Still—there is the vast business of which some of the Board to this day cannot form a conception, and what its future may be will depend upon the sagacity and resolution of OUR generation—not upon traditions drawn from a different era.

Poor Gell, he had found a foe and not a friend. He was writing to a Conservative, and a traditionalist, likely to interpret such an appeal as both sycophantic and disloyal. Cannan was also an extremely methodical man, and his stamina could match that of Bartholomew Price. He spoke, when he spoke at all, in cadences strange to Gell's ear. He was Bywater's friend, having quietly assumed equality much as Bywater had with Pattison, without preliminary discipleship. The two were a deadly combination, for they had command of the ironical mode, later defined with great specificity by the Fowlers in *Modern English Usage*. The aim was 'exclusiveness', the means 'mystification', the audience 'an inner circle'. Gell, who was earnest and extroverted and a Justice of the Peace, felt thoroughly excluded and mystified. Their diversions might be cosy evenings talking Aristotle over a pipe, but in a curious way they were also more irreverent, more flippant, and less serious than he was himself. The keen interest Cannan always showed in the Press evidently got on Gell's nerves. He did not hesitate to tell Cannan that in answering some of his questions he was wasting precious time. Or on occasion he would profess not to understand the question, ready though he would be to answer it if Cannan could make himself clear.

Gell was more ill than he thought in the winter of 1896 and did not return to the office until March, after a prolonged convalescence in the South of France. Business was almost at a standstill, and Doble hardly fit to carry on. In February the Vice-Chancellor had asked Cannan to 'help poor Doble in his secretarial labours till Gill's return. I am afraid the poor fellow needs all the help he can get.' For the rest of 1896 Gell was exceptionally busy, with the opening of the New York Branch, the setting-up of a new insurance scheme for Press employees, with the new buildings in Walton Street that Hart's extension of the printing works made necessary. He was as usual having trouble with his royalty accounts, and all statements to editors and authors were late. The office consisted of himself and a secretary, Doble, and the chief clerk and accountant, W. J. Jeeves. These, together with the warehouseman, constituted the whole of the salaried staff. The wages staff consisted of nine men, four of whom were employed in the warehouse and two in the High Street depot. Their combined weekly wages were £7. 9s. 0d. This pathetically small force had somehow or other to prepare annually the authors' and editors' accounts which by 1897 numbered 700. They might be estimated profit, actual profit, royalty, or commission accounts.

On top of this there was the usual correspondence of a busy publishing house to deal with. Authors were more than usually tiresome. Gladstone was pestering Gell with proposals for a new edition of Butler's *Analogy*, and was brutally told that it was premature: the old man was eighty-nine and died the next year. Sir William Hunter brightly opined that the current famine in India offered a good opportunity for advertising his *Brief History of the Indian Peoples*. W. P. Ker, renowned for his taciturnity, was talking too much, and York Powell and Cannan were hatching some sort of an anthology of English verse behind his back. Small wonder that everybody was unwell. Doble went into hospital. Mr. Jeeves was 'extremely shaky' and compelled to rest. Gell had to try to redistribute the work among the junior staff as best he could. Further appeals for help were addressed to the Delegates. Unable to take a holiday he struggled on for another year, but it had become too much for him. Horace Hart too was away, recuperating from a breakdown. On 20 October 1897 Gell wrote his last letter as Secretary to the Vice-Chancellor, Magrath, begging the Delegates to excuse his absence at the first meeting of term. He had stayed on to complete the authors' and editors' accounts in the absence of Doble and Jeeves, and this was his first opportunity to get a few days' holiday. He hoped that Jeeves was sufficiently recovered to pull through to the end of the year, and because of the new arrangements he had made he now had no more than he could fairly do—for the first time for many autumns.

It had been an exacting year but not all Gell's energies had gone into shoring up the collapsing office. Milner's appointment as High Commissioner for South Africa was as disturbing to him as any local events. Possibly years of separation lay ahead. He busied himself furiously organizing the grand farewell dinner in London, but a tormenting question was forming in his mind: should he go too? Milner wanted him. There were great opportunities in the South African administration and the Colonial Secretary, Joseph Chamberlain, had intimated that the Imperial Secretaryship in Cape Town might be within his reach. He was almost ready to take the job, but there was a consideration of deadly familiarity. He would be surrendering an income of £1,800 a year, and a house of his own. Milner urged him to make up his mind. If he decided against, neither Chamberlain nor Lord Selborne, Under-Secretary for the Colonies and Milner's friend, would forget him, he wrote reassuringly, and in any case he had 'the qualities which command their own terms'. A few days later Milner

Dictionary Murray

W. A. Craigie

Henry Bradley

C. T. Onions

wrote again. Chamberlain had decided that he dare not approach the Treasury for higher salaries—'So I must begin to run my Empire with Second Division clerks.' They became known later as 'the Kindergarten', young Oxford men of high ideals who never knew they had been got on the cheap.

At the next meeting of the Delegates the Vice-Chancellor expressed the opinion that the work of the Secretary's office was beyond the strength of the existing staff, and a committee consisting of himself, Price, and Markby was appointed to consider ways of relieving the Secretary of some part of his responsibilities. A week later on the recommendation of the committee it was agreed to appoint H. T. Gerrans to the staff. The necessary arrangements were expected to be of 'some delicacy and complexity', but it was understood that Gerrans would be willing to accept this undefined post. Markby visited Gell at Langley Lodge, and came away assured that he would welcome Gerrans not as a subordinate but as a colleague. He respected him as a man accustomed to administrative routines. It was in the Delegates' mind that there should in effect be two Secretaries, for with the expansion of the business it would be necessary for one of them to be absent from Oxford from time to time, and it was essential that the other should be equally capable of looking after the shop.

But the Delegates had acted too late. Within a few days they received a printed communication from Edith Lyttelton Gell, written with all the acerbity that characterized her husband's letters when he was displeased. By the direction of Dr. Lauder Brunton, an eminent physician, Gell was absolutely forbidden to attend to any matter of business whatsoever. Although entirely free from any organic complaint, 'he has succumbed to a period of prolonged over-strain', and in order to avoid a grave and possibly irretrievable collapse she must apply for the six months' leave of absence insisted upon by the specialist and by the local doctor. Mrs. Gell continued at some length: the familiar technique of recrimination, of reminding the Delegates of what they had left undone, and even the choice of words, suggest that Philip Lyttelton Gell still had the strength left to fire his parting shots. 'I think it my duty to recall to the Delegates' memory', it was written, 'that by the Doctor's certificate presented two years ago, the importance of so re-arranging matters at the Press as to ensure to the Secretary a period of at least six weeks uninterrupted holiday in the year (without Press business constantly following him) was clearly stated, and I was then assured that measures should be taken on his return to ensure this minimum.' But instead of this he found on his return that Doble had completely broken down, and that his absence naturally threw upon the Secretary a double load. Fresh assurances had been given the previous March that a competent assistant would be appointed to strengthen the crippled staff. 'I understand', wrote Mrs. Gell, 'that the Delegates have now some such scheme in contemplation. It will be a matter of great regret to Mr. Gell, that after awaiting so long the step now proposed, he should be peremptorily forbidden to discuss for the present the important question to which the

I

Vice-Chancellor refers. As many of the Delegates are aware, he has long urged that the situation was an impossible one, and was most anxious to have devoted the last Long Vacation to the re-arrangements involved in the initiation of a new Member of the Staff.'

The Delegates read the letter, and one from the local doctor expressing his own fears of 'a grave and possibly irretrievable collapse' if the specialist's instructions were not obeyed. The Vice-Chancellor told them that there was no time to be lost. He recommended that an agreement be made with Gerrans for a period of five years at a salary of a thousand guineas, and that for the time being he should undertake all Gell's duties. The Delegates refused to be stampeded. They deferred consideration until the next meeting. In the meantime Markby was to consult the solicitor, Mr. Williams, about the legal position. The question was whether Gell could be given notice and it was answered by the solicitor with a certain equivoca-tion. In his contract, which did not expire until October 1901, there was a clause stating that if 'Mr. Gell shall from any cause (except temporary illness) become incapable of performing his duties then it shall be lawful for the Delegates to peremptorily determine the agreement, provided that in case such incapacity is through no fault or default of Mr. Gell he shall be entitled to six calendar months' notice in writing of such determination'. The legal position seemed clear enough. Gell was patently unable to perform his duties, his illness appeared to be more than temporary, but his incapacity could not be attributed to any fault or default on his part. It was in order to give him six months' notice. But to be effective the notice must be in writing and must be served upon him personally, or upon somebody authorized to accept it on his behalf. If the former, nobody could foresee the consequences on Gell's precarious state of mind. On the other hand if Mr. Gell declined to act at all or to appoint a legal adviser the Delegates would be faced with an impasse. Having communicated his opinion to the Board, Mr. Williams took fright. He was afraid that he might have appeared too hostile to Gell, towards whom he felt personally a very great regard and respect—feelings, he knew, shared by all the Delegates. He had also thought of a very alarming outcome, that Gell on learning of the fate intended for him might return to the office even at the peril of his life. He might repudiate his wife's letter and claim that his absence had been due only to temporary illness. In view of these fearsome possibilities, it would perhaps be prudent to do nothing for sixty days, after which there would be no possibility of claiming temporary incapacity and six months' notice could be served.

The Delegates were divided among themselves, Price, Cannan, and Bywater actively opposed to Gell, Gerrans and Markby anxiously concerned that justice should be seen to be done, others perhaps indifferent or bored. They had lost the services of the Vice-Chancellor, who had retired to his bed, telling Markby that the Delegates would have to finish the Gell business without him. As an emergency measure Gerrans was asked to act as Secretary for the next six months. He was not yet forty. After a week he had to report to Price, now acting as Chairman of the Delegates in the absence of the Vice-Chancellor, that it was proving too much for him. He had his other college and University duties to perform, but he had been confident enough that he had the physical ability to carry out what the Delegates proposed. 'During the latter part of the week', he wrote, 'serious doubts arose in my mind, and my fatigue and quasi-collapse today have rendered it quite clear that I cannot comply with the request of the Board without breaking down.' The Secretary's office was becoming a major health hazard. Only Price and Cannan appeared immune. J. C. Masterman, who remembered Gerrans in 1910 when he was in his early fifties, described him as a remarkable man 'with a great dome-like head set on a sturdy and substantial body'. He was not a man to be easily crushed.

Nine days having elapsed, a reply to Mrs. Gell's letter was concocted: it was brief and omitted even a token expression of sympathy. She was asked to empower Mr. Gell's legal adviser to meet the legal adviser of the Delegates. This she declined to do without knowing the nature of the questions involved. Markby, acting on the Vice-Chancellor's instructions, told her that it was not possible to furnish her with the points the Delegates thought might need to be discussed, at least not without summoning a special meeting of the Delegates, which would involve further delay. Mrs. Gell expressed bewilderment. The Delegates had discussed the question of leave of absence at two successive meetings. Surely they had decided whether to grant it or not. She was compelled to infer 'that it is the intention of the Delegates to make Mr. Lyttelton Gell's condition an opportunity for discussing matters seriously affecting his position, while he himself is strictly forbidden to deal with them.' She could hardly believe this to be their intention.

The Delegates appeared quite unable to act, and again Markby betook himself to London to confer with Williams. This time the advice was less equivocal. Leave of absence should be granted, and the aim of the Delegates should be to show that they had done everything that they could properly do for Gell, in order to strengthen their position when the end of the six months came. The solicitor was now not sure that it could be proved that Gell was more than temporarily incapacitated, and to give him notice would in any case lay the Delegates open to 'the charge of having acted very cruelly towards an old servant'. At last, therefore, he was granted leave, at a reduced salary of £600. Markby informed Mrs. Gell, and added: 'The Delegates also think that they are bound to notice the suggestion put forward more than once, in one shape or other, in the course of the correspondence, that the Delegates are in some way responsible for the breakdown in Mr. Gell's health. The Delegates feel sure that if you had been fully informed as to the facts, this suggestion would not have been made, and they have no hesitation in assuring you that there is no real foundation for such a suggestion.'

This particular deadlock broken, the Delegates were able to make plans in order to keep the business functioning. The whole of the Michaelmas term of 1897 had been taken up with the dilemma posed by Gell's abandonment of his post. In December it was resolved that Bartholomew Price should undertake the general direction of the Secretary's office during the six months, that Gerrans and Cannan should act as Pro-Secretaries, and that Doble should be granted four weeks' leave of absence. With Price now almost eighty, and Gerrans suspicious of his own health, it was upon 'the sagacity and resolution' of Cannan that the future of the Press now depended.

On Christmas eve, 1897, he wrote in a mellow mood from the Secretary's room to some of his authors. 'Gell is away invalided', he told Gilbert Murray, 'and I am sitting in the office contemplating the list of Books in Progress.' He inquired about the edition of Euripides promised for the autumn, and assured him that there would be no delay before presenting it to an 'excited and appetent public'. He reminded Sir Thomas Raleigh, Clerk of the Privy Council, Gell's friend and legal adviser, of the new edition he was preparing of Cornewall Lewis's *Remarks on the Use and Abuse of some Political Terms*, awaited by 'an interested and appetent public'. York Powell he bombarded with questions, about an editor for selections from the Sacred Books of the East, about possible translations of the Eddas, for information about Celtic heathendom, about his English ballads, and his school history of England—ending, brightly, 'This is a Christmas Card.' He was evidently very much at home.

It was clear however that, unlike Gerrans, he would not be able to work with Gell as a colleague, and as his grip tightened there was only one choice before the Delegates. They took it finally on 25 February 1898, after the leave of absence had exceeded sixty days. They resolved that it was not desirable that Gell should return to his duties as Secretary. The resolution was communicated to his brother Henry, who was asked to use his discretion in breaking the news. Dr. Gell, however, would not be a party to any such arrangement. Unable to penetrate the barriers Gell had created about him, Cannan wrote a letter for the Vice-Chancellor to sign addressed to Gell. It was to be kept by the Pro-Secretaries and might be used in case Gell were to turn up at the office with the intention of resuming his job.

Gell was called back to England from the South of France early in April on the death of his father. He went to Buxted Rectory in Sussex, his father's home for many years, where his brother Henry told him that the Delegates had 'a grave and unexpected communication to make' to him. So Gell put it in an informal and temperate note to Gerrans, informing him that he was referring the matter to his solicitors. Gerrans replied by sending him the letter in the Pro-Secretaries' keeping signed by the Vice-Chancellor. Gell wrote to the Vice-Chancellor on 22 April informing him that his health was happily restored; under the circumstances it was 'somewhat difficult to account for the Resolution of the Delegates'. But from then on he prudently left everything to his solicitor, Mr. Holloms, who talked ominously of a case of 'wrongful dismissal'. As such it would not be a proper subject for arbitration. The Delegates had put themselves legally in the wrong by their resolution of 25 February, and a jury would be justified in assessing the damages at £6,300, the full balance of salary for the unexpired term of the agreement, or at an annuity of £600 a year for life. The Delegates were offering £400.

The end of the story can be told in Gell's own words, as he told it in a long letter to Milner, the first part of which concerns the loss of his father whom Milner greatly respected.

There appears to have been a great battle in my absence—Magrath Price and Cannan determined to seize the opportunity to plant Cannan permanently in the Office in some quite impossible plan of Dual or multiple control—Markby and others equally determined that as leave of absence had been formally granted to me nothing modifying my position and Agreement could be resolved on in my absence. The latter party however were defeated by a bare majority. Markby thereupon cut the whole concern—(at any rate for the present year) and Magrath in his heedless way passed a Resolution—without even consulting their lawyers—terminating my Agreement, so as to start again as they thought with their hands untied. The ground stated was my absence thro' ill health for more than two months. They did not even realize that *leave* of absence on a reduced salary precluded such a course. That was in February. They then lost their nerve, or Cannan lost his supporters—for they could not agree upon any further step. But the Vice-Chancellor kept the Resolution up his sleeve to be fired off at me directly I returned, and I received it from him in the middle of the Vacation, when it was two months old. No kind of explanation or proposition or overture accompanied it. The letter was in Cannan's writing and signed by Magrath. It had been kept secret from everyone. It was imagined by some that this gracious act would lead me into negociations:—not I think by Cannan himself. My mind was clear in two minutes:—I had already grave doubts whether I might not in the end have to resign. And now the Delegates had simultaneously made my relations with them hopeless, and given themselves away by a Breach of Contract. I declined any personal discussion and asked Holloms to make the best bargain he could. Holloms was very anxious to compel them to withdraw their Resolution: but I am sure *you* will feel I did right in declining this course. On the contrary I wished to pin them to their blunder.

Well the Delegates tendered me £5600. I maintained that considering my relations with the Press and the University, I was reluctant to discuss the matter as a question of damages: that if they based their action on my temporary failure in health, my health had suffered thro' the conditions of their service, and that a pension was the only appropriate settlement.

The Delegates caught at my suggestion, and further offered a laudatory Resolution. As to the amount of pension, neither Holloms nor Raleigh have been able to screw them up to what *they* thought fair—£600 a year. They have stuck at £400, wh. is a strong position. . . . So here I am, a gentleman at large! If we are to live *here* without worry, I must earn £600 a year by Directorships. If they don't turn up, we must let the house next year.

I should have no reserves, were it not for the mingled astonishment and regret of my staff. They all say things have been in chaos, and that they have been 'longing for my return'. The University is simply bewildered. The opposition had positively been hinting that I was a hopeless wreck etc.—and here I am again, fit buoyant, ready to work but standing aside to everybody's perplexity, whilst the Press is known to be in difficulties—(Hart being still away)—my work being divided between two of the Delegates; and when the University learns that owing to their fatuous policy the

Delegates have had to pay me for doing nothing the very sum wh. they declined to allow me for a business assistant—they will wonder more!

Milner was 'immensely delighted'. Work at the Press had for far too long been a danger to his friend's health and peace of mind. 'On the whole', he wrote, 'I don't think there is any fate so enviable as that of being unjustly "sacked" in a civilized country.' He urged him to keep Langley Lodge 'out of malice': he would so like to see Gell *'flâner* about Oxford as a gentleman at large, while they are floundering'.

But Gell went jauntily on his way, leaving behind the troublesome shadow of his former self. He had never been, in the cliché beloved of efficiency experts, the right man in the right place at the right time. He had not had much of a chance since Jowett threw him in at the deep end. But now old friends began to rally round and new opportunities opened up. The Prince of Wales and Joseph Chamberlain were told that he would be the ideal man to make an Imperial Institute in London a vital social and commercial centre for colonists. It was work dear to his heart, and he was prepared to make sacrifices, but such work called for £2,000 a year at least. The directorships proved the answer. The Rhodesia Cold Storage and Trading Co. Ltd., the British Exploration of Australasia Ltd., and the British South Africa Company satisfied in the end his imperial longings without obliging him to leave the country. Of the last he was a director from 1899 until 1925, becoming Chairman in 1917 on the death of Jameson, the ex-raider and former Prime Minister of Cape Colony, and finally President. He regained the family seat in Derbyshire, the splendid sprawling Tudor pile of Hopton Hall, which had been temporarily lost in a neighbourly feud. His wife, the Honourable Edith Mary, fourth daughter of the 8th Viscount Midleton, compiled best sellers for the London business. In 1926 he died, and was not even short-listed by Chapman and Milford for inclusion in *The Dictionary of National Biography*.

PART IV

CAESAR AND THE ALLIGATOR

1. Making the Press what it ought to be

CHARLES CANNAN was educated at Clifton College, went up to Corpus as a scholar in 1877, duly completed his double first four years later, and became classical tutor and Dean at Trinity when his former headmaster at Clifton, Dr. Percival, became President of the college. He was thirty-nine when he gave up teaching to become Secretary. While still a Delegate he had confided to York Powell, who in turn confided to Cannan's friend Arthur Quiller-Couch, that he was going to make the Clarendon Press 'what it ought to be: the first Press in the world', and according to Powell he had already taken an important step in the right direction: he was 'learning to suffer fools gladly'. In his early days, Quiller-Couch admitted, 'You risked being made painfully aware that he did not. A fool—and he could scent one from afar—was too fatally meat and drink to him.' He learned rather to exclude fools from his environment than to suffer them, though he retained a gift for making somebody not already a fool feel that he had become one. Cannan was another who could blight a man's confidence by silence. He may have made the Press the first in the world, but to do so he needed to create a man in his own image. He created Humphrey Milford.

Cannan's education was complete at an early age. At twenty-five he appeared to have devoured the whole of English literature as well as the classics. After that he tended to return to a few old favourites—Defoe, Peacock, John Galt, and Susan Ferrier, who wrote novels of Scottish life. Cannan was born in Richmond, Surrey, but his father came from Kirkcudbrightshire, and a General Cannan had taken charge at Killiecrankie. He made no attempt to keep up with the 'moderns', in whom only York Powell among those associated with the Press showed much interest. Later he confined himself, outside office hours, to Aristotle and the Dictionary, and newspapers of all descriptions to which he was addicted. He gave much thought to Rugby football, and according to Q supplied 'no small part of the intelligence which revolutionized "Rugger" at Oxford'. He could lecture on the 'loose scrum'. He was also a passionate Alpine climber. In every other walk of life he was notably dispassionate.

R. W. Chapman, who had been awed by him, contributed an acrobatic, even breath-taking article to *The Dictionary of National Biography*. 'His manner was formidable; his tone was dry and even cynical; his last weapon, which he used ruthlessly, was silence; his enthusiasms were unspoken; he had a mean opinion of human intelligence in general, and not a very high one of human probity. This is, perhaps, not the description of a great man, or of a lovable one; yet Cannan was both. Those who knew him well became aware that they had to do with a man of great intellectual power and subtlety; of rare force of will; of unselfish devotion to the things he loved; and of a singularly tender heart.'

Chapman must have pondered long over those semicolons, and the word 'perhaps'. He worked with Cannan for many years, and eventually succeeded him, but he never got to know him well. In another attempt to sum him up he rebutted the charge that this awesomely remote figure could be intemperately clever at the expense of those excluded from his intimacy. In his obituary for *The Times* he wrote: 'There can seldom have been a mind so acute, that was so completely master of its own dexterities; he was preternaturally clever, but his wit was always under government.' He came to be known, nevertheless, as 'the Alligator'.

Fortunately he was a superb letter-writer. Chapman, an authority on this subject, put him in a class by himself. As he moved in an extremely narrow circle, seldom left Oxford, and was so taciturn, this was a considerable asset: a repressed cordiality was released and his letters, as Chapman said, 'won us a host of friends'. Unlike either Price or Gell, he chose always to write as a responsible individual rather than as a spokesman for the Board—unless he were simply turning a book down. For that purpose he, Gerrans, and Doble soon settled upon a formula, a terse but dignified communication that might be a little more comforting to the author than a bare rejection slip, the use of which the Press has always eschewed. It ran: 'Dear Sir, The Delegates of the Press have considered your suggestion that they should publish ——, and they desire me to reply to you, conveying their thanks for the suggestion you have been so good as to make to them, and their regret that they do not find themselves able to accept it.'

Some of the first bits and pieces of the neglected business he had to pick up after Gell's departure may have struck Cannan as significant. Before that Christmas of 1897 he found that Clark's edition of Aubrey's *Brief Lives* was printed and ready, but that there was nothing he could do about it until the Delegates met again towards the end of January to determine the price and the quality of binding. There was a dispute going on with the distinguished scholar W. P. Ker, then Professor at University College, London, and Fellow of All Souls, who was under contract to produce an edition of Dryden's prose works with notes. He had supplied copy for the text during the summer, but Gell had refused to have it set up without the notes. Ker was not prepared to produce the notes until he had seen the text in proof. The two men (contemporaries at Balliol in the 1870s), had been stubbornly refusing to give way. Doble told Cannan that the compositors needed work, and suggested that it would not be unreasonable to grant Ker his wish—though the principle was bad, and the practice still worse, for Ker continued to withhold his notes after the concession had been granted. At the time, faced by one of his first decisions, Cannan could only write to Price: 'Can I venture to give the order, or must we wait for the Delegates?' What with one thing and another they had also forgotten to arrange for the special binding of the latest part of the Dictionary which was to be presented to the Queen. York Powell ought to have attended to the matter, but by December with nothing done Cannan had to act on his own initiative. He decided that it would be quicker to leave it all to Frowde. 'He seems to know that the Queen likes bright colours, and I dare say that he will hit off her taste very well.'

Time and again there would arise those questions of no great moment which had traditionally been referred to the Delegates for an answer. With the sanction of Price, now eighty years of age, Cannan could sometimes risk a short cut. But it was very soon apparent to him that the business could not continue to be conducted along traditional lines. It took a man steeped in the tradition to make the transition to a greater autonomy of the executive palatable to the Delegates. It still seems odd that even in retrospect Cannan never recognized Gell's predicament. But, enjoying the complete confidence and understanding of the Delegates, he himself so effortlessly overcame the same predicament that he soon forgot that it had ever existed. Over the next twenty years the role of the Delegates outside Finance Committee diminished until it consisted very largely of the selection of books to be published by the Clarendon Press, many of which were actually initiated by the permanent staff. The details of administration were handled in the office, just as Gell had always said they should be.

It is again a part of the Press legend that with the departure of Gell all the massive energies of the age were suddenly released. It seemed so to Humphrey Milford in later years. Coming to the Press at the end of the depression of the 1890s, he recalled that it was almost at a standstill—'at the lowest ebb both in resources and in reputation: from this position of insignificance it was rescued by Cannan'. From their relative perspectives there was little difference between Gell's recollection of the Press as he found it, and that of his successor. It had some modest reputation for the publication of learned works, but outside academic circles, to the general reader and in the book trade, the only well-known Oxford books were the Bibles and Prayer Books. It had to be galvanized afresh by Cannan, as it had once been by Jowett. It was understandable that Gell's achievement, such as it was, should be disregarded. That 'dead-lift' by which he had heaved the Press into the nineties and which he believed would never need to be done again, did need to be done again, not once but many times.

Nevertheless at the end of the century the Press was far from moribund and its reputation had never been so high. Horace Hart had transformed the printing business, Frowde was transforming the London publishing and binding business, and somewhat outside the Delegates' ken activity became increasingly feverish as the century ran out. A million Bibles a year still left a vast spare capacity that demanded to be filled. The manufacturing departments, including the Paper-Mill, were showing an exuberance that could not yet be matched on the publishing side, but Frowde found his list rapidly diversifying and multiplying. There was no time to await instructions from headquarters. The machines had to be fed. But the fame of the Dictionary, if nothing else, preserved the image of massive and unshakeable respectability. In 1897 *The Times* could say that 'The liberal and enlightened management, with an eye to the best interests of learning as well as to commercial profit, that has now for many years marked the administration of the Clarendon Press, is signally illustrated by the encouragement given and the facilities provided for carrying out the work of compiling this great dictionary... It is the greatest enterprise which has ever been undertaken by the Clarendon Press, the greatest effort probably which any University, it may be any printing press, has taken in hand since the invention of printing.' Nobody at that time could doubt that the Press had reached its highest pitch of prosperity and usefulness.

At the Paris Exhibition of 1900 it was proving how competitive it could be, and how alert to the advantages of publicity. The display of books included sets of the Dictionary up to date, six volumes of Edward Arber's 'British Anthologies' on India paper, a special exhibit of higher educational books, and forty-seven unique editions ranging in price from £4 for an Oxford Miniature *Milton* to £150 for *A Century of Oxford Almanacks*. The paper display again concentrated on the miracles of India paper. The Press was awarded three Grands Prix, for binding, paper, and higher educational books: no other publisher won any at all. The next year the exhibits from Paris were shown in the Examination Schools in Oxford and at Amen Corner, and attracted wide coverage in the press. *The Times* recorded, 'In no department have the ever-increasing activities of the University of Oxford been more vigorous and successful than in its printing press. Within the lifetime of men still in middle age the Clarendon Press, to use the alternative term, has developed from a comparatively small concern to one of the greatest in the world.'

The superb British craftsmanship that enabled the Oxford binding-house in Aldersgate Street to compete with the great continental firms was greatly admired. 'Happily there are still people in the world who love a good binding,' wrote the *Pall Mall Gazette*, 'who feel a strange contentment at seeing their author worthily housed.... People, therefore, who like luxury in literature, who feel ashamed when their poets go shabby, will turn with especial pleasure to the exhibition at Amen Corner.' The period of 'literary luxury' was ending, but for some years the workers at Aldersgate Street were allowed a free hand in matters of design, despite occasional interference from York Powell, and contributed enormously to the prestige of the Press. It was said that the skins of 100,000 animals were used yearly to bind the Bible alone—roughly speaking, an average-sized goat would cover ten Bibles. One of the most highly prized bindings was Levant morocco, a goatskin made into leather by processes perfected in France, and of the calf bindings the best was known as 'Russia', being the undyed skin of Russian cows exported by the house of Savin. This could be distinguished from imitations, such as English calf, by its incomparable smell, which nobody was able to match. Pigskin, sheepskin, and sealskin were also used. (Book-loving vegetarians like Furnivall—and indeed Bernard Shaw, with whom temperamentally he had something in common—were cruelly tested.) Huge quantities of gold leaf were needed for lettering and ornaments and gilt edges, and the sweepings from the binding-house floor once yielded a lump of gold that was sold for £130. For luxury bindings the sheets were sewn with silk instead of thread, and headbands of silk were fitted by accomplished needlewomen. A large modern American sewing-machine was available and a hydraulic press for rolling the sheets, but these were for cheap books and nothing to boast about.

Oxford printing has been traditionally somewhat austere, not seeking after effect; to hint in any way that the matter is less important than the form is in bad typographical taste. A mid-twentieth-century Printer to the University, Charles Batey, explained in simple terms what a book should be: 'The type should be legible, properly disposed on the page, and well inked: the paper should be opaque, of a right colour, kindly to the eye, and pleasant to the touch; and the leaves should be secured in a safe binding, suitably lettered with the book's title. The whole should be of convenient weight, not burdensome; the book should open easily, and without alarms or crackles, and lie quite flat: and to all demands it should respond in a quiet gentlemanly way; and, as we read on, it should withdraw itself from our consciousness, leaving us alone with the author.'

Not all the productions of the Press in this adventurous era met these requirements. The Ellen Terry Edition of Shakespeare in forty volumes on India paper, for instance, was enough to alarm anyone with failing sight: the page measured 2 inches by $1\frac{1}{2}$. In 1897 the Oxford Thumb Classics began to make their miniature appearances. *The Imitation of Christ*, Keble's *Christian Year*, *The Vicar of Wakefield*, and the *Compleat Angler* were printed in 128mo ($2\frac{1}{2} \times 1\frac{3}{4} \times \frac{3}{8}$ inches). Typographical ingenuity and India paper made everything possible, and every folly could be catered for. Turning books into playthings or keepsakes was not strictly speaking part of the Delegates' policy. But all the popular classics published by the Press came to be available in a variety of different formats, bindings, on India paper or not, and of course at different prices. By 1914 there were four editions of the complete works of Dickens available: The Oxford India Paper Dickens in seventeen volumes at 4s. each, The Eighteenpenny Illustrated Dickens (20 volumes), The Shilling Dickens, and The Fireside Dickens in twenty-two volumes at prices ranging from 87s. to 41s. according to binding. The first two volumes of 'The Fireside Edition' had been issued jointly in 1901 with Chapman and Hall, and described as the 'copyright' edition. If Hart's machine rooms were short of work, Frowde would order reprints before they were needed, paying for them however only when the existing impression was exhausted and stock was delivered in the normal way.

The preoccupation with novel formats and Hart's readiness to oblige led to the proliferation of series claiming the name of 'Oxford'. These were generally selections of verse or prose, sometimes of particular poets, sometimes on a chosen theme such as friendship, gardens, or grief, and they were elegantly and cheaply produced. The Oxford Moment Series in 1910, selections from Marcus Aurelius, Emerson, E. W. Wilcox to name but a few, suggests that by that time the choice of titles was becoming a problem, and certainly the word 'Oxford' had ceased to indicate major works specifically sponsored or authorized by the Delegates. Steps had eventually to be taken to prevent further devaluation. 'Oxford' denotes works which either represent 'to an unusual degree an "Oxford" standard', or are expected 'to have lasting if not permanent value', to use a later definition.

An Oxford Catalogue of 1905 consisted of 105 pages, of which eleven were devoted to a 'Select List of Mr. Frowde's Publications'. Heading the list was Joseph Wright's *English Dialect Dictionary*, 5,000 pages in six volumes. Wright, who succeeded Max Müller as Professor of Comparative Philology in 1901, was of origins so humble that by comparison Murray and Bradley belonged to the privileged classes. He began work at the age of 6 as a quarryman's donkey boy in Bradford, earning 18*d.* a week. At 11, when his father died, he was making £1 a week as a wool sorter and was able to support his mother and two younger brothers. At 15, the Franco-Prussian War was the talk of Bradford, and in order to keep pace with events Wright taught himself to read the newspapers. From then on it was plain sailing. At 21 he had saved £140 and spent three months in Heidelberg, where he acquired an interest in mathematics, which he taught for a while on his return home. A further visit to Heidelberg diverted him to comparative philology; a brief stay in Leipzig aroused an interest in Lithuanian; and in 1887 Max Müller discovered him and brought him to Oxford as a lecturer to the Association for the Higher Education of Women. He was also appointed a special lecturer in Teutonic philology. His next task was to write the books needed for teaching the subject, and over the next few years the Press published his grammars and primers on Old High German, Middle High German, and Gothic.

The idea of a dictionary had been projected by the English Dialect Society in 1873: some 1,000 voluntary helpers had been recruited, about a million slips had accumulated. Wright was the obvious man to edit it—the only man, in Skeat's view—and the Clarendon Press the obvious publisher to publish it. Unfortunately this was the 1890s and the idea of another dictionary sent a thrill of horror through the Board of Delegates. Price and Gell were relatively unflinching, both indeed anxious to support the project, but hearts were faint, reality had to be faced. The Delegates 'have a very hard experience of the vast interval which separates the *materials* for a Dictionary from a finished product,' Gell explained, 'and they are quite unable to commit themselves to any fresh responsibility in this direction.'

Wright, though bitterly disappointed, bravely resolved to carry on. He secured a government grant, raised subscriptions, and invested all his personal savings. Wanly apologetic, the Press offered him a small office in Walton Street adjoining that of the Secretary. The great work, printed by Hart, was published between 1896 and 1905. It could not carry the Clarendon Press imprint, but Frowde marketed it with a particular solicitude, forgoing part of his commission because Wright by his own network of publicity had saved him so much labour. It was one of the first books to be sold on the instalment plan. Today the market is mostly in Japan. Even as he began his work Wright had said that pure dialect was, with the spread of education and improvement in communications, fast disappearing. He was only just in time.

Second on Frowde's list came Hart's *Rules for Compositors and Readers at the University Press Oxford*, followed by Collins's *Authors' and Printers' Dictionary*, two of the most influential books ever published by the Press. The former, as a small booklet, had been in circulation since 1893, though the 'Rules' themselves had emerged gradually over many years. Its sole purpose was to secure uniformity in the style of books printed at the Press. Copies were given freely to all who asked, until it was discovered that some were being sold in London. 'As it seems more than complaisant to provide gratuitously what may afterwards be sold for profit', Hart decided that he had no alternative but to publish his 'little book'. In the course of many editions, and with the connivance of Skeat, Murray, Bradley, and several eminent classical scholars, it acquired an authority that could hardly be gainsaid. However arbitrary some of its injunctions, Hart's word on punctuation, italicization, division of words, capitalization, spelling, etc. was final. The instruction was to follow 'Rules'—unless an author were exceptionally adamant and insisted against all reason that the compositor should follow copy. Even then, as likely as not, the Printer's reader would apply the Rules at a later stage, and much vexation could ensue. Hart's practice on the punctuation of quotations has mystified many authors over the years. Gladstone himself waged a losing battle with him over the spelling of 'forgo'. He wished to include in a list of errata to Butler's *Works* a 'correction' of the spelling. Hart responded by sending him a copy of Skeat's *Dictionary*, showing that 'forgo' was right in the sense in which he was using the word and could not therefore be corrected. It was only after reference to Murray that Gladstone wrote to Hart: 'Personally I am inclined to prefer forego, on its merits; but authority must carry the day. *I give in.*' Hart, and Murray, were less successful in their campaign for the spelling of 'dispatch': for 'despatch' there was no justification at all, as it derived from a simple slip by Dr. Johnson, who although he knew that dispatch was correct aberrantly mis-spelt and misplaced the word in his dictionary. Hart rigorously applied his Rule, but it was noticed that 'despatch' was creeping insidiously into the newspapers and was even used by the Post Office itself.

Collins's Dictionary was equally idiosyncratic, a source of constant wonder to its users for, although highly selective, it uncannily yielded information and advice reasonably to be expected only from a very much more comprehensive compilation. It was Collins who invented the 'Oxford comma', for which he obtained support from Herbert Spencer. In his entry '"and" *or*, ", and"', he quoted Spencer's verdict on whether to write 'black, white, and green', with the comma after *white*: 'inasmuch as when enumerating these colours ... the white is just as much to be emphasized as the other two, it needs the pause after it just as much as the black does.' On '-ise' and '-ize' endings Collins, again with Spencer's backing, came down firmly in favour of the latter: it was absurd to have the letter in the alphabet and not to use it where phonetically appropriate. The thirty-seventh edition of Hart appeared in 1967, and the eleventh edition of Collins in 1973.

Frowde was a Plymouth Brother, but eclectic in his choice of devotional works. Many were published at the author's expense and circulated among friends or in a particular parish. Some, like *My Morning Counsellor* and *My Evening Counsellor* by M. Kimmont Esq., caught on, in which case Frowde would buy the author out. Diversification of the list occurred in other ways. Not before time the Delegates had ordained that sermons should not be published by the Press. Frowde, with the infant New York Branch in mind, thought that an exception might be made for the Bishop of Albany. Cannan and Doble were sympathetic, but did not think that the rule could be overcome by the simple expedient of calling them lectures. It was better to devise a new imprint, and they suggested it should read 'Printed at Oxford England BY HORACE HART M.A. PRINTER TO THE UNIVERSITY. And sold by the Oxford University Press, American Branch.'

In Oxford the Delegates, under some pressure from the new School of English Literature, had embarked on major editions of the English poets and dramatists, which were to conform to the most exacting standards of scholarship. They might take many years to produce. Meanwhile the famished masses were crying out for literature, and the London publishers were falling over each other in their eagerness to feed them. It would have been singularly unworldly and unbusinesslike had Oxford chosen to stand aside. In 1896 the first six volumes of Oxford Poets had appeared without their full academic dress. They were available in three editions, including a miniature 'suitable for storage in the waistcoat pocket'. Edward Arber had also appeared. A former Admiralty clerk he had entered the academic world through King's College, London, and become Professor of English Literature at Mason College, Birmingham. From this experience he concluded that the study of English was being gravely handicapped by the lack of reliable texts. The Early English Text Society was doing its best to make Middle English literature accessible, and Arber determined to do the same for the later literature. His mission resulted in a plethora of anthologies and new editions. Arber saw himself as a pioneer, both in his aim of making good literature available cheaply to the widest public, and in his method of maintaining the highest scholarly standards. Early in 1899 Frowde announced the 'British Anthologies', which were to consist of 2,500 poems arranged in ten volumes, beginning with 'Dunbar and his times,

1401-1508', and ending with 'Cowper and his times, 1775-1800'. They were to be based on the earliest and most authoritative texts, and Professor Arber's thirty years' experience would ensure their scholarly accuracy. The volumes were called eventually just 'English Songs', and sold at a shilling each. Like many comparable Garlands, Treasuries, Pageants, and Clusters of Gems, his anthologies fell short of the standards Oxford was trying to establish. 'A disastrous performance', wrote Quiller-Couch to Charles Cannan. Public demand was the only justification for these productions, which diminished in number as the unending series of Oxford Standard Authors was able to base itself on more dependable texts.

In 1900 the Clarendon Press published 56 new titles. In 1904 the tally was 100, and in 1909 it reached 223. Cannan used to say, 'I do not think the University can produce enough books to ruin us.' He was often mysterious in his utterances, which were memorable for that reason. This may have been a sardonic comment on the productivity of Oxford scholars or a sanguine reflection on the capacity of the Press to absorb whatever might be put before it at a time when new areas of research were being constantly opened up. It indicates too a broader view of the dichotomous functions of the University Press. The best of Oxford scholarship would always have to be accommodated. In the future that might become a serious challenge, but it could be met if the Press became a truly national, and indeed international, institution. It would publish in every field and at every level, finding the best scholars wherever they might be. And Oxford books must be made to sell all over the world. In this period it became an affront to conscience to think that any part of the British Empire should be deprived of the benefits of British civilization—and that manifestly included Oxford books. As a writer in the *Fortnightly Review* in October 1900 crankily reminded his readers, these islands were but a seventeenth part of the territory under the sway of Her Most Gracious Majesty—a territory that covered one-fifth of the habitable world. He estimated that, at the moment of writing, its population was 387,013,954—potentially a substantial market—and it was one of the burdens of empire that the spiritual as well as the material needs of Her Majesty's subjects should be served. This was far from being the sort of visionary or eccentric babble of which nothing was likely to come. Over the next fifteen years branches were established in Canada (1904), Australia (1908), India (1912), and South Africa (1915) with the primary purpose of selling that notoriously unvendible commodity, the Clarendon Press book. That it was possible to sell any at all was due to some far-sighted departures from precedent by Charles Cannan and his colleagues.

Domestically, the narrower concept of the intellectual sovereignty of the Press was expressed by the theologian and Biblical scholar William Sanday, Lady Margaret Professor of Divinity since 1893 and Delegate since 1896, a man said to be slow in arriving at conclusions though tenacious of them when once reached. He composed during August 1900 a contemplative memorandum on the principles to be followed in the acceptance or rejection of books. In that year Max Müller died, and it was fitting that Sanday should grapple afresh with the dilemma he had never satisfactorily resolved. It seemed to Sanday that in the matter of selection the element of chance was rather greater than it should be, that Delegates were guided individually by different principles, and it was often a matter of accident which of these principles prevailed. The principles themselves, however, were of a fundamental kind. 'I suppose that we should all be agreed that our position is different from that of an ordinary publisher; but it is no doubt an open question for how much the difference should count. And I seem to be conscious that I might be in some cases laying more stress on the elements in our business which distinguish it from that of an ordinary publisher where others might lay more stress on those which the two forms of business have in common.' The conclusion he was gradually approaching was that, in the absence of any centralized body with a responsible Minister at its head and an Academy at his side drawing upon the public funds, it fell to the Press to keep in view 'not only the ordinary conditions of publishing but the *whole policy of the higher education*. I would venture to say that if our country is to hold its own in the competition with other countries, there should be somewhere within it *a real centre of knowledge for every subject of substantial importance. . . .*'

This assumption of responsibility for the national culture becomes less breath-taking when Sanday can be seen to be plodding back to the ancient debate about learning and education, unremunerative and remunerative books. Not only that, he had been moved to these meditations by two particular books which he hoped the other Delegates would agree to publish. One was a translation, galling though it was to have to put up with one, of Noldeke's *Syriac Grammar*, for the apparatus for the study of Syriac was inadequate. The other was a translation with introduction and notes of the Sibylline Oracles. The generalities about 'a centre of knowledge' were justified, he felt, by these two particular cases. The more recondite subjects are just those in which there is most new knowledge and in which there is the greatest likelihood that significant new discoveries may be made. 'The real importance of subjects', wrote Sanday, 'is often almost in inverse ratio to the number of students. The most frequented subjects are usually those in which it is only a question of restating old knowledge.' This was an extreme assertion of a position which has never been left wholly defenceless. Max Müller had been forced to conclude that there should be two publishing departments. Cannan, aware that some sort of split was already occurring, was determined to have it both ways. He would not dismiss the recondite, nor would he fear restating old knowledge. Sanday concluded with words that seem mysteriously to paraphrase Cannan's observations on the University's power to ruin the Press: 'I wish I had more fears that the offers of such books would be beyond our power of coping with them.' Whatever he was trying to say, the Delegates declined to publish either of the books he had on offer.

Henry Frowde, Publisher to the University, 1880–1913

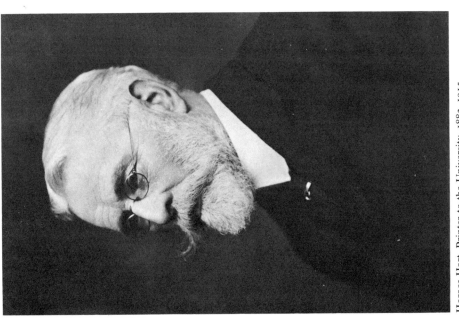

Horace Hart, Printer to the University, 1883–1915

Charles Cannan, Secretary, 1898–1919

Humphrey Milford, Winchester and New College, joined the Press as Assistant Secretary immediately after taking his first in Greats in 1900, at the age of 23. He was a slim, handsome, athletic young man, a tennis player of distinction who competed at Wimbledon. He did not have time to acquire the donnish manner and remained outwardly a man of the world during the years that Cannan was moulding his inner self in the image of his own. Doble continued his conscientious martyrdom, and for the first time the 'office' acquired a genuine collective identity, far exceeding in the initiative it seized anything that Gell had contemplated. As it was now clear that the whole of the world's literature not actually in copyright was available for publication, the opportunities were unlimited: all that mattered was that the right editor should be chosen and that the text published should be up to the Oxford standard.

Milford, however, was destined from the start for London, ultimately to be Frowde's successor. He was to be the man Gell had always been looking for. Frowde himself was not due to retire until 1909, and had indicated that he did not intend to do so even then, but his responsibilities were growing, and being allowed to grow, and by the time Milford's Oxford grooming was complete he was very urgently needed.

The further development of the London business was at the expense of the Bible Press. In 1905 the Delegates instructed Horace Hart to make over to Frowde all the plates for the Oxford Poets. A year later it was decided to transfer to the London publisher financial responsibility for the printing of Bibles and Prayer Books and for maintaining stocks. It was a grievous blow to Hart's self-esteem, and a mortal one to the Bible Press itself. Its function henceforward was merely to execute orders from London; deprived of all the accounting and supervision of stock it was deprived of its *raison d'être*, and in 1906 the Learned Press and the Bible Press were finally merged into one after 228 years. For Frowde, who respected Hart, these transactions were painful and prolonged. He was, however, so accustomed to his eminence by now that he accepted the extra responsibilities as a natural outcome of it, and became even more whiskery, patriarchal, and benign.

Cannan's attitude towards him appears to have changed from amused condescension to affectionate respect. His immense labour on hymn-books, Prayer Books, and Bibles would seem occupation enough for two men. His limitations were, however, as plain to Cannan as they had been to Gell. It was not just that he lacked a first in Greats, he was not even an autodidact, like Longman, Macmillan, or Dent, with a passionate concern for literature and its dissemination. He loved books, but when it came down to it, the glue and threads and dyed cloths that held them together, the discounts and incentives that persuaded booksellers to stock them, the advertisements and reviews that might persuade people to buy them, came between him and the printed word. When he opened a book he looked first at the margins. Plymouth Brethren were in any case suspicious of secular literature. Edmund Gosse in *Father and Son* recalled a preacher who had

K

denounced the Stratford Tercentenary as 'A blasphemous celebration of the birth of Shakespeare, a lost soul now suffering for his sins in hell'. Frowde was broad minded enough to traffic in that lost soul, and nobody complained about his business acumen. Even if not precisely the man that Cannan would have chosen to represent the University of Oxford to the world outside—as Milford precisely was—there is no doubt that in middle age, when little more could have been expected of him, he assumed a new dimension. He saw new horizons and acquired an imperialistic mission. Towards his fellow publishers he adopted a manner of kindly sagacity, but did not feel that it would be proper for him to join their Association.

When he heard of what was intended, Frowde wrote to Sir William Markby, 'as to a personal friend, confidentially and freely', as Markby had invited him to do. After a lengthy and rather awesome preamble, he conceded that nobody could be better fitted than Milford to conduct the business successfully, once he had acquired the necessary experience and grasped the supreme importance of maintaining good relations with the trade. But there were two or three aspects of the matter upon which he proposed to write with great freedom. The first concerned Milford's prospects. 'You have assured me', he wrote, 'that it is the desire of the Delegates that my retirement should not be hastened, so I hardly think it will be wise to let Mr. Milford assume that my post will very soon be vacant. . . . As a matter of fact, I do not wish to retire, and do not suppose I shall have any such wish in 1909.'

His second point went directly to the heart of the matter, and the prose became sonorous. 'The ties which exist between Mr. Cannan and Mr. Milford are very close. Their methods are the same. The two men appear to me to think with one mind and speak with one voice, and, if Mr. Milford is to be located in London, perhaps I had better state what I understand to be my official relations with Mr. Cannan. . . . My relations with the Secretary for the time being were explained to me by the late Dr. Price when I took up the London management more than 31 years ago. He told me that the control of the London business . . . would rest wholly with me, that I should be subject to the Board of Delegates, but only to their Secretary in so far as he represented the Board, and he assured me that I need have no fear under that head, because it was an unalterable condition that the Secretary must reside in Oxford. . . . With regard to the present Secretary it is only on those rare occasions when he is made the channel for conveying the orders of the Delegates to me that I regard myself as subject to him. . . . I consider that if Mr. Milford is to enter my employment and to work cordially and successfully with me it will be necessary for him to sever his official connexion with Mr. Cannan and to transfer his allegiance to me.'

Having already bound Milford to himself in a way that could not be affected by formal oaths of allegiance, Cannan had confidence in the future. He intended in due course to allow him all the freedom of action Frowde was asserting for himself. The changes that the Delegates were inaugurating, Frowde conceded, added considerably to his work, and made the extra help being proffered essential and unavoidable. With Milford's departure in 1906, R. W. Chapman became Assistant Secretary in Oxford.

2. The Oxford Book of English Verse

ONE of the first and more famous deviations from the principle of publishing exclusively works of original scholarship or school-books was *The Oxford Book of English Verse*. The editor, Arthur Quiller-Couch, was not strictly speaking academically respectable at that or indeed at any other time. He had failed to get a first in Greats despite Cannan's tutoring, and in some desperation, with a mother, brother, sister, and intended wife to support, he had plunged into the writing of a historical romance about the Cornish coast, in imitation of Stevenson. The bursar of his college advised him to show the manuscript to Gell, who could be expected to recognize another *Treasure Island* if he saw one. He recommended an approach to Cassells. The book, *Dead Man's Rock*, was a success, and Q produced a dozen novels in as many years. He also became reader for the firm. A prolific journalist too, he was soon able to live comfortably as a freelance writer at The Haven in Fowey, in his ancestral county of Cornwall.

As an old Cliftonian, a Trinity man, and also a regular contributor to the *Oxford Magazine*, which Cannan for a time edited, Q was a man whom Cannan suffered gladly. They had their private jokes, formally mispronounced each other's names (Q was Mr. Cowch), and bowed ceremonially when they met. Their correspondence tended to be unbusinesslike by former Press standards, if not by Macmillans'.

The idea of an anthology of English verse probably originated with York Powell, and it was Cannan who suggested that Q should edit it. (Q later described him as its 'onlie begetter'.) In February 1897 Gell got the impression that something had been going on behind his back. He had received a letter from Q and a carefully drawn up scheme, annotated by York Powell, which indicated that matters were further advanced than he had imagined. He wrote to Cannan complaining about the duplication of correspondence. Cannan replied soothingly. He had really been writing to Q about something else. He had, admittedly, happened to mention that Palgrave's *Golden Treasury* was 'passé', and it was time for a new anthology, but in any case he had spoken to Gell about it first—'nobody can say I ever wrote a letter to anyone if I could induce any one else to write it instead'.

The scheme presented by Q, which had obviously been much discussed, was based on two fundamental principles: that the existence of India paper made possible a far larger collection than had hitherto been attempted in one volume; and that the popularity of *The Golden Treasury* left no opening for another anthology unless it could be given some quite fresh characteristics. 'The two conditions help each other,' Q explained, 'or rather the second compels you to be different from Palgrave, and the first helps you to be different.'

The 1891 edition of Palgrave contained 339 items, and covered only three and a half centuries of English poetry, starting with Wyatt and Surrey. Using India paper it would be easy to include in 'a handy little volume' at least twice as many items and to cover the whole range of English poetry from the beginning to the present day. The economy of bulk would even allow a challenge to Mackay's *Thousand and One Gems* which, in spite of double columns and an awkward shape, sold well. India paper once again appeared to make all things possible.

Q chose to confine himself for the most part to lyrical poetry, 'the whole province of the British Lyre'. He then went into details about the size and shape and type and the poets neglected by Palgrave to whom justice would have to be done. He concluded that, as the Press would probably wish the book to make its way into schools, licentious verse had better be rigidly excluded. 'Luckily English poets have done it so badly, almost without an exception, that the editor will find this easy.' York Powell agreed in principle, though he thought Dryden should be excepted. 'But don't let it be childish,' he scribbled; 'keep the adult in view, the nun or less intelligent person not too much.'

There were many anthologies in existence but *The Golden Treasury* was regarded as the only serious rival. It would clearly not be too difficult to improve upon it; that in itself, however, would not necessarily cause a change of heart in a faithful public. Cannan regarded it as a dated piece of frippery, the outcome somehow of the Great Exhibition of 1851, although it was not published until 1861. Ever since it had been under fire from the critics. The first edition was notable for some striking omissions. Blake, Donne, Swift, Chatterton, and Emily Brontë failed to find a place: Coleridge just scraped through with one poem and a severe reprimand from the editor for 'serious imperfections in clearness, unity and truth'. Later editions compromised and the idiosyncrasies became less blatant but it remained a curiously unbalanced selection.

'Lyra Britannica' would allow the editor enough space to be generous even to those poems or poets he disliked. Cannan's maxim, impressed at some time or other on the editor of every 'Oxford Book', was that anthologies must include anthology pieces, old favourites the public would expect to find there. The temptation to omit a poem on the grounds that it was already hackneyed was strong in editors who felt that the Oxford imprint was licence to explore new ground. Q, however, was sensitive to popular taste. In his first list he was prepared to admit Burns's 'A man's a man for a' that', which he detested, because 'no Scotsman will do without it'. York Powell, however, struck it out as 'poor stuff'. He also deleted Blanco White's 'Sonnet to Night', calling it 'overrated', a notable understatement.

Coleridge had described it as the finest and most grandly conceived sonnet in the language, and Leigh Hunt raved that 'it stands supreme perhaps above all in any language, nor can we ponder it too deeply or with too hopeful a reverence'. Q acquiesced but did not forget; he slipped it into the second edition in 1939.

The plans were carefully worked out and estimates had been prepared for a volume of some 850 pages before the proposal was presented to the Delegates. This in itself was unusual. The Delegates were accustomed to having the initiative, or at least the opportunity to debate an idea virtually from its inception. Cannan told Gell that he thought it would go through without trouble, but that Gell would have to negotiate terms with Q that were satisfactory to the Delegates. He was evidently a little uneasy about this, fearing that Q, as a professional writer, might ask too much. 'Though I think it should be a Delegates book if possible,' he wrote, 'I shouldn't mind it's going to F. [Frowde] if that proved to work better. But *Q* believes (strange to say) in the C.P. and that's worth something to us in the negotiations.' In March 1897 the Delegates resolved to proceed with the work 'as likely to be remunerative', and in April they approved the terms negotiated by Gell—£100 advance, 3*d*. per copy on all copies sold until expenses had been covered, rising to 6*d*., with 3*d*. on copies sold for export. This was an ingenious arrangement which Q subsequently regretted.

Q continued to write novels and articles, plays as well, but by March 1900 his selection was nearing completion, specimens had been produced by the printer, and publication in time for Christmas was contemplated. 'I'm going a mucker on Landor', he told Cannan. 'It may be a symptom of middle age, but he seems to me the deuce of a chap.'

There were still many details to be settled, however. Q found himself hindered by York Powell's insistence on the original spelling in the earlier poems. The attempt to understand Skeat's theory of Middle English spelling made him bilious, and by July he was prepared for publication to be held over until 1901 while he painfully pursued the original spelling in every instance. 'To my bewildered mind', he wrote, 'this craze for antique unsystematised and almost haphazard spelling is the bloodiest [carefully deleted, presumably in the office] nonsense. The same fellow will spell the same word differently in two consecutive stanzas ... meaning no harm, just careless: and why we should perpetuate his casual errors is more than I can get explained. However let us strive to be perfect; even though we achieve silliness on the way.' Somebody did explain to him and a compromise was reached which he explains in the preface. 'In the very earliest poems inflection and spelling are structural, and to modernize is to destroy', he writes confidently. But he would modernize as soon as modernity permitted: 'this seemed wiser than to discourage many readers for the sake of diverting others by a scent of antiquity which ... should breathe of something rarer than an odd arrangement of type.'

Q became stubborn and opinionated with age, but in preparing his first anthology he showed great patience and a measure of docility in dealing with York Powell, who was constantly holding up progress, if only by failing to answer letters. When he did intervene, Q went to considerable pains to oblige, and he scarcely dared to make a move without his approval. He was prepared to accept from him 'in its proper birthday place' a late contribution, 'Fra bank to bank', if somebody would find out the date of Alex. Bryde, 'or whatever his name is outside of Y.P.'s handwriting'. Mark Alexander Boyd's *Sonet* was duly included. In August Q was correcting proofs and supplying new copy at the same time, and writing rather desperately to anybody who might be left in the office to ask '1) when is Mr. Cannan expected home and 2) where Prof. York Powell is wandering?' The latter had disappeared with Q's numbered list of poems and Q had lost count. He thought that Crabbe began about 500 but could only guess.

Another problem that was not resolved until the last minute was that of the title. 'Lyra Britannica' having fallen out of favour, Q suggested 'The Oxford Anthology', 'The Oxford Book of English Verse', 'The Golden Book of English Verse', and 'The Pageant of English Poetry', with a preference for the second. But by September he had reverted to 'Lyra Britannica', having come to understand that 'The Oxford Book of English Verse' would not do because it would be popularly shortened to 'The Oxford Book'—'which is—alike in the advertisements of the C.P. and on the shield of the University—the Bible'. He was suddenly full of doubts. Would 'Lyra Britannica' fairly cover the Irishmen? Garland, Caskets, Pageants, Garners, Choirs, Museum, Gallery, he babbled to Cannan—'Orchestrion Oxoniense', British Bards on India Paper, The Greater Anthology, The Muse's Garden, the Oxford Album, Pierides, Lyra Laureata, Lyra Aurea... The man was at his wit's end. Surprised by the objection to 'The Oxford Book' but apparently almost persuaded by it, Cannan consulted Frowde, who informed him not very helpfully that a 'Lyra Britannica' had been in Longmans' Catalogue in 1868. He added that he kept in stock in leather bindings 'Lyra Anglicana', 'Lyra Consolatioris', 'Lyra Apostolica', and 'Lyra Innocentium'. As an afterthought he said that he could not 'conceive how "Oxford Book of English Verse" could be objected to because of the Bible. Was it because portions of the Bible are translated from Hebrew Poetry or because the text is broken up into "verse"?' His bewilderment solved the problem. It was 20 September 1900.

Early in October Q sent York Powell manuscript copy as far as Meredith, and there were about ninety poems still to come. He was well ahead of the printer, so he thought, but being driven frantic in his quest for permissions from copyright holders. Doble was helping as best he could, York Powell and Cannan were using their influence wherever possible. 'If you are going grey over copyrights,' wrote Q to Cannan, 'I am going daft. Swinburne, Yeats, and some others simply neglect to answer letters. Our only way is to go on and print whatever is permitted.... Set aside all that is doubtful, say for 2 days and print at end if by vigorous work at the telegraph I can extract permissions hitherto delayed. . . . I wrote to Swinburne and Yeats, for instance, weeks ago: and the trouble generally has been dire.'

The telegrams began to have their effect. Swinburne, Yeats, A. E., and Gosse granted permission. But 'look here', wrote Q, 'I don't want Jean Ingelow's *High Tide* omitted on any excuse whatever. I don't see why I should pay for it—as it is, you'll have to sell 100,000 before you repay me for grey hairs and shortened life: but I will raise a subscription rather than lose it. It's Ha'porths of Tar, Sir, after I've made you an anthology the like of which is not.' The poem never got in. With Frowde reminding them that the season was already so far advanced that every day was vital, with the printer further ahead than Q thought ('For Heaven's sake drive them', he had begged Cannan) and bombarding him with proofs due for almost immediate return, nerves were beginning to fray. But at least a lesson was being learned: it is wiser to apply for permissions at a much earlier stage.

The next trouble was the binding. Frowde wrote, 'I am afraid Mr. Couch cannot have Oxford blue for his Anthology.' He had never succeeded in getting the cloth makers to produce it, and blue was his most troublesome colour. 'Please . . . send me a sample of the true Oxford blue of the present time,' he asked Cannan, 'for I am told it is getting darker.' Q, in the midst of his other worries, was not a little outraged. The best samples available did not please him. 'True Oxford blue is a rich blue-*purple*, not afraid of its colour and not dingy at all', he explained. The samples were prophetic of what things might come to if the Clarendon Press did not correct the trend. He advised sending a boy out to hunt for a bit of genuine old Oxford ribbon.

The worst alarm of all was occasioned by Frowde when he received unbound dummy copies on ordinary paper and discovered just what sort of a monstrosity Cannan was allowing to emerge. There were 1,168 pages and he doubted whether it would be possible to bind the book. He proposed to treat one of the dummies by keeping it under a press for at least twelve hours in the hope of being able to 'smash' the paper into shape. But he was not optimistic. On receiving this news on 9 October Cannan in some dismay stopped production and concluded that drastic cuts would have to be made. He had in fact foreseen this problem at the start. In his first letter to Gell about the project he had asked whether there was any 'dodge' whereby they could have a great deal of poetry in a small space on India paper, and a manageable cheap book for possible adoption in schools which would have to be on ordinary paper. Gell's answer had been that it would have to be divided up for schools, but Cannan had never accepted this. He now sent a telegram to Q informing him of the dilemma. Q replied at once that he was prepared to come to Oxford by the night mail if necessary, or to telephone at stated times. He supplied a list of poems that could be omitted. Cannan was still contemplating the gruesome task of amputation when, late the next day, he received a telegram from Frowde which read, 'I have satisfied myself that the smashing of Couch will not seriously injure the paper, and the proportions of the volume of 1168 pages will be fairly good. I do not therefore recommend you to injure the book by cutting out good matter.'

The book was published towards the end of October, a mere 1,000 copies having been printed on India paper, and 2,000 on 'dry'. The price of the former was 10s. 6d. and of the latter 7s. 6d., and Q observed that his threepenny bits were beginning to look very small. By the beginning of December Frowde had disposed of 653 copies of the India paper and 1,407 of the dry, but most of these he assumed to be still on the booksellers' shelves. Q denounced the British public as an ass, which could not be made to believe that a small volume was worth money for being small. He suggested that if Frowde were depressed over sales he should try binding the India paper edition in cheap leather: 'the difference between leather and cloth is the sort of obvious thing to impress their silly minds.' Frowde followed his advice and within a few days produced half a dozen varieties of binding, for the more expensive of which he charged 15s., making Q's threepenny bits look even smaller. The book began to move, and before Christmas another 2,000 copies of the India paper edition had been printed.

The original object of the enterprise appears to have been forgotten in Oxford by the time of publication. If it had not been for India paper the book would never have been made, but Frowde was instructed to send out for review dry copies only. 'What we want', Doble told him, ignoring one of Gell's old maxims that it was important to be of the same mind when publishing a book as when initiating it three or four years earlier, 'is that the literary points should be criticized first and that the manufacturing points of view should be considered afterwards.' Frowde obeyed with extreme reluctance. It was a splendid opportunity lost for, as he pointed out, a book can only be published once. With his own publications it was his practice to send out a copy on each type of paper to the best newspapers by way of contrast, and to make the ordinary edition serve for the inferior journals. He took advantage of his special bindings to try belatedly to attract attention to the special advantages of India paper. He carried some specimens round to the Foreign Office and showed them to Lord Salisbury, Chancellor of the University. 'He was greatly interested', he reported to Cannan, 'and expressed much gratification at having been allowed to see them. He spent half an hour in examining them and asked various questions about our India paper etc. He was not sure whether or no he was nominally a Delegate of the Press, and I could not enlighten him, so he was forced to content himself with his inferior title of Chancellor.'

The Oxford Book of English Verse went through twenty-one impressions and had sold over half a million copies by the time a second edition appeared in 1939, when Q was 'at a loss what to do with a fashion of morose disparagement'. It continued to sell even after the publication of *The New Oxford Book of English Verse* in 1972. Q produced *The Oxford Book of Ballads*, which Cannan had proposed to the Delegates in 1897 but with York Powell as editor, and in 1912 *The Oxford Book of Victorian Verse*. By 1914 there were Oxford Books of French, Italian, German, Latin, and Spanish Verse, and also one of Canadian verse published by the Canada Branch.

3. Fell Types and Facsimile Reprints

THE Fell types had been much neglected by the Press, and the old punches and material lay unused in a cellar in their old oak boxes. They had been brought out once in 1867 by Henry Latham to produce the Clarendon Press Series edition of Catullus in Fell Small Pica, but Latham appears to have been thriftily using what was available. Their aesthetic qualities were scarcely appreciated until the gifted amateur, the Revd. C. H. O. Daniel, Provost of Worcester College, began using them on his private hand press in the 1870s. He printed very small editions of obscure literary texts to give to his friends. In 1883 he began printing Robert Bridges's poems, and this led to more Fell types being bought from the Press, and a modest revival of interest in them. Bridges designed the Yattendon Hymnal, which he edited with his friend F. E. Woodridge during the 1890s. He chose Peter de Walpergen's music type, which had been cut for Dean Aldrich some two centuries before and never used. This splendid production greatly impressed both churchmen and bibliophiles. It was completed as *The Yattendon Hymnal* in 1899, printed and also sold by Horace Hart. The following year Hart himself printed 150 copies of his *Notes on A Century of Typography at the University Press Oxford 1693-1794*, in which he reproduced the specimens of Fell types issued between 1670 and 1686. There was then already an occasional demand for them by London publishers. Hart had busied himself on this work for many years, both putting in order the ancient punches and matrices belonging to the Press, and gathering new information concerning its early history. He had produced much more than a 'manager's record—a compilation necessary for the proper administration of the University Press', as he put it. The first five copies for presentation—none were for sale—went to Cannan, York Powell, the Revd. C. H. O. Daniel, Falconer Madan, and C. E. Doble. But it was another two years before the refurbished Fell type was used in a major University publication, in *The Order of Service for the Coronation* of 1902.

It was not in the nature of Cannan and his colleagues to neglect an asset, but the old types could not be so easily exploited as India paper, valuable though they appeared to be. For ceremonial purposes, or for occasional printing, they were admirable, but as Harry Carter has put it, 'There is a gulf between antiquarian interest in a typeface and willingness to read a book in it.' Photographic or type-facsimiles were, however, not uncommon. The First Folio of Shakespeare was reproduced in facsimile four times in the nineteenth century, first in type in 1806 and by photolithography in 1866. The Oxford collotype facsimile of 1902 at 5 guineas or 6 guineas was sold out in advance of publication and added substantially to the year's profits. The first four copies were presented to the King, the German Emperor, the President of the United States, and the Duke of Devonshire who had lent his copy of the Folio.

To many English textual scholars facsimiles came to be seen as their essential working tools. It was argued that, ideally, the whole corpus of printed English literature up to at least 1800 ought to be available in this form. If the best editions were used the 'final' text, which proved so elusive to the classical scholars, would have been established, and the commentaries which followed would simply embody the current state of knowledge. But the English classics were still tumbling from the presses in a disorderly and headlong fashion, not at all to Cannan's fastidious classical taste. It was Quiller-Couch who saw how to imbue them with a dignity that would persuade Cannan to regard them as one of the more solemn responsibilities of the Press. 'I want the prospect of my middle age to be cheered', he wrote, 'by a long vista of authoritative English Classical Texts, and am sure they would bring the Press as much honour and profit as the Greek and Latin texts you are now issuing.' This was written in December 1903. At the next meeting of Delegates in January 1904 Cannan put forward, as emanating from 'the office', a proposal for a series of Tudor and Stuart reprints. The matter was deferred. At the next meeting he tried again, and the Delegates resolved, in the nearest approach to levity to be recorded in their minutes, 'to give favourable, but not too favourable, consideration to any suggestion made by the Secretary'.

Cannan thereupon began to plan carefully, to draw up lists, to print elaborate instructions for editors, and to consult with Horace Hart. It had occurred to him that this was the opportunity to make use of the Fell types. Among the first titles to appear on his lists were Meres's *Palladis Tamia* (1598), Pepys's *Memoires of the Royal Navy* (1690), Evelyn's *Sculptura* (1662), Turbervile's *Noble Art of Venery or Hunting* (1576), and Faithorne's *Art of Graving and Etching* (1662). The more he thought about it the more esoteric the titles became: Peacham's *The Compleat Gentleman*, Fortescue's *Forest of Histories* (1571), Pettie's *Petite Pallace of Pettie his Pleasure* (1576), and Howell's *Devises*. The general reader was being put ruthlessly in his place. Milford himself remained sceptical, already envisaging the day after his move to London when he would be called upon to sell the books.

The aim of the series was to reproduce all the essential qualities of sixteenth- and seventeenth-century printing. 'But a reprint is not necessarily a facsimile,' Cannan conceded in his prospectus, 'and it is thought that to reproduce mere eccentricities or actual defects would be pedantic and tiresome, especially as the form of the books does not admit of critical footnotes.' Obvious misprints would be corrected, but for the rest the original text was to be reproduced exactly. The old spelling was to be retained, even to the point of keeping different spellings of the same word on the same page.

Q had been so thoroughly converted by York Powell from his earlier view that retaining the original spelling was 'the bloodiest nonsense' that he more than once felt the need to preach to Cannan on the subject. There was nothing arbitrary about the old spelling, he now insisted: 'There was an educated spelling of each period and print the texts in that. By doing this we should be performing what an English Academy ought to have undertaken years ago.' With uncharacteristic docility Cannan accepted his view, and the tricks and contrivances of the early compositors were faithfully reproduced. These were to be reprints, not editions, and the distinction was to be clearly maintained. Anything in the nature of a commentary would break down the barrier separating the two, and so textual criticism was rigorously eschewed. A brief introduction only was allowed.

The titles for the Tudor and Stuart Library were not put forward as likely to be unremunerative, a classification still applied though with increasing irregularity. Despite the Delegates' misgivings, Cannan appears to have been persuaded by Q that the series, which could be continued indefinitely, would bring fame and distinction: it would be a thing 'no gentleman's library should be without'. No heed was given to the competition. W. H. Henley was editing a Tudor series for Benn, and the 'Mermaid Dramatists' edited by Havelock Ellis had been in existence for over a decade. The Oxford series would be unique because of the rarity of some of the texts it would be resurrecting, and because the Fell types enabled the Press to reproduce the old books in the old style. To do justice to them the Wolvercote Mill made a paper from pure linen rag which gave them a brilliance that had long since faded from the old editions, if they had ever possessed it.

Cannan also gave much thought to a suitable binding. Some calf supplied by Frowde pleased him by its appearance but not by its smell. Having kept it for some time in the hope that it would go away he had to report that it still smelt of old boots and would not do. He wanted something cheap, but not cloth, which would be anachronistic—something florid with a good deal of gilt, and perhaps roses. 'Tell the designer to think of the Field of the Cloth of Gold', he asked Frowde, 'or tapestries at Audley End, or something.' He had finally to settle for an imitation Tudor binding in exceptionally tough paper which nobody knew what to call: in the General Catalogue of 1916 it was noted that it had been more than once described by reviewers as leather.

It was expected to sell these necessarily expensive volumes to students, as well as to bibliophiles. If the production of the books afforded Hart some consolation after the injuries done to his pride by the transfer of responsibilities to London, the appearance of the first four titles in time for Christmas 1906 filled Milford with gloom. His understanding with Cannan was such that he felt free to tell him what he thought, and what the reaction of the public was likely to be. For Pepys's *Memoires of the Royal Navy* he foresaw 'disgust of the scabrous that it is not more Diary'. Evelyn's *Sculptura*: 'or The History, and Art of Chalcography and Engraving in Copper' would induce 'dumb despair . . . at the reappearance of this dead dog with a new tail'. Sir Henry Knyvett's *Defence of the Realme* (1596), published for the first time, would be greeted with horror for it recommended universal military service, and as for Howell's 'Devises' it would come as a disappointment even to those familiar with his other works: nobody could claim that he had been more than 'a tolerable minor poet'. So

Milford was able to report quite cheerfully on sales some months later. They had not been quite so bad as feared—and Howell especially had surpassed all expectations and beat Evelyn by one. The scores were Knyvett 132, Pepys 125, Howell 77, Evelyn 76.

These four books had been accepted as experimental by the Delegates, and it might be thought that the experiment had failed. Nevertheless titles continued to be added to the series, and it was reactivated again in the inter-war years. R. W. Chapman was convinced that it would eventually be recognized 'as the really swagger gift-book series'. There is a stubborn almost imperishable belief among book lovers that attractive, out-of-the-way books must sell eventually, that the rarity and obscurity of a work that excites the bibliophile will also entice the public at large to buy it. The series moreover was so respectfully received, and met so much with the approval of the new breed of bibliographers, that it became a duty to scholarship to continue it. There could have been no higher praise than that received by Hart from Bruce Rogers, the great designer and typographer. Writing from America in 1909, he described the series as 'about the perfection of modern book making'. The different volumes, in all their variety, 'so successfully avoid all pretence or mannerism that they attain the very acme of style'. Rogers went on, 'It is no exaggeration to say that I'd rather have that series to my credit than the accomplishments of any of the private presses of recent years.'

4. Sir Walter Raleigh and the Oxford English School

THE death of York Powell in 1904 left a vacancy among the Delegates that no one man could be expected to fill. He was replaced by the Dean of Christ Church, Thomas B. Strong, a theologian with a taste for music. The Delegacy in consequence consisted of classicists, theologians, and lawyers, with a Professor of Mineralogy, Sir Henry Miers who became Principal of London University, and a mathematician with wide interests, Henry Gerrans. Markby and Bywater were the only survivors from the days of Bartholomew Price. York Powell had doubled as historian and literary adviser, and the Delegacy was now conspicuously weak in both these fields. In 1905 it was decided to invite Walter Raleigh, the recently appointed Professor of English Literature, to act as literary adviser for a fee of £100 a year for three years.

Raleigh accepted with alacrity. 'I am deeply gratified,' he wrote to Cannan, 'and I will not refuse, though I do wish that I could think that they have shown themselves to be good men of business in this affair. If I could find a gold-mine for them, I would. As it is, I fear that my chief function is to suggest to them, at their own charges, further works of unremunerative benevolence. I shall not be at ease until I have introduced them to some enterprise that is both virtuous and profitable.'

Raleigh was indeed a mixed blessing. He was not made a Delegate—not until shortly before his death in 1921—and was certainly no business man. When his appointment as adviser was renewed in 1908 he wrote, 'I propose to continue the practice of afternoon calling. I don't want to be a Delegate, if I may stay in the engine-room.' Raleigh, perhaps because of his illustrious namesake, had a taste for nautical metaphors. Although he regarded Cannan as captain of the ship, he described him too as 'always working hard in the engine-room. When there were arrivals, and celebrations and votes of thanks . . . he would just put his head up for a moment in the companion way to see that things were going well and then would vanish below. Many people never knew he was there.'

Raleigh was highly popular with everybody at the Press, where the regular visits were enjoyed by Cannan, Milford, Doble, and Chapman as a welcome relief from routine work. Only after his move to London did Milford begin to worry about what unsaleable item Raleigh might come up with next, but over the next twenty years he contributed as much to the London business as to the Clarendon Press. Of the many critical editions of the English classics he initiated the majority appeared in the 'Oxford Poets' series or the 'Oxford Miscellany' or the 'Oxford Library of Prose and Verse', which catered for the 'incurious lovers' of literature, under the Frowde imprint.

Raleigh had held three university chairs before coming to Oxford. The first had been at Aligarh, where he was able to observe the depressing effects of an alien literature and an inflexible curriculum upon students struggling to acquire some mechanical aptitude for passing examinations. Ten years in Liverpool and four years in Glasgow did little to change his mind about the general fatuity of the examination system, which in the provinces had given English literature the reputation of being a crammer school. In Oxford the English School had got off to a sickly start. There were still many who held that English literature could not be taught, that it was a 'soft option' despite the efforts of the philologists, and the fact that in 1904 the candidates consisted of fifteen women and only five men told its own story. There was an appalling shortage of teachers. Ernest de Selincourt was indefatigable, and at times appeared to be carrying the teaching burden almost alone. With the help of Napier, the Merton Professor of English Language and Literature, Joseph Wright of the Dialect Dictionary, C. H. Firth the Regius Professor of Modern History, and the Clarendon Press, Raleigh proceeded gradually to transform it into one of the most popular schools in the University.

Raleigh has been unkindly described by John Gross in *The Rise and Fall of the Man of Letters* as a frustrated writer, with a grudge against literature. It is true that after coming to Oxford he wrote little and his projected major work on Chaucer was never finished—a familiar enough tale. He was still working on his book on Shakespeare for Macmillan and there are many heartfelt references to 'weary Willie' in his early correspondence with the Press. He showed generally a robust promiscuity of taste. 'I know good literature,' he once wrote. 'I haven't been in the kitchen, I daresay, but I have flattened my nose for days against the window, and I have smelt it.' An inveterate habit of referring to Shakespeare, Blake, or Wordsworth as 'Bill' has caused him to be condemned as a middle brow. So perhaps he was, but a middle brow was what was needed by the Press at the time. Moreover, when literary criticism was reaching a degree of acrimony not known since the beginning of the nineteenth century, he was extraordinarily benevolent in judgement, reluctant to say in public—though not in private—a harsh word about anybody. Systems and institutions he detested, but whoever laboured at all adequately in the field of English studies could depend upon his encouragement. This was important, for many English scholars found their own colleagues highly incompatible, and it was no time for the infant English School or for the Oxford Press to appear to be taking sides.

The great advantage of Raleigh from Cannan's point of view was not only that he appeared to command confidence amongst scholars of different persuasions but that he had behind him the wide experience of teaching in the provinces, where the study of English was further advanced than in Oxford. There the debate would continue about how the teaching of the Classics could be reconciled with the introduction of English literature, which traditionally a student was supposed to pick up for himself—as indeed he frequently did—and how English could be converted into an academic discipline that would both train the mind and promote the advancement of knowledge at the highest level. In Cambridge the same debate had been postponed. In the provinces English literature had long been accepted as an alternative to the Classics, as a humanizing influence to counter the deadening trends of contemporary life. The industrial revolution was seen as a threat to the continuity of English culture, which could be avoided by instruction in all that was noblest and most beautiful and sublime in the country's heritage. Lofty thoughts could brace the soul against the soot and tedium of daily life. Matthew Arnold imagined literature as an alternative to religion. Long ago, the Revd. Vicesimus Knox had written of the benefits of polite literature to the mercantile classes: 'nothing perhaps contributes more to liberalize their minds, and prevent that narrowness which is too often the consequence of a life attached, from the earliest age, to the pursuits of lucre.' Though in practice the courses and stereotyped exams designed to promote this ideal frequently impeded its realization, the importance attached to good literature, which had not always been regarded as polite or respectable, had widespread consequences in creating a reading public.

In academic Oxford the idea that English literature could be improving in this sense was for a time almost tantamount to a charge of illiteracy. To Charles Cannan too it must have seemed a little strange, for not only had he himself 'done' English literature at an early age but he knew in a secret corner of his mind that all the achievements of English literature paled into insignificance when compared with those of the Master, Aristotle. Raleigh was of great value therefore because he could apply with assurance the common touch. Some of the books that resulted were trifles by old Clarendon Press standards, mere belles-lettres. But the view gained ground that an unedited author was a rebuke, and a reminder that an editor should be sought forthwith. One of the first of the countless notes and jottings that accumulated into mountainous files during R. W. Chapman's thirty-six years at the Press read simply: 'We ought to be plugging away at cheap texts.' It was addressed to Raleigh, who was doing just that.

It was in its way an exhilarating experience for the Press to open its doors to men from what must have seemed all walks of life—obscure lecturers in provincial universities, teachers of belles-lettres, reviewers and journalists, even common or garden novelists. Anybody could join in. Doble was editing the plays of Goldsmith, Stow's *Survey of London*, Swift's *Journal to Stella*; Milford edited Cowper and later Clough; Chapman is probably best known as the editor of Jane Austen, Boswell, and Johnson.

The major editions of the English authors rumbled slowly on: F. S. Boas's *Kyd* (1901); Warwick Bond's *Lyly* (1902); Hutchinson's *Shelley* (1904); Buxton Forman's *Keats* (1906); George Saintsbury's *Minor Poets of the Caroline Period* in three volumes (1905-16); and Grierson's *Donne* (1912), brought to the Press by Raleigh. He himself contributed *The Complete Works of George Savile* in 1912, but his strength did not lie in textual scholarship. The Oxford English Texts grew out of two earlier series, the Spenser and the Marlowe series, and originally included the Tudor and Stuart Library. The dramatists appeared in a uniform edition, but the elaborate and inscrutable design of the first General Catalogue of 1916 based on Aristotelian principles caused them to be separated from the 'Oxford English Texts' proper.

The success of the Oxford Classical Texts had bred confidence and a sense of authority: the application of comparable standards to English authors was probably the most important contribution to scholarship made by the Press during these years. 'The laborious co-operation of editors, printers, and publishers, with much assistance kindly given by scholars resident in Oxford and elsewhere'—to use the words of innumerable prospectuses—would bring to the Oxford English Texts the same distinction and prestige. To establish a proper approach to the editing of these texts was no easy matter, however. Old techniques for the editing of manuscripts had to be adapted to the editing of early printed books: new techniques had to be learned. Haste usually led to disaster, but there was another peril. The more able the editor, paradoxically, the more difficult and immense his task might become. An editor of genius could discern problems that might take years to resolve. The great Oxford edition of Ben Jonson by Professor C. H. Herford and Percy Simpson was accepted in 1903, in the expectation that copy would be ready for the printer in 1905. It crept on at a snail's pace for nearly fifty years.

Simpson, a schoolmaster in London when the project began, was brought to Oxford by Raleigh and Cannan, who felt that his gifts could be put to better advantage under their personal guidance. He supplemented a meagre income from the Press by lecturing. He also published an influential little book, *Shakespeare's Punctuation*, and in 1913 started a class for graduate students on the 'new' bibliography and the principles of textual criticism. From the point of view of the English School it had been a wise move, but like the earlier importations of Murray, Bradley, and Craigie—the men who represented 'English' in Oxford before the emergence of the School—it did not bring immediate results. Indeed, apart from the Dictionary, no other Oxford book was quite so long in preparation.

In 1923 Chapman, perhaps a little tipsy at the prospect of progress, sent a statement he thought might be used by the *Times Literary Supplement*: 'It is announced that the printing of the long-expected edition of Ben Jonson by Professor Herford and Mr. Percy Simpson has at last begun. The editors, whose researches have spread, extensively over a quarter of a century and all known copies and manuscripts in all libraries, intensively into un-penetrated and all but impenetrable recesses of learning, have at least completed their prolegomena, and as it is well known that the best scholars write their prefaces only when their work is done, it is permissible to hope that the future course of the work will be through smooth waters.' The Prolegomena was published in two volumes in 1925, and the years passed. In 1931 Herford died. Simpson was old and far from the end, but in a totally unexpected act of defiant gallantry he married a woman twenty years younger than himself, and gained thereby a new lease of life. Evelyn Simpson, a distinguished scholar and an authority on Donne's prose works, became junior editor in 1937. The last three volumes of the text and two volumes of commentary could never have been published had she not first devised ways of hurrying Simpson along and finally taken charge of his massive accumulation of material herself. The work was completed with the publication of the eleventh volume in 1951.

Raleigh looked for quicker results and generally obtained them. He did not ask too much from his editors—a text of sorts, a preface, a few matter-of-fact notes. He was still trying generally, in the tradition of Jowett, to avoid what could be called 'editions', preferring exact reprints from existing texts. He was saddened when the abandonment of the Fell types for the Tudor and Stuart Library meant discarding the long S, for it made it 'impossible for the Press to produce a reprint of any monument of English literature without (all unconsciously) producing an edition'.

Raleigh sought out the most distinguished authors of the day, not to persuade them to write books, or even to edit them. In his letters the imagery of gaffs and hooks appears, and what indeed he was looking for was a 'catch'. The quest for a famous name to adorn a title-page, and more or less incidentally to write a preface, became a habit that endured for many years after Raleigh had departed. One of his first bids was simply for the right to reissue Swinburne's essay on Blake, temporarily out of print. The Oxford English Text edition by John Sampson had recently appeared, and also *The Lyrical Poems* with an introduction by Raleigh in the Oxford Library of Prose and Poetry. In 1905 he addressed Swinburne on behalf of the Delegates, though without their authorization, in his most fulsome style: 'It would be a pride and pleasure to them if by their means the noblest monument ever raised to the genius of Blake might be brought within the reach of the growing number of his readers and lovers.' Swinburne replied courteously but he was committed to Chatto. Another author who got away was 'Jo' Conrad, from whom Raleigh had tried to get a preface to *Typee*. But he had high hopes of 'the best living English prose-writer', W. H. Hudson. 'Nobody reads him and he is poor,' Raleigh told Cannan; 'his reputation will come, but it hasn't come yet,—a rare and wonderful chance.' No response came from W. H. Hudson. It is doubtful whether the Press ever discovered his address. The first letter conveying Raleigh's enormous admiration for his work was returned by a bemused American lecturer of the same name.

Thomas Hardy was obviously the man to edit William Barnes, the Dorsetshire dialect poet who campaigned relentlessly for the anglicization of English. Hardy agreed, but for a long time nothing happened. Eventually Raleigh met him at a weekend at Lord Curzon's, and was able to persuade him to write the preface and prepare his glossarial notes. What Hardy was doing there is not clear from Raleigh's report to Cannan: he was evidently not being a social success, but Raleigh was delighted. 'I rejoice in T. Hardy, and am glad I didn't hustle him. When I met him at Curzon's I merely told him that Barnes would have to go unprefaced. The people at Curzon's complained that Hardy didn't talk worth a cent. He told me that one has to be very careful about talking, for people get your ideas if you talk, and bring them out over their own signatures. So he sat under a tree and corrected proofs.' Raleigh, a loquacious man, was much impressed by Hardy's resolution: it occurred to him that he himself would write more if he could learn to keep quiet. The edition of Barnes was published in 1908. Amongst his other recruits from outside the academic world were Mark Rutherford, who edited a selection from Johnson's *Rambler*; Arthur Symons with *Select Poems of John Clare*; and E. V. Lucas who did *The Hambledon Men*: 'John Nyren's Young Cricketer's Tutor', for the Oxford Library of Prose and Poetry.

This 'Library' was the most curious and incoherent of series. It began in Oxford but Milford took it with him among his personal belongings when he moved to London. It included *Echoes from the Oxford Magazine, More Echoes from the Oxford Magazine*, three volumes of Japanese classics, and a clutch of Walter Raleigh's favourites—or 'leaden pigs', as Milford sometimes called them—including *The Heroine, or Adventures of a Fair Romance Reader* by E. S. Barrett, first published in 1813, and Cobbett's *Grammar of the English Language* of 1817. Milford looked dismally upon the Tudor and Stuart Library, but he also included type-facsimiles of nineteenth- and eighteenth-century poets, despite Frowde's warning of public apathy. *Poems by Keats, 1820, Poems by Shelley, 1820, Browning's Men and Women, 1855*, were three of the 'nine particular stars' in the series, reproduced 'so that the reader may have before him what the

L

contemporaries of the poet saw on the pages fresh from the Press'. Raleigh never claimed to be a business man. Cannan, Milford, and Chapman in certain contexts modestly did, but once they had decided on a text to be reprinted they became strangely obdurate, not amenable to commercial reasoning. Oxford breeding prevailed: if the public did not want the books that was the public's loss. Frowde did all he could to dissuade both Cannan and Milford from going ahead with a type-facsimile of the 'Kilmarnock Burns, 1786'. After consulting the principal Scottish and London book-sellers he was quite sure that there was no need for it. 'It is difficult these days to find subscribers for any kind of facsimile,' he wrote; they appealed 'neither to the Scholar nor to the Man in the Street'. Moreover an excellent facsimile of the 'Kilmarnock Burns' already existed. If it had to be done, he concluded sadly, no more than 250 copies should be printed. But no attention was paid to him.

Milford was quite Raleigh's match when it came to dredging up the neglected and abandoned books of the early nineteenth century. Bad taste can be cultivated as a mark of intellectual distinction so long as it is confined to the obscure writers of an earlier age. Few people can have been reading the 'pretty songs' of Barry Cornwall (B. W. Procter) in 1907, but Milford was and he pronounced them not nearly as bad as was commonly made out. 'I think a surprisingly good book ought to be made out of these second and third rate early Victorians,' he wrote to Cannan, and suggested that a 'retained' researcher should be put to work. Writers to be considered might be Frederick Tennyson, Tennyson-Turner, Beddoes, M. Howitt, Mrs. Norton, 'and other even more obscure persons'. Lyttelton Gell would still from time to time take luncheon with Frowde at Amen Corner. As he glanced at the lists of recent publications he reflected that something exceedingly strange had happened to the Delegates since he had been their obedient servant.

To the young bibliographer, W. W. Greg, recently appointed general editor of the Malone Society publications, Raleigh addressed himself with some formality. 'The Press, I am sure, would like to join you to its company', he wrote on 4 May 1906, thus commencing an association that was to last for fifty years. What was needed, he explained, was a book of early English drama which would be a kind of preface to the latest issue of Shakespeare. Greg replied by return that he had long hoped to leave as his life's work a history of the rise of dramatic art in England, and Raleigh's invitation suggested a first step towards the realization of his dream. 'I don't know whether the Press will be inclined to put up with my angles and sharp corners', he wrote warily. Even so, he concluded, 'May I without impertinence say how delighted I am to find you taking an active part in the direction of the Press at Oxford. With men like you and Bradley (Henry, I mean) to advise them they ought to be able to start a tradition in English literature which would do more to set a standard of modern scholarship than anything there has been so far.'

He was not altogether happy, however, about the Press's general policy.

It appeared to be aiming at two incompatible ideals—'The "final" text for the use of linguistic scholars and the reading edition for the lovers of literature.' This was precisely what it was aiming at, making use of its two imprints, and hoping that in time the lovers of literature would be able to enjoy the best and most authoritative texts, disencumbered of too elaborate an apparatus, but 'final' nevertheless. It was the discovery that the two ideals were not incompatible that had created in the two halves of the Press a mood almost manic, which nobody fanned more enthusiastically than Raleigh himself.

Greg was treading carefully, for he could not know whether Raleigh knew that he was already corresponding with Cannan over his notorious review of Churton Collins's edition of Greene's Plays and Poems, a matter considered important enough to be referred to the Delegates. Only a few days earlier he had admitted to Cannan that he had been distinctly unfortunate in his connections with the Press, having had to find fault with every important Elizabethan work that had come to his notice. 'I shall be much disappointed', he added, as one of the few who was to live to see the day, 'if I am not able to take a very different view of the "Ben Jonson", when it appears.' It must have crossed his mind that his letters, even the review itself, had so impressed Cannan that he had instructed Raleigh to approach him at once with this new proposal. But this was not so. Raleigh was pursuing a premeditated course and Cannan adopting a position of such serene neutrality that he would not in any case have seen fit to interfere.

The feud with Collins was of some significance, for it was a declaration of civil war within the realm of English studies and established an honourable tradition of savagery that persists to the present day. The bibliographer took arms against the literary critic, who found himself of a sudden denounced as an amateur. In this case the victim, Collins, belonged to an earlier but equally savage tradition in which the literary critic was the professional whose mission was to topple the dilettante from any place of authority or repute. His first encounter with the Press was in 1878 when he took issue with Price and Kitchin over the Clarendon Press Series edition of Milton by R. C. Browne, M.A., declaring it worthless. Mark Pattison ransacked his memory and the *University Calendar* in an attempt to identify this Collins, but he could not recall anyone of the name quite so brashly acrimonious. His contributions to the *Quarterly* and *Saturday Review* made his views on the pitiful state of English literary criticism more widely known. Edmund Gosse suffered terribly at his hands when he published his Clark Lectures at Cambridge in 1885, *From Shakespeare to Pope*. Collins in his review made it all too obvious that Gosse had not read, perhaps never even looked at, some of the books on which he was pronouncing well-mannered literary judgements. Collins developed the technique, still popular amongst academic reviewers, of rounding with great solemnity on the publisher, once he had demonstrated beyond reasonable doubt that the hapless author or editor was unfit to plead. 'That such a book as this should have been permitted to go forth into the world with the *imprimatur* of the University of Cambridge affords matter for very grave reflection.' The conclusion is generally that the offending book should be withdrawn at once before it utterly pollutes the streams of learning. A more modern version might read: 'If this book had been issued by a commercial publisher or even by a minor university press, it could perhaps be overlooked. But it appears bearing the imprimatur of one of the world's most ancient academic presses . . . it comes to us with the official sanction of . . . it is advertised and distributed by the world's largest publishing house, with offices from Melbourne to Nairobi and Toronto to Kuala Lumpur. . . .' In such words the spirit of Churton Collins lives on, and also the disciplined pernicketiness of Walter W. Greg.

'You Elizabethans appear to be good fighters!', wrote Cannan in his time to Greg. 'I am not sure that the prudent course for the publisher is not to keep out of the period.' 'My occupation would be gone,' Greg replied. But Cannan had his misgivings. It had taken five years to get Collins's *Greene* through the Press, and as Doble knew too well he was not an easy man to work with. His approach to editorial work is an indication of how much was then expected of the printer. Each of the plays was to be printed *literatim*, and all the numerous variants were to be recorded. Thus copy was presented in what Collins regarded as a perfectly straightforward way, his instructions quite clear. The text transcribed was that of the first quarto: in the left-hand margin in black ink were the readings from the second quarto, and in the right-hand margin in red those from the third quarto. 'So that all that was required', he wrote to Doble, 'was an *intelligent* printer to set up the variants according to these instructions.' He had been told not only by F. J. Furnivall but by York Powell that there was no question of the printer being unable to do so. Doble and Cannan thought otherwise, and decided to ask J. C. Smith of Glasgow, editor of Spenser and of a highly successful *Book of Verse for Boys and Girls*, to prepare the copy for the printer. Smith made hundreds of amendments and suggestions both in Collins's manuscript and in what was already in proof, and generally assumed the role of editor, even preparing his own notes regardless of what Collins had done. Not surprisingly Collins reacted violently. 'Now it has come to Mr. Smith versus myself,' he wrote to Doble, 'you approving of Mr. Smith. This is simply an impossible and intolerable state of things.' He could legitimately object to a change in editorial principles, but he had one other serious complaint to make. He was an exceedingly busy man with little time to spare for editorial work, yet the printer showed no consideration whatsoever. Proofs invariably came in just at the time when he was in the middle of his hard daily grind or when he was thoroughly exhausted by it.

A long series of compromises, mostly on the part of the Press, ensured that work continued, but in the end Cannan resolved that he and Henry Bradley would have the last say on the final proofs. Between them they would resolve all outstanding queries, arbitrate between conjectural emendations, and make sure that the book was printed and bound before Collins set eyes on it again. Cannan could not have been surprised by Greg's review, though he may have hoped that they would not be so comprehensively caught out.

After his catalogue of errors Greg concluded, 'It is high time that it should be understood that so long as we entrust our old authors to arm-chair editors who are content with second-hand knowledge of textual sources, so long will English scholarship in England afford undesirable amusement to the learned world.' The article appeared in the first issue in 1905 of the *Modern Language Review* edited in Cambridge, but at the time Greg was writing to Cannan and Raleigh the issue had been mysteriously withdrawn from circulation. It was not known why, but that somebody was threatening a libel suit seemed the most likely explanation. The rumour, distorted by Furnivall, reached Collins that it was his own edition that was being withdrawn, and he wrote in high agitation to Cannan, who reassured him. Cannan also had to assure Greg that as far as he knew nobody was threatening libel, and Collins himself confirmed this. Greg was ingenuous enough to send Cannan a letter he had had from Collins, which he thought showed that there was no ill feeling. He apparently failed altogether to notice the wicked gleam behind Collins's concluding words. After thanking him for a 'truly excellent and most helpful review', he added that 'it happened by a really strange coincidence that when Mr. Milford at the Clarendon Press directed my attention to your review which I had not seen that I had just posted to the Literary Editor of the *Tribune* a notice of your book on Pastoral Poetry in which I had been obliged to take as unfavourable a view of your literary qualifications as you had taken of my philological.'

In the *Tribune* Greg's book, published by A. H. Bullen, had been described as 'not so much a treatise as an aggregate of bewildered jottings', belonging to a sub-species of literature having its origin in University theses and prize essays, 'the essential note of which is mediocrity'. To Cannan he expressed indifference and contempt for the habits, occupations, and achievements of 'the genus literary Muck-worm'. Greg wrote to the *Tribune* and the quarrel went on. It was all quite apt, and amusing to the onlooker. Twenty years before, Collins had been called 'a louse upon the locks of literature' by Tennyson, who was defending Gosse, and in a further absurdly miscalculated article Collins had tried to show that honest criticism of a book need not be taken personally. As an example he gave his good friend Swinburne, whose critical opinions and literary style he had recently been obliged to condemn as wild. Yet Swinburne had taken no offence at all and their friendship remained unaffected. It turned out that Swinburne had not been aware of Collins's criticisms until his attention was so smugly called to them. The friendship thereupon came to an end.

Collins regarded Greg as scarcely different from, and certainly no better than, the philologists, whom he hated even more than the dilettanti. Their discipline, if such it could be called, did nothing for literature. On the contrary, wrote Collins, 'it too often induces or confirms that peculiar woodenness and opacity, that singular coarseness of feeling and purblindness of moral and intellectual vision, which has in all ages been the characteristic of mere philologists. . . .' In corresponding with Greg, and copying his letters conscientiously to the Press ('this is fun', he noted in an aside to Milford), his tone was carefully ingratiating. He pretended that the factual material for Greg's review had been prepared by somebody else, who was performing a useful service and should be encouraged. It was unfortunate that Greg, because of his literary disabilities, was unable to make better use of it. Their debate might even have been of some interest to the general public had it not been for the appalling dreariness of Greg's prose. 'May I venture to suggest', he wrote, 'that while the research part is going on you might be reading say the Second Philippic or the Letters of Junius which would certainly tend to brighten up your style and impose a little real life and acid into it.'

Cannan was not unfamiliar with the aggressive instincts of his classical colleagues, but this was a relatively new battlefield and the tactics were cut-throat. He was probably not being entirely flippant when he talked of withdrawing from the Elizabethan period, and there was something to be said for Raleigh's policy of playing safe, and keeping out of the textual minefields. But it was declared policy to make available the most authoritative texts based on the most scientific methods. Looking back in 1930 in his presidential address to the Bibliographical Society Greg himself attached considerable importance to this incident. 'The recognition of the value of bibliographical study at Oxford is, I believe, primarily due to the University Press, and even so perhaps to a fortunate accident. There was a time when the belief prevailed there that anyone with a good classical education on the broad lines of the Oxford tradition was sufficiently equipped to undertake the editing of any English author. Of course, this simple faith was bound sooner or later to lead to disaster, and one day a book appeared that was a real disgrace, and which received well-merited castigation. The Secretary to the Delegates at the time was a gentleman who combined a valuable capacity for learning by experience with a useful gift of forcible language. He at once saw the need for an English scholar on whose help and judgement the Press could rely.' The editor of the *Library* in which the address was printed then intervened, and the story had to be completed in a footnote added later. 'What Charles Cannan said was, "My God, we've got to get in a bloody expert!" "And I", added Percy Simpson, "am the bloody expert."'

The story does not seem entirely plausible. What Cannan did was to bring to the Delegates' attention the two reviews, and they 'agreed to express no opinion upon either question'. Cannan would not be unduly impressed by the arguments, and his 'mean opinion of human intelligence in general' was always quite sufficient to steady his nerve. Henry Bradley (who observed that Greg had missed an education by going to Cambridge) and Raleigh remained his guides, and Percy Simpson was paid £200 to

Sir Walter Raleigh and the Oxford English School   139

concentrate exclusively for nine months on Ben Jonson and help redeem the reputation of the Press.

Raleigh was equally unruffled. Two years later all was forgotten. 'His bark is enormous,' Raleigh wrote of Greg, 'but I don't think he will bite.' Meanwhile, although a proposed history of English literature by Churton Collins had been respectfully declined, his edition of Sir Philip Sidney's *Apologie for Poetry* had been accepted and published without misadventure. In 1908 this mordant gospeller for English studies, who had suffered all his life from periods of acute depression, fell into a dike near Lowestoft after an overdose of sleeping pills and was drowned.

The Elizabethan and pre-Elizabethan period was not abandoned: new recruits were brought in to deal with it, notably Greg's mentor R. W. McKerrow who was to produce an edition of Shakespeare's source-plays, A. W. Pollard, and W. P. Ker. But the more the bibliographers refined and advanced their special techniques the more difficult it was for them to engage in editing. Indeed as time went by this ceased to be one of their functions. It was no more their business than to compile bibliographies, which was 'mere prostitution' in Greg's view, sometimes imposed upon them in the dark age of the science by professors of literature 'too slovenly and too indolent to do the drudgery of their own work for themselves'. What Greg himself was doing during these years remained a mystery. It was reported once that his book would turn out to be 1,000 pages. Raleigh pleaded with him to make light of his task. 'I am only afraid that you will do it too well, and spend weeks of labour where hours would meet the case', he wrote. 'I know that you *may* find, that, in some cases, you have practically to recreate the text. But I hope these cases may be few. Most of your textual work could, I believe, be done on the proofs.' It was Raleigh's successor in the chair, G. S. Gordon, in his inaugural lecture, who said 'We cannot much longer expect the Clarendon Press to train, and to train on proof-sheets, half the editors of England. It has been hitherto our only training school.'

Greg in fact was simply compiling a list of early English plays, not editing them at all. He had moved back from the printed drama of the Elizabethan age to the earlier religious drama preserved in manuscript, and was pondering the bibliographical issues involved. This task in one form and another occupied him for thirty years. 'I wandered long in darkness,' he confessed, 'and was late to see the light.' An introduction and some notes to Shakespeare's *Merry Wives of Windsor* for the Tudor and Stuart Library were all that Raleigh was able to get out of him in the years preceding the First World War. But he, McKerrow, and A. W. Pollard made a generation of literary critics neurotically apprehensive of their own armchairs.

5. Building the London Business

MILFORD was given £70 by the Delegates in 1906 to facilitate his move to London and a salary of £700 when he got there. Frowde by then was earning £1,800, the highest-paid man in the Press since Lyttelton Gell. His contract had allowed for an additional payment when the annual net profits of the London and Oxford businesses exceeded 10 per cent of capital, but he had received nothing on this basis since the bad year of 1892. Before then he had mustered some £2,000 which was traceable to the Revised Version. On settling his pension in 1904, H. T. Gerrans drafted a statement for Finance Committee which welcomed the opportunity of bringing to the special notice of the Delegates 'the long and brilliant services of Mr. Frowde'. This was not allowed to stand. Gerrans's version was revised by Monro to read 'long and distinguished services'. In Oxford, Hart earned on average £1,680, and Cannan allowed the Delegates to pay him £1,200 a year.

The Delegates at this time adopted, or accepted, a policy radically different from that of the Syndics in Cambridge. The latter retained control over all publishing, and their manager in London was concerned solely with sales and promotion. The Delegates on the other hand abdicated direct responsibility for a substantial part of the Oxford list. It is impossible to say to what extent Cannan was behind this decisive development, but if he were to build 'the First Press in the world' he needed a free hand. And once Milford's energies were fully engaged it was too late to draw back. The activities of the London business were only rarely brought to the attention of the Delegates. Perhaps a man like Gell, a stickler for the rules however much he deplored them, would have felt obliged to seek instruction and authority. Cannan simply saw that it was a matter beyond their time and competence. Their agendas were still far too long. Meeting once a fortnight they might be confronted by as many as fifty new proposals or suggestions each one of which had to be considered and either rejected, deferred for further consideration, accepted with or without conditions, or occasionally referred to Frowde. The practice of using outside advisers rather than depending on individual Delegates, which had so often meant York Powell or Ingram Bywater, did not lessen their load: for they had to select the adviser, evaluate his report, and determine his fee—all matters which would subsequently be left to the office. For them to attempt to cope with the outpourings of the London business was quite out of the question.

Cambridge may have felt that as a University Press it was not in a position to compete with the London publishers, and that it was prudent to concentrate on academic respectability and the highest standards of production. The competition did indeed appear ferocious during the Edwardian period, when so many series of cheap reprints were being put out. The ultimate in cheap books had come with George Newnes's 'Penny Library of Famous Books' in 1896, but there had been some reaction against the inevitable shoddiness of such productions, and publishers like

Nelsons (under the guidance of John Buchan), Cassells, Collins, Methuens, Routledge, and Dent had their 'Little Libraries', their 'Muses' Library', their 'People's Library of Classics', or their 'Universal Library', all designed with some degree of elegance, for which a market was assured. Even those publishers who did not regard it as part of their vocation to supply the public with edifying literature saw such series as an insurance against the risks of publishing new books. By the turn of the century it was estimated that there were at least eighty series of cheap reprints of the English classics issuing from British publishers. Neither Cannan nor Milford appears to have been in the least perturbed by the competition. Anything another publisher might do could easily be matched, and indeed with the market so infinitely extendible, both at home and overseas, it could perhaps still be, as Macmillan had said, that these series were not exactly jostling each other. At the time it seemed that, whatever might be written in some obscure learned journal, the Press could do no wrong. 'Any edition of any work that bears the hall-mark of the Oxford University Press needs nothing else to recommend it', wrote the *Westminster Gazette*, and to Cannan and Milford this was no more than a truism. For the Oxford University Press it might be thought that the competition from outside was of less concern than the competition within. The multiplication of its own series meant that the Press was jostling itself.

One of the most characteristically spectacular publishing achievements of 1906 was the launching of the Everyman's Library by J. M. Dent. In February the first fifty titles were published simultaneously, and by the end of the year 152 titles had appeared. Dent was a book-binder's apprentice from Darlington who had set up business as a publisher in 1894. The Everyman's Library was edited by Ernest Rhys, an excellent choice that came about by mistake, Dent being under the impression that he was consulting a Celtic scholar of the same name. Rhys shared Dent's grave messianic fervour and believed that salvation was based on good works, which he estimated at a thousand. The Library would contain the thousand greatest books ever written. It was a noble enterprise. The design of the books was calculated to induce in the reader feelings of reverence. There was about them a kind of hushed piety.

It so happened that shortly before the Everyman's Library appeared Frowde had acquired sixty-six volumes of World's Classics, following the bankruptcy of Grant Richards, who might have been one of the most successful publishers of his day if he had had a stern accountant to go with him and be his guide. He had amongst other things published *The Shropshire Lad* and the first edition of *Little Black Sambo*—copies of this racist classic in far from mint condition would fetch over £100 in 1975. His first World's Classic had been *Jane Eyre* and his last, No. 66, Borrow's *Lavengro*. The first Oxford volume was Anne Brontë's *Tenant of Wildfell Hall*, followed by Thoreau's *Walden*, and the fourth volume of Gibbon's *Decline and Fall*. They appeared on ordinary paper at 1s. each—the same price as Everyman's—and in pocket editions on India paper, at

1*s*. 3*d*. Bookcases were available from the publisher in fumed oak or mahogany.

In comparison with Rhys's Everyman's Library the processes of selection were whimsical, and the smaller format was not compatible with the reverential approach to Great Literature. Everyman sought a solemn bond between publisher and reader, World's Classics were a kind of flirtation. Nobody could foresee what would come next, or detect any signs of a balanced editorial policy. *Mrs. Caudle's Curtain Lectures* by Douglas Jerrold had gone down well enough in the *Punch* of the 1840s, but it was not what was generally understood as a classic, nor was Richard Cobbold's *Margaret Catchpole*. Jane Porter's *The Scottish Chiefs* and John Galt's *The Entail, or the Lairds of Grippy* could scarcely be accounted for without a knowledge of Charles Cannan's private reading habits, and Milford's taste for adventure stories can alone explain the inclusion of Mayne Reid's *The Rifle Rangers* and *The Scalp Hunters*. (F. R. Leavis was to deplore the literary tastes of the 'Greats man'.) Nevertheless in due course most of the acknowledged classics found a place, the English poets were fully represented, and many of the more idiosyncratic choices settled down comfortably to enjoy their improved status in the world of letters. It was natural for the public to assume that a World's Classic must be worth reading for some reason or another, and in any case they were extremely agreeable little books to handle and to have on the shelf.

'Who reads and buys *The World's Classics*?', asked the *Periodical* in 1907. 'We do not profess to know, but the fact remains that nearly two million copies have been sold.' One answer was certainly young people. This was the golden age of reading generally, and the golden age of reading particularly in youth. A few generations later the age group that was devouring World's Classics and all the other classics had been converted into the student market, which was nibbling on students' textbooks. Unthreatened by further examinations, literate young people who had enjoyed the benefits of a sixth-form education could read to themselves and to each other with bated rapture and discover new worlds. It was not uncommon for members of the lower middle classes to quote extensively from their favourite poets when in love. Longfellow, curiously enough, was the best-selling poet in World's Classics after Shakespeare, though he was said to be kept mostly for Sundays.

The World's Classics once and for all established the Press in general publishing. They also served to broaden Frowde's literary horizons. Hitherto it might be said that for him the only good author was a dead author whose copyrights had run out. Copyright-watching was one of his favourite occupations. So eager was he to publish a selection of Browning's earlier poems that he took legal advice in order to ensure absolute precision of timing. The latest of the poems he wished to include had been published in 1864, and the law at that time gave copyright for a period of 42 years. Frowde's problem, however, was whether the law covered printing as well as publication: could he not have the book printed and ready for sale within hours if not minutes of the expiration of copyright? He was told that he might have the poems set up in type, but that they should not be printed before the copyright ran out, at midnight on 20 August 1906. He was equally quick off the mark with Walter Savage Landor who was entering the public domain at about the same time.

The World's Classics gave him the opportunity to cultivate living authors. Theodore Watts-Dunton, a writer whose reputation had steadily diminished, was the only living novelist to be represented, Grant Richards having chosen to include *Aylwin*. Frowde approached George Meredith, hoping to include a number of his books, beginning with *The Ordeal of Richard Feverel*. Unfortunately the terms he was able to offer were unlikely to attract any author already enjoying a measure of success. The price at which the books were sold left the barest margin of profit, and he could offer little inducement other than a promise of the widest circulation among a new public. 'My experience proves that a cheap edition of a copyright work in sixpenny or shilling form does not injure its sales in a better style,' he told a sceptical Meredith. Frowde was thinking in terms of £20 for every 10,000 copies printed, and few authors regard themselves as charitable organizations. However, Watts-Dunton brought Frowde into contact with the ageing Swinburne, whom he nursed solicitously at his home in Putney. Lunch with Swinburne was pleasing to Frowde's vanity, although its consequence was the appearance in the World's Classics of *Joseph and his Brethren*, a dramatic poem by Charles Wells first published in 1824, to which Swinburne had written an introduction in 1876. Frowde found himself unable to resist the suggestion that he should reissue it. He did, however, persuade Swinburne to write the introduction to the World's Classics edition of Shakespeare's Complete Works.

Nobody dealt more forthrightly than Frowde with the perennial problem of expurgation. Indeed for him it did not exist. The new generation of scholars was resolutely opposed to it, but well into the twentieth century a double standard prevailed. Expensive complete texts could be made available for the élite, for 'ripe scholars': for the masses expurgated editions would be required reading for many years to come. As Noel Perrin pointed out in *Dr. Bowdler's Legacy*, the Victorian cult of delicate sensibility was so widespread that it was necessary to expurgate for commercial reasons, to provide family reading. Swinburne once said that no man ever did better service to Shakespeare than Bowdler himself. The Clarendon Press was severely criticized by the new bibliographers for allowing the bowdlerization of sixteenth- and seventeenth-century writers. Walter Raleigh complained bitterly about Clark's edition of Aubrey's *Brief Lives*, in which despite the editor's protestations many of Raleigh's favourite passages had disappeared into a row of dots. Raleigh in fact had come to suspect that the whole nineteenth-century cult of modesty and embarrassment was a sham, a by now visible affectation. Deliberating with Milford over a volume of 'Rustic Ballads', some necessarily bawdy, he asked, 'Do they really shock any one?' He very much doubted it. 'As a tribute of social esteem we expect one another to be shocked—it is a subtle form of flattery; and no more than mere politeness to show symptoms of shock when they are expected from our delicacy of fibre.' He would not have written so to Frowde, who would have found the argument incomprehensible. And Raleigh, a broad-minded man with no strong impulse to push points to their logical conclusion, did concede that it was after all a matter of taste. 'To every one his weakness', he wrote to Milford, agreeing to certain omissions. '*I* can't stand smells in literature.'

Frowde would have agreed entirely with Francis Palgrave's pronouncement of the 1870s: 'Much that was admissible centuries since, or at least sought admission, has now, by a law against which protest is idle, lapsed into the indecorous.' The twentieth century was beginning its indecorous course, but for Frowde there was no difference at all between moral principles and common business sense. He would, for instance, promote the works of Tolstoy, within reason. A collection of twenty-four short stories newly translated by L. and A. Maude for the World's Classics was published as *Twenty-three Tales* in 1906. He wrote uncompromisingly to Aylmer Maude: 'The tale "Francoise" the copy for which I now return had better be omitted from our book, and I shall be glad if you can find some other to take its place; if not we must have 23 only. To include it would mean a very much reduced sale for the book; nor should we be promoting the study of Tolstoy's works such as we desire to do.'

His new series afforded Frowde considerable satisfaction. It was a challenge commercially, and it involved work on which he could expect enthusiastic co-operation from Milford. He was uncertain, however, of its acceptability to the Delegates. He wished to present to each a complete set, but he understood that 'some of them may be unwilling to give house room to cheap reprints of this character'. He left it to Cannan's discretion to decide on suitable recipients.

In terms of profitability and of sales nothing could yet quite match the long line of devotional books that continued to pour from the London business. They carried such titles as *Voices of Comfort*, *The Bow in the Cloud*, *A Book of Sorrow*, and *Whisperings from the Great*. The most successful of all these anthologies, apart from Palgrave's *Treasury of Sacred Song*, was the Hon. Mrs. Lyttelton Gell's *The Cloud of Witness*, 'a daily sequence of great thoughts from many minds, following the Christian season'. It sold inordinately, available in about twenty different styles. Published in 1904 there was still a lively demand for it during the Second World War. Mrs. Gell was further responsible for *The More Excellent Way: Words of the Wise on the Life of Love, a Sequence of Meditations*, and *The Vision of Righteousness, aids to Meditation for Daily Use*. These Milford referred to, outrageously as 'Mrs. Gell's tosh-books'.

6. Medical and Juvenile: the Joint Venture

IN 1905 Sir William Osler, recently elected Regius Professor of Medicine at Oxford, was made a Delegate. It was an enterprising appointment. Osler had an international reputation and immense influence. He was widely held to be the greatest clinician of his time and had written the standard textbook on clinical medicine, *The Principles and Practice of Medicine*, published by Appletons in New York in 1892. He was also an enthusiastic medical historian and a bibliophile who could hold his own even in the company of Ingram Bywater. In 1929 the Press published *Bibliotheca Osleriana*, which listed 7,600 items from his private library. Throughout his life he searched for rare early impressions of *The Anatomy of Melancholy*, and his collection of the works of Sir Thomas Browne was as complete as any one lifetime would permit. Osler was a Canadian, who had held the Chair of Medicine at McGill, before becoming Professor of Clinical Medicine at the University of Pennsylvania and then physician-in-chief at the Johns Hopkins Hospital in Baltimore. In Oxford he was generally thought of as an American, and the first task assigned to him by the Delegates was to report on a proposal for a book on international law for no other reason than that the author, a J. B. Scott, was an American. Osler made a few discreet inquiries and established that Scott was a reputable and hard-working scholar. He proved to be a most indefatigable editor of documents and became Director of the Carnegie Endowment for International Peace. In itself of no particular significance, it was reassuring for the Delegates to feel that the grape-vine, long perfected as a system of communication in Oxford and much improved throughout the United Kingdom, could also be made to work successfully in America with the help of their new recruit.

H. A. L. Fisher remarked that Oxford 'does not easily capitulate to strangers, especially if their claim to distinction rests upon scientific rather than on literary grounds, but Osler left Oxford no choice, and from the first the surrender of the University was absolute and immediate'. Osler himself capitulated to the University and to the University Press, wherein he saw larger opportunities. 'I have become deeply interested in the University Press', he wrote to a friend, 'of which I am one of the managers. The meetings form a sort of literary seminar, and we really have great sport, particularly with the expert opinions sent in upon works which are offered. It is an immense business. We employ 700 people.'

Osler advised on many matters. In the last year of his life, 1919, he was writing to Milford, 'There is (will be) much money to the publisher of proper Motor Itineraries of this country, combining the delightful features of the old road maps (with the hotels and country houses named and marked) and such modern aspects as gradients, repair shops, etc.' But it was the appearance of the first issue of the *Quarterly Journal of Medicine* in 1906, with Osler as senior editor and main contributor, that began the transformation of the Press into one of the largest publishers of medical books in the country. The start was almost from scratch.

Sir Henry Acland, who had occupied the Chair from 1857 to 1894, had been a man of artistic temperament, and a lifelong friend of Ruskin. He found the Oxford Medical School in much the same state it had been in when the first Regius Professor had been appointed by Henry VIII, and his task had been to shake off the dust to make way for a little modern equipment, which he effectively did. But he was strongly opposed to any form of specialization, believing that the first responsibility of the University was to provide a liberal education in the arts for all its students. Purely professional medical studies should be carried on somewhere else, and Oxford could certainly not be expected to pioneer research. His successor was a distinguished physiologist, Burdon-Sanderson, under whom Osler studied as a young man in London. On behalf of his subject, Burdon-Sanderson had edited a volume called *Memoirs on the Physiology of Nerves*, consisting of papers by German and French scholars, but the Oxford Medical School did not produce books of its own. *English Medicine in Anglo-Saxon Times, Surgical Instruments in Greek and Roman Times, Studies in the Medicine of Ancient India*—such were the titles that studded the list. Fascinated though Osler was by the history of his subject there was clearly nothing there that might help him to teach it. Osler's appointment as a Delegate was timely, for the London business was just about to embark on what became known as the 'Joint Venture'. In co-operation with Hodder & Stoughton, the Oxford University Press acquired two entirely new departments: juvenile and medical.

A long tradition and Gerrans's enthusiasm ensured that educational books continued to be published from Oxford. Some were highly success-ful: J. C. Smith's *Book of Verse for Boys and Girls* outsold Q's *Oxford Book of English Verse*, and A. J. Herbertson's Oxford Geographies were constantly reprinting, often in impressions of 25,000 copies at a time. In the space of three years fifty volumes of the Oxford Modern French Series and the Oxford Higher French Series were published, designed to make the best French literature available to the higher forms of the public schools, to university students, and to the general reader. The novels of Flaubert, George Sand, Stendhal, and the works of some licentious poets could be read 'in the family circle or in the schoolroom without any fear of *les convenances* being outraged', as one journal approvingly put it. But too little attention was still given to junior or middle schools and, though much was achieved, educational publishing tended to be haphazard. Cannan was not interested: at least he was said by Chapman to be 'eager but not enthusiastic', which must amount to the same thing. So the processes of organic growth were given a sudden jolt when Milford established himself at Amen Corner and got to know the people next door, notably Ernest Hodder Williams.

With remarkably little ado they entered into a form of partnership to produce children's books under the joint imprint of Henry Frowde and Hodder & Stoughton. Hodder's problem was a shortage of capital, which had prevented them entering the school-book field. Milford's appetite was whetted by the thought of entering the lucrative juvenile market with what were euphemistically called 'prize books'. Literature for the amusement and entertainment of children had undoubtedly been neglected in Oxford, where it was difficult to reconcile it with the purposes of a University Press. But 'recreative' literature could be educational as well. Moreover as educational publishing in Oxford was uncoordinated, weak at the elementary level and too often neither fish nor fowl, as he had told Gerrans, Milford could claim to be making good a flaw in the general structure. Two editors were appointed, Herbert Ely and Charles James L'Estrange. Between them they produced hundreds of books under the name of Herbert Strang (or, when they felt so inclined, Mrs. Herbert Strang), and they remained with the Press, known as 'the heavenly twins', until retirement in 1938. The joint venture with Hodder & Stoughton for elementary juvenile books ceased in 1916 when all the stocks were sold to O.U.P. At a stroke Milford had created a semi-autonomous department of the Press which has endured and more often than not flourished until the present day. The readers, arithmetics, poetry books, the annuals and tales for tiny tots, sprang in their tens of thousands from the joint venture, and the output became so great that in the end even the General Catalogue stopped trying to keep abreast of it.

Milford and Ernest Hodder Williams next launched a brand-new series of medical publications. Osler was in Oxford, and it was hoped not only to profit from his advice and co-operation but to use his name as general advisory editor. Hodder Williams knew Dr. J. Keogh Murphy, admirably qualified to be acting editor. In November 1906 Milford arranged for the two men to meet, and he anxiously awaited a report from Cannan on Osler's reactions. They were apparently favourable. By the end of the year another contract had been signed between Frowde and Hodder & Stoughton, and between the two publishers and Dr. Murphy. Milford received £100 a year as a fee and everything was arranged on a fifty-fifty basis.

In 1907 *A System of Medicine* edited by Osler in seven volumes was announced, as an intimation that there were to be no half measures, and an important series of manuals began to appear—Burghard's *System of Operative Surgery*, and *A System of Syphilis* in six volumes. As important for the growth of the Press as the acquisition of the World's Classics was the purchase of Young J. Pentland's business in 1908, which brought in a number of important titles, among them the massive and perpetual best sellers, Cunningham's *Text-Book* and *Manual* of anatomy.

Towards the end of his life Osler was planning what became *The Oxford Loose-Leaf Medicine*. It was edited by Henry A. Christian, Emeritus Professor of Physics at Harvard University, and published in 1920 by the New York branch, which immediately assumed a new dimension. Its only publication hitherto had been the Scofield Bible. *Oxford Medicine* was in twenty-one volumes, consisting originally of nearly 300 monographs by more than 200 authors. It was the first loose-leaf medical work ever published. The principle was ingeniously simple. By issuing regular supplements it could be kept always up to date: subscribers had only to discard the old pages and insert the new. To the Oxford travellers it was like a return to frontier days. A vast new territory lay before them. In thousands of small towns throughout America there might be no bookshop, but there would always be a doctor.

The joint medical venture lasted until 1923, when O.U.P. bought all Hodders' stock and interests. The series had prospered from the start, and again Frowde and Milford had brought into being a new department of the Press which always enjoyed a considerable degree of independence. Milford was later to do the same with his music department.

7. The Clarendon Aristotle

A LONDON book might be conceived, edited, printed, and published in the interval between two Delegates' meetings. The equanimity with which Cannan, naturally brisk and incisive, endured the creeping paralysis that afflicted one of his bravest endeavours in Oxford, the translation of Aristotle, was remarkable. He had just as much to be aggravated by as Lyttelton Gell when what should have proved so congenial a task proved so peculiarly troublesome.

It was undertaken in collaboration with Balliol College, the Jowett Trustees. Jowett had left the copyright of all his writings to the College, and had stated in his will that the income accruing from them should go to 'the making of new translations of Greek authors'. Aristotle was the author he had particularly in mind. At the same time the Clarendon Press had been offered a number of translations of parts of Aristotle's works, and the Delegates were willing to publish them if competent editors were appointed. The circumstances were ideal for the coming-together of the two institutions.

Balliol College meetings and Delegates' meetings were necessary to settle the details, and as vacations tended to intervene progress was necessarily slow, though punctuated by moments of panic haste when it was hoped that a step forward might be made. If Markby had not been a member of both committees, deliberations might have been indefinitely protracted. W. D. Ross and J. A. Smith, the Master of Balliol, were appointed editors, and were to be paid £50 each a year. That was a start. For the next two and a half years draft agreements passed back and forth. There was no particular problem but the college, and the editors, were anxious that everything should be done correctly. It was not always easy to remember what had

R. W. Chapman, Horace Hart, H. T. Gerrans, John Armstrong (Manager of the New York Branch), Charles Cannan

The young Humphrey Milford

already been done, and if there were uncertainty it was safer to go back to the beginning and start again. 'Making an agreement with J. A. Smith is the most capital joke I have come across for a long time', Cannan commented to Markby.

He wanted an understanding that at least one complete volume should be published each year. The editors were to provide copy ready for the printer and the Press was to publish at its own risk. Any profits were to be divided equally, despite a recurrent plea from Balliol for 60 per cent, and frequent promptings from Cannan that they would be well advised to take a royalty. Payment of translators was much discussed. They should do it for glory, in Cannan's view, but if they were to be paid it should be on publication, and not on delivery of the manuscript, or even on return of the proofs. This seemed prudent to the Bursar of Balliol, who had recently noticed a bill of £43. 15s. 6d. owing to Lyttelton Gell. A selection of Jowett's essays had been edited by Gell, partly printed, but never published because of disagreement among the literary executors. By May 1907 a final agreement had been drawn up for the Clarendon Aristotle and signed by the Vice-Chancellor on behalf of the Delegates. It was passed to Balliol for completion. Years later it was discovered that, worn out by their long and fastidious exertions, the Trustees had forgotten to sign it, and no valid agreement existed.

Cannan had begun buoyantly enough, telling the Delegates that the project would prove that 'we know more than the Germans', and reminding everyone that the Aristotle Society had been meeting weekly for twenty-five years. As the Aristotle Society was very largely Ingram Bywater, to whom the memory of Jowett was distasteful, it was not easy to turn it to advantage. Bywater had for long refused to be parted from his translation of the *Poetics*: he hugged it to himself, though Cannan begged him to let him send it to the printer. When he finally did release it for publication in 1909 it appeared independently, not in Jowett's posthumous series.

Even before the negotiations with Balliol began, Cannan had been trying to decide what to do with a translation of part of Aristotle's treatise *Parva Naturalia*, by J. I. Beare of Dublin. In December 1904 he felt optimistic enough to reveal to Beare the plans for 'an organized campaign and regular siege of the whole corpus of the Master. And I may tell you in confidence that it is pretty certain that soon after the new year we shall have arranged for a more or less periodical publication of Aristotelia. We think that the difficulty of the author is so great, and his extent so wide that nothing but regular sap and mine all round his circumference will suffice.' The appointment of the two editors allowed him to get Beare's manuscript off his desk and into their hands. He told Bywater that he could sleep more easily as a result.

Some two years later it appeared to be ready for the printer, and then it was only a matter of days before the work was in proof. The proofs puzzled J. I. Beare in Dublin. Footnotes had sprouted where he had not intended them to be. As usual Cannan had taken a strong line about footnotes,

M

insisting that they should be kept to a minimum: 'we are not aiming at finality'. It seemed to Mr. Beare that there had been a departure from the editorial principles as he understood them, and he found himself in much the same position as Churton Collins after the ransacking of his edition of Greene. For what had happened was that as a result of correspondence with the editors Beare had written notes to justify his own versions to them, not expecting these notes to be printed. The editors had kept his notes, and added notes of their own contradicting him. The proofs, as Beare pointed out to Cannan, looked ridiculous. The relationship of editors to translator was like that of a lecturer to his student bringing up his exercises for correction. Beare very temperately protested.

Cannan looked mournfully at the proofs. It would be improper to criticize his editors, but he did allow himself to remark that there was only one Bywater. He then took it upon himself to re-edit the translation and to enter into a long correspondence with Beare, who was astonished by his insight and erudition, and delighted to find an ally. Meanwhile the other translations scheduled for the series were all being held up by the craving for 'finality' and by disagreements between the various parties. In 1906 Frowde had an inquiry from a customer about the new Aristotle series that the Press was issuing. '"Issuing" is a good joke', Cannan replied. 'All Aristotelians are quarrelsome except the Secretary and he is only saved by association with mild business men.' He did not deny that they might be in labour with something, but he had already recognized the onset of paralysis and no forecasts could be made. Beare's part of the *Parva Naturalia* was eventually published in 1908, and other volumes slowly crept into print. But only in the context of a hundred years war could Cannan's military metaphors be deemed appropriate. In 1919 R. W. Chapman wrote him a note about lack of progress, conveying Ross's hopes that Cannan would use his influence to get things moving again. At the bottom, scribbled in pencil by a frail hand, are the words 'C.C. quite exhausted'. The series was concluded in 1952.

8. The Fowlers and the Dictionary

TRANSLATIONS were a new departure for the Press. Cannan was not much attracted by them in general. A suggestion from a Professor at Yale that the Oxford Classical Texts should be issued with translations on facing pages, and with explanatory notes, puzzled him considerably. Students of English literature would find them useful, he was told. Cannan could not imagine how or why. It would be impossible to get an English class to have anything to do with the difficult Greek, and nobody wanted simply a crib. 'Perhaps the mere sight of the Greek type will be educational', he mused to Frowde, concluding that the project should be left to the Americans, who at least appeared to understand it. Frowde could import copies with his own imprint if he felt so inclined. But Cannan demanded a fee of £1,200 plus royalties if use were made of the existing plates, and that ended the matter. Six years later in 1912 the Loeb Classics began to appear, and though they were dismissed at first as too expensive at 5s. a volume they did not turn out to be quite so useless as Cannan had supposed.

The rule was that the Clarendon Press should not publish translations because they could be of no possible use to scholars who would have no difficulty reading the originals. Jowett's *Plato* had at times proved an embarrassment, an unfortunate precedent that had to be explained away on the grounds that it was primarily a commentary which happened to have a translation attached to it. The rule was relaxed in the post-Gell era, when the general reader had established his right to some consideration from Oxford. Even so when the Oxford Library of Translations began to appear early in the twentieth century it was stressed that the books had not been written to order, 'but produced for the delight of the writers themselves by the students of their favourite authors'. Quite serious scholars might choose to while away their leisure hours in such fond pursuits, translating Caesar's *Gallic War* for instance, and their efforts could be presented as harmless diversions. The Oxford Library included translations of *Beowulf*, Dante, Machiavelli, and Heine, as well as of the Greek and Latin authors. One of the first titles to appear in 1905 was a translation of Lucian, complete in four volumes 'except for some works considered spurious and some omissions by way of expurgation', by H. W. and F. G. Fowler. 'Who are these Fowlers?', the *New York Times* asked, as many people were to ask in years to come. It concluded that they were women, for the translation was 'dainty as well as accurate and finished'.

Neither Cannan nor Milford could easily have answered the question. They never met the Fowlers and could not very well in the course of their correspondence satisfy the curiosity the two brothers naturally aroused. Whoever they were it had gradually to be accepted that they had attached themselves to the Press for life, and when one Fowler died in 1918, it turned out that there was another and as yet unsuspected one to continue the association.

Before *Lucian* was published the senior partner, Henry Waldon Fowler, had presented Cannan with a description of their next work. 'We have just begun to collect materials for a little book which we think might serve a useful purpose, but which would perhaps not be in your line. This is a sort of English composition manual, from the negative point of view, for journalists and amateur writers. There is a vast number of writers nowadays who have something to say and know how to make it lively or picturesque, but being uneducated cannot write a page without a blunder or cacophony or piece of verbiage or false pathos or clumsiness or avoidable dulness.... It might possibly, we think, be mildly entertaining as well as serviceable.'

Cannan liked the idea immediately. It was indeed one of his own, but he had never found the right person to do such a book. 'We in the office would welcome an antibarbarus', he wrote, 'and we don't suppose there would be the least difficulty in getting the Delegates' approval—though they—good cautious men would like no doubt to see the book or a specimen of it.' There were two publics, he explained: 'one is the schools which desire something in the nature of a Rhetoric (in the old sense). The other is that which you have in mind; the editor of the Spectator and the people who write in the *Times*.'

The Fowlers took this so much to heart that they persisted in calling the book 'The New Solecist: for sixth form boys and journalists'. The prospects for any book under such a title would have been deservedly poor, and no better under any of the other titles the Fowlers were able to think up— 'Solecisms and Journalism', 'Solecisms and Literary Blemishes', 'The Unmaking of English', 'The English of the Times' (with compliments to *The Times*). The struggle to find a title was much more prolonged than it had been for Q's anthology, and when eventually printing was held up because the title-page was blank, minds everywhere seemed to go blank too. It was after all a very unusual book. The Delegates had originally accepted it as 'The Antibarbarus', a kind of dictionary of common blunders and moot points in syntax. Milford reported to Bradley that the office was bitterly divided over the question of what to call it, and begged him to think of something. All Bradley could suggest was 'Good and Bad English'. Somehow or other, at the last minute, the office was able to settle its differences and come up with 'The King's English': it turned out that there were two other books on the market with the same title, but that was of no consequence.

The King's English, published in 1906, was never really suitable for schools, and it was taking a narrow view to suppose that it would serve as a guide for journalists. Mature writers found parts of it difficult, and parts perverse, but for anybody who had ever tried to put pen to paper it was either an indispensable guide or a threat to mental health. On old problems like ending sentences with a preposition, the distinctions between 'which and that' and 'will' and 'shall', 'different from' and 'different to', the permissible uses of a split infinitive, the Fowlers had something tantalizing and original to say. They were frequently somewhat disconcerting. 'The ironical use of *somewhat* for *very* is so hackneyed as to be practically an apology for dulness.' The only reassuring aspect of the book was the abundant evidence it provided that everybody made mistakes.

The Fowlers were criticized for deepening the division between colloquial and written English, for being precisionists at heart and inflexible grammarians, for imposing rules which if followed would actually mar a writer's style and render it graceless, not to say self-conscious. On behalf of his fellow professionals, Desmond MacCarthy in reviewing a later edition wrote, 'it is clear that such rules must often involve the consideration of barely perceptible subtleties which waste the writer's time.' Many questions were better left to the ear and judgement of the author. The Fowlers were sensitive to criticism. From the beginning they had realized that as their examples were taken from some of the best authors as well as the best journals and newspapers they would be open to the charge of presumption. (The authors most frequently pilloried in *The King's English* were Marie Corelli, with forty-four quotations, Emerson (39), Borrow (38), J. R. Green (35), Dickens (30).) For that reason they had wanted to remain anonymous. 'We have occasionally to reprove writers of repute,' H. W. Fowler explained succinctly to Cannan, 'which is more presumptuous in two who are by their names just known to be unknown than in an imaginary one about whom it is unknown whether he is known or not.' Cannan was not persuaded and wanted no meekness. He had been persuaded by Henry Bradley that they had nothing to fear. 'We were a little nervous', he admitted to Henry Fowler after the first specimens had been approved by Bradley, 'about the reception the ultra expert would give it, but he was much more gracious than we dared to hope.' He therefore took as his text, frequently repeated, 'The elementary laws do not apologize: neither does the Clarendon Press apologize'. The only occasion he had to rebuke the Fowlers was when he read an appendix they had written for the second edition, which was to appear six months after the first had been published. 'I am I must confess distressed', he wrote, 'by discovering in it "apologetic remarks". . . . The book has a great chance of establishing itself, if the public can be persuaded that it is always right.' Argument, or concessions to critics, would undermine confidence and allow the public to believe that it could 'continue to live at random (and what is worse, not buy the book)'. Henry Fowler apologized: 'I am sorry we have forgotten the Dogma of Infallibility; but we are ready to return to the true faith.'

The hunting of solecisms became a sport in which Cannan, Milford, and Chapman delighted for many years. It partly accounted for Cannan's addiction to newspapers. Chapman gleefully pursued misuses of the word 'case', and Milford kept an eye open for 'ases', rejoicing once in some lines in a letter from Clement Shorter to *The Times*: 'It is not so much a question as to what poets have written about the simple country life as to how far they have cared to endure it.' Reporting this exciting find to Oxford he pointed out that the author, 'in his own beastly idiom, should have written "as as to how far . . ."'. Cannan toyed with an article on German English—'the Germans are very poor linguists, poor things'—and kept a scrapbook, of Americanisms in particular, from which he supplied the Fowlers with 'heaps of filth of various degrees of abomination'. The *Oxford Magazine* also joined in the game, and the Fowlers appeared to as well, but in a very different spirit and temper.

Henry Fowler had been a schoolteacher, and the instinct of both brothers was to teach and correct, not to deride. They wrote in sorrow rather than contempt. Misuse of the language was certainly a serious matter, but there was no cruelty in them, only an innate strictness. Yet there was established between the two men living humbly in Guernsey and the small élite of the University Press in Oxford a lasting *rapport*. Most importantly Cannan had found the answer to the question he and the Delegates had been asking for years: who could compile a 'short dictionary', using what had already been done for the big dictionary and filling in the gaps themselves. Other people had been tried without success. The temptation to get Bradley and Craigie to do it had been resisted. But it was high time that the Press began to recover some of its investment in the *O.E.D.* The way to do it had been clear, but lexicographers were scarce. Knowing only the work they had done for the Press and nothing about their background or qualifications, Cannan willed that the Fowlers should henceforth be lexicographers.

In 1906 they considered the matter in their customarily grave and modest manner, and concluded that it would take five years. Cannan had heard lexicographers' promises before, but he had also been more than once surprised by the Fowlers' unfailing punctuality. It would certainly not take less than five years, and he was prepared to accept that as a provisional deadline. The *Concise Oxford Dictionary* was published in 1911, and that was as close to a miracle as anything Cannan experienced.

The end of the big dictionary was almost in sight. Observing the bearded figure of James Murray proceeding on his tricycle through the streets of Oxford one day in 1908, Sir William Osler remarked to a friend, 'The University pays me my salary to keep that old man alive till his eightieth birthday in 1917 when the Dictionary will be finished.' It had not in fact got beyond R when the *Concise* was printed. Bradley was battling his way through S, but the final part, 'Sweep–Szmikite', did not appear until 1919, when C. T. Onions had joined the team. Every month the Delegates studied the score sheet. In October 1903 it read

Dr. Murray	—pages composed—	$18\frac{2}{3}$
Dr. Bradley	— ,, ,,	$7\frac{2}{3}$
Mr. Craigie	— ,, ,,	$8\frac{2}{3}$
Dr. Murray	—average compared with Webster—	$10 \cdot 66$
Dr. Bradley	— ,, ,, ,, ,,	$-18 \cdot 4$
Mr. Craigie	— ,, ,, ,, ,,	$- 4 \cdot 72$

The Delegates' comments are not recorded: on this occasion there were perhaps cries of 'well played, Craigie', and groans over Bradley's verbosity. But the very next report showed that although Craigie had completed 11 pages his average compared to Webster had shot up to 33·00. It was as always bewildering, unpredictable, inexplicable, but there was little the Delegates could do. When Bradley dropped again to $7\frac{2}{3}$ pages in June 1905 it was agreed to remonstrate with him upon his slow rate of progress, but he was by then so esteemed a member of the University and of the Press that it was no more than a gesture, and perhaps an ironical reproach to Cannan for allowing *The King's English* to take up too much of his time. The Delegates no longer sought to intervene. They and their Secretary recognized that the editors were not fools: it was the language itself that was insane.

Cannan read proofs of the Dictionary for pleasure and instruction, and not with a copy of Webster and a measuring rod in his hand, nor indeed with a time-clock ticking beside him. Like many others he had come to the conclusion that he would not live to see it finished. He would have given his full assent to a letter written by Lord Aldenham to Bartholomew Price in June 1897. 'In all but speed the O.E.D. goes on splendidly! I hope the Delegates will harden their hearts and shut their eyes to the Balance.

'Surely Efficiency is of more consequence than Expedition.

'Some of us won't see the letter Z finished, nor indeed many earlier letters; but I don't see that *that* is of any weight.'

Efficiency was achieved after a fashion, though the physical separation of the dictionary staff—Murray's Scriptorium was in the Banbury Road, Craigie's Dictionary room in the Old Ashmolean, and Bradley was housed for a time in the Clarendon Press—did not contribute to it. Bradley had worked as Murray's assistant for only a year before becoming an independent editor, with responsibility for the letter E. Craigie had worked with Murray for four years before being sent out as an advance party to settle Q in 1901. It cannot be said that Murray altogether trusted either of them. They were brilliant undoubtedly, but had they his stamina, patience, and dedication, or even his powers of succinct definition? His resolve to produce as much himself as Craigie and Bradley together sustained him in his unending labours, though the task was made easier by Bradley's other preoccupations and by Craigie's acceptance first of a lectureship in the Scandinavian languages and then of the Rawlinson and Bosworth Chair of Anglo-Saxon. Bradley was never a quick worker. His friend Robert Bridges said that he had the utmost difficulty in making up his mind about anything. He spoke slowly, with painful deliberation, and the only man among those who finished his sentences for him who got them right was, he maintained, Craigie.

In 1901 two complete volumes were published, Volume IV by Bradley, Volume V by Murray, the last to appear for seven years. Volume H–K was one of Murray's most heroic achievements, its 1,274 pages representing little more than three years' work. Bradley's volume F–G, on the other hand, had taken him since 1894. R. M. Leonard recorded in the *Periodical* that 'a Chinaman in Singapore, on opening a school for his countrymen, announces that he is prepared, among other things, to teach English "up to the letter G"'. Leonard had already started on an exercise that was to divert him for many years. By reaching 'Infer' the Dictionary now ran to 16,516 columns $10\frac{1}{2}$ inches long. Set on end the type would extend upwards for two and a half miles, four times the height of Snowdon, fourteen times that of the Eiffel Tower. The lines already in print if placed end to end would stretch for 72 miles—from Charing Cross to Folkestone.

Though sales were invariably disappointing, the prestige of the Dictionary continued to grow enormously. It was being quoted and used as a work of ultimate authority in the law courts, in Parliament, by the President of the United States. Appearing as it did there were those who could actually read it, who awaited each part of the long-running serial with an eager curiosity. Murray moved excitingly from O to P, Craigie from Q to

R. Bradley's excursions in the early part of S yielded his article on 'set', the longest in the Dictionary, and acclaimed a masterpiece. The eyes of the world were on these three men in Oxford, and their eighteen assistants.

For Cannan there was a 'less vexatious discrepancy between expenditure and results', particularly after Lord Aldenham's son had used his influence to procure £5,000 from the Goldsmiths' Company in 1905 to help cover the expenses of Volume VI. When that volume was eventually published in 1908, with most of the next volume already issued in parts, it seemed an altogether happy event. Instead of calling sombre attention to how much was still to be done, after so great an expenditure of time and money, as the earlier volumes did, it now became possible to foresee the end. Falconer Madan reckoned that 'the greatest literary work ever produced at Oxford' would be finished in 1912. 'That nothing may be wanting to this noble work,' he wrote, 'the open page of any portion of it displays a more pictorial effect, owing to the skilful use of type of various kinds, size, and appearance, than any printed page elsewhere in existence.' In the same year Murray accepted a knighthood, with many agitated misgivings. Academic honours he craved, but to be a plain knight, 'as if I were a brewer or a local mayor', struck him as a questionable distinction. Moreover the tradesmen would put up their prices.

He and Craigie were less sanguine than Madan about the date for completion. On finishing R in March 1910, Craigie estimated that there was still another seven years' work ahead of them, and it was not until 1913 that Murray made public his ill-kept secret. 'I have got to the stage', he said, 'when I can estimate the end. In all human probability the *Oxford Dictionary* will be finished on my eightieth birthday, four years from now.' In 1879 it had been thought that the Dictionary would take ten years to complete. Despite all human probability, in 1917 it was still to take ten years to complete.

But comparison with other dictionaries being prepared on the Continent now suggested that the pace set by Oxford was little short of headlong. Even the Germans could not begin to match it. The first part of *Deutsches Wörterbuch*, originated by Jacob and Wilhelm Grimm, had been published in 1852, and the work was still far from finished. About a sixth remained to be done in 1913. The *Ordbok Öfver Svenska Språket* for the Swedish Academy began to be published in 1893; after twenty years only A had been done and a few fragments from B, C, and D. The Dutch *Woordenboek* had been in progress since 1850 and had barely reached the half-way mark. This was the kind of comforting perspective much needed but not available in the early days of illusion and of impossible targets, of physical breakdown and despair.

The Fowlers had before them, as their starting-point, some 300,000 words already defined, getting on for a million quotations, and over 10,000 pages of the *Oxford English Dictionary*. Their target was a concise dictionary of about 1,000 pages. They treated the articles in *O.E.D.* 'rather as quarries to be drawn upon than as structures to be reproduced in little'. In his preface to the second edition of 1929, Henry Fowler wrote, 'When we began, more than twenty years ago, the work that took shape as *The Concise Oxford Dictionary*, we were plunging into the sea of lexicography without having been first taught to swim.' But with the massive example of *O.E.D.* to guide them the Fowlers never appear to have been in any difficulty. Nobody went to Guernsey to instruct them, nor was it ever suggested that they should venture to Oxford. Their main anxiety was that the book might be a failure, because it differed considerably from other dictionaries in the use it made of illustrative quotations. Possibly no one would want it. 'We have no fancy for being paid for unsaleable stuff', Henry Fowler wrote. 'We should be easier in our minds if we received half only of each instalment.' 'But indeed you are too modest', Chapman replied. 'We have hopes of making money (after many days, no doubt) as well as reputation out of it.' It was then being called the 3s. 6d. dictionary. At that price it might indeed be many days before the Press started making money. But once having determined the price, the Press did not allow itself to be deflected by estimates and printers' bills, which showed that this possibly unmarketable article would have to sell 25,000 copies to clear its first costs. Cannan took the risk with equanimity. Failure would have convinced everybody that dictionary-making in any form was money down the drain. But after many days the Press did begin to make money out of it and eventually sales settled down at about 300,000 copies a year. The Fowlers had been paid £380 for their work by the time the book was published, and over the next ten years £370 in annual bonuses.

Henry Fowler believed that a man ought to be able to live on £100 a year. As he had inherited £120 a year from his father, he was over-endowed by his own standards, and inclined to disembarrass himself of superfluous wealth through charity. After a relatively undistinguished undergraduate career at Balliol he had carried away with him a tepid testimonial from Jowett: 'He is quite a gentleman in manner and feeling and has good sense and good taste.' Jowett added that he thought Mr. Fowler had 'a natural aptitude for the profession of Schoolmaster', and that was the profession he followed, for seventeen years, at Sedbergh. In 1899, at the age of 41, he resigned on a matter of principle, and began a new life of assiduous journalism in London. He lived in Chelsea. Every day without fail he ran at nine or ten miles an hour to the Serpentine for his morning bathe. In one Christmas Day race he was badly cut about the chest by ice. He had a recurrent dream that he was having tea with Queen Victoria, but otherwise it was an uneventful life. In 1903 he went to join his brother Frank in Guernsey. He had often remarked that his family had a defective sense of clannishness.

Frank was twelve years younger, and since leaving Cambridge with a first in Classics had done little except grow tomatoes, rather half-heartedly, and build himself a small granite cottage. When Henry arrived they built a similar cottage within shouting distance some fifty yards away, and from there the two anchorites produced their *Lucian, The King's English,* and *The*

Concise Oxford Dictionary. Each morning Henry ran a mile down to the sea and a steep mile back. The rest of the day he worked, often out of doors, wearing a football jersey and shorts. In 1908, on his fiftieth birthday, he married a lady of forty-six, a nurse.

9. History in Rag-time

IN 1911 there appeared at last *A History of England* for schools. It was written by C. R. L. Fletcher, an Oxford historian who had become a Delegate in 1905. In the early stages it had threatened to go the same way as York Powell's ill-fated venture, and Goldwin Smith's. Fletcher had already written a school history for John Murray, creating a rut into which he repeatedly sank back. His early efforts to break fresh ground were an embarrassment to Cannan and Milford, whose forebodings were confirmed by the advisers to whom they sent the manuscript. Fletcher's political opinions were discomfiting even to a staunch conservative like Cannan. He was an excitable Tory imperialist, anti-Papist and anti-Irish, a chauvinist, a royalist, to whom all that was most dear depended on the Royal Navy. Cannan told him he must not try to compete with himself, and after all it was not so very paradoxical, given the constancy of his views, that he should find he had said most of what he had to say before. But Fletcher was determined. There must be more to British history than that. The elementary schools had not heard the last of him yet.

Cannan might have been able to fend Fletcher off, awkward though it was to be faced by a Delegate promoting his own book, but he was quite undone when Fletcher produced a collaborator, none other than Rudyard Kipling. Moreover, as Fletcher now tantalizingly suggested that he might approach another publisher, Cannan had to invite Kipling to stay with him and use all his skills of persuasion to secure the book for himself. A generous provision of new poems to punctuate and adorn Fletcher's prose narrative would certainly result in something different. It could be a lucrative little venture which would do the nation's children no great harm. Cannan decided to go ahead. In January 1911 the printer was ready to start, and Fletcher wrote to ask whether the book had ever been passed by the Delegates. If not it should be soon, but he would not wish to be there when the matter was brought up. In R. W. Chapman's hand are the stupefying words—'Agreed to go on keeping it dark at present'. It had become a conspiracy, a misdemeanour without precedent if it were to carry the Clarendon Press imprint. Presumably Cannan was still not sure. His bolt-hatch if needed would be through the Henry Frowde and Hodder & Stoughton imprint, but he was reluctant to let it go.

Kipling had long been an enthusiastic motorist. His early jaunts in Sussex, when he boasted a magnificent one-thousand-two-hundred-guinea car, had given Henry James much food for thought. By 1911 he had moved on to higher things and was motoring in the more inaccessible parts of the Pyrenees when proofs appeared. Fletcher badly needed to consult him about commas. The printer's reader had been punctuating Kipling's verses as he had Fletcher's prose, introducing amongst other things the Oxford comma. Fletcher could not abide it. 'May your reader who inserts commas where I had specially left them out (e.g. Lancashire, Devon, and Cornwall) be fried alive,' he wrote in his usual robust vein to Cannan, 'with the author of the "King's English" told off to keep him from dying too quick.' Kipling, though he did not approve, was more accommodating. 'I abhor an abundance of commas but if it's the Clarendon Use put em in. I think it makes the sentences sloppy.' An interesting problem for the textual critic.

Kipling contributed twenty-three poems in varying styles, some of them undoubtedly effective. However they may appear on the printed page, their possible impact in the classroom might well give those of a liberal disposition cause for alarm. Fletcher, himself a propagandist, had cannily slotted Kipling in so that points that might have been questioned by a shrewd child were suddenly taken out of the realm of argument by Kipling's snappy jingles and a roll of drums. Explaining 'Danegeld', Fletcher scolds Ethelred for having listened to his 'wise men', who were 'as useless as the House of Commons would be today if there were a big invasion. . . . A country in such a plight wants a *man* to lead it to war.' Whereupon Kipling intervenes

> It is always a temptation to an armed and agile nation,
>   To call upon a neighbour and to say:—
> 'We invaded you last night—we are quite prepared to fight,
>   Unless you pay us cash to go away.'
>
> And that is called asking for Dane-geld,
>   And the people who ask it explain
> That you've only to pay 'em the Dane-geld
>   And then you'll get rid of the Dane!
>
>   *   *   *
>
> It is wrong to put temptation in the path of any nation,
>   For fear they should succumb and go astray,
> So when you are requested to pay up or be molested,
>   You will find it better policy to say:—
>
> 'We never pay any one Dane-geld,
>   No matter how trifling the cost,
> For the end of that game is oppression and shame,
>   And the nation that plays it is lost!'

Under the dull heading 'Imported Food', Fletcher makes a point he was most anxious to hammer home: 'It is our duty to keep our navy so strong that it must be for ever impossible for us to be defeated at sea.' The words in themselves were not likely to inflame the imagination of a child, but

Kipling's splendid poem 'Big Steamers' that follows was of incalculable potency. Perhaps W. H. Auden read it at school.

> 'Oh, where are you going to, all you Big Steamers,
>   With England's own coal, up and down the salt seas?'
> 'We are going to fetch you your bread and your butter,
>   Your beef, pork, and mutton, eggs, apples, and cheese.'
>
> *   *   *
>
> 'Then what can I do for you, all you Big Steamers,
>   Oh, what can I do for your comfort and good?'
> 'Send out your big warships to watch your big waters,
>   That no one may stop us from bringing you food.
>
> *'For the bread that you eat and the biscuits you nibble,*
>   *The sweets that you suck and the joints that you carve,*
> *They are brought to you daily by all us Big Steamers,*
>   *And if any one hinders our coming you'll starve!'*

The book was published in June 1911 — an unusual time for a school-book — in two editions, one of 25,000 copies, crown 8vo, in cloth at 1s. 8d., the other of 5,000 copies, quarto with additional illustrations, at 7s. 6d. It had an extraordinary reception. It was acclaimed as a masterpiece, as 'the most popular book of the year' by the *Glasgow News*, and 'the chief literary event of Coronation Year' by the *Church Family Newspaper*. During the summer it was at the top of the *Daily Graphic*'s monthly best-seller list for 'general literature', ahead of the *C.O.D.* and of Dr. Sanday's *Christology and Personality*. Some reviewers, however, were prejudiced. 'History in Rag-time' was the title given to it by the *New York Times*: 'Granted the need of a rag-time history,' the reviewer wrote, 'Mr. Fletcher and Mr. Kipling stand out above all mankind as the two persons ideally and conspicuously fitted for the task.' But he was not prepared to grant the need. The *Star*, instead of appreciating that it instilled in the mind a proper sense of patriotism and breathed a healthy imperialistic spirit, declared it 'almost too bad to be true'. The *Weekly Times and Echo* asked, 'Who is it that has tempted Mr. K. to leave his "last" and prostitute his genius to this petty political balderdash?' The colour plates were described as gaudy — Cannan was colour-blind and could make mistakes in such matters — but the Press itself generally escaped censure, books at this level apparently not yet being regarded as the University's responsibility to the same extent as advanced works of scholarship. Equally the Press paid less heed to the newspapers than to the scholarly journals, though in the severity of its rebuke the *Manchester Guardian* review would seem to have merited the Delegates' attention as much as Greg's review of Churton Collins. 'But for the rah, tah, tah and the bounce the book would be dreary reading,' the reviewer wrote. 'As a work of history it is as nearly worthless as a book can be; as a work designed to influence the minds of children it is the most pernicious we have seen.' The *Manchester Guardian* was regarded as pernicious itself, however, amongst sound Conservatives and it is unlikely that Fletcher would have allowed it in his house. Cannan was on his side. 'I suppose we must conclude', he wrote of another review, 'that no Radical is to be trusted to know a fact when he sees it.'

Then to Fletcher's excitement there came a message from Buckingham Palace. The Queen—Queen Mary—was pained to read that William IV had 'as a young man . . . been nicknamed "Silly Billy"'. It was required that the last words should be changed to read 'served in the Navy'. Though he was described earlier in the same sentence as 'a stupid honest old gentleman' this was allowed, perhaps on grounds of historical accuracy. 'It is almost worth making such a blunder to have it pointed out by the Queen', Fletcher gloated to Cannan, who, however, was not amused. If it were a matter of royal command the only way in which the offending words could be changed was by printing a four-page cancel, a tiresome and pointless operation since so many copies had already been sold. There was even a possibility that he might have to call in unsold stock from the booksellers. It seemed to him that two Silly Billys were involved. Fletcher's suggestion that an erratum slip should be inserted at the appropriate place was plainly absurd. Fortunately there came in due course what was interpreted as a clear command not to reprint on the Queen's account. The correction could be made in subsequent impressions. Fletcher in the meantime had managed to recollect his source, a story told by his grandfather of a famous lunatic at Bedlam, to see whom William IV had once been taken. The lunatic pointed at him and called out 'Silly Billy! Silly Billy!' 'By Gad he knows me,' said William. 'Oh yes,' said the keeper, 'he has his lucid intervals.'

Fletcher watched over the book like a possessive mother for the rest of his life. During the First World War he was anxious to add a supplementary chapter, in which credit could be given for the war effort, slackers exposed, and the Irish further chastised. Kipling thought it would be better to win the war first. In 1919 Fletcher was meeting unexpected resistance from the Press: the new chapter would spoil the balance, he was evasively told. It continued to be an obsession with him. The Labour Party and the ungovernable working classes were added to his list of *bêtes noires*. The country generally was falling into the hands of scoundrels. Kipling disowned him in the most courteous fashion, allowing a new edition if the Press so wished, but only if it were made clear that he was in no way responsible for views not his own—'and may it be prosperous exceedingly and may you be right'. But the Assistant Secretary of the day, John Johnson, supported by Gerrans and other Delegates, was firm. With regret, and with a sense that the Press he so much admired and wished to help had fallen victim to narrow-mindedness, Fletcher determined to approach John Murray, in the hope that he would agree to publish the chapter separately.

But in 1929 he was making another attempt to persuade the Press to agree to a new edition with his concluding chapter, now further revised. Kipling repeated what he had said ten years earlier. 'As you know I didn't do anything at all much beyond the verses,' he wrote. 'You lie', Fletcher replied. 'Some of the most valuable prose suggestions, and all the pretty little love-poems in prose to England were yours.' Ageing, but more convinced than ever of the truths he had to convey, Fletcher found to his chagrin that he was not being allowed to make himself heard. It was a bitter experience. The Press, now in the person of Kenneth Sisam, had dug in its heels. Nonplussed, for after all only unteachable radicals or inferior races were likely to find his chapter contentious, Fletcher brooded and began to think of posterity. The unlucky chapter would be among the papers he left behind. To Sisam he wrote, 'I should like you therefore, or Milford, to send a line which I can pin on to it giving some plausible reason why it was not printed in my life time: some words which exonerate the Clarendon Press from the accusation of being afraid of public opinion (for I think you may quite fairly play the card that the *University* as such has to have respect for contemporary opinion). I fear that if you leave it to me to do I might say something unkind, and I don't want to do that or to do anything which would be interpreted as disloyal to the Press which I have loved so much and which has been so good to me.'

Sisam was obliged to ponder the question as a matter of principle, though there was no way of reconciling the principle he now enunciated with whatever principles had governed the publication of the book in 1911. 'In a book for schools', he explained, 'the publisher (in this case the University) is given a much fuller responsibility; and we take the view that, as an institution, we ought not to issue schoolbooks that would give offence to a considerable section of our clients, e.g. the Irish.... Teachers in fact assume that a book with our imprint has undergone a certain censorship, behind which they may shelter; and however stupid a censorship may be, there is something to be said for it in the case of schoolbooks and of juvenilia generally.' To Milford he wrote, 'I have done my best, but told him to apply to your golden pen if it isn't right. Strange that he doesn't see how much better the fire would be: but he really loves that chapter, and I am afraid its rejection cuts him to the heart.'

10. Views from the Outside

Two distinguished 'outsiders' joined the O.U.P. in the years immediately before the First World War—the young Basil Blackwell and the young Geoffrey Faber. Sir Basil went to Amen Corner in September 1911. Frowde, who knew his father well, had suggested that he might spend a year with the Press in London 'to gain some insight into publishing'. It was 'one of the most delightful years of my life', Blackwell later recalled. 'No man can have had a more gracious introduction into the mysteries of publishing.' His stay was extended to sixteen months at the request of the Press, and he still felt rather proud about that many years later. 'The lasting impression made on me at Amen Corner', he wrote, 'was one of reverence for scholarship and enthusiasm for any books which might advance its cause.'

There was nothing gracious about the habitation at Amen Corner itself. Ever since 1883 Frowde had been battling for more space, which could be gained only by renting adjoining premises. This usually meant acquiring them piecemeal, or at best perhaps the entire top floor of a neighbouring building. At one time he was burrowing his way through the office of the Chief Beadle of the Stationers' Company, and there was a constant knocking of holes in walls. In the end, by successive accretions, Amen Corner stretched from Paternoster Row at one end to Ludgate Hill at the other. Distances were great, communication a severe problem. It was an easy place to get lost in. Those who worked there generally kept to their own offices for safety and had little knowledge of what was going on in other parts of the warren.

Blackwell's apprenticeship, however, was gracious enough. He was invited to complete a selection of 'English Essays 1600–1900' for the World's Classics and to see it through the Press. He shared the honour of the title-page with Stanley Makower who had died before the selection was complete. He was able to visit the London Library and the Reading Room of the British Museum at will. His narrow office was little more than a converted corridor leading from the showroom, but it afforded a view of the more stately and roomy offices of Humphrey Milford and Frowde, both of whom were flanked and protected by secretaries. 'We did not see much of Milford', Blackwell wrote. 'He was shy but, in my experience, always kindly and with an infallible eye for a misprint.' Frowde was remoter still. 'In the inner sanctum was Henry Frowde, a numinous figure with a spade beard, always dressed in grey with a frock coat, except on those occasions when we would find hanging up in the cloakroom a blue serge suit, which gave warning that he was to entertain someone to lunch, and that the cloakroom was forbidden territory between 12.30 and 3.0 p.m., when the blue suit was seen to be hanging up again.'

Faber only saw him once, when he sent for every member of the staff in turn on the day of his formal retirement, and presented each with an inscribed copy of the Two-Version Bible. 'A patriarchal figure, with a flowing beard, Frowde was the cartoonist's ideal embodiment of the evangelical piety and the shrewd practical sense which together characterized the London book trade of the last century and gave Paternoster Row its peculiar atmosphere, at once vigorous and musty.'

Blackwell found a companion in R. M. Leonard who, having once satisfied himself that though an Oxford graduate Blackwell was not supercilious, proved affable and informative. He was a keen Frowde observer, and was occasionally consulted by the patriarch on matters of importance, such as whether he would be justified in buying his youngest daughter a bicycle for her twenty-first birthday. Leonard told Blackwell that the best way to get a rise in salary was to approach the publisher's secretary, Mr. Curtis, confess to being troubled with religious doubts, and ask to seek the aid of Henry Frowde. 'That good man would devote the greatest care to setting you right, but then you must be careful to say "Thank you, Sir, you have removed my difficulties". This was deemed to be worth 5s. a week.'

For Geoffrey Faber it was an entirely different experience. He was just finished at Oxford, and properly equipped with a first in Classical Moderations and Greats. Ambitious, eager to learn everything he could about publishing and to learn it quickly, this was no sunny interlude before returning to the family business but a serious and apprehensive step into an unknown future. He was perhaps destined, if all went well, to be Milford's assistant, possibly even his successor. It took him a little while to realize that Milford, at thirty-six, was only twelve years his senior. His approach consequently was a good deal less light-hearted than that of Blackwell. He started work at Amen Corner on 1 January 1913, and the fact that this was the year of Frowde's retirement and of Milford's succession seemed to him looking back to have been not without significance. By then the title of 'Caesar' had been bestowed upon Milford by one of his younger editors.

In 'A Fragment of Autobiography', published in the *Bookseller* in 1953, a few months after Milford's death, feelings pent up for forty years were allowed to come out. Faber remained always a little in awe of Milford: 'He was about as near perfection, in his own right and way, as a man can be', he wrote. After the war he became a friend, and Faber liked to think that Milford watched his emergence as a successful publisher with something akin to affectionate pride. Even so, in his account of the Oxford University Press as it had appeared to a frustrated employee forty years before there rankled still a sense not so much that he had failed but that Milford had failed him.

The gist of his complaint was that he learned nothing while there that was to be of the slightest use to him in later life. On his first morning, he records, he was 'summoned into the Presence, given some catalogues, a few extremely terse instructions', and shown to his allotted desk. Within half an hour he was at work compiling a list of Oxford books, cutting up bits of printed paper and gumming them on to blank foolscap sheets. It was a tedious job, he did not know why he was doing it, and he became extremely depressed. His narrow office was warmed by an ancient electric heater. It so dried up the air that he began to suffer from sneezing fits, convulsions appallingly prolonged. When they were over he was incapable of speech or reason for quite a while. As time passed they became more frequent and more prostrating: the fear that Milford might discover him in the throes or aftermath of a fit preyed upon his mind. At last somebody suggested putting a biscuit tin filled with water on top of the stove. The sneezing stopped immediately. 'I have often reflected', Faber wrote, 'that this was the only real piece of technical knowledge I acquired in my 21 months' apprenticeship at Amen Corner.'

The Quad, c. 1900

Q. (Sir Arthur Quiller-Couch)

The first weeks were only made tolerable by the presence of Basil Blackwell, full of the insouciant joys of youth. He was able to initiate Faber into at least some of the mysteries. Frederick Hall, later to become Printer to the University, told them about design and typography, and even gave lessons in 'casting-off'. Faber discovered that he was the only man in the entire organization, Milford not excepted, who knew how to draw up an estimate. Looking back it seemed to him almost unbelievable, but it was true. If so, it can only have been because Cannan neglected to tell Milford, and Milford in any event did not want to know. Nobody really believed in estimates.

With Blackwell's departure Faber's depression deepened. His catalogue was finished and there was nothing for him to do. He observed jealously that everybody else seemed to be busy, though he was unable to find out what they did. Later he discovered that they were not as busy as he had supposed. 'One morning, I came to the end of my endurance', he continues. 'I left my desk, went through the show-room, up the steps to Milford's room and knocked at the door. "Hah, Faber! What is it?" "I have finished that catalogue, Sir. May I have something else to do?" There was a short but very highly charged silence. "I don't engage first-class men to ask me to tell them what to do. Your brain ought to be pullulating with ideas. Go away and use it."'

Utterly abashed, still quite ignorant even of what his job was supposed to be, and therefore of what his brain should be pullulating with, Faber consulted the man who knew how to do estimates, Fred Hall. 'What you must do', he said, 'is to get Milford to send you down to the Clarendon Press for six months. I'm not going to be here for always; and it's a shocking state of affairs that nobody else in the place knows the first thing about printing or binding or paper.' This seemed sensible advice to Faber: the only problem was whether he could muster the courage to face Milford again. Eventually he did so. His request to go to Oxford to learn something about book-production was instantly turned down with one of Milford's characteristic utterances: 'A first-class man is a Greek among the barbarians.' Nothing more was said.

In the early summer of 1914 Faber put in for an Ancient History Fellowship at Wadham. His old tutor, to whom he confessed his dissatisfaction with the Press, thought there would be no harm in trying. If he did not get it he would be all right where he was. The Press would not throw him out. On the day the results of the election were known Milford entered his room and asked for news. Faber told him that somebody else had been elected. Milford fidgeted and would not meet his eye. 'I'm sorry,' he said, 'I hoped you'd get it. You'd better go at Michaelmas. You aren't happy here.' So Geoffrey Faber's career in publishing seemed to have come abruptly to an end. He had failed. It was still a few months before 4 August 1914.

Faber had not taken to the idea of being at once ignorant and superior. It seemed to him then, and in 1953, that it was very wrong to think that a

N

'first-class man' fresh from a University should see himself in that light unless he had 'already learned the technique' of his new calling. If he had not done so, it was his first duty and essential task to learn what the 'barbarians' knew that he did not. 'How simple, and obvious, this must now seem to everybody!', he reflected. 'How could it conceivably be denied? But, forty years ago, Milford denied it to me, as if it were a proposition too foolish even to be argued, and condemned me, for the rest of my life, to use other men's brains instead of my own.'

The true nature of Milford's arrogance and the hierarchical intellectual structure imposed by Oxford largely escaped Faber. Milford had absolute confidence in his own brains, but saw no reason to exercise them unnecessarily. He was after all a literary man. What was the point of paying somebody to be Printer in Oxford and then trying to learn the craft oneself? Faber's attitude was incomprehensible to a man reared by Cannan, whose own taciturnity prevented him from ever explaining to others what had to be done or how. Milford and Cannan shared a wonderful confidence in the efficacy of sound academic training, which taught a man how to pick up all he needed to know on any subject whatever. Cannan himself had learned the business without any overt pursuit of knowledge, and he expected others to do the same. 'If it comes to mere ability in handling affairs the man with Greek will always come out top', Q once remarked, and though he would not have put it so crudely Cannan shared the faith. R. W. Chapman recalled being interviewed for the job of Assistant Secretary. He was very nervous and the interview had not been prospering when it was interrupted by a telephone call from Milford in London. That over, Chapman ventured to ask what he would be required to do, should he be appointed. After a silence Cannan said, 'You heard me just now: that sort of thing.' Demoralized, Chapman accepted the finality of the answer and went away wondering.

The belief that no special training, particularly of a technical kind, was necessary for a publisher was not unknown outside the Oxford University Press. Publishing after all was a gentleman's profession. A distinguished head of a modern London publishing house used to say that he did not want to know anything about printing techniques, for fear that it might deter him as a publisher from asking the impossible. The belief may have been stronger in Oxford because of the unusual organization of the business. Frowde over the years acquired great expertise and used it to good effect in producing his own books. He was his own production manager, firm and clear in his instructions to Hart. As far as Oxford books were concerned, however, his advice was sought only on matters of binding, pricing, publicity, and sales. There was nothing in the nature of a production department in the Oxford publishing business. Cannan, Chapman, or Doble would decide on the format of the book, perhaps even its type, but they did not need to concern themselves unduly with technical matters which could easily be dealt with by Hart. It was true enough that Milford himself during his apprentice years in Oxford had learned remarkably little about the fundamental processes involved in the production of a book: 'never take two responsibilities' was a maxim deeply impressed upon him by Cannan. In a later period Faber might have been allowed to go on a course, but a stubborn conviction that publishing, like English literature, cannot be taught has never been entirely extinguished. Later practice was to put any new editorial recruit to work reading files. After six months of that he would be allowed to write his first letters to authors, which would be carefully checked and corrected before going out, and to bear some of the responsibilities for seeing a book through the Press. Many trained in London, probably destined for a post overseas, saw scarcely anything of Oxford, so the figures of Secretary and Delegates, representing the ultimate authority, remained to them as mysterious and unapproachable as the occupants of Kafka's Castle.

Faber glimpsed something in the relations between London and Oxford that seemed to him extremely obscure. If they were not made more so they were at least epitomized by the gnomic memoranda sent to London from Oxford, the obscurely allusive communications from Cannan and Chapman—those from the latter often indecipherable as well. Only Milford, to whom they were usually addressed, seemed fully to understand them. As an Oxford man Faber too knew how to relish allusiveness, deliberate avoidance of plain statement. But it seemed to him there was something behind 'these verbal quiddities, something elusive and impalpable and most difficult to define or describe, but indubitably there, and exceedingly tough'. The only line of correspondence that he could remember after forty years was a note from Chapman explaining why he would not be coming up to London: 'I think', he had written, 'I can't eat leeks two days running.' The very fact that they had stayed in his mind for so long suggested that the words had a sinister power to haunt. It was not surprising, when he put his mind to it, that he could make little of them. His bewilderment was not unlike that of Lyttelton Gell, and he too could claim to be a 'Jowett' man, if only because he wrote his biography.

It was said that Cannan was the only person to know the difference between the Oxford University Press and the Clarendon Press, and nobody dared to ask him what it was. Faber also put his mind to this tantalizing question, but only in the fullness of time and of hindsight was he able to make anything of it. Milford, he concluded, had been deliberately blurring the distinction. The Alligator and Caesar were one, as Frowde had long ago perceived, and it was their dominating personalities that had shaped the complex institution in which he was unable to find a place. His final verdict on Cannan, however, was an interesting mixture of hindsight and an awareness of recent charges, publicized in the late 1940s, that the Press had divorced itself from the University. He related that particular debate to his own brief experience forty years before.

'Cannan was a deliberate obscurantist,' he wrote unforgivingly in 1953, 'a determined autocrat, whose whole power had been consciously directed for years to the primary object of isolating the University Press from

University criticism. His success in this direction was astonishing; but it led, inevitably, to a kind of wall-building round the Press in which everybody was compelled to take part. The Press became a complete end in itself, and everybody in its employ was expected so to think of it. Any selfish aim, or personal desire, was an unmentionable, unthinkable, heresy.'

And in his view it was the attempt after Frowde's retirement to transplant this attitude, just tolerable perhaps in Oxford, to Amen Corner that was at the root of the trouble. Amen Corner should have existed to make money for the Clarendon Press to spend on the promotion of learning. It had no other justification, yet it felt itself to be superior to the commercial London book trade which it ought in fact to have been trying to emulate. Faber blamed Milford for this. He was absolute master in his own house, at the same time selfless administrator of a large business held in trust for the Delegates of the Clarendon Press—'an august body whose collective opinion I am sure that he rightly held in small respect'. Frowde's honest commercialism was put aside, and the idea of devoted service to a great institution, involving the sacrifice of personal ambition, was inappropriately fostered in London too.

Milford remained unfathomable to Faber. There was no visible evidence of planning, of mature consideration, of anything that could be described as a publishing policy. Instead there were sudden leaps into the unknown. He was an intuitive creature, and consequently unpredictable. The swiftness of his decisions could deceive the eye, but from the Joint Venture of 1905 until the purchase of the Home University Library in 1941 they appear to have been generally right. Once a decision was made he placed extraordinary trust in the man chosen to implement it, leaving him to find his own way. But the enigma of his personality remains. He was described by his successor, Geoffrey Cumberlege, as a man of intermittent charm. In his article for *The Dictionary of National Biography* A. L. P. Norrington wrote: 'His personality was strongly marked but elusive. What he said or did was seen to be characteristic, yet could not easily be predicted, and he inspired a lively but wary devotion in his staff.'

He probably learned more than he realized from Frowde, who to the very end of his career seemed determined to demonstrate a capacity for unlimited growth. Every year that passed he invited some new and massive demand upon his resources, particularly those of his sales staff, and his ramshackle warehousing facilities. In 1908 he took over the publications of the Early English Text Society, which Furnivall had founded in 1864: there were some 250 separate titles, most of them so slow-selling that they could be expected to stay in print for the rest of the century. In 1909 he issued his first volume for Yale University Press, in 1910 for Harvard, in 1911 for Columbia, in 1912 for Princeton. By then some 300 people were employed at Amen Corner. Getting on for 500 titles were issued by the O.U.P. in 1913 under one or other of the twenty-three imprints then in use. The total number of books published by British publishers that year was about 12,000.

The capacity of individual scholars to cope with the advance of knowledge such superabundance indicated was strained. The tendency to specialization and to collaborative works of learning increased. The Cambridge Modern History (1902–12), the Cambridge History of English Literature (1907–16), and the Cambridge Medieval History (1911–36) were produced by teams of experts. The Oxford Survey of the British Empire was a similar enterprise, with seventy-three contributors. Published on the eve of war, the six volumes took pride of place on page 1 of the first General Catalogue. This and the many other books on the Dominions and on India in particular were regarded by Cannan as perhaps the major achievement of the Clarendon Press in the old era. Of the Survey, he wrote, it 'must always be a standard book, for it gives a complete picture drawn at first hand by those who knew the Empire in its last year of peace, and even its statistics need never be revised, as they are the last of the old order of things and will always be wanted for comparison'.

It was a period for erecting monuments of scholarship, a period too of heroic illusions when the definitive still seemed within reach. The classical and literary scholars edited their texts, the historians edited documents, speeches, or the works of their predecessors—Burke, Carlyle, and Macaulay were in great demand. *The Letters of Horace Walpole* edited by Mrs. Paget Toynbee, over 7,000 pages in sixteen volumes, was published with astonishing celerity between 1903 and 1905. (Some twenty-five years later so much new material had come to light that the Yale edition was under way, to be completed in thirty-four volumes in 1965.) One of the great Oxford scholars of his day, P. S. Allen, was editing the letters of Erasmus. Very tentatively, in 1898, the Delegates had agreed to publish two volumes of 500 pages each. Allen went off to scour the libraries of Europe and by the time he had gathered the material for the first volume it was clear that he was dealing with but a small fragment of the whole. Bishop Stubbs and Ingram Bywater sat sternly in judgement: like the lexicographers he had consistently failed to observe the limits. But by then the Delegates' attitude had come to seem one of niggling and old-fashioned parsimony. Monuments of scholarship took many decades and many volumes to complete, as the Dictionary had taught them well, but the lessons to be learned were patience and an unstinting recognition of the magnitude of a man's life's work. In 1906, Cannan wrote to Allen: 'The Delegates are very brave.' They had consented to seven volumes, and he hoped to publish one every two and a half years. For Cannan the object was to finish the job, come what may (whilst warning Allen of that 'Better which is an enemy of the Good'). As a contribution to expenses £100 was offered for 1906, a token of goodwill, and neither Cannan nor his successors complained that each volume appeared on average every $3\frac{1}{2}$ years, and that even with the devoted help of his wife and H. W. Garrod the twelfth and concluding volume was not published until 1947.

In the summer of 1914, Sir James Murray and Henry Bradley received degrees of D.Litt. *honoris causa*, and C. T. Onions on becoming Joint Editor received an honorary M.A. Edward Prince of Wales, an eighteen-year-old undergraduate at Magdalen, visited the Press in Walton Street and so much appreciated it that he came again the next day with the Queen and Princess Mary. A painstaking letter to Hart thanking him for the traditional keepsake was read to the Delegates, and recorded in their minutes.

> This will ever remain to me a souvenir of one of the most interesting $1\frac{1}{2}$ hours I have ever spent.
> What wonderful machines are invented nowadays, and I had not the least conception that as many as 800 hands were employed in the Press.
> Please thank Mr. Cannan very much for so kindly proposing to let me have the six volumes of the new geographical survey; I have always been very interested in Geography and maps.

In that long hot summer the Delegates reached an extraordinary decision. While Frowde had been hacking his way towards Ludgate, the Press in Oxford had also had to contend with a critical shortage of space. The need to accommodate more people, more machines, more stock, was making the problem increasingly grave. The architects' estimates for new buildings of the size required were, however, high. A more economic solution presented itself. It was decided to roof over the quadrangle. Plans were drawn up and approved in May 1914. The quadrangle contained a pond, with lilies and rushes, and trees and shrubs in 'vases' in each corner; the grass had been carefully tended since 1830. There was also a magnificent copper beech. It may have been an anachronism, this pastoral refuge at the heart of a great factory, and the Press quadrangle did not perhaps compare with Tom Quad at Christ Church or the Great Court at Trinity, Cambridge. Nevertheless it was a quadrangle and there is a basic architectural law hallowed by tradition that quadrangles are open spaces. Unfortunately there was a grimmer law concerning the maximization of the utilization of space, and Horace Hart believed it to be inexorable. But with the war the scheme was shelved: eventually it was dropped, and the architects' fee was written off. Today the copper beech is higher than the surrounding buildings, and the printing works have spread deep into Jericho. Suggestions occasionally put forward that the parking of cars in the quad might help to resolve a contemporary dilemma are answered in a word: desecration. Cannan would not be so kindly remembered by his heirs if he had allowed one of the country's better-looking factories to be converted into the simulacrum of a prison.

Despite such aberrations in its domestic policies, the O.U.P. by 1914 had firmly established itself as a national institution with a responsibility to survive in the interest of civilization as a whole. Rupert Brooke, in a twilit humour, moved by Grierson's edition of Donne, commended the future to its keeping. Looking sad-eyed upon the world for objects to praise, he found 'Charing Cross Bridge by night, the dancing of Miss Ethel Levey, the Lucretian hexameter, the beer at an inn in Royston . . . the sausages at another inn above Princes Risborough, and the Clarendon Press editions of the English poets. But the beer and the sausages will change, and Miss Levey one day will die, and Charing Cross Bridge will fall; so the Clarendon Press books will be the only thing our evil generation may show to the cursory eyes of posterity, to prove it was not wholly bad.'

PART V

THE GREAT WAR

1. The Pamphlet War

O N 4 August 1914 sixty-three men of the Territorial Army marched out through the Press gates, seen off by Cannan. There were about 575 adult males employed at Oxford, with over 200 women and boys. More than 300 men had enlisted by 1917 and from Amen Corner about 100, or a third of the staff. Yet the output of the Press remained extraordinarily high, and when necessary great feats of speed could still be performed. The demand for the Bible reached a new peak as it became an essential piece of military equipment, though cynics questioned whether on India paper it retained its traditional bullet-stopping properties. Well over a million copies a year of the New Testament were supplied for 'use in the field'. Within a few weeks of the outbreak of war the 'Knapsack' Bible was on sale again, as it had been during the Boer War, bound in khaki with the Union Jack in gilt, or in navy blue adorned with a gilt anchor. It was bound up with the Church Hymnary or with the Scottish Metrical Psalms.

The Oxford Faculty of Modern History rose to the occasion in spectacular fashion. *Why We are at War: Great Britain's Case*, a work of 264 pages including an appendix of original documents, was written during August by Ernest Barker, H. W. C. Davis, C. R. L. Fletcher, Arthur Hassall, L. G. Wickham Legg, and F. Morgan. It was published on 14 September and, by the time the Delegates retrospectively approved publication at their first meeting of the new term on 16 October, it was in its seventh impression. At the instance of the Government it was translated into French, Italian, Swedish, Danish, Spanish, and German. All the translations were done in Oxford and the translators gave their services freely. The Press printed and published these editions and arranged for their distribution abroad. It was fulfilling in a small way the role performed by the overseas service of the B.B.C. in the Second World War. In November 1915, in fulfilment of a promise made in the preface, a cheque for £728. 1s. 0d. was sent to the Belgian Minister in London together with a letter signed by Cannan and the six authors—one of the rare occasions when Cannan was moved to put aside his rule of anonymity. In the preface it had been said that 'Any profits arising from the sale of this work will be sent to the Belgian Relief Fund, as a mark of sympathy and respect for the Belgian nation, and especially for the University of Louvain.' In 1920 a second and final payment of £176. 3s. 9d. was sent.

Why We are at War was surprisingly sober and dispassionate, the six historians keeping their heads when all about them was a mindless fervour. Throughout Europe those who had called themselves patriots were discovering for the first time what patriotism really meant. It was a transcendent passion, a transcendental religion. Those who had not called themselves patriots, like Stefan Zweig in Germany, who as a citizen of Europe had regarded himself as above it, were overwhelmed just the same and realized that for many experience of the war would be the greatest event of their lives. Scholars were by no means immune. The Oxford Pamphlets began to pour from the Press, written with intense conviction, and a spontaneity that distinguished them from works written later to manipulate public opinion or promote the war effort. Gilbert Murray, Regius Professor of Greek, pursued the cause of peace throughout a long life. He hated nationalism, had opposed the South African war, and as he explained in his pamphlet of 1914, *How can War ever be Right?*, he had put the most intense feeling into his translation of Euripides' *Trojan Women*, the first great denunciation of war in European literature. But without changing his convictions he could say, 'I believe firmly that we were right to declare war against Germany on August 4, 1914.' He lost in consequence the friendship of Bertrand Russell, one of the few with complete immunity from the contemporary fever.

Eighty-seven Oxford Pamphlets had appeared by September 1915, when the series was said to be complete. Some were practical and instructional— C. S. Orwin on *The Farmer in War Time*; others generally educational and informative, like Arnold Toynbee's *Greek Policy since 1882* or Paul Vinogradoff's *Russia: The Psychology of a Nation*. H. A. L. Fisher, then Vice-Chancellor of Sheffield University, contributed *The Value of Small States*. Sir William Osler wrote a chilling piece, *Bacilli and Bullets*, proving that the risk of being killed in combat was small when compared with that of dying of enteric or typhoid fever on the way to the front. C. R. L. Fletcher put in two rapid bursts in *The Germans, Their Empire and how they have made it*, followed by *and what they covet*. Ernest Barker and others took on Nietzsche and Treitschke, who could be regarded as the ultimate villains of the piece. It was noted that in the index to the latter's *Politik*, under 'war' there were the following heads: 'its sanctity'; 'to be conceived as an ordinance set by God'; 'is the most powerful maker of nations'; 'is politics *par excellence*'.

Help in the pamphlet war also came from Macmillans, and in a long series of papers published in the *Round Table*. The specialists tried to put their expert knowledge at the disposal of the community as a whole. 'In the way of political education there has never been anything like it since Britain became a nation', wrote Sir William Sanday, author of Pamphlet No. 1, *The Deeper Causes of the War*. But the Germans were equally active. When their pamphlets began to appear in Britain at the end of 1914 it was disconcerting to find how many of them were signed by distinguished professors whose names until then had commanded nothing but respect. Ulrich von Wilamowitz-Moellendorff, the 'prince of scholars' revered by Gilbert Murray, was amongst them; and the theologians Adolf von Harnack and Ernst Troëltsch; and the jurist Otto von Gierke; and the historians Eduard Meyer and Erich Marcks.

The list was a long one, and for an Englishman the pamphlets made melancholy and monotonous reading. It was not a time for seeing both sides of a question, and only two conclusions could be drawn from them. These eminent Germans had, quite suddenly it seemed, acquired a deep loathing for the British people. Other countries they could understand and up to a point forgive. But the malice, greed, envy, and hypocrisy of the British made them the best hated of all Germany's enemies. This was clear if inexplicable. But equally strange was the fact that these learned men had disregarded the essential principles of scholarship: they had not returned to their sources, they had failed to consult the most authentic documents. How else could they have arrived at such patently false conclusions? So much, it was felt, for the much vaunted science of Germany. Oxford men, of course, had always had their suspicions. 'Horror of everything German was of very ancient date', wrote Tuckwell, recalling an hour-and-a-half sermon by Tatham, Rector of Lincoln, in which he had wished 'all the Jarman critics at the bottom of the Jarman ocean'. Pusey and the Tractarians had spotted there the source of all corruption, and even Jowett who had introduced the German philosophers into Balliol sided with France in the Franco-Prussian War. The jingoism and anti-German feeling of the 1890s and early twentieth century had infected Charles Cannan, so that even the Oxford Classical Texts and the Oxford Aristotle, works supposedly of pure scholarship, were not unconnected with the spirit of nationalism. 'So much German work is sham and insincere whenever one tests it,' wrote York Powell in 1895, 'and they brag so over their work. They sicken me as the Americans do. I am getting more and more jingo.' The Oxford dons were ready for the war when it came.

To the Lady Margaret Professor of Divinity, William Sanday, it seemed that the war had brought many blessings, for which all civilized men should be thankful. 'A great seriousness has come down over all the combatant nations', he wrote in *The Meaning of the War*. 'All Europe was in need of some such sobering and solemnizing influence ... It seemed as if the higher aims of the spirit were being drowned in gross and growing materialism. All this has been changed.' The war saw the triumph and vindication of Christianity. As the casualty lists lengthened and the courage of the volunteers remained unwavering, it was borne in upon William Sanday that the world was a more fundamentally Christian place than he had ever supposed. Men and women everywhere had shown themselves capable of rising to the greatest heights that Christianity could possibly require of them. And of the dead he wrote, 'If our feelings towards them are not the counterpart of the very best that Christianity can evoke in us, I do not know what else they are.' It takes all sorts to unmake a world.

The public appetite for pamphlets subsided, and so too did the appetite for Milford's patriotic anthologies, or productions such as *The Patriots' Diary*, in which R. M. Leonard listed 250 battles and 'warlike movements', 200 great events, 250 birthdays, and 300 deaths. With Hodder & Stoughton Milford continued to publish the Young Patriot Readers for the schools of the Empire. The Press in Oxford turned its attention to the history of the belligerent nations, a series that outlasted the war itself, to the learned books on which a start had already been made, to the steadily increasing demands of the Government, and to the general problems of survival.

2. Volunteers and New Recruits

BY the end of 1914 Cannan had practically no staff left. Horace Hart had been ill since the summer, and on top of his other responsibilities Cannan had been acting as Controller of the printing business. Chapman remained for the time being, but was soon to go into the army. With him in the large office overlooking the quad and the round pond were only Mr. Durham, the accountant (with seventeen years' experience behind him and twenty-three ahead), and Mr. New, the chief clerk. It was then that Cannan commandeered his three daughters, Dorothea, Joanna, and May. 'I shall need you all', he told them. 'You had better come up to the Press.' They were intelligent and well educated and could type. It did not occur either to the girls or to their father that they might be paid. There was, after all, a war on. They were volunteers. Through long experience, they were better qualified than most to interpret their father's unspoken requests. A greater problem was Chapman's handwriting. He wrote his letters standing up, dropping the awful drafts into a tray to be typed. In the first batch she encountered May Cannan could not read a single word: he appeared to use a private shorthand.

In *Grey Ghosts and Voices*, May Wedderburn Cannan recalled those days, and indeed even earlier days, for she remembered her father walking with Bywater who she thought was Aristotle, and she remembered the death of Queen Victoria. 'Everyone went into black', she wrote, 'and father spent a great deal of time on the telephone, for when the Sovereign died there was a new prayer book which was something to do with "the press-in-London" and up in Walton Street the great presses turned and turned.' In 1914 her sister Dorothea was given special responsibility for the *Journal of Theological Studies*, Joanna for the *Quarterly Journal of Medicine*, and May for the General Catalogue. The fire burned in the grate, the presses thudded beneath them, and life in the main office was cosy, busy, and cheerful. 'I loved the place,' May Cannan wrote. 'I loved the coming and going, the dust and the smell of proofs with the printer's ink still wet on them; the darkness that spread from the windows on those winter evenings; the mounting tension as the end of the day came near and the post must go out. . . . I knew I was happy. It was a great and learned Press and I was a very small cog in one part of it.'

In 1915 a new Assistant Secretary was found to take the place of R. W. Chapman. He was John de Monins Johnson, aged thirty-three, a papyrologist with no previous experience of publishing. He had read Arabic after taking his degree in Oxford, and spent two years in the Egyptian Civil Service. Before the war he had been exploring in Egypt, where he found the earliest known manuscript of Theocritus. A strained heart kept him out of the forces and he was introduced to the Press by the archaeologist D. G. Hogarth, a Delegate since 1912. Johnson was to prove a man of autocratic tendencies and uncertain temper. His personality did not lend itself to harmonious relations with others. In his first years at the Press, however, he was not allowed to spoil the pleasant atmosphere: he was held in check by Dorothea Cannan, whom he married in 1917. He was to become in due course Printer to the University, though Cannan had it in mind that he might be needed as Controller of the Paper-Mill if the newly appointed A. D. Clapperton enlisted.

The services of Hogarth as a Delegate were lost when he was sent out to direct the Arab Bureau in Cairo in 1915. He had been a restless traveller in pre-war years, *Times* correspondent in Crete during the revolution there and in Thessaly on the eve of the Greco-Turkish War. He had also excavated in Crete with Sir Arthur Evans. But his knowledge of Arabia, on which he was now a recognized expert, was based on secondary sources, mostly Charles Doughty, whom he had rediscovered and whose life he wrote. He arrived in Cairo with the rank of Commander in the Royal Naval Volunteer Reserve. He was responsible for the Arab campaigns conducted in the field by the man he had taught archaeology, T. E. Lawrence. On leave in Oxford in 1916 he briskly abolished the slavery of the Cannan daughters, insisting that they be paid 30 shillings a week.

At the same time a very different, but in its way equally remarkable, campaign was being waged by the Fowlers. In their seclusion in Guernsey the war had come as a very painful surprise. Temperamentally pacifist, they nevertheless saw that their country was in peril and needed them. They came to the conclusion that their place was at the front. As Henry was by then fifty-seven years old it was an improper conclusion to draw, but the morning swim, the brisk run to the sea and back, and natural abstinence, had preserved in him the vigour of a much younger man. He gave his age as forty-four and enlisted in the 'Sportsmen's Battalion' without further questioning. Frank was only forty-five but not so robust: he enlisted too, rather less buoyantly. By December 1915 their battalion was deemed fit for service and drafted to France. There these two extremely fastidious gentlemen spent several weeks heaving coal, getting soaked to the skin, and living in quarters unsuitable for any civilized man. Henry Fowler was cruelly punished by the military authorities once it was discovered that he had lied about his age. In every bid he made to get to the front he was thwarted by some implacably benign medical officer explaining to him that he was too old for trench-work. Briefly they got as far as the support trenches, and were exposed to snipers' bullets and shell-fire, but Henry was depressed by a rumour that nobody over forty would be allowed into the front line itself. 'We have been coal-heaving this morning', he wrote to his wife. 'That is the way a grateful country rewards respectable old gentlemen of 57 who are fools enough to think they can fight for it.' It was clear that they had made a mistake. 'Of course Frank and I are much more useful to the country writing books for the Oxford University Press than washing dishes and the like, even if one job is done in uniform and the other out of it.' And it pained Henry to reflect that while he was doing no good for himself or anybody else he was costing 'the silly old country' £100 a year.

In February 1916 the authors of *The King's English* drew themselves up to their full height and addressed their commanding officer as follows:

Pte H. W. Fowler (M.A. Oxon., late scholar of Balliol: age 58) and Pte F. G. Fowler (M.A. Cantab., late scholar of Peterhouse; age 46) have been engaged for some years in Guernsey on literary work of definite public utility for the Oxford University Press (Secretary C. Cannan Esq., Oxford). They enlisted in April 1915 at great inconvenience and with pecuniary loss in the belief that soldiers were needed for active service, being officially encouraged to mis-state their ages as a patriotic act. . . . They are now held at the base at Étaples, performing only such menial or unmilitary duties as dishwashing, coal-heaving, and porterage, for which they are unfitted by habits and age. They suggest that such conversion of persons who undertook purely from patriotic motives the duties of soldiers on active service into unwilling menials or servants is an incredibly ungenerous policy on the part of the military authorities, especially when the victims are advanced in years and of a class unused to the kind of work imposed on them, and that such ungenerous treatment must, when it becomes generally known at the end of the war, bring grave discredit on those responsible for it.

(Signed) H. W. Fowler, M.A.
        F. G. Fowler, M.A.
        authors of *Translation of Lucian*, 4 vols.;
        The King's English; *The Concise Oxf. Dict.*

In June 1916 the army conceded that Henry Fowler had done his bit and he was discharged, still as tough as nails. Frank, whose health had broken down, found himself as a younger man inextricably in the army's clutches. At Étaples he had developed an ominous cough, before long he was spitting blood. Sent back to England, he was in and out of military hospitals but never managed to regain civilian life. He died of consumption in May 1918 before his discharge could be effected. Henry Fowler wrote in bitterness and sorrow to the *Westminster Gazette*, charging the Army authorities with responsibility for his death. 'The relentless persistency of the Army in clinging to its used-up human material, which it will not even be at the pains of sorting out and flinging on the scrap-heap when the expense of its upkeep is greater than its military worth, has doubtless cost the country many lives that deserved keeping in existence for their peace-time value.' Henry Fowler returned to Guernsey to resume work alone on *Modern English Usage* and *The Pocket Oxford Dictionary*.

There were few able-bodied men left in Oxford and Kenneth Sisam, a young New Zealand Rhodes scholar, was not one of them. But Cannan had his eye on him. He had been lecturing on Old and Early English whilst still an undergraduate at Merton, as assistant to Professor Napier. When Napier died in 1916, Sisam had for a couple of years been more or less in charge of the teaching of English language. J. R. R. Tolkien always said it had been his particular good fortune to attend his lectures. Sisam's B.Litt. thesis, 'An Edition of the Salisbury Psalter', was examined by Bradley and Craigie and found satisfactory. But this precocious young scholar was a chronic invalid. He worked for a time on the Dictionary under Bradley, but the labour was too great for him. A large man, with a powerful constitution, toughened by his early years in the New Zealand bush, a devotee of cricket and rugby, he had fallen victim to the Oxford climate and at the age of twenty-seven was utterly debilitated. 'When I first came to England', he once wrote, 'I used to wonder at the feebleness of the English physique but now I just marvel that they have the strength to stand their climate.' Cannan, whom he had never met, came to his rescue when not only his health but his money was running out. He was offered a retaining fee and employed on light labours for the Press. One of his first tasks was to revise Skeat's edition of *Havelock*, which he did in three weeks. Cannan also arranged for him to be examined by Osler who diagnosed, in Sisam's words, 'internal nervous affection the result of run down, and in no way dangerous'. Sisam survived, to become rugged and indefatigable in later life. He was the man to see the Press through the next World War.

3. Cannan Repels Invaders

REGULAR annual contributions continued to be made to the University Chest but they were reduced to £2,000 a year during Cannan's time, on the general ground that there never really was a 'surplus' and profits earned should be put back into the business. The University chose this moment of exceptional stress to prepare a statute that greatly alarmed and dismayed the Delegates. Money was short and, without as it seemed to them due warning, Council proposed to take over the surplus funds of all delegacies and committees, and to assert in a new statute a claim by the University to dispose of such funds for University purposes in any way that it saw fit. The claim was extraordinary and without precedent. Preparations had been afoot in the University since the end of 1913, but not until 17 March

1915 did the Hebdomadal Council present its proposals to the various delegacies, requesting their comments by 1 May.

In a letter signed by the Vice-Chancellor it was pointed out that all these bodies were the creation of the University, that their success was 'largely due to the credit and reputation of the University', and that they had no separate legal identity. It was the kind of situation that Gell had always feared. To Cannan it seemed that the achievement of fifty years might suddenly have to be written off. He said categorically that he would never have assumed office in 1898 if the proposed statute had been in effect. Unwilling though he was to think of the Press as in any way small, it had to be admitted that the University of which it was a part was by definition larger. With the experience of one small state at the hands of a superior power never far from his mind, Cannan set out during the Easter vacation of 1915 to muster his depleted forces to repel the invader. He drafted a long memorandum, which despite signs of breathlessness remains a remarkable and courageous document. Council had had eighteen months to prepare its case: Cannan had barely six weeks.

The various delegacies and committees appointed by the University had in fact a semi-legal status. They had been created by statutes, and as long as the statutes remained unaltered they could retain their separate funds. They were in effect agents acting on the instructions of their principal, the University, to transact its business. Legal opinion, based solely on the University Statute Book, was that the instructions themselves had created a legal trust between the principal and the agents, with the result that the principal was debarred, as he would not have been in an ordinary business, from 'calling for his moneys'. Hence the need for a statute. Disabilities created by statute could be removed by statute: the principal could 'revoke his instructions and so give himself the freedom with which he has by his instructions parted'.

The Delegates, however, saw the constitutional problem in a different light. It was argued firstly that the right of the Press to take profits from its business activities was not created by statute but by a whole series of charters, by Acts of Parliament, and by an abundance of legal opinions and decisions. These, like tradition itself, were grave things to tamper with, and the word 'hitherto' appeared like a rash upon the page. 'The University has hitherto avoided a too curious examination into its rights,' the memorandum noted approvingly. But it warned that if the statute were passed the University would have to face 'difficult questions which have hitherto been properly allowed to slumber'. The defence of University rights would be hampered if the University were to put upon its Statute Book 'a naked claim to overrule, in view of other University necessities, the discretion hitherto accorded to the Delegates'.

The whole of the Delegates' business, it was pointed out, was based on the assumption that their earnings were at their disposal, and it was on this assumption that they had entered into their commitments and planned their policies for the future. They had made contracts with authors, with other businesses, with their own officers. The Delegacy itself had 'attracted the services of not the feeblest brains and the least energetic workers to be found among the academic body'. These men were willing to take large responsibilities, because they had faith in the power of the Board to form and to persevere in a permanent policy, not varying, or even legally subject to variation, according to the occasional pressure of other needs upon the University. Moreover they asked for no payment, as boards of directors of other businesses normally did. The financial credit of the Press stood high, but the legal basis of that credit would be fundamentally altered by the statute, and in consequence a larger working capital would be required. The immediate financial loss to the University would on this ground alone be far greater than any conceivable gain in the future.

Cannan evidently suspected that there was even more to the proposed statute than met the eye. Its object might be not only to gain some financial advantage but to assert the control of the University over the work of the Press. As always the difficulty lay in determining the identity of the University. It could be located in Council, in Congregation, in the University Chest, or in the Board of Finance, but as far as the Press was concerned the Delegates believed that they were the University as the immediate representatives of Convocation. In any case it would be totally mistaken to suppose that the statute would lead to an increase in University control. If some committee of overseers were appointed it would have to grow gradually over the years into something indistinguishable from the Board of Delegates that already existed. There would in the end be no change, just a prolonged period of uncertainty and confusion. But more likely it would be found necessary to bring in partners to administer the business, a reversal of the policy the Delegates had followed for so long and the Syndics in Cambridge were still following. The work of fifty years would have been wasted, and the University would find once again that it was not master in its own printing-house.

The case for the Delegates was vigorously stated. To add a little extra weight it was also pointed out that the Press had no surplus, that the war had brought the book trade almost to a standstill, and that it was not wise policy to create an impression that funds might be made available by statute when no such funds existed at all. Furthermore the rights and privileges of the Press were shared with the Cambridge University Press. 'As the defence of the two Universities has been and must be conducted in common, it would not be proper for this University to move without notice and conference.' This was perhaps the most telling argument of all, and the most bold. The Delegates insisted that they claimed no real independence. But there was the implication that the long history of the Press, its long experience of legislation and litigation in defence of its rights and privileges, made the Delegates to a substantial extent custodians of the rights of the University itself.

The Vice-Chancellor of the day was the Dean of Christ Church, Thomas B. Strong, who had been a Delegate since 1904 and remained one

H. W. Fowler in Guernsey in working togs

C. R. Fletcher

until 1937 except for an interlude of five years when he was Bishop of Ripon. In 1915 he found himself very nearly torn asunder, as chairman of the two conflicting bodies. But the Delegates' spirited defence of their position, supported by a number of similar though less portentously elaborate replies from other bodies, was effective. Council informed the Board of Finance, from which the proposal had originated, that it would be unfortunate to invite opposition on such a scale, and accepted that the practical differences which the various delegacies foresaw were real enough. That was the end of the proposal, and nothing more was heard of it.

4. Passing of the Old Order

THE deaths of Sir William Markby, C. E. Doble, Ingram Bywater, Sir James Murray, and Horace Hart in the first year or so of the war emphasized the discontinuity of events. The devoted, long-suffering Doble, who died in 1914, had been an editor in most of the various senses of the word. He had acquired a general bibliographical knowledge that made him particularly valuable to Frowde. When it had been agreed that Frowde should publish the Oxford Poets and other miscellaneous books, making his own arrangements with the printing business, it had also been resolved that the Secretary's office was to make all 'editorial arrangements'. It was probably never quite clear to Frowde, or to anybody else, quite what this meant. But in practice it very often meant leaving everything to Doble. Frowde bought the paper, and gave the printing order; Doble provided the copy. If, for instance, Frowde chose to reprint *The Compleat Angler*, and do so as cheaply as possible, forgoing the illustrious name to append to a preface, Doble was the man who knew which was the best text of which edition to use, and where amendment might be needed. If called upon, he would modernize the spelling and punctuation for the incurious lover of literature. His work on manuscripts and proof sheets at Oxford was greatly added to in his later years by his editorial responsibilities for London reprints.

Ingram Bywater had remained a Delegate until the end, though in his last years he did not often leave his London home. R. W. Chapman, living 'a nomadic and semi-barbarous existence' in Macedonia, was having it harshly borne in upon him that an era was passing. Bywater became the centrepiece of his nostalgia. He was the quintessential scholar whose learning could never be surpassed, was unlikely even to be approached by future generations. The memory of him was polished and burnished until it shone with a golden glow and represented the lights of home and of a civilization ended. In the essay eventually published in Chapman's little book *Portrait of a Scholar* the effulgence of his style does not conceal the possibility that others might not share his feelings about the great man. He remembered fondly 'the innocent arrogance of his mind' and the 'mordant

O

perspicacity of his judgements', qualities that did not endear him to some. 'His copious memory was stored with the lapses of other scholars', wrote Chapman, adding hastily that to suppose he was avidly preoccupied with minutiae, and inordinately solaced by professional scandal, was a risible travesty. There were after all few more exciting pursuits than textual criticism. 'The graces of civilization and the delights of learning are far from me now,' he elegized in Snevce. Yet there was still solace in a few good books, 'and the best odes of Horace, the best things in Boswell or Elia, often awake memories of Attic nights. Memories and visions, in which gleaming mahogany and old morocco are seen darkling in a haze of smoke, and an old man in his big chair by the fire draws forth, for my pleasure and his, the hoarded treasures of his rich old mind.'

Sir James Murray died in Oxford in July 1915, two years short of the eightieth birthday on which he had once hoped to celebrate the completion of the Dictionary. It was thirty-three years since the first instalment of copy had been sent to the printer. In the end he and his staff had dealt with more than half the English vocabulary, had written four complete volumes and portions of three others, and he had over the full distance averaged nearly 220 pages a year. He is known to have lost only one word—'bondmaid'. It was found, a homeless stray, long after 'Battenlie–Bozzom' had been published. On his death it was reckoned that a tenth of the Dictionary remained to be done by Bradley, Craigie, and Onions.

Horace Hart suffered a nervous breakdown in August 1914, and never recovered sufficiently to be able to return to work or to be able to survive without it. In January 1915, writing from Torquay, he reluctantly offered his resignation, and at the age of 75 he had to move from his house overlooking the quad to one he had bought on Boar's Hill. He received many letters of sympathy, or of congratulations on having completed his term, and acknowledgement of his long service to the Press was dutifully and sincerely made. One letter had a particular warmth and a touch of old comradeship lacking in the others. It came from Lyttelton Gell.

The announcement of your retirement from Active Service comes to me with somewhat of a shock, for I find it impossible to realize that over 30 years have gone by since you first showed me round the Press in November '83. Yet those were the days when there was no Strong Room,—when our Fire Insurance Policies were in a Mediaeval muddle,—and the Stocks were all over the place:—no telephones, no speaking-tubes, no typewriters, and even a stenographer was deemed too 'Commercial'. . . . Do you recollect the monotony of the old Press type, and the traditional Clarendon Press page, and all the efforts you made to equip the Press with the variety of Type which has lifted its Typography up to its present level?

It is equally difficult for me to realize that now more years have flown since we parted Company than the 14 years we worked together, and I do not doubt there is a great deal more to show. Yet that 'dead-lift' required to modernize the Press would not have to be faced twice, and probably there is no one left except myself who has the least conception of the extraordinary transformation and the rapid expansion effected in those days.

It took a good deal out of all concerned, but however things may have proceeded since 1898, you have every reason to be proud of your special part in the enormous stride which separated the Press of 1898 from the Press of 1883, when Jowett first stirred the fire and set us all running.

From the point of view of personal advantage and position and emancipation from the harassing intrigues and jealousies of some people, it might be thought fortunate that I had to turn my back upon it all, and launch out afresh into the bigger and deeper waters of the City. Yet the wrench of parting with the colleagues, and the staff, and the interests that I left behind, is not forgotten.

Now that your turn has come, I trust that all your hard work for the last 32 years has left you with health to enjoy your well-earned rest, and that you feel your own work will be carried on successfully.

I can see from the Advertisements that the Press has developed an activity and elasticity which in the past the Delegates would have disallowed, and I hope the expansion brings Revenue to the University in these days of poverty. As for the N.E.D. our Critics used to insist 20 years ago that with 'a little more energy and better organization', it could be finished off in no time! Still the end seems now to be in sight. . . .

Hart was found drowned in a shallow pond in a neighbour's garden in December 1916.

5. Business as Usual

THE Cannan daughters suggested putting up a sign, 'Business as Usual'. That, their father thought, would be a bit much. Business was becoming increasingly unusual. The Printer was engaged on work for the Naval Intelligence Department which required speed, accuracy, and above all secrecy. Elaborate security arrangements were introduced. A few learned books wended their way through the press, but increasingly slowly as other work intervened and the shortage of materials of all kinds became more acute. Manuscripts began to pile up in the Strongroom to await the return to normality.

The public mood had changed by 1916, but not that of C. R. L. Fletcher. Discovering that Fiedler's *Oxford Book of German Verse* had been reprinted, he wrote an enraged letter to the Vice-Chancellor. He had been told that there was a demand for the book in the United States, and that export sales helped the war effort. 'I think there is reason to fear', he wrote, 'that the University and the Delegates will . . . lose far more in the public esteem than they will gain in cash. Even were the gain from the sales of such a book likely to be enormous, no pecuniary advantage ought to be allowed to compensate for such an outrage on the feeling of patriotic citizens.' The protest was duly entered upon the Delegates' minutes.

The New York Branch did well with *The Oxford Book of German Verse*. It did well generally. In 1917 it showed profits of over £20,000; the five home businesses between them had little more than £6,000 to show for the year's trading. The Scofield Reference Bible had been published in 1909, the first Branch publication, though its planning and preparation had been carefully supervised by Frowde. The revised edition of 1917 was entirely an American production. It largely accounted for the enhanced profits of that year, and of many years to come. It was edited by the Revd. C. I. Scofield with the help of eight consulting editors, and provided 'a new system of connected topical references to all the greater themes of Scripture, with annotations . . . definitions . . . helps at hard places, explanations of seeming discrepancies, and a new system of paragraphs'. It was the only important Oxford book to originate in the United States before the appearance of *The Oxford Loose-Leaf Medicine* in 1920.

The reading public in Britain, its appetite for books about the war sated, was uplifted in 1916 by the tercentenary commemoration of Shakespeare's death. Something special was called for, and despite depleted staffs and diminishing supplies of paper the publishers did their best to provide it. The Clarendon Press had a trump card up its sleeve. In 1907 the Delegates had approved a proposal for a collaborative book on Shakespeare's England under Walter Raleigh's supervision. Raleigh had allowed it to fall into the hands of Sir Sidney Lee, a notable editor in his time and a veteran of *The Dictionary of National Biography*. In his search for something to do Geoffrey Faber had discovered that this was an old project perpetually going to sleep, 'through Lee's unbelievable powers of procrastination'. He made it his job to visit Lee from time to time and always found him hard at work on some other task altogether. Faber did not achieve very much, but he got his first glimpse of what he regarded as the literary heights he had come to London hoping to explore. The project had now to be forcibly reawakened. C. T. Onions supplanted Lee as editor and vigorous efforts were made to stir the laggards among the forty-three contributors. The Poet Laureate, Robert Bridges, composed an ode. After several months of intensive bustle the copy was ready early in 1916 and the book was published with masterly timing in April. It was in two large volumes of some 1,200 pages with 195 illustrations and it cost 25s. Contributors included Raleigh, E. K. Chambers, D. Nichol Smith, R. B. McKerrow, Percy Simpson, C. H. Firth, and Henry Bradley. There was no editor's name on the title-page, and Sidney Lee's only contribution was a short piece on 'Bearbaiting, Bullbaiting, and Cockfighting'. How the Press had managed to conceive and execute so ambitious a project in the middle of a war was a mystery to the public. 'What it cost the Press from start to finish is anybody's guess', wrote Faber, looking back on his own modest part in the enterprise.

At the same time Milford was engaged on an even more complex operation for the Shakespeare Tercentenary Committee. This was *A Book of Homage to Shakespeare* edited by Israel Gollancz. The homage was international, and for most people unintelligible. There were 166 contri- butions written in some thirty different languages, dead and alive, including Sanskrit, Chinese, Finnish, and Armenian. Only the Germans were excluded. The first of nearly 600 pages were set up on 10 March 1916, and the book was ready on 1 May. So great was the capacity Hart had created that, even working well below it, such prodigious feats—as they now appear—could be achieved. In fact in the last two years of the war when, in the memories of those who remained, work at the Press was almost at a standstill, enough books were published to make necessary an eighty-seven-page supplement to the General Catalogue of 1916. The tiny staff in Oxford produced 259 titles, and the London lists were swollen with the increased output of the American University Presses, which included the Harvard Oriental Series, many volumes of which were printed in Oxford, and the Harvard Business Studies. The Carnegie Endowment for International Peace spawned a whole library of books on international law. Milford issued two volumes of verse by members of his own staff, Charles Williams's *Poems of Conformity* which he professed not to understand, and E. V. Rieu's *The Tryst and other Poems*. Mr. and Mrs. Herbert Strang were as prolific as ever. New series abounded: the Something to Do Series in nine volumes and the Dumpy Series in sixteen; not to mention the Peek-a-Boo and Madam Mouse and the Happy Hour Series, and one called simply the Two Shilling net Limp Series.

Work on the Dictionary went on. Another 432 pages were published, bringing the total up to 13,864. Onions's article on 'super-' was savoured by the connoisseurs and thought to be one of the best yet, rivalling Bradley's 'set'. One book to afford Cannan particular satisfaction was A. C. Clark's *The Descent of Manuscripts*, progress on which had frequently been interrupted. Printed on the best paper and according to the highest standards, this learned work appeared at last in 1918.

Towards the end of the war there was a new spate of pamphlets on the League of Nations circulated through the Ministry of Information. It was claimed that more translations of Grey's pamphlet were published in a shorter time than of any other document in history. Raleigh continued sniping until the end. In *Some Gains of the War*, published in 1918, he considered the richness of the English language and its literature, and compared it with the barren wastes of German letters. Furthermore, he observed, 'I fear there is no German word for "fair-play".'

6. The Dictionary of National Biography

I⊤ was towards the end of 1917 that the University was presented with *The Dictionary of National Biography*. The great work had been begun in 1882 and George Smith, the founder, had miraculously kept his original promise of quarterly publication to complete it with the sixty-third volume in 1900. A three-volume supplement appeared in 1901, the year of Smith's death, and the standard twenty-two-volume edition was published in 1908-9. In addition there was the supplement edited by Sir Sidney Lee, in three volumes, covering the decade 1901–11. The *D.N.B.* was presented to the University by the Smith family. Osler, an old friend, could claim some credit. The rest of the Smith & Elder business had been taken over by John Murray. One of the daughters wrote to Osler: 'You have always taken so kindly an interest in the matter that I should like to tell you we are all agreed to offer the Dictionary to the University of Oxford.' The gift was accepted by decree of Convocation with proper expressions of gratitude. The benefactors were thanked in particular for having imposed no onerous or detailed conditions, as donors sometimes do. In the hands of the Delegates this great treasure of the national inheritance would, like the *O.E.D.*, be safe.

'Clearly a damnosa hereditas', reflected R. W. Chapman twenty years later. The gift had consisted of the copyright, the stock which had dwindled to vanishing point, and stereotype plates. It carried therefore a double liability: that of reprinting and keeping in print the main work in twenty-two volumes, and that of maintaining its continuation into the twentieth century along the lines already laid down by the first decennial supplement. Smith's family did not pretend that it was, in a commercial sense, a gift. As Chapman put it, 'they took the line, very properly, that private enterprise had done enough and that it was time for a National Dictionary to pass into the keeping of a national institution. . . . The University has always taken the view that if it fails to initiate a great enterprise, it should seize any opportunity of making amends by espousing it when it becomes derelict.' There is little evidence that the University ever took this view, and perhaps Chapman was enjoying an ironical allusion to the famous lost causes. His attitude was not unlike that of some of the Delegates during the early days of the *O.E.D.* When someone once called the *D.N.B.* a white elephant, Milford replied, 'Very likely; but that is the sort of animal that ought to be in our stable.'

For Cannan there was a further contingent liability, and a serious one, in the person of Sir Sidney Lee. His failure to produce *Shakespeare's England* was not forgotten. The remarkable efficiency and dispatch with which he and Sir Leslie Stephen had produced the *D.N.B.* was not entirely forgotten either. Only taskmasters of rare authority and dedication could have ensured the punctual publication of one volume each quarter for sixteen years. Lee, moreover, had been responsible for the 1901–11 decennial supplement. Even in 1917 he was concerned that work should start on its successor, though the decade had run little more than half its course. More seriously he and his friends, notably Professor C. H. Firth who had been appointed the Delegates' principal adviser on the Dictionary, urged the importance of regarding the main work as a 'living organism'. This was a view that had to be treated most warily. It meant constant revision, making good omissions, correcting errors—revision on a scale that would have been impossible without re-setting the entire work. The expense would have been enormous. Cannan adopted what he called 'sandbag resistance', both to the proposed revision and to the idea that Sidney Lee should have anything to do with it. 'The doctrine that the Dictionary was a living organism', Chapman wrote in 1936, 'and that constant attention should be given to its uninterrupted growth was, I think, evolved after 1917. . . . I would make the point that an organism can hardly be said to live which has been stereotyped.'

Unable to penetrate Cannan's defences and faced by an obstinate silence from the Delegates, Lee remained frustrated until after the war, merely allowing it to be known that trouble was brewing. There were said to be 'cabals at the Athenaeum'. His opportunity came when the 1901-11 supplement in its original three-volume form went out of print, and was replaced according to precedent by a single-volume uncorrected reprint. Lee addressed a long diatribe to *The Times*, reminiscent of some of Furnivall's outbursts, suggesting that the Press had laid its cold avaricious hands on a national asset and intended to draw the revenues without shouldering the responsibilities. The Delegates had put themselves out of court by refusing to co-operate with the former editor and his staff, and nothing remained for the friends of History but to wait for the copyright to expire in 1931. But by then the fire in Lee had finally been extinguished. Shortly after the war the Delegates agreed to continue the Dictionary by means of decennial volumes, and by 1927 the 1912-21 volume was ready for publication. An article on Lee by Sir Charles Firth was prefixed to it as a special tribute: not having died until 1926 he did not properly qualify for inclusion.

The problem of the revision of the main *D.N.B.* remained, however, and still remains unsolved. The 'living organism' theory never quite lost its hold, and as time passed the lists of errors and omissions grew. So too did the estimates for embarking on a full-scale overhaul, from tens of thousands, to hundreds of thousands, eventually into millions. The authority of the work as a whole remained almost embarrassingly unimpaired, for there was a general reluctance to admit the fallibility of so indispensable a work of reference, for which in a man's lifetime there could be no alternative.

7. The Death of Cannan

CANNAN had always intended to retire in 1918 at the age of 60, but he carried on to see the Press back on its feet again, the men restored in their jobs. He was weary and unwell. A diminutive man, he became more shrunken with the years, though his head was large and there was always a touch of self-importance about the paunch. One of Milford's new recruits, Major Geoffrey Cumberlege, recalls a visit to Oxford shortly after the war ended. He reported to the Secretary in the tower at the Clarendon Press after driving from London in his second-hand car. 'The interview was unforgettable,' he wrote many years later. 'Behind a huge roll-top desk was almost hidden a very small grey-haired man. . . . I stood patiently beside the desk but he paid no attention to me whatever and just kept on writing. Finally, after minutes had passed and without looking up, he said "I suppose you are Cumberlege. Have you a car?"' Being assured that he had, Cannan said, 'Then you had better go up to Iffley Road where Percy Simpson lives. His house is on fire. See what you can do.' Cumberlege went about his business. On future occasions he found that it was his duty to escort Cannan from Amen Corner to the underground station after his weekly visits to Milford. The precise purpose of this courteous exercise was never quite clear to him, but as very much the junior officer he felt that it would have been improper to speak without being spoken to. As a result no words were ever exchanged during these journeys, except for the merest formalities.

Cannan died a sad man. In November 1918 his daughter May became engaged to Quiller-Couch's son, Bevil, to the great satisfaction of both the parents. She had known him for most of her life, and it had always been his intention to marry her if he survived the war. It was a source of deep mortification to her that, in the belief that he might spare her anxiety, he did not propose until after the war was over. On active service in France throughout, he came through only to die of pneumonia early in 1919.

May Cannan remembered the bleak winter evening when she went round to the Press to tell Chapman, who now occupied the tower room, that her father was dying. 'He couldn't bear the young going out to die; and yours, that was too much', was all Chapman said. Sir Walter Raleigh said much the same. 'He was obliged to protect himself,' he wrote, 'or life would have hurt him too much. So he wore a sort of shell, made of irony and wit and other hard material.' But in the end life did hurt him too much: 'he hated staying behind and seeing the young men go'. Sir William Osler could not save him, for he too was on his death-bed.

Almost the whole staff of the Clarendon Press either attended the funeral or lined the streets between his house and the Church of St. Peter-in-the-East. As all the tributes show, this remote, taciturn, totally undemonstrative man had inspired loyalty and affection in an unexpectedly large number of people. Raleigh was surprised to find, given his preference for hiding in the engine-room, how many knew what his work and influence had meant to Oxford. Controlling the fortunes of the Press during the period of its great expansion, his main achievement was in the relaxing of those controls that had inhibited its growth. He saw that major works of scholarship could no longer be subsidized exclusively by sales of the Bible, nor by school-books, nor yet in his day by the offspring of the great Dictionary, or by reference books. The patrons of learning were now the middle classes. Cannan established the indispensable relationship with the general reader through the imprints of Frowde and Milford. For that he got no credit. The credit and a substantial measure of public gratitude went to the London publisher. Frowde's name was still almost synonymous with the Oxford University Press to Aldous Huxley in 1925, when he credited him with the invention of India paper, which made it possible to get 'a million words of reading matter into a rucksack and hardly feel the difference'.

The popular view was summed up in two articles in the *Sphere* magazine and *The Times*. The writer in the *Sphere* explained the difference between the Clarendon Press and the Oxford University Press. The former produced the 'literature of education—the literature that makes for the academic mind'. Those books produced by the Oxford University Press 'are the books that give that education its real fulness by humanising it'. Cannan may have appeared to epitomize the academic mind, but it was a mind in fact very open to suggestion and his ambition was to make the Clarendon Press 'what it ought to be: the first Press in the world'. To do so a way had to be found to reach that large class of reader described in the article in *The Times* in the early 1920s as dilettanti—'persons of a name often carrying reproach among researchers, but indispensable to them nevertheless. . . . They help to form the necessary special public and tend to create the necessary general opinion without which advanced study would become either socially useless or financially impossible. The policy of the Oxford University Press is a vindication of the race of *dilettanti*. It encourages them; and as their numbers increase the potentialities for human happiness increase. If all that could be said of the Oxford University Press was that it fostered the spirit of dilettantism, it is by no means certain, in the present state of the world's civilization, that it would be small praise.'

The *Times Literary Supplement*, reviewing the last edition of the *Oxford University Roll of Service*, had a word to say about the work of the Press: 'Probably no European Press did more to propagate historical and ethical truth about the war. The death of its Secretary, Charles Cannan, a year ago, has left an inconsolable regret among all those more fortunate Oxford men, old and young, who had the honour to be acquainted with one of the finest characters and most piercing intelligences of our time. He was a very great man, and is alive today in the spirit of the institution which he enriched with his personality and his life.'

PART VI

THE INTER-WAR YEARS

1. Reconstruction

IT had taken about fifty years to create the vast and diverse business of the modern Press. The more flexible and adventurous policies of Cannan, Frowde's transformation from humble warehouseman into one of the most eminent publishers of his day, the emergence of Milford, the apparently limitless productivity of the manufacturing departments, and finally the establishment of branches in the U.S.A. and throughout the Empire, completed the processes begun by Price. But to Chapman after his return in 1919 it seemed for a time that the great structure that had been created was unlikely to endure.

He was heavy hearted as he contemplated the ravages of the war, the death of Cannan, the days that would never come again. Rising costs made him fear for the whole future of academic publishing. It was a bleaker prospect even than that of 1945. Then the vast demand for books far exceeded the supply. Chapman was preoccupied with the possibility that the market, for learned books at least, had collapsed. A book which before the war could have been produced at a very modest loss now incurred a loss roughly five times as great. The purchasing power of his public had certainly not kept pace with costs. How could the impoverished professional man continue to buy books in anything like the quantities to which he had once been accustomed? The result could only be lower printing numbers, higher prices, and more and more unremunerative books until the Press sank into bankruptcy and the tides of barbarism washed all away.

In *Some Account of the Oxford University Press* (1921) these forebodings expressed themselves in an outright appeal for help. The Delegates, he wrote, 'have done their best to keep down prices; and the book-buying public, on its side, has made heroic efforts to pay the increased prices which it has been necessary to ask. . . . The Delegates have no hesitation, therefore, in calling the attention of librarians, and of those who are responsible for the provision of library funds, to their urgent need of continued and increased support.'

The previous year the same forebodings had prompted an article in the

Athenaeum, later used as a preface to Collins's *Authors' and Printers' Dictionary.* It developed into a magisterial rebuke to all those authors who were tempted by the 'specious mutability of print' to make unnecessary corrections in proof: 'It should be a point of honour not to inflict upon printer and publisher the burden of irritating afterthoughts and infirm vacillations.' But it began by stressing the dangers of rising costs to the book trade and by urging heroic remedies for grave ills, namely shorter books. The English reading public would have to accustom itself to flimsy, perhaps even to paper, bindings; to smaller and closer type and narrower margins. But such economies, though important, would make no vital difference. 'You cannot make books cheap by making them nasty.' The only way was by printing more copies or by printing fewer words. He did not expect to be able to print more copies of the average Clarendon Press book, so he recommended the latter course. 'If the effect of economic pressure is to make authors study compression, and readers, attention, the gain will be great. The prolixity of modern writing, fostered by cheap paper and print, by the habit of making books out of articles and lectures, by the use of typewriters and stenographers, is a positive evil; and it has so reacted upon most readers that they have become incapable of assimilating close thought or a terse style.'

Neither the immediate future nor the present was quite so bad as Chapman supposed. It was generally assumed that Oxford would have to face a prolonged period of convalescence. In the event it returned to normal at an alarming pace. By 1920 there were more students in residence than ever before, and the University was forced at last to appeal to the Government for help in order to accommodate and teach them all. The state responded generously; in so far as it was responsible for the provision of library funds it may be said to have answered Chapman's appeal too. Moreover the annual payments of £2,000 to the University came to an end in 1921. The immediate justification was shortage of cash, but the 1922 Royal Commission on the two Universities largely endorsed the decision by stating that the first call on the funds of the Press should be for the publication of learned works by members of the University. As an international publishing house this implied a restraint on its activities that was never welcome, but three years later the Government Grants Committee, under the chairmanship of Sir William McCormick, took an ampler view. It concluded that the two University Presses, with some help from the better commercial publishers, were adequately supplying the national need for works of learning. The Committee would not, therefore, help other universities to set up presses of their own, nor would it expect those in Oxford and Cambridge to make contributions to their Universities to supplement or make good the Government grant.

In 1919 the output of the Clarendon Press seemed meagre: only 111 new titles were published, the lowest number recorded in peacetime between 1905 and the present day. But the General Catalogue of 1922 had swollen by forty pages as a result of 1,490 additions to the list in 1920 and

1921. Major works of scholarship remained scarce, but a start had been made on the short books that Chapman saw as the answer to economic crisis.

Oxford Tracts on Economic Subjects consisted of four pages and cost $1\frac{1}{2}d$.: a set of seven in an envelope with introduction could be had for $10\frac{1}{2}d$., and 100 for 10s. 6d. A new series called 'The World of To-day: A Guide for all Through Current Problems and Events' was launched by Milford. Volumes were of sixty-four pages and at 2s. 6d. by no means cheap. Throughout the inter-war years World's Classics of whatever length could be bought for 2s. Oxford complemented the London current affairs series with one called 'The World's Manuals', sub-titled simply 'A Series of Introductory Volumes'. These too were priced at 2s. 6d., and though none of the authors achieved a target of sixty-four pages they were undoubtedly made to study compression. Some of them, like R. G. Collingwood, emerged chastened but triumphant. After furious labour, and 'incredible self-denial about purple patches, adjectives, and explanations of obscure points', he presented *Outlines of a Philosophy of Art* in 34,975 words—matching exactly, he claimed, the record he had set himself earlier with *Roman Britain*.

Within five years there were thirty-five World's Manuals divided into various categories. Collingwood appeared under Art, Religion, and Philosophy, together with C. E. M. Joad's *Introduction to Modern Philosophy* (112 pp.). He also appeared under History and Geography with Ernest Barker's *The Crusades* (112 pp.) and W. R. Kermack's *The Expansion of Britain*. Under Languages and Literature there were books on Chinese and Persian, Prince Mirsky's *Modern Russian Literature*, and H. A. R. Gibb's *Arabic Literature*. Social Science included *Karl Marx's 'Capital'* by A. D. Lindsay, *Population* by A. M. Carr-Saunders, and *Modern Political Theory* by Joad. Books of this kind were a new departure for the Clarendon Press. Many of them endured, even after the series itself was discontinued. Only in Science and the History of Science does the heavy hand of tradition prevail, the old nervous recoil from modernity. Among the first titles were *Greek Biology and Greek Medicine* by Charles Singer, *Mathematics and Physical Science* (in Classical Antiquity), and *Chemistry to the Time of Dalton*.

Neither scholars nor Chapman's newly impoverished professional man, the book lovers and book buyers of the pre-war era, needed 'introductory volumes', and the interests of the latter were assumed to be mostly classical or literary. In 1920 the new Honours School of P.P.E.—Philosophy, Politics, and Economics—was inaugurated. To the traditionalists it was obvious that it would attract an inferior class of student, that it reflected a general decline in civilized values. But in the post-war era allowances had to be made, and it could not be denied that the world was become a more complicated place. Economics was no longer a subject a gentleman could pick up as he went along. Even so the World's Manuals and The World of To-day series were not aimed primarily at undergraduates either. With them the Press entered the field of adult education. At least that was the intention of John Johnson, who had links with the Workers' Educational Association, founded before the war, and a general concern for the 'self-improving' public. Specifically they had been intended for the 'Continuation Schools', proposed in H. A. L. Fisher's Education Act of 1918. The Act had raised the school-leaving age to 14, and recommended part-time education up to 16. Cuts in public expenditure made the continuation schools almost immediately obsolete, but a growing number of people—growing for the best part of a century—sought to prolong their education in whatever way they could.

The World's Manuals, as a series, were not a success, though by the mid 1930s they numbered forty-eight. A powerful editorial team of sixteen leading scholars had been assembled, apparently rallying to the cause of peace as vigorously as they had risen to the challenge of war. Many were Delegates. Cyril Bailey, classicist and editor of Lucretius; H. W. C. Davis, modern historian and editor of the *D.N.B.* Supplement; G. S. Gordon, Professor of English Literature in succession to Raleigh and editor of the new Oxford Shakespeare; W. D. Ross, Aristotelian; N. V. Sidgwick, chemist; and R. G. Collingwood, whose destiny had been revealed to him by Kant's *Theory of Ethics* when he was eight. Also on the team were Ernest Barker, C. T. Onions, Richard Livingstone, Charles Singer, Julian Huxley, and David Nichol Smith, who had succeeded Raleigh as the Press's principal adviser on English literature. This cluster of eminent names graced the first page of the General Catalogue until the Second World War, but failed understandably to impose an identity on the series comparable with that of the Home University Library, founded by Thornton Butterworth Ltd. in 1911, and eventually taken over by the Press in 1941.

Johnson was more successful in another venture, again aimed at the W.E.A. and University Extension courses. In 1920 he suggested to Richard Livingstone a composite work, 'The Debt of Greece'. Within a year it had been written, printed, and published as *The Legacy of Greece*, the only snag having been a doubt whether Dean Inge would write the chapter on Religion, without which it was feared the book would not be regarded as authoritative. *The Legacy of Rome* followed, edited by Cyril Bailey. It took longer, partly because Johnson allowed himself to be carried away by his enthusiasm for illustrations. He had a talent for lay-out and design hitherto rare in the publishing business, but a growing taste for lavishly illustrated books was at odds with the current economy drive. Particularly with school-books, where cost was vital, his pictorial ambitions could be positively dangerous. He became increasingly reluctant to publish anything without pictures. Even Carr-Saunders's World's Manual on *Population* was not felt to be complete without a portrait of Malthus. For *The Legacy of Rome* he allowed seventy-six illustrations, more than twice the number for *Greece*.

Bailey in the course of editing became aware of an ambiguity in the word 'legacy', which was to harass future editors as well. *The Concise Oxford Dictionary* defined it as 'material or immaterial thing handed down by predecessor'. It might be taken to mean the inheritance of the testator, and a contributor would attempt merely a valuation of the total assets of the latter. The writer on Roman agriculture rated it so low as to imply that his contribution was superfluous. The Rt. Hon. H. H. Asquith in his introduction irritatingly dwelt on aspects of Roman life for which the future was not appreciably indebted; Bailey complained that it had a 'rather dampening effect'. But these were minor set-backs and in about eighteen months the book of over 500 pages was produced.

The great age of the 'man of letters' was passing, the age of specialization had begun, but Oxford was not yet conforming to the pattern. The war had interrupted research and in the 1920s there were many scholars—historians, classicists, and literary men—who could write elegantly and with facility for the general reader. They carried their scholarship lightly, though some would say that they had less of a burden to bear than, for instance, Ingram Bywater. But to men such as Gilbert Murray, Richard Livingstone, Arnold Toynbee, A. E. Zimmern, Charles Singer, Dean Inge, Ernest Barker, C. Foligno, and F. de Zulueta the cause appeared to be a good one. They observed their deadlines and specifications of length and accepted with a mild affectation of surprise a cheque for £10 in the end. The first two Legacy volumes turned out to be an unexpected commercial success. After 8,000 copies had been sold Chapman saw that they were 'quite a little gold mine', and authorized a bonus payment of £10 to each contributor. By 1939 there were 'Legacies' of India, the Middle Ages, Israel, and Islam.

The instructional, even at times inspirational nature of post-war Oxford books was evident in the prodigious output of F. S. Marvin, to whom posterity has been unkind. A Chief Inspector of Schools in the West Riding, he wrote for 'intelligent teachers and teachers in training colleges'. He had no patience with the disillusionment of the times: just as for Sir William Sanday the war had confirmed his faith in the infinite perfectibility of man. For Milford he edited and partly wrote nine volumes of essays called 'The Unity Series'. The first, *The Unity of Western Civilization* which appeared during the war, covered the ground from 'Unity in Prehistoric Times' by J. L. Myres to 'A World State' by J. A. Hobson, concluding with an essay by Marvin on 'The Growth of Humanity'. *Progress in History* (1920) followed the same pattern. *The Evolution of World-Peace* (1921) began with an essay by Marvin and Arnold Toynbee on 'Alexander and Hellenism', and moved on to 'An Apology for a World Utopia' by H. G. Wells and 'The Teaching of History and World Peace' by Eileen Power. A second edition in 1933 carried an epilogue by Gilbert Murray. There were many distinguished contributors flushed by new visions of sanity and peace the League of Nations had conjured up. In 1919 Marvin had published *The Century of Hope* with the Clarendon Press, an account of western progress since 1815, the contemplation of which induced in him visions of yet more centuries of hope to come. It was too much for the reviewer in the *Times Literary Supplement*. What would one of those nineteenth-century meliorists Marvin so much admired find if he were to return to the world today? He would find poverty, starvation, illiteracy, disease, hatred among peoples. 'He might hear, what has not been heard for countless ages of history, the hyaena howling in South-Eastern Europe, drawn from far off by the infinite abundance of dead.' The book survived the next war and remained in print until 1953.

The hyena was clearly to be heard in *Movements in European History*, published early in 1921. V. H. Collins was responsible at Amen Corner for books for secondary schools. He worked under Milford but his position was anomalous, for secondary education was the province of the Clarendon Press and strictly speaking he was answerable to Oxford. It was he who initiated the World's Manuals for the continuation schools which Johnson took over. It was also his idea to invite D. H. Lawrence, a former teacher like himself with whom he was acquainted, to do a history book for schools: more remarkably, he obtained Milford's approval, though Lawrence was not a historian, or a novelist whose name he then wished to be associated with the University Press. But Lawrence's fortunes were at their lowest ebb in 1918. The harassment he had suffered during the war, and the prosecution and suppression of the *Rainbow* in 1915, had affected him morally and financially. Milford was sympathetic as a matter of principle: he could not as a matter of taste help Lawrence by publishing *Women in Love*, though Lawrence was without a publisher at the time.

Lawrence started work in July 1918, clear as to his purpose: the 'history' was to be along modern lines. 'At the present moment, history must either be graphic or scientific,' he began. 'The old bad history is abolished. The old bad history consisted of a register of facts. It drew up a chart of human events, as one might draw up a chart of the currants in a plum-pudding, merely because they happen promiscuously to be there. No more of this.' Lawrence was addressing children in the junior forms of grammar schools, or the upper forms of primary schools.

The book was finished in April 1919 and the draft was presumably read at Amen Corner by Collins and others. No records survive, but there may have been some doubts about its suitability, for the Press was slower in making up its mind than was usual in those days. The manuscript was referred to Fletcher, who with creditable breadth of mind—many of Lawrence's opinions were abhorrent to him—approved it with only minor reservations about 'dates and names'. One name in particular presented a problem, that of the author himself. Milford, for reasons which Lawrence understood and readily accepted, would not allow it on the title-page. The book was published in February 1921 under the pseudonym 'Lawrence H. Davison'.

It was moderately successful. The first impression of 2,000 copies sold out in about two years, and the next 2,000 showed that sales were still picking

up. At that point the book caught the eye and aroused the predatory
instincts of Johnson. It fell within his province and he proposed to bring out
a second edition, fully illustrated. Lawrence was asked to write an epilogue
to bring it up to date and to suggest possible illustrations. An epilogue was
easy, but he felt pestered by the request for illustrations and wrote to a
friend, 'I suppose you don't know off-hand where one could find a few
suitable things that the Oxford Press might reproduce?—They're an
incompetent show, if ever there was one. But pleasant with it.'

The Oxford Press found the epilogue decidedly unpleasant, not greatly to
Lawrence's surprise. Sisam edited out the more offensive passages before
showing it to Fletcher, who read it with considerable impatience. Passages
in it seemed to him a libel upon the British, and indeed upon humanity. But
Fletcher had a personal interest in epilogues and, outraged though he was,
could not bring himself to say that it should be discarded. He concluded
that 'if Sisam's passages, or most of them, are removed, I don't think what is
left is any worse nonsense than one may read every day; though the style is
epileptic (at the twenty-seventh iteration of *growing tip* I almost screamed
aloud) . . .'.

The reaction is understandable. Writing at great speed Lawrence had
lost himself in an impenetrable silvan metaphor, from which the 'growing
tip' seemed the only way out. 'The War, called now the Great War, came in
1914, and smashed the growing tip of European civilization', he began, and
so he went on. He recalled the ideas of Progress, of free competition, of
equality of opportunity: 'Since the War these words make us feel sick, they
have proved such a swindle . . . We none of us believe in our ideals any more.
Our ideal, our leading ideas, our growing tip were shot away in the Great
War . . . the old leading tip was shot to smithereens.' The name of Lloyd
George, a former Prime Minister, was coupled with that of Horatio
Bottomley, a current convict, to symbolize the 'Voice of the People', to be
remembered only with shame: 'Let us hope never to hear it again in full
blast, the Voice of the Herd.' Out of the wood at last, he briefly expounds
natural aristocracy, the aristocracy of the soul, and appeals to every boy
and girl to 'make the great historical change inside himself and herself, to
care supremely for nothing but the spark of *noblesse* that is in him and in
her, and to follow only the leader who is a star of the new, *natural Noblesse*'.

A child progressing from Fletcher and Kipling's *History of England* to
Lawrence's *Movements* would surely experience a curious sense of dislocation. The Press did something to mitigate the shock by refusing to print
the epilogues to either book. Lawrence's survived amongst his papers, with
no explanatory letter of rejection, and was published for the first time in
1971, when the book was reissued with an introduction, giving all the facts,
by James T. Boulton.

The impulse of authors and publishers after the war was to get back to
work and to make up for lost time. As university teaching itself had become
more onerous, there were fewer scholars immediately tempted to embark

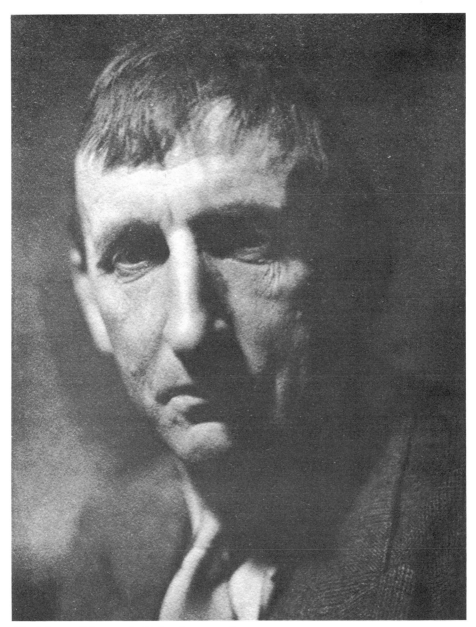

John Johnson, Printer to the University, 1925–46

R. W. Chapman, Secretary, 1920-42

on major research which might take many years. It was some time before
the quintessential Clarendon Press books reappeared and there were no
substantial additions to the Oxford English Texts between 1915, when both
F. W. Moorman's edition of Herrick and L. C. Martin's Henry Vaughan
were published, and 1926, when de Selincourt's edition of *The Prelude*
appeared. The third and concluding volume of Saintsbury's *Minor Poets of
the Caroline Period* came out in 1921, after a gap of fifteen years.

But Chapman and Milford were still determined to realize the catholic
policy of the pre-war years—to publish virtually everything that could be
called English literature, major or minor, up to some moment in the
nineteenth century increasingly difficult to determine. They were unde-
terred by public apathy. Replying to an article in the *Athenaeum* called 'Our
Inaccessible Heritage', which had deplored the lack of cheap editions of the
earlier writers, Chapman could point out firstly that there was no such lack,
and secondly that the sales of *England's Parnassus, or the Choysest Flowers
of our Moderne Poets* (at 7s. 6d. for 600 pages) had in recent years varied
between 27 and 4. Production, he explained, could not be much accelerated
without an increase in demand. 'We confess that we were unprepared to
find things quite so bad as this,' the *Athenaeum* granted.

In the face of chronically poor sales Chapman persisted in believing that
what the connoisseur needed, and what the public wanted, was type-
facsimiles, even of nineteenth-century works lacking any claim to typographical distinction. He is possibly the only literary critic to have defended
the 'three-decker' novel, generally regarded as a pernicious conspiracy
between publisher and librarian to keep up the price of fiction. Fine
dramatic points might be lost, he thought, by bundling books together in
one crowded volume. Of his own favourite novelist he wrote, 'Those who
have once read *Pride and Prejudice* in three slim duodecimos, with
a ha'porth of large type to the page, will not easily reconcile themselves
to the inelegance of the modern reprint.' The Printer could not easily
have reconciled himself to such a view, but in both his reading and his
writing Chapman tended to attach less weight to content than to style.
As far as Sisam was concerned, facsimiles could safely be left to the
camera.

Kenneth Sisam was appointed Junior Assistant Secretary in 1922.
Though always valetudinarian, he had recovered his strength if not his
appetite. Throughout his mature life he had an aversion to food, and his
sturdy constitution appears to have reconciled itself to a dismally meagre
diet. He took no lunch and manoeuvred resolutely to avoid dining out.
Travel abroad was particularly perilous, and in America he went in terror of
hospitality. It was his fate, however, to spend the last years of the war at the
Ministry of Food. In 1919, in recognition of his services, he was appointed
Director of Bacon Contracts, and when the disposal of bacon stocks had
been completed he was appointed Vice-Chairman of the Bacon Claims
Committee. For a man whose main interests hitherto had been in Early and
Middle English literature it was valuable experience, to which later as a

P

publisher he did not hesitate to attach weight. While Chapman had been messing about in Macedonia, dreaming of Bywater and dabbling with Greek particles, he had been engaged on work of undeniably national importance. He had gained invaluable business, administrative, and legal experience, which few scholars were privileged to possess. He knew how things worked. Chapman and Johnson, Fletcher and Hogarth, were among those eager to lure him back to Oxford, but the Civil Service was reluctant to lose him. It could also offer a higher salary. This was not a determining factor, however, and there was no doubt where in the end his heart would draw him.

He was a man who, like Cannan, preferred the engine-room. Though a colonial, lacking a public school education and unable always to catch the secret harmonies familiar to Chapman and Milford, the traditions of the Press seemed from the start to be embodied in him, and it was he who in due course handed them on. His relationship with Chapman was curious. Their interests and habits were entirely different: they have been described as two men who never met, though they worked closely and harmoniously together for nearly twenty years. Sisam came to assume the role of senior civil servant, content to let Chapman play minister.

Johnson's feverish energies and his hectic pursuit of new books had much to do with the rapid recovery and expansion of the Press after the war. His relations with authors were good, with his colleagues sometimes prickly. In 1925, on the death of Frederick Hall, he was appointed Printer and moved downstairs. He was forty-three, old to be learning a complex new trade, though he had shown as a publisher an exceptional interest in the technical aspects of typography. He admitted that the change was the most sudden, the most startling that he had ever had to face. 'I was become a tradesman,' the former papyrologist recalled, 'dependent on the whim of others, on their contentment or discontent.' But it seemed to him in the end a change from 'something almost artificial in life to something which was more human, and therefore more real'. Downstairs, amongst the 800 employees, many from families associated with the Press for generations, proud equally of the ancient traditions of their craft and their modern machinery, was the true heart of the business. Upstairs, the publishing side came to be dismissed as the 'post-office'.

Johnson was the last of the true autocrats, a stern disciplinarian who abhorred mirth. His secretary, G. E. Durham, was not permitted to sit down while taking dictation but had to rest his notebook on the mantelpiece in front of the fire. More than once, to Johnson's irritation, he fainted from the heat. The species is now rare in Britain. Johnson, despite his very different background, was in the old tradition of Oxford printers. Factory discipline was 'dour and hard', one of his graduate readers recalled, 'as suited also John Johnson's temperament'. Yet he could also show the most delicate consideration, especially to women.

Chapman, who allowed himself no breath of criticism of the Press in his own published work, wrote of the pride the 'work-people' took in the scholarly excellence of the books on which their labour was spent. 'The Press is, in all its parts, conscious at once of its unity and of its relation to the University of which it is an integral part.' The graduate reader, who had experienced the long hours and poor pay and the servile status of the work, wrote, 'No one who has not experienced it will understand the difference, in Oxford, between a job with university standing and one without. No iron curtain is more impenetrable than the one between the printing and publishing sides of the University Press.' Johnson did not hasten the coming of democracy. It was not the happiest of Chapman's decisions to appoint a man who not only lacked experience (which as it turned out did not matter), but one careless of the human touch.

Chapman remained essentially a bookman and scholar, but as Secretary he had immediately to attend to more material concerns. The new machines installed by Hart nearly thirty years before were all wearing out at once. But perhaps the timely purchase of several valuable freehold properties was, as Chapman modestly claimed, his most lasting contribution. The Walton Street building had been conceived on the grand scale, with possibilities of expansion to meet all foreseeable demands. But the unforeseeable had arrived and the machines were crowding out the books. In the early 1920s the total stock of Clarendon Press books alone, bound and unbound, was approaching five million. They were stacked in every corner. Walton Street expanded to include a new bindery, and a greatly enlarged Monotype department, but that was no answer to the problem of stock. 'The Delegates of the twentieth century,' Chapman wrote, 'when they found themselves driven to the conclusion that the space available in Walton Street would all be wanted for manufacture, and that provision for storage must be found elsewhere, felt themselves bound to emulate their predecessors and to take a long view.' Some of them, Chapman chose not to record, had taken a decidedly short view only a few years earlier and agreed to roof over the quad. After the war, however, they acquired a large freehold estate north of Oxford which, like the architects of Walton Street, they believed equal to any development foreseen or not foreseen. On it was built a warehouse, and ten acres were placed at the disposal of the Press Amalgamated Athletic Clubs as a sports ground. With the help of a gift of £1,000 from an anonymous Press author (C. R. L. Fletcher, in fact), tennis-courts, bowling-green, cricket and football pitches were laid out. The area was named Jordan Hill by Chapman, for those hoary old quires had gone out from Jericho unto Jordan.

In London it was decided not to renew the lease on Amen Corner, and two adjacent houses in Warwick Square on the former site of Newgate prison were purchased. Their conversion into Amen House, the London headquarters from 1924 to 1965, was protracted and costly. In addition a piece of vacant ground was bought at the back adjoining the Old Bailey; on it was built a seven-floor warehouse which could store some three-quarters of a million books. The bindery in Aldersgate Street was still turning out leather bindings, and there was a quire warehouse in Old Street. By the end of the decade, however, it was necessary to start building a much larger warehouse in Neasden, in the north-west suburbs of London. The Great War seemed after all only a brief hiatus in the inexorable growth. But there was to be another one with the Depression, and this heavy capital expenditure in Oxford and London was completed only just in time.

2. Passage to India

BETWEEN the wars offices were opened (and closed) in Leipzig, Copenhagen, and Paris, but no new overseas branch was established. The impetus that began in an imperialist era was regained in the period of colonial independence. The primary and explicit purpose of a branch was the distribution of Clarendon Press and London books. In the United States, Canada, Australia, and South Africa this was not an entirely unrewarding or thankless task, for there was always the Bible: the branches arose out of Frowde's conviction that once the Press was face to face with its customers it could do the bulk of the Bible trade.

In India, the situation was different. At the age of 24, E. V. Rieu of Balliol had been sent out to open a branch in Bombay in 1912, travelling circuitously by the Trans-Siberian railway in order to meet the Press representative in Shanghai and, if suspicions of incompetence formed in London proved correct, to dismiss him. This the young Rieu did. In India he soon realized that the primary function of a branch could not be fulfilled: that even for the 'Rulers of India' series, or for Vincent Smith's *History of India*, or Dubois's classic *Hindu Manners*, there was but a small demand. Some school-books could be adapted, but if the secondary function were to be observed—that of making a profit—he had to create new books specifically designed for local requirements. With the help of Bartholomew of Edinburgh he produced the Indian School Atlas, which was successful. His triumph was to be invited by the Government of the Central Provinces in 1916 to produce a series of Readers in Gujarati and Marathi for schools: within a year half a million copies were ready for distribution. But during the war Rieu became increasingly cut off. He roamed the sub-continent, and even further afield, dutifully sending his reports to Amen Corner, where it was extraordinarily difficult to know what to make of them. The problems he faced could not easily be imagined, and nobody ever visited him. By the end of the war he was a sick man, and a replacement was needed.

Major G. F. J. Cumberlege, D.S.O., of Worcester College, returned to England in January 1919 with the intention of resuming his pre-war plans for joining the Egyptian Civil Service. Dining one evening in his old college he was asked by the Dean whether he would like a job in India. A few days later he was being interviewed by Milford. Before he had had time to take stock of his situation, or the army leave to which he was entitled, he was reporting for duty at Amen Corner. He was to sail for India as soon as a berth could be found. Rieu was calling piteously from his sick-bed for urgent relief, but it was not until September 1919 that Cumberlege was able to book a passage and go to the rescue. This allowed time for his training at Amen Corner. Rieu, suffering from malaria and boils, was too ill to train him on arrival, leaving almost immediately for home. He made his name many years later as a translator of Homer and editor of the series of Penguin translations. He died in 1972 at the age of 85.

Cumberlege took over a 'successful and growing business', Chapman wrote confidently in 1921, but Cumberlege could see no evidence of it. Not having had time to learn anything from Rieu he appeared to be starting from scratch. Even before leaving London the very existence of the Branch had puzzled him. In the small tropical dungeon of an office in Bombay where Rieu had languished he was even more perplexed: 'I would ask why the O.U.P. was in India; to make money, or to be educational missionaries, or just to further the distribution of Oxford and London books?' These questions were to be aired in public a quarter of a century later, when Cumberlege was one of those called upon to answer them. At the time he felt that he himself received no satisfactory answer. It was taken for granted that the Branch should be profitable. There was also a more ideological view, that the services rendered by Oxford to the Indian Empire could be enhanced by the activities of its Press. But whatever it was trying to do the Press was not in Cumberlege's view doing it successfully. No Bibles, no children's books, and no trade books were really saleable. If he were lucky he might get occasional orders for some of the smaller dictionaries, and odd copies of Anson's *Contract* could be sold in a few universities. But he was in no position to compete even with the local English bookseller, who got better terms from London than the Branch. He also appeared to be better informed of forthcoming Oxford titles, some of which Cumberlege only knew about when he saw them displayed on his shelves.

It took rare courage and determination even to recognize the magnitude of the challenge. As Rieu had discovered, it could only be met by producing books locally, strictly designed for the Departments of Education in the various Provinces. A glimpse of the possibilities open to him came when a 'Stories Retold' version of *Ivanhoe* was set for matriculation in Madras, thus guaranteeing an immediate sale of 20,000 copies. The market was almost entirely for educational books, and the biggest demand of all was for books at primary level in the vernacular. The Central Provinces Readers continued to be a stand-by. In due course books in Assamese, Bengali, Hindi, Kannada, Malayalam, Punjabi, Tamil, Telagu, and Urdu appeared, and the Press was able to compete with the 'Bazaar' publishers and show profits that afforded satisfaction in London. More spacious premises were found in Bombay, and offices were opened in Madras and Calcutta. But it was desperately hard work, only made endurable by the experience and dedication of the Indian staff. By the time he had grappled with the problems of publishing in India—not least of which were the white ants and

cockroaches that devoured his stock—Cumberlege was ready for anything. He was the natural choice when drastic measures were needed to
rescue the New York Branch at the time of the Depression. He spent seven
years in India. In 1923 Milford wrote to say that he was sending out 'a
nice and intelligent' Winchester and Trinity scholar called A. L. P. Norrington, who had recently joined the Press. It had been decided that a year
or two in India would be excellent training. 'Thomas' (now Sir Arthur)
Norrington became Junior Assistant Secretary in Oxford in 1925 and
eventually Secretary in 1948; Cumberlege succeeded Milford as Publisher
in 1945.

3. The London Business

MILFORD never found it necessary to assert his independence, as Frowde
had once thought it prudent to do. The diarchy of Secretary and Publisher
became even more pronounced between the wars: the principle of the
equipollence of the two officers was firmly stated. Whereas Cannan never
wrote an unnecessary letter, Chapman was a compulsive jotter of notes:
often accused of secretiveness he was also excessively communicative, and
more so with Milford than with his own staff, generally too busy to be as
companionable as he could have wished. 'I know that you are tolerant of
my prattle,' he wrote. There was an almost daily exchange of information
and gossip.

Milford had assembled a team that needed little guidance, men only too
happy to be left to go their own way. He was 'Caesar' and they asked
no impertinent questions, though newcomers continued to be perplexed
by lack of instruction. Cumberlege's first task was to correct proofs of
Chapman's *Selections from Boswell*. This was hand-set in Fell and nobody
had told him about the peculiarities and irregularities of that type. So he
busily applied, as he believed, Hart's Rules and marked the proofs for
unaligned words and letters. Chapman's note to Milford was brief: 'Your
Mr. Cumberlege seems to be playing the April fool. This seems the only
explanation for his proof-reading.'

The mind of Charles Williams pullulated constantly. He had joined the
Press in London in 1908 at the age of 22 and he remained with it until his
death in 1945. Novelist, poet, dramatist, biographer, critic, and theologian,
he left no record of himself as a publisher. 'He created about him an
atmosphere that must be unique in the history of business houses', wrote
one of his colleagues, without elaboration. It must certainly have been very
unusual. Few if any of those who worked with him could understand either
his theology or his poetry, or even his novels; his most intimate friends and
admirers had to confess that his work was obscure. This did not prevent the
Press from publishing most of his poetry and critical work. The novels,
described by Chapman as 'spiritual shockers' (by the author as 'metaphysi-

cal thrillers'), were published by Gollancz, for whom he also compiled *A New Book of English Verse*. In 1936 he wrote *Thomas Cranmer of Canterbury*, the play to be performed in the Chapter House at Canterbury following T. S. Eliot's *Murder in the Cathedral* of the previous year. Though no great master of light verse he wrote ingenious masques for performance by the staff at Amen House: 'Caesar's chair' played a prominent part, obeisance was paid to an invisible presence.

Obscurity was becoming acceptable in so far as it was 'modern', but Williams's obscurity was of a different order. Both his idiom and his metaphysics were strange, and he appeared to belong to no recognizable tradition. Those not immediately moved by the 'soaring and gorgeous novelty' of his technique generally remained bewildered. For their benefit his friend C. S. Lewis offered pellucid guidance: 'In him the tradition which had begun by being pantheistic, revolutionary, and antinomian becomes Nicene, hierarchical, severe. It is not a Celtic Twilight, but a Celtic Noon.' Lewis had no doubt that he would in the end 'stand as the great English poet of this age'.

The two men met after Lewis had written to say how much he had enjoyed Williams's novel *The Place of the Lion*, just as Williams was about to write the same about Lewis's *Allegory of Love*. When the Amen House staff moved to Oxford at the beginning of the Second World War they met regularly, and a circle of friends gathered twice a week in their favourite pub, The Eagle and Child, to drink cider, read from their own work, or play the 'quotation game', at which Williams excelled. Among those of his friends who contributed to the memorial volume published in 1947 were Dorothy L. Sayers, J. R. R. Tolkien, C. S. Lewis, H. O. Barfield, and Gervase Mathew. They knew that Williams had spent all his working life at the Oxford University Press, but over this he and they appeared to prefer to draw a veil. It had nothing to do with their own experience of him. He talked about books, but not about publishing, and it would certainly not have occurred to him to attempt to turn his literary acquaintance to the advantage of the Press, to presume to treat his friends as potential 'authors'. A more orthodoxly competitive editor might have expressed a professional interest in the sequel to *The Hobbit*, early chapters of which Tolkien would occasionally read aloud.

His own literary activities must also have absorbed a good deal of his energies. Altogether he published some thirty books, and innumerable articles and memoirs. In Oxford he lectured for the depleted English Faculty during the war, besides doing tutorial work. In 1941 he took over the editorship of the *Periodical*, but it would seem that he courted obscurity within the Press, escaping much of the office routine that makes up the average editor's day. A deeply religious man, it was he who bestowed the name of Caesar on Milford. Yet his colleague, Gerard Hopkins, who worked with him for over twenty years, wrote: 'His affection for the Oxford University Press was, to no small extent, the moving force of his life. It shared, it symbolized, the fervent religious faith and the happy domestic love which rounded his existence. The City of God in which he never ceased to dwell, contained Amen House as its noblest human monument, and all who lived and worked in it were citizens with him.' On the other hand, in his *D.N.B.* article on Williams, Hopkins admitted that his duties at the Press, though carried out with enthusiasm and prudence, occupied a relatively small part of his life. For C. S. Lewis his death was the greatest loss that he had ever known: it prompted his book *The Problem of Pain.*

Gerard Hopkins, nephew of Gerard Manley Hopkins, was also a man of letters. He joined the Press at the end of the First World War and remained as editorial adviser with responsibility for publicity until retirement in 1958. He wrote seven novels, and his many translations from the French (particularly the novels of Mauriac) brought him distinction as Chevalier de la Légion d'Honneur. For translating he had a remarkable facility. With the French text beside him he might appear to be copy-typing, but the copy that emerged from his typewriter was good English prose, if a little remote at times from the meaning of the original. He was genial and unworldly, feeling little sympathy for those who followed their profession in too competitive a fashion. For him as for Charles Williams it was contrary to propriety, and to what the Press should represent, to put business before good manners. But he had a disarming way with literary editors and got good publicity. It was he who contrived for an advertisement in the *Times Literary Supplement* a memorable image likening the growth of the Oxford University Press to that of a great banyan tree with tremendous roots—and suckers in every field.

Frederick Page, who for most of thirty-seven years shared a room with Charles Williams, edited amongst other books the Oxford Illustrated Trollope with Michael Sadleir, the *Selected Letters* of Keats, and with Edmund Blunden *The Essays of Elia* for the World's Classics. His interest in the nineteenth century brought him as well as Chapman and Milford into frequent contact with the book-collector and forger of genius, Thomas Wise. Not until 1934, when he was already old and ailing, were Wise's misdemeanours publicly exposed. Even after his guilt had been proved beyond reasonable doubt, Milford and Page persisted in half-believing in his innocence, until they themselves risked being charged with collusion. An impression was allowed to get abroad that 'Oxford' was supporting Wise for reasons best known to itself; eventually vigorous disclaimers had to be made. It had simply been impossible for such honest men as they to believe in the enormity of his deception.

Amen Corner was itself by now an amorphous architectural sprawl, and this led perhaps to a certain want of cohesion in the London Business. The move to Amen House in 1924 secured more rational, and certainly more elegant premises. The opening was celebrated with great pomp and rhetoric. A grand luncheon was held and the speeches must have kept the distinguished guests until late in the afternoon. Nothing quite like it had occurred before in the annals of the Press, and the occasion, fully reported in the newspapers, was made into a kind of triumph, hardly to be explained in terms of a simple change of address. If Milford had written all the speeches himself it could not have been more greatly to his satisfaction.

The Archbishop of Canterbury (Dr. Randall Davidson) recalled the invention of printing long ago and all the many developments since then that had culminated in the great institution they were contemplating that day. Mr. Asquith paid tribute to the enlightened policy of successive Boards of Delegates and their Secretaries, singling out 'for especial mention and for deep regret the name of our lamented friend Mr. Cannan'. Lord Curzon, Chancellor of the University, could not forbear to say that he understood that Oxford men were sparsely represented in the Labour Government of the day. Even so he was sure that Labour looked upon Oxford not only with sympathy, but with enthusiasm. 'Many Labour men have had their training at Oxford University,' he said, 'if not always in the colleges, then in other excellent institutions, while we, on our part, have done our best to go out into the world, and carry such sources of illumination as we have in our possession to the labouring classes of this country.' He spoke also of the quality of Oxford paper and printing, not only repeating an old boast but doing so in words oddly reminiscent of Rupert Brooke: 'And when other books—and thank God it is so—when the vast majority of other books disappear, when the paper on which they are printed degenerates into pulp, when the type fades out and becomes obscure, and when nobody is left with anything to read except the publications of the Oxford University Press, then shall we attain the full measure of our reward.'

Winding up, as it were, for the opposition, the Chancellor of Cambridge University, Lord Balfour, said that he was always pleased to listen to Oxford men praising each other. He felt he must advise all those who cared for posterity to desert the Cambridge Press, or any of the great publishing houses, and make at once for Oxford. He only regretted that if they took his advice the new building they were there to celebrate would prove quite inadequate to deal with the crowd of seekers after immortality.

It was a great day in the history of the Press, the speakers had said, and as the guests dispersed on that March afternoon they were no doubt fuzzily inclined, even if they could not say precisely why, to agree.

In 1925 thirty new titles were added to the World's Classics and some half-million copies sold. Milford went on springing surprises. He had always found Trollope enjoyable, at a time when Trollope was generally out of favour. *The Three Clerks* had appeared in 1907; *The Warden* was included in 1918; and from then on there was a steady accumulation. With the help of Stanley Baldwin, Milford eventually prevailed upon the public to start buying and reading Trollope again. He had a more immediate success with the novels and stories of Constance Holme, in his view disgracefully neglected. Having failed to persuade another publisher to risk reissuing her works, he drove *The Lonely Plough* into the World's Classics, and its success was such that over the next few years seven other books by her were added.

Milford was a voracious reader of detective stories and never left on a journey without laying in a supply which would ensure a ration of at least two a day. He caused two anthologies, called *Crime and Detection*, to be included in the series and also instructed V. H. Collins to compile *Ghosts and Marvels*: 'Selections of Uncanny Tales from Defoe to Algernon Blackwood.' Joined in a strange companionship were such works as Richard Livingstone's editions of Plato and Thucydides, and *Speeches and Documents on the British Dominions, 1918–1931*, edited by Arthur Berriedale Keith, the most remarkable and versatile of scholars. Keith was a lawyer, Regius Professor of Sanskrit and Comparative Philology, and lecturer on the constitution of the British Empire. His *History of Sanskrit Literature*, first published in 1920, endures; so too his work on the colonies and dominions.

Perhaps Milford's best-known discovery was Flora Thompson, whose trilogy *Lark Rise to Candleford* did in fact become a classic with the passage of time. When, after his retirement, an informal attempt was made by friends and colleagues to determine the most important new book—excluding Clarendon Press books—issued by Milford during his thirty-two years as Publisher, opinion was divided between Toynbee's *A Study of History* and *Lark Rise to Candleford*. 'Milford's list is as personal', wrote Chapman, 'as anything ever is which emanates from that extraordinarily homogeneous plurality Amen House, where all pulses take their time from Caesar's.' He was referring to his list of candidates for inclusion in the 1920s volume of the *D.N.B.*, but the words would equally apply to the World's Classics.

Williams's taste in poetry was generally conventional, despite the eccentricity of his own. For a long time the Poet Laureate, Robert Bridges, and Lascelles Abercrombie were the only living writers to be included among the Oxford Poets. Slim volumes of contemporary verse decorated the main list in genteel style. In 1918, however, Milford published *The Poems of Gerard Manley Hopkins*, edited by Bridges. Hopkins, a Jesuit priest, had died in 1889, and although one or two poems had appeared in anthologies his work was generally unknown. The experience of being confronted all at once with a fully matured and highly original poet was disconcerting: it was felt that had it been possible to observe his development step by step in the normal way it would have been easier to assimilate him. Despite the recommendations of the Poet Laureate—who himself found much that was repugnant in his old friend's verse—the first edition of the poems made little impact. The *New Statesman* conceded that 'Father Hopkins's poetry is to eye, ear and mind the strangest that has been published in England—the poetry of Mr. Doughty not excepted—in modern times.' But it could not be recommended to the ordinary reader. John Middleton Murry in the *Athenaeum* speculated on whether the failure of his whole achievement was due to the starvation of experience which his vocation imposed upon him, and concluded that it was. The first edition of 750 copies was not sold out for more than ten years. In 1930, nevertheless, the Press ventured on a second edition, with an appendix of additional poems and an introduction by Charles Williams. It was greeted as something long-awaited. Hopkins was acclaimed as a great liberating influence on English verse. The *Times Literary Supplement* clamoured for the publication of all his prose writings as well, for everything possible should be done to make his work more generally known and to spread the fame 'of this poet of true genius'. In due course his correspondence, his journals and papers, his sermons and devotional writings, were published by the Press, and numerous critical studies sprouted about him.

Bridges was less successful in promoting the poems of another friend, Digby Dolben, though he persuaded Milford to publish them, and also to have half a dozen copies manufactured in America to secure copyright there. In 1929, when Bridges was eighty-five, *The Testament of Beauty* was published. It appeared first in an *édition de luxe* of 250 copies printed to the design of Stanley Morison, with a dedication to the King designed by Eric Gill. This poem of 4,376 lines, sprinkled with obscure Bridgean words —eterne, fust, illachrymable, languörous, muliebrous, vastidity—and seething with thoughts and emotions of unimaginable loftiness, was an immediate success. The ordinary edition was reprinted four times within three weeks, and even after the first excitement had subsided it continued to sell some 4,000 copies a month. Bridges was a greatly respected Poet Laureate and a national monument, but this alone does not explain the demand for this extraordinary work. It had a grandeur fast disappearing from the world: soon there would be no poets left who could write that Beauty was 'the eternal spouse of the Wisdom of God and Angel of his Presence'. Once having compared it to Wordsworth's *Prelude* the critics hardly knew what to say. H. W. Garrod chose to define its essential quality as 'a certain sweet and gentle seriousness'. It was 'the only great poem that has appeared in living memory'. Lascelles Abercrombie thought that Bridges had devised a system of versification that would be of capital importance for the future. And the *Periodical* rejoiced, for it was the best seller of any poem that living man had known.

In 1930 Milford suggested to Abercrombie that he might compile an 'Oxford' book of modern, twentieth-century verse. Abercrombie agreed. It would, he thought, be 'a delightful pie to cook'. He was to have the assistance of Milford's niece, Anne Bradby (later Anne Ridler). After four years, however, Charles Williams had to report to Milford that Abercrombie had made little progress and was in a state of considerable muddle and distress. For one thing it had occurred to him that the anthology would lose him a host of friends. A new editor was needed and it had to be decided whether to seek another 'Name' or to forgo the Name in the hope that 'Oxford Book' and 'Modern Verse' would in themselves be sufficient to sell the book. It could be compiled in the office. Somewhere between a Name and anonymity came the young poet Dylan Thomas, whose poems had been reluctantly declined not long before ('very physiologically modern', Williams explained). Milford consulted Sisam. There was little difference between anonymous and Dylan Thomas, in his view, and somebody well known to reviewers seemed to him essential. So Williams drew up a list, headed by W. B. Yeats, 'who would be the one name which would awe all sides'. His second preference, on the assumption that T. S. Eliot was committed to Fabers, was Aldous Huxley. He was too modest to mention his own name, but he was an obvious candidate. Chapman and Sisam favoured Yeats, expensive though he was known to be. An approach was made through his agent and Yeats agreed.

It was accepted that an anthology of modern verse was the responsibility of Amen House, even though as an 'Oxford Book' it would carry the Clarendon Press imprint. In Oxford the modern poets were not much read and Sisam and Chapman could only offer general advice. The former issued the usual solemn warning against omitting popular favourites. 'At Amen House I think you are all inclined to the highbrow attitude in poetry,' he wrote to Milford. It would be as well to impress upon the editor at the start—for he would get little help from his publisher as he went along—that a popular book for ordinary people to enjoy was intended. 'After all, Yeats has immediately reminded you through a literary agent that even the most spiritual poets need money.' It was an ironic reversal of roles, and there is no evidence that Milford passed on the Assistant Secretary's instructions, or that he needed to.

In the spring of 1935 Yeats went to work, reading assiduously, an ageing man of sixty-nine attempting to capture the spirit of the age. Ezra Pound tired him out; he could not keep his attention fixed on G. M. Hopkins for more than a few minutes at a time; Wilfred Owen disgusted him; in T. S. Eliot there was a flatness; and the social passions of Day Lewis and MacNeice seemed to have little to do with poetry. But there were exciting compensations. Some of W. J. Turner's poems were 'exquisite', and he delighted in a young poet called George Barker. By June he was 'going a mucker', as Q would have said, on Dorothy Wellesley, whose poetry he had just discovered, and with whom he formed a friendship that lasted until his death. Friendship would not affect his judgement, he had told Charles Williams: unlike Abercrombie, he could fearlessly exclude the work of old friends like Richard Aldington and J. C. Squire. But he found that he had given more space to Dorothy Wellesley than to anybody else and had to explain to her that this would not do. 'People would think it was friendship,' he wrote, 'especially as, I think, you come immediately before T. S. Eliot.'

By November the selection was almost complete, but as usual there was trouble obtaining permissions, a task entrusted to Yeats which proved beyond his powers. It took several months to sort out the muddle he got into. Not until 1 May 1936 was Williams able to send a complete manuscript to Sisam. 'The whole book varies most amazingly,' he wrote, 'from the most imbecilic simple poems of Masefield and Drinkwater to Mr. Empson. You cannot, however, say that it has not a great deal of very popular stuff in it.' Uncomplainingly Sisam passed the copy to the printer and the book was published in November 1936.

Neither the Press nor Yeats expected to escape controversy, and it followed in abundance. *The Times* described the choice of Yeats as editor as 'a happy inspiration'; the *Spectator* as opportunism on the part of the Delegates. The anthology itself was criticized as tantalizing and un-integrated, shapeless and perfunctory. The poor representation of Kipling and Pound was attributed by the *Spectator* reviewer to the niggardliness of the Clarendon Press. 'As I had a fixed sum for payment of authors I decided on my own responsibility that I could not afford more of these expensive writers', Yeats replied, which hardly exculpated the Press. The same fate posthumously befell Yeats himself who, for financial reasons, was under-represented in a number of anthologies, including the *Oxford Book of Irish Verse*.

The most extravagant charges came from Lord Alfred Douglas, who sent a telegram to Yeats with copies to the newspapers and leading literary figures:

Your omission of my work from the absurdly-named Oxford Book of Modern Verse is exactly typical of the attitude of the minor to the major poet. For example Thomas Moore, the Yeats of the 19th century, would undoubtedly have excluded Keats and Shelley from any anthology he had compiled. And why drag in Oxford? Would not shoneen Irish be a more correct description?

Douglas also wrote to Milford telling him that his ridiculous anthology would 'remain as a monument to the ineptitude of the Oxford University Press, as conducted by you, for all time'. He quoted a letter he had received from Sir Arthur Quiller-Couch, who had written, 'It must be the "Oxford" that stirs your gall. You should take it as a high compliment that you are not in Mr. Yeats' gallery. He was a poet once: but adulation has turned his head, and Lord! *what* an anthology and *what* a Preface.' There were some who regarded the preface as a more important contribution to English literature than most of the poems that followed it.

Yeats was not displeased by the uproar, which helped sales, and he regarded vindictive criticism as proof that he had somehow got to the heart of the matter. The surprising amount of space allotted to Oliver St. John Gogarty, with more poems than anybody else, and to Dorothy Wellesley, was noted by the critics, but Yeats saw no reason to apologize or explain, and he was sure he had been right to omit altogether Wilfred Owen— 'whom I consider unworthy of the poets' corner of a country newspaper', he told Dorothy Wellesley. 'There is every excuse for him, but none for those who like him.' He had indeed omitted all war poems on the ground that 'passing suffering is not a theme for poetry'.

The general question appeared to be whether working poets were properly qualified to act as anthologists. Their selections would tell the reader more about themselves than the state of current literature. All the other Oxford Books of English verse had been compiled either by Q, a sort of professional anthologist, or by scholars or literary critics whose reputations did not extend far beyond the academic world. Sir Edmund Chambers had done the sixteenth century, H. J. C. Grierson and G. Bullough the seventeenth, Nicol Smith the eighteenth, and Milford himself the Romantic period. Sisam's insistence on a 'Name' for the 1900–35 volume suggests that he doubted the saleability of contemporary verse and also whether it could be fully understood by anybody but a practitioner. Despite the idiosyncrasies of Yeats's selection he was not apparently displeased with it, certainly not by its sales. And when some thirty years later the need was felt to replace both Q's original anthology and to bring out a new book of modern verse the same instinct prevailed: the former was entrusted to a scholar, the latter to a poet.

4. The Music Department

V. H. COLLINS was something more than the 'Educational Manager'. He was informally responsible for training new recruits, not by inducting them into the many mysteries of the business but by subjecting what letters they were permitted to write to a deadly scrutiny. Geoffrey Cumberlege was placed in his charge when he first joined the Press in 1919: a kindly man, he recalled later, but an 'incurable schoolmaster'. Heavily armed with coloured pencils, he would treat every draft letter placed before him as an exercise: it emerged a mass of coloured corrections. In 1921 a senior assistant to the Educational Manager was appointed, a young man named Hubert Foss. He was twenty-two, and had been a teacher in a preparatory school and assistant editor of a journal called *Land and Water*. He was not particularly interested in education: he was passionately interested in music.

The Oxford History of Music in six volumes, edited by Sir W. H. Hadow, had been published between 1901 and 1905. It seemed a milestone of sorts at the time. In nineteenth-century Oxford the idea that music might in any sense be educational would not have been entertained. The influence and interest of Gerrans and Bishop Strong caused a few other music books to be published by the Clarendon Press, but Cannan was tone-deaf as well as colour-blind, and Chapman indifferent. Milford, however, was not without musical taste and in 1923 he chose to start a special music department. When asked later to explain why this department should be in London rather than Oxford, for it was not profitable, Chapman could only say that he himself was as ignorant of music as his predecessor, whereas Milford had personal and business relations with cathedral organists and hymnologists. And he also had Hubert Foss.

It was perhaps the boldest and most imaginative of all Milford's innovations. There is no direct evidence that Foss was responsible for the original decision. Indeed there is no evidence that Milford knew anything about the music trade or was even aware that sheet music was a very different commodity from books—that it was impossible to sell music through ordinary book trade channels, which were all he had available. However, there was always one way of entering a new field, by dispossessing a current occupant. He acquired The Anglo-French Music Co. Ltd., together with most of its staff and its premises in Wimpole Street. He engaged Norman Peterkin, a composer of good if modest reputation, as sales manager. He was then in a position to withdraw from the scene. The stage belonged to Hubert Foss, and the virtuoso performance he proceeded to give astonished not only his employers but the whole musical world.

His work was hectic but inspired. Books and scores poured out at a rate of some 200 titles a year: the 1931 Music Catalogue listed over 1,750. He came nearer than any other single man, Milford said, to ruining the Press. In 1933, when asked by the Delegates to justify his conduct of the London business during the slump, Milford admitted that to have cut or abolished the music department would have been a rational economy, one dictated, it could be argued, by common sense. But though it had failed dramatically to pay its way, it had under Foss done more for British music in ten years than the rest of the London music publishers had in thirty. He begged to be excused this one extravagance.

Medical books, juvenile and elementary, later overseas education, were all separate departments which could be assimilated within the traditional structure of a publishing house. They also corresponded roughly with the policy of the Delegates, for they were sources of revenue which enabled the Clarendon Press to go about its proper business. The music department was always different, not simply in the way it functioned, but in its purpose. It was an anachronism, and as it grew it reflected in microcosm the anachronistic growth of the Press itself. To begin with it did not apply commercial standards. Chapman conceded that it was as impossible for it to do so as it was for the Delegates in the field of *literae humaniores*. It would be quite out of character for a University Press to publish popular music— the equivalent of publishing popular fiction. On the other hand it could not publish the standard classics, which were mass-produced and marketed by the established music publishers: there was no scope then for textual criticism that might establish one score as intrinsically superior to any other. Brass bands moreover seemed to move in a rather private world of their own. It was on contemporary English composers that Foss concentrated, and for many their work was obscure and displeasing. He was publishing for a minority, performing the same essential service as the Clarendon Press, and the most cherished items on his list were likely to be among the most unremunerative.

Chapman looked benignly on the new department. It completed, he felt, the 'academicization' of the London business begun with the appointment of an Oxford graduate as Assistant Publisher in 1906. To Sisam it offended against tradition and logic. It was clearly a 'spending' department, and the whole point of the London business was to provide revenue. 'It is a subject of public wonder and admiration that they produce so much apparently unremunerative work', he wrote caustically, even perhaps a little enviously, to Chapman in 1929 when money was short. At the time he was affronted by a suggestion that the Delegates might relieve the department of an embarrassment by publishing a learned book on ancient Greek music. It had been sent in the first place to Foss, who was being allowed to give the impression of having money to burn, and Sisam saw no reason to help him out. Milford admitted that there was a problem and that, although this particular work might have the hallmarks of a Clarendon Press book, his new department, by assuming for itself peculiar responsibilities, had eliminated the familiar distinction between learned and general publishing.

It was clear, however, that sooner or later the department would have to become self-supporting if it were not to be brought directly under the Delegates' control. It did so in the end by following the example of the parent body. The largest part of its publishing came to be of educational and tuitional works. It produced music courses at all levels for schools, textbooks for music colleges and colleges of education, and for universities. Then the wireless created a whole new breed of general reader before whom Foss could display his extraordinary assortment of wares. And the department produced reference books. So in due course it ceased to be a spending department. In 1937 Milford was able to report a loss of only £2,200 and by 1939 it was paying its way. It had, admittedly, taken longer than expected. But the greatest triumph of all was that among the contemporary composers whom Foss had discovered or encouraged were some of the best sellers of the day, and of many days to come.

The most prolific of his authors was Percy Scholes, who was also one of the first to recognize the magnitude of Milford's achievement. 'What you are doing is too big for us to grasp all at once,' he wrote in 1928, 'but when we do grasp it I think the Press will stand ahead of every music-publishing house in the country.' Scholes was music critic for the *Observer*, a regular broadcaster, musical editor of the *Radio Times*, and author of *The 'Radio Times' Music Handbook* published by the Press. In 1938, by which time he had been able to give up journalism and retire to Switzerland, the encyclopedic work on which he had been engaged for many years was published as *The Oxford Companion to Music*.

Foss developed the list by introducing series, such as 'The Musical Pilgrim Series'. Sir Henry Wood's *The Gentle Art of Singing* was published in four volumes in 1927–8. In the 1930s Foss published Sir Donald Tovey's six volumes of *Essays in Musical Analysis*. The list of books on music became enormous, but the music itself was the great achievement. In 1925, Vaughan Williams became an Oxford composer, with a setting for voice and piano of four poems by Walt Whitman. Within a year or so an informal understanding had been reached by which the Press agreed to publish whatever he wrote. An enduring and close relationship grew up between the two men. When Foss resigned in 1941, Vaughan Williams wrote, 'I did not know how much I counted on you. I know that I owe any success I have had more to you (except H. P. Allen)[1] than to anyone else.'

Foss also published the young William Walton, starting modestly in 1927 with piano duet arrangements of *Portsmouth Point* and the first suite from *Façade*. With Walton formal contracts had to be negotiated at regular intervals, but all his mature works were published by the Press. In 1929 Foss launched Constant Lambert with *The Rio Grande*, and among other young composers he published and encouraged were Peter Warlock, E. J. Moeran, Rubbra, Alan Rawsthorne, Benjamin Britten, and John Gardner. Established composers—Holst, Ethel Smythe, Ireland—also joined the Oxford list.

The department moved in 1932 to 36 Soho Square, and in 1950 to 44 Conduit Street, where it remains. Foss left early in the war, unwilling to tolerate the restraints being imposed upon him. He became a free-lance writer, a popular broadcaster, and organized concerts for the forces. He died in 1953 at the age of 54. The man who came close to ruining it left the Press a handsome legacy. The centenary of Vaughan Williams's birth and Walton's seventieth birthday fell in 1972. The celebrations proved the soundness of his investment: quite a little gold-mine, in fact, as Chapman would have said.

5. Overseas Education

In 1915, E. C. Parnwell joined the Press in London at the age of 16, as a clerk in the educational department under Vere Collins. In 1926 he was told by Milford to 'become expert in education overseas'. He was provided with an office, a table and two chairs, an in-tray and an out-tray, and an Oxford Wall Map of the World. That was the only positive instruction and guidance he had from Milford about starting what was to prove the most important new venture of the inter-war years.

All Parnwell's experience had been in secondary education, and although it extended to the education of Europeans in Australia and South Africa he had not been introduced to the problems of 'Native Education', of which he was hardly aware. Presumably it was an inkling that much was being said on the subject that decided Milford that he needed an expert. Longmans were already in the field, Macmillans not far behind. An Advisory Committee on Education had been set up by the Colonial Office some years earlier. *Native Education in Africa*, a Colonial Office paper, and the Phelps-Stokes report on education in tropical countries were published in 1927, and the International African Institute was founded soon after.

By 1928 it was time for Parnwell to leave his desk and set out on his

[1] Sir Hugh Percy Allen (1869-1946), Professor of Music in Oxford and Director of the Royal College of Music.

Q

travels. He went first to South Africa. He was to make a survey of native education there and also to investigate the way in which the Press's interests were being managed by the Branch. He was surprised to find the Cape Town office in the hands of a man of seventy-four called Charles Mellor, who appeared to have been left there by an oversight. He duly reported to Milford that the business was not being run as energetically as might be wished, but Milford took no immediate action. He requested Parnwell not to cause him to cross bridges before he got to them: 'A judicious hesitation, Mr. Parnwell, may allow a difficulty to solve itself without intervention.' It was never known whether the letter he eventually wrote proposing retirement reached Mellor before or after his death from excessive tea-drinking.

Travelling through South Africa and Rhodesia Parnwell acquired his first glimmerings of an obvious truth not previously brought to his attention. In his business experience hitherto, French or German was taught as the 'second' language, and despite an abundance of textbooks not always very successfully. In Africa children were being taught English as their second language, with virtually no suitable textbooks, by teachers whose own English was barely intelligible. Evidently there were vast opportunities for the publisher if he could find the man to write the books that were so badly needed. Parnwell soon discovered that there were a few outstanding pioneers at work in different parts of the world, notably Lawrence Faucett in China and Michael West in Bengal. West had in fact already approached the O.U.P. in India, but his proposals for a series of experimental readers had not found favour. By the time Parnwell had acquired his expertise West's New Method Readers, the New Method Course, and other supplementary readers had been published by Longmans and were in use throughout the tropics. For the moment there appeared to be no possibility of competition.

Lacking a suitable author, Parnwell produced a little book himself for schools in Malta at the request of the Director of Education there. He also prepared word lists of his own, marking some 2,000 words in *The Pocket Oxford Dictionary* which represented in his view a minimum vocabulary. Word counts and word-frequency lists had been and were being compiled by the experts, but Parnwell preferred his own, and was later assured that it differed only slightly from the more scientific compilations. On the basis of it he proposed to build an elementary English course for African schools. But at this moment one of the experts turned up in person at Amen House to offer his services, Lawrence Faucett. He had tried to interest Longmans, but because they were already committed to West, and Faucett's course was not then complete, he had been turned away. His method was similar to that of West, but the emphasis was on the spoken rather than the written word. With his help Parnwell was able to start publishing the Oxford English Course in 1931, five years after he had been given his special assignment. During that time much money had been spent on salaries, travelling expenses, and eventually on production costs. There was nothing, except Parnwell's little booklet for Malta, to show for it, and no receipts had been recorded. Milford never intervened. Even after some dozens of books of the Oxford English Course had appeared, together with two teachers' handbooks and sixteen graded supplementary readers, the new department, by now known as O.E. (Overseas Education), thrived only modestly. Parnwell campaigned in the Middle East, but only in Turkey, where Faucett had been employed as organizer of English teaching, could he make much headway against the competition.

In 1935 he turned again to Africa. The Educational Adviser to the Secretary of State and the Protestant Missions in Kenya recommended to him Sister Isabelle Frémont, an experienced educationalist who could adapt Faucett's books for East Africa. After discussing plans with her in Nairobi he went on to Malaya, Hong Kong, Shanghai, and Japan, tirelessly hawking the Oxford English Course across the world. The principal of a school in Hong Kong examined his wares respectfully, but sighed that they were not enough. He had to teach school subjects through the medium of English, but the vocabulary and idiom of the standard textbooks were far wider than could be acquired from the Oxford Course. So far Parnwell had had no clear plan, beyond the provision of suitable materials for the teaching of English in elementary schools. Now he had suddenly a vision of what had to be done: he was to provide an endless variety of reading-books based on controlled vocabulary with simple glosses of 'unknown' words, simplified textbooks, and graded English dictionaries. The scope of O.E. could indeed be extended indefinitely, until it achieved what nobody initially could have dared forecast. By bridging the linguistic and cultural gap between primary and university education, it could help to rear in Africa and Asia a host of new readers of Clarendon Press books, and thus fulfil the original purpose of every department of the Press as laid down by its founding fathers. Much had to be done before the millennium could be reached, but henceforth Parnwell's main preoccupation was the broadening of the O.E. programme with more advanced books to which Sisam gave the generic title 'Oxford Progressive English'.

On his return from the Far East Parnwell found that he had lost Faucett, victim of a mental breakdown. He had, however, found F. G. French, once headmaster of Rangoon High School and then an Inspector of Schools. He continued the work of adapting Faucett's elementary course, while Parnwell branched out with the Oxford English Readers for Africa, a series of history books written by T. R. Batten while teaching in Nigeria, and a set of four textbooks of General Science for Tropical Schools. He planned 'An Approach to English Literature' in five volumes, for long a remarkably successful series. It was compiled by H. B. Drake. In the first volume the chosen passages had to be violently adapted so as to build on a standard vocabulary of 1,500 words at a fixed rate of so many words to a page. The second volume required less brutal treatment, and by the fifth, when the vocabulary had reached 3,000 words, the pupil would be able to tackle the texts with the help of a simplified dictionary. It was unfortunate that the Press had not at that time a suitable dictionary to offer, but Michael West's *New Method Dictionary* was available from Longmans. The dictionary that O.E. was seeking arrived unexpectedly during the war in the form of printed sheets smuggled out of Japan by A. S. Hornby. But by then there was not enough paper available to print it.

In 1935 the department sold in all £5,000 worth of books. By 1940 an annual turnover of £10,000 had been reached, and at the end of the war £40,000. It was still only the beginning for O.E. In the next ten years the turnover went from £40,000 to £400,000, to become a decade later roughly a quarter of that of the business as a whole. The department had, moreover, established itself as the training ground of future branch managers.

6. The *D.N.B.* Supplement

CANNAN'S sandbag resistance gone, something had to be done about the *D.N.B.* The main work itself had to be reprinted from plates at a cost of £8,000: sales were in the region of 100 sets a year. It was estimated that some 4,000 sets were in existence, the majority of them in sixty-six parts rather than the twenty-two volumes, which confused the page references in the index and epitome, now to be called *The Concise Dictionary of National Biography*. To revise the whole work would cost, it was calculated, £100,000—a figure that remained constant though notional throughout the inter-war years.

The immediate matter of concern was the continuation of the Dictionary into the twentieth century. Despite the feud with Lee and Firth, the Delegates agreed in 1920 that work should begin on a 1912–21 volume. It would have to be on a much more modest scale, however, than Lee's 1901–11 supplement of more than 2,000 pages which included 1,660 lives. Peering into the nineteenth century Chapman noted that the annual rate of admission, at a peak in the 1870s, had then begun to decline, and for the nineties was well below the annual average for the century as a whole—by his reckoning 113 as opposed to 133. Lee had then wrecked such balanced and meaningful calculations by allowing the annual rate to go beyond 160; his own lack of judgement rather than the worthiness of those who gained entry was apparent. If this unhappy precedent were followed, the twentieth century would yield more than 15,000 worthies and the *D.N.B.* would prove an even more serious case of elephantiasis than the *O.E.D.* itself.

Chapman did not expect the twentieth century to merit such attention. He saw no reason why the decline that had set in during the nineties should not continue: the evidence suggested acceleration. But the problem was how to persuade the public, the Smith family, and Sir Sidney Lee that a much smaller selection with shorter articles was not a mean and disreputable economy but the result of an enlightened and considered policy.

Chapman had discovered that 1917 was a particularly lean year in which no career had come to fulfilment. Convinced that he was living in an age of mediocrity, he wanted to 'grasp that nettle', as he put it; his diagnosis could be put to the public in justification of short measure. 'Too dangerous, I timidly submit', Milford wrote, and Sisam argued that the 'mediocrity' theme would not help sales. One of his editors, H. W. C. Davis, simply did not agree. Chapman admitted that it was difficult to prove, but he 'hoped it might confuse the public mind'—it was not unusual for Chapman's honest convictions to run through devious channels. But he was overruled. It would be plain to everybody that continuation on the scale of Lee was out of the question, and Chapman had to content himself with expressing the Delegates' conviction that the value of the Dictionary would be enhanced rather than impaired 'by the maintenance of a high standard of eminence in the persons to be commemorated'.

Whatever the misgivings, the work on the succeeding decennial volumes proved congenial. The solemn task of selection induced high spirits, and occasional flippancy; the awesome responsibility of holding the keys to eternity proving too much at times for Chapman's and Milford's sense of the ludicrous. But they went in genuine fear of an oversight, or an injustice, and concealed behind an Olympian smirk their striving for Olympian detachment.

The lives written by Leslie Stephen himself could be taken as a model: his instructions to contributors had been 'No flowers, by request'. To write on friends and contemporaries with a proper objectivity was exceedingly difficult, however, and led to an adaptation of the obituary style which required a special kind of ambiguity, frequent use of 'nevertheless', of the deft *non sequitur*, and contradictory adjectives. Chapman's own contribution on Bywater might also be considered exemplary, if only because in trying to evoke the memory of his old friend he forgot to mention certain basic facts: that he had, for instance, been Regius Professor of Greek for fifteen years.

Class lists were kept, first-class candidates being entitled to two pages, second-class to one page, and third-class half a page. A very small group of 'supermen' could claim up to six pages—Kitchener, Joseph Chamberlain, Milner, and W. G. Grace amongst them. In practice the contributors did not always fill the allotted space. By far the largest class was the fourth, the failures who had nevertheless earned consideration. Particular attention was paid to them as the decade passed, in case a change in reputation had occurred: lists of 'Resuscitated Rejects' were circulated and reconsidered at regular intervals.

Actual preparation of the Supplement was in the hands of the two editors, Davis and J. R. H. Weaver of Trinity, but Chapman's intervention was often sought, or at least could not be avoided. He regarded the 1920s as altogether more 'rich' than the previous decade, and no longer talked of an age of mediocrity. He was regularly in touch with Geoffrey Dawson, editor of *The Times*, and through him with the 'Chief of Morgue', or the

'Gravedigger', whom Dawson preferred to call 'the colleague in charge of our memoirs'. The 'Resuscitated Rejects' were the subject of many cryptic notes that passed between Chapman and Milford as they went through the lists. 'Harrison, Frederic. Two columns. Positivist. I can't tell you what he was or did but I seem always to have known his name,' Chapman scribbled. Or, 'Hornby, A. N. "A great Cricketer." We can't admit many of this large class.' Milford protested: 'Yes—as the greatest master of the short run, and remembering Thompson's "O my Hornby and my Barlow long ago."' He did not get in. Chapman was more impressed by Milford's support of Spofforth: 'Yes! Australia would leave the Empire if the Demon Bowler were omitted.' Of a distinguished publisher, Sir Algernon Methuen, Chapman wrote, 'I am not lenient to publishers'; of a 'noted' anthropologist he observed, 'I think *noted* excludes'; of a Duke, 'Certainly not; an absurd person'. G. R. Sims, strongly backed by E. V. Lucas who believed with others that he had been Jack the Ripper, was rejected at the third count.

The allocation of space also required a keen discernment. Politicians or military men might be judged by rank attained, but the reputations of writers and artists were notably fickle. Weaver was full of doubts about D. H. Lawrence. 'I wondered what would be thought about him—even twenty years hence. However, a great deal is said about him *now*, and no doubt we ought to reflect that.' One omission that Chapman later regretted was Horace Hart. The bibliographer, A. W. Pollard, had referred to him in an article as a 'great Printer'. 'We were afraid of rating domestic gods too high', wrote Chapman. He still doubted whether he really had been a great printer: Johnson told him that he had been 'a great commercial printer', which perhaps took true greatness away from him. But he had certainly been a pioneer in typographical research.

7. A Stable of Dictionaries

A CHAPMAN scrawl addressed to Sisam read, 'We must do anything, agree to anything, ignore anything, to keep him in his admirable rut.' It referred to Henry Fowler, to whom he had offered domestic help (see opposite). Sisam was the fourth Oxford man with whom Fowler had to deal, and it must have been a matter of some wonder that with each new correspondent he not only met his match in scholarship but encountered somebody with rare literary and philological qualities who understood immediately what he was about. The only change, and that of the times, was that he now found himself addressed as 'Dear Fowler' instead of 'My Dear Sir'.

In 1924 *The Pocket Oxford Dictionary* was published, bearing on its title-page the names of both the brothers. By then Henry was at work on the 'Idiom Dictionary', which he had first proposed in 1909. Ever since the

6 Nov. 1926   (486.K.S.)

Dear Chapman

My half-hour from 7.0 to 7.30 this morning was spent in (1) a two-mile run along the road, (2) a swim in my next-door neighbour's pond — exactly as some 48 years ago I used to run round the Parks & cool myself in (is there such a place now?) Parson's Pleasure. That I am still in condition for such freaks I attribute to having had for nearly 30 years no servants to reduce me to a sedentary & all-literary existence. And now you seem to say: Let us give you a servant, & the means of slow suicide & quick lexicography. Not if I know it; I must go my slow way.

However, I am getting a little more pace on with A.O.D., & now completion of the *C.O.D.* he had been saying that he wished to bid goodbye to straightforward lexicography. Dictionary-making would be so much more agreeable if you could leave out the useless and obvious words, and just concentrate on the idiomatic. He would write a dictionary for the 'kind of Englishman who has idioms floating in his head in a jumbled state, and knows it'. On putting the idea to Chapman he got the reply: 'A Utopian dictionary would sell very well—in Utopia.' That, it seemed to Fowler, disposed of the matter. He was surprised a couple of years later when Chapman asked him what had become of the old idea. He reminded him of the forgotten quip, and Chapman had to explain that he had not meant to be taken seriously. Although Fowler was never able to say goodbye for long to lexicography, by 1925 he had found time to put all but the finishing touch to the 'Idiom Dictionary'. As before, the provisional title had become so familiar that not until the title-page was in hand was any serious thought given to it. Sisam then suggested 'A Dictionary of English Usage'. Fowler thought that in self-defence 'modern' ought to be inserted. In the dedication 'To the Memory of My Brother', Henry Fowler described the book as the last fruit of the partnership that began in 1903 with the translation of Lucian.

Modern English Usage was reprinted four times in 1926, once in an impression of 50,000 copies for the United States where Putnam's put out a special edition. It retains, more than fifty years later, a good deal of its original authority: Fowler had promised Cannan at the start to 'assume a cheerful attitude of infallibility'. The quality of the work is best described, however, in his own definition of 'idiosyncrasy'—a 'peculiar mixture'. It is difficult to quarrel with the *O.E.D.*, but one can argue with Fowler nearly all the way from his instructions on the use of 'a' and 'an', to his cheerful dismissal of the second 'z' in 'fizz'. Somerset Maugham complained that he had no ear, that he 'did not see that simplicity may sometimes make concessions to euphony'. Yet nobody can safely disregard Fowler's warnings. Some of the articles became famous—'vogue words' were all the vogue at one time, and the spotting of 'genteelisms' became a kind of cult, that article being one of the most provocative, and indeed fallible. Many of the genteelisms listed are ineradicable; the 'chiropodist' has long since ousted the 'corn-cutter' from the dictionaries. But there is always the possibility that Fowler may have been right at the time. He was resisting the trend towards magniloquent titles that proved irresistible in the end.

In 1925 Fowler at last moved from Guernsey to live at Hinton St. George, near Crewkerne in Somerset. The task the Press wished to assign to him was the preparation of what became known as 'The Quarto Dictionary', an 'unconcise' dictionary of current English of about 1,500 pages. It was asking a great deal. He was at the same time doing a second edition of *C.O.D.*, published in 1929. He escaped *The Little Oxford Dictionary* (1930), an abridgement of an abridgement of an abridgement—a task, as he put it, like pulling out the hairs of one's own head one by one. He was called in, however, to help finish off *The Shorter Oxford English Dictionary*. For five years he gathered materials for the 'Quarto' without ever quite committing himself to the task. He had found a collaborator in Colonel Le Mesurier, who had been corresponding with him since reading *Modern English Usage* in India: he was particularly good at defining technical words, on which Fowler felt unsure. 'Le Mesurier understands *things* which were always rather a mystery to our O.E.D. staff', Sisam told Chapman. The third brother, A. J. Fowler, whose existence had been unsuspected at the Press, was introduced into the correspondence. He was said to share the family affliction.

It was not until January 1930, however, that Henry Fowler wrote with any enthusiasm about the project. He agreed that it was time for the Quarto to come down from the clouds, and he would set to work 'de-telegraphesing'. In May he wanted to give up—it would take ten years: 'To put a man of 72 to such a job is a flying in the face of the actuaries.' In any case, he added once more, 'I am no true lexicographer.' Chapman drew upon all the eloquence he could command, and Fowler was helpless. 'After that', he wrote, 'what can I say but that you have given me a grand send-off? and what can I do but get to sea without more ado?' In August he wrote again to Chapman: 'My wife, after a six-year struggle, which seemed always on the point of turning in our favour, with cancer, was suddenly a few weeks ago pronounced incurable.' She died a few weeks later. But by the following February he could report that the oculist and doctor had told him that 'both eye and I have rather better than the ordinary expectation of life at 73, which Whitaker says is 7·25, and that would bring me to 80.'

Every Christmas Fowler received a cheque from the Press. These cheques, Sisam explained, were 'thank-offerings for the success of those of your great works which are contractually the Delegates' property'. Now he offered a further £200 a year for the Quarto. This seemed absurd to Fowler, and he protested. 'I am one of the few people who have had no occasion to complain of "these hard days".' He might accept £100, but Sisam, who greatly admired disinterestedness and had himself as an adviser refused fees on the ground that they put up the price of books, insisted that this was not enough. 'All right,' Fowler wrote, 'if you insist on making a millionaire of me, do so.' He accepted £200 a year for ten years, out of which he was to pay his brother and Le Mesurier.

In 1931 specimen pages were set up to nobody's satisfaction. A two-tier system had been adopted, the lower half of the page containing technical and ephemeral words, mostly Le Mesurier's work. It meant two alphabets and it was clear that it did not work. In 1932 the doctor's report on Fowler was bad. He was told to cut out the morning run, the cold bath, the lawn-mowing and weight-lifting, and to eat nothing more meaty than chicken. Six months later there were signs of improvement, and in November 1933 he was back in full harness with his two partners and expected to finish in six years. On Boxing Day of that year he died.

Sisam was determined that the idea of the Dictionary should live on. A. J. Fowler and Le Mesurier continued to work on it until their deaths, and in the course of time the dictionary claimed more victims. After the war Chapman dabbled in it, but no satisfactory editor could be found and it was never finished. The file was finally closed in 1971.

The completion of the big Dictionary in 1928 had been an occasion for only modest celebration. The end had been so protracted that too much jubilation would have been out of place. The alphabet had been exhausted with the publication of XYZ in 1921. In 1926 Unright–Uzzle and Wilga–Wise were published and there was only one part left to come, the infamous Wise–Wyzen. H. L. Mencken in the American press wrote that his spies in Oxford had told him that plans were under way for celebrating its completion with 'military exercises, boxing matches between the dons, orations in Latin, Greek, English and the Oxford dialect, yelling contests between the different Colleges and a series of medieval drinking bouts'. But the world had to wait two more years for William Craigie to finish Wise–Wyzen. Somebody said that he bestrode the Atlantic like a colossus, and this was not an advantageous posture from the point of view of the *O.E.D.* Professor of Anglo-Saxon in Oxford from 1916 to 1925, Professor of English at the University of Chicago since then, his time had been too fully occupied. In 1928 there were at least orations in Latin, however, as the honorary degree of D.Litt. was conferred at Oxford on Sir William Alexander Craigie, Charles Talbut Onions, Humphrey Sumner Milford, Robert William Chapman, and John Johnson, who provided the Public Orator with an occasion to recall the memory of his much-loved father-in-law, whom they would have wished, had he been alive, to take the chief part in the day's celebrations. Murray, Gell, Bradley, and Hart stirred unquietly in their graves.

R. M. Leonard, who had been keeping the score for thirty-two years, could now complete the record. The twelve volumes defined 414,825 words, and contained 1,827,306 illustrative quotations. The type, last heard of as stretching from London to Folkestone if placed end to end, would finally have extended over 178 miles: Leonard estimated that there were 227,779,589 letters and figures, not counting punctuation marks. The Dictionary had been finished seventy years after its inception, or a mere forty-four years after the publication of the first part of A, easily outpacing the German, Swedish, and Dutch contenders. The speeches of the 1897 dinner were recalled, and *The Times* leader describing it as the greatest effort since the invention of printing. But for the most part the superlatives had been exhausted. Arnold Bennett called it 'the longest sensational serial ever written'. To Sisam, however, who had been reading each episode as it came out since his boyhood in New Zealand, it was not the end. A supplement was already in preparation, and after that there would be other supplements. At a dinner given by the Goldsmiths' Company, the Prime Minister, Stanley Baldwin, in proposing the toast to the editors and staff, said, 'If ever a work was destined for eternity the Dictionary is it, because no sooner have we, like myself, the second generation of subscribers, drawn our last cheque, had it cashed, and seen it honoured, and had the last volume delivered, than we are told the supplements are about to begin.'

And there were not only supplements but the whole stable of dictionaries of differing dimensions in different languages for which Sisam was responsible. Sisam distrusted lexicographers. His own experience at the Old Ashmolean must have given him an insight into their lonely habits and it was intolerable for him to contemplate the pace at which they worked, disappearing for days in Bodley in pursuit of an impossible perfection. Workers on historical dictionaries were at particular risk, caught in the terrible undertow of words. He had much higher hopes of the 'Quarto' dictionary than of *The Shorter Oxford English Dictionary*. But where were the people with the necessary skills who could endure, as Murray and his colleagues had done, the appalling drudgery? 'The position of Dictionaries is desperate,' he told Fowler in 1925. 'So few lexicographers will perform.' The revised Liddell & Scott and the new Latin dictionary to replace Lewis & Short moved on at a snail's pace. With Fowler gone, Sisam's attempts to build up a dependable and permanent dictionary staff were not particularly successful. Some of the lexicographers he found were old, had high blood pressure, and died of natural causes. One cut his throat. Another, in whom the utmost confidence was initially placed, carried eccentricity to such extremes that he finished up calling himself the Seer of Barras, and writing an endless epic poem in which Sisam figured as the Antichrist.

When the *O.E.D.* was finished rueful attempts were made to count the cost. The debit balance appeared to be in the region of £375,000, but nobody knew quite what that meant. Overheads were not included, and the value of money had changed since the first outlay. Whatever the actual figure, Chapman made it appreciably worse when he decided in the 1930s to reprint 10,000 sets of the Dictionary, supposedly for all time. There were 6,000 sheets left at Jordan Hill on the outbreak of war. It was thought that if the worst came to the worst they would make an excellent air-raid shelter.

8. Companions

SISAM was responsible both for bringing respectability to, if not actually creating, the Press's scientific list, and for an important advance in the range of reference books, which joined the dictionaries, Oxford books of verse, and the established series for schools as the 'bread-and-butter lines' of Oxford publishing. He stumbled upon the idea for the 'Oxford Companion to English Literature' without knowing that he had done so, and thereby opened up a range of possibilities that is still being explored. Sir Paul Harvey was a civil servant who had retired early to Mayfield, in Sussex. He laid no claims to being a literary man, saw himself in fact as the common reader, though by ordinary standards he was exceptionally well read in the Classics and English and French literature. He had completed an index for a history of the Persian Gulf in 1927 and as usual was impatient for more work. Sisam threw out as a possibility a new book along the lines of Brewer's *Dictionary of Phrase and Fable,* originally published in 1870, fondly known to more than one generation as 'old P and F'. As well as explaining English phrases and slang terms it had listed characters in fiction and provided much various and useful information. Sisam's casual suggestion startled Harvey. 'You have not before mentioned to me the idea of a new Brewer', he wrote, 'and perhaps you would be good enough to develop a little your idea of what the book should do.'

Sisam rose bravely to the challenge. 'Your last letter put me in a quandary', he admitted, 'because I really had not a very clear idea of what I meant by a new Brewer. But I have been thinking it over, and begin to see some boundaries. The book I have in mind would not be, like Brewer, a dictionary of phrase and fable with a number of facts. It would be quite precisely a reader's companion to English literature; in one volume of 1,000 pages if necessary.' He then went on to consider the contents: every English author of any importance; certain foreign authors commonly quoted; some characters from legend and mythology; something about classical authors; finally, 'the really exciting part of the book', allusions. Sisam reckoned the book would be worth £500, and that it would take three years to write: he offered £100 a year for three years, the balance on completion.

At first Harvey worried about his competence, sure that Sisam overrated it. 'But perhaps more competent people can employ their time to better advantage', he reflected, and agreed that three years should finish the job. His business was to carry out Sisam's conception. That must be the guiding principle, he insisted, for no two people would conceive such a book in quite the same way. He had made an abstract of the instructions contained in Sisam's letter of 23 November 1927, and kept it on his table. It was more than a guide: these were his orders, and they could not be countermanded even by Sisam himself.

Sisam did not at once appreciate that his first thoughts had become Harvey's last. From time to time he had new ideas. Romantic heroes and early English saints should perhaps go in. And what about social and sporting events, like Wimbledon and the Quorn? Such suggestions appalled and bewildered Harvey. He was working his way through Beaumont and Fletcher's fifty-two plays and found that his deplorable health prevented him from dealing with more than three five-act plays in a day; they merited only a few lines, some none at all, but the shorter the article the greater the labour of condensation. To have Sisam introducing new ideas at this stage was intolerable. 'I have tried to penetrate myself with your conception of what this book should be', he explained again to Sisam, who then began to grasp something of what he had done. Either he had taken possession of Harvey, or Harvey had taken possession of him. 'I am rather horrified to find', he wrote, 'that you take my original proposals for the backbone of the book as a complete and minute plan, which may not be varied.' It was a difficult situation. He wanted to help but he stood implacably in his own way. Harvey, fearing that at any moment some new deviation might be contemplated, asked to be left alone for two years. Sisam dropped the correspondence. Possibly, he thought, Harvey would never finish.

But Harvey, immensely diligent and methodical, was always punctual despite complaints of constant ill health. By 1931 the bulk of the manuscript had been received and enthusiastically approved. Sisam was prepared to call it a great work. Some articles were diffuse, some superfluous, but he did not mind: they could be attended to in subsequent editions, making space for new matter. Nevertheless a year was spent filling gaps, checking the facts, studying suggestions made by advisers, particularly C. R. L. Fletcher. This was done on proof sheets. Fletcher became enthusiastic, and suggested adding fifty or more articles on incidents in English history. Harvey took all criticisms gratefully, but could not always agree to additions. 'He has some kind of code or constitution for the book, and has often made me the answer "This is excluded by rule so-and-so",' Sisam told Fletcher, again forgetting that the code was his own.

Fletcher complained about the excessive number of American entries: his inclination was to scrap the lot, on the ground that it was a companion to English literature. 'We have to make a little money where we decently can in these difficult days to pay for more learned books', Sisam explained, and just at that time Chapman and Milford were in America carrying proofs. They showed them to Cumberlege and the first sign of trouble came in a cable from Cumberlege asking Sisam to hold up the printing. It had been agreed in New York that there was no reason why he should not have the galleys read for conspicuous American omissions. Cumberlege asked his literary adviser, Ben Ray Redman, to read the proofs for this purpose. He wondered whether Sir Paul would have any objection to Redman's name appearing on the title-page—in smaller letters, of course. He told Sisam that he had had a note from Chapman saying 'I have no doubt Harvey (and Sisam) will welcome reinforcement (within limits!) from U.S.A.'

Sisam was determined to publish the book in time for Christmas 1932. Suggestions in May that from the American point of view the work was not yet begun were far from welcome. Moreover, his own confidence in Harvey's common sense increased with every batch of criticisms that reached him from his many advisers. Each time they reflected the particular interests of the man, and the critics differed more among themselves than they did from Harvey. Wherever a compromise seemed called for it turned out that Harvey in his own way had already reached it. Sisam assured Cumberlege that he would do everything possible to accommodate Redman's contribution but time was running short. He did not dare to tell Harvey at once of this unexpected development. Despite pleas from Cumberlege that it would be better to publish the following year than to put out an incomplete book, Sisam went ahead. As the proofs were paged, space for Redman's reinforcement diminished, and in the end Sisam reckoned that they amounted in all to little more than five pages. He conducted the negotiations with patience and equanimity until called upon to pay Redman's fee; that he thought was exorbitant and he grieved aloud.

Despite his liking for the book Fletcher did not expect it to sell. Sisam had mentioned a second edition, but he doubted whether it would ever run to one. 'I see you expect me to lose £1000,' Sisam wrote. 'Well, I am not sure of that. You see, I had some years in the selling of bacon, often very inferior bacon, which gives me a feeling for what people will buy, whether I like it myself or not, and although the world is full of gloom at the moment, I have the "hunch" that this will be a pretty big seller. . . . Think how a journalist will revel in it, or a solver of cross-word puzzles, or an American lady in search of learned dinner table conversation! Two years ago I would have reckoned to make the £1000 on the first edition instead of losing it, but it is true that times are hard.'

It was a pretty big seller, and Sisam was pretty pleased with himself, however he chose to justify the book to Fletcher. Admittedly it could not claim to be an original work of scholarship or even educational in a strict sense, but he now had plans for further similar compilations. Much of the usefulness of Harvey's *Companion* in fact lay in its lack of originality. He had a firm critical sense, but did not always trust it: he tried to confine himself as far as possible to the facts. Like the Fowlers when they embarked on lexicography, he had had to learn his job in the course of compiling the book. He achieved an extraordinary impersonality. His evaluations—'an acknowledged masterpiece', 'not now highly regarded'—are entirely conventional, and there is no way of determining whether he enjoyed reading one book more than another. He was the ideal compiler of Companions. Later workers in the genre have mastered the adroit interpolation which makes their presence felt without diminishing the objectivity the genre demands. 'Has produced works that are far from negligible . . . has perhaps received something less than his due' might read in another context 'a genius, shamefully neglected'. Harvey did not allow himself such liberties: in any case he was not sure.

A second edition appeared in 1937. Sir Paul Harvey went on to compile *The Oxford Companion to Classical Literature*, and under heavy pressure from Sisam consented to do at least part of a Companion to French Literature. He drew the line at the end of the eighteenth century: beyond that he would need a collaborator. He worked on his part throughout the war and in 1947 sent the complete manuscript on slips to the Press for safe-keeping.

In January 1935 in New York a young Harvard graduate, James D. Hart, was on his way to catch a Fifth Avenue bus when he found himself passing the Oxford University Press. On an impulse he went in, with no exact purpose in mind except to point out the want of a Companion to American Literature. He was met by Margaret Nicholson, who later translated Fowler into *Modern American Usage*. She 'listened with remarkable sympathy', Hart recalled, and took him to see the general editor, Howard Lowry. 'He was astonishingly attentive to me and proposed that I prepare a few sample entries that very evening to bring back the next day so that they might be seen by Geoffrey Cumberlege. The reception I had from Cumberlege was somewhat frostier but he took the entries and before long I heard that the Oxford Press would publish my work.'

The New York Branch had been looking for the right man ever since the failure to americanize Harvey satisfactorily, and had almost despaired of finding him when Hart walked in. Some early specimens were sent to Oxford and London, where they were generally approved, with the injunction that the more 'worldly' points in American life and literature should not be overlooked. 'I was rather startled', wrote Lowry, 'to have the London office suggesting that Roxy, the movie magnate, the Cliff Dwellers in Chicago, etc., should be mentioned.' Sisam's initial insistence on the importance of 'allusions' had by then permeated the Press. Five and a half years after his first appearance Hart presented Lowry with the complete manuscript.

There is no broad area of knowledge that cannot yield a Companion, and since the war the series has thrived. Sometimes the word itself seemed inapt—in relation to the Christian Church, for instance: that Companion was called *The Oxford Dictionary of the Christian Church*. In recent years have appeared Companions to Art, to the Decorative Arts, to Sports and Games, to Film, to Science, to German Literature, to Ships and the Sea, to Canadian History and Literature. Each one sets out to achieve the impossible—to be comprehensive. All of them could trace their ancestry back to the letter written by Sisam in November 1927.

9. Science

IN the same year, 1927, Sisam became involved in a very different enterprise, but one of equal importance for the future. There were two physicists in Cambridge, Ralph Fowler and P. Kapitza, who were thinking of starting a series of monographs on physics. One of Milford's travellers for technical books was J. G. Crowther, who had wide scientific interests and a wide acquaintance with scientists. He knew Kapitza, discussed the projected series with him during the summer, and reported enthusiastically to Sisam. He in his turn consulted the Delegate N. V. Sidgwick, a chemist, whose important book *Electronic Theory of Valency* was published in 1927. The idea struck them as feasible, though there were obvious objections: the editors were Cambridge men; for an Oxford series F. A. Lindemann ought to be involved; and Kapitza seemed to have in mind volumes of essays, which in principle Sisam opposed. It was obviously something worth bearing in mind, but no immediate decision was taken.

Crowther was assiduous in pursuit, however. Fowler and Kapitza had decided to go ahead, and he was determined to hold on to them as long as possible even though no commitment had come from Oxford. Towards the end of 1927 Fowler told him that they had had offers from other publishers, and would soon have to decide whether to follow them up. During the Christmas vacation Sisam found himself faced by an ultimatum. He had until 1 January to make up his mind. Sidgwick was out of Oxford and the Delegates had had their last meeting of the year.

On 30 December he composed a difficult letter to Fowler. He began by admitting that the plan was not too clear in his mind. Indeed he was on entirely unfamiliar ground. The only constructive thought that came to him was that Einstein would be a good author to have. And he noted that Eddington's *Stars and Atoms*, published that year by the Clarendon Press, had got off to a good start. He decided that he had better concentrate on terms and financial matters, which might allow him to appear businesslike without revealing too fully his ignorance of the subject, and of the exact nature of the proposal. Works in the series, he suggested, would be contributions to learning; they could not be expected to do more than pay their way, and that not at once; all concerned would have to write off a good deal 'as service to the subject'. Even so he was prepared to go into details about possible royalty arrangements. He also considered the desirable length of the volumes, and advised that no doctoral dissertations should be included. In the end he had managed to write a substantial letter that could leave Fowler in no doubt as to his interest in the series, but in considerable doubt as to where precisely he stood.

As soon as Sidgwick returned Sisam was in touch with him. He admitted that he had become considerably entangled, though he had tried to keep 'completely quiet, not seeing my way'. There now seemed no alternative but to go to Cambridge to discuss the issue thoroughly. He was clearly apprehensive about such an excursion into dangerous and alien territory. 'I dare not face these lions alone,' he wrote, 'as I know nothing about physics, and would not be able to conceal my ignorance. But it looks as if a field day in Cambridge . . . is the only way out. I sedulously avoid going there; and last time Norrington went, the police caught him for parking his car in the wrong place. So perhaps we had better take an armoured car.'

The raid on the Cavendish Laboratory in Cambridge took place on 6 March 1928, and was a success. Whatever his misgivings, Sisam returned to base with his confidence fully restored. Kapitza was a Pole, perhaps a little excitable, and he had not been impressed by his judgement and publishing sense. But Fowler was 'a huge fellow of great energy and swiftness of mind, and I should think the great man in mathematical physics in ten years' time'. He also had a clearer picture of the series itself: it was to be genuinely international, and the object was to find the leaders, the young men especially, in various branches of research and to persuade them to write monographs on the subjects they had pioneered. 'The International Series of Monographs on Physics' was to be confined to original work of real importance. Fowler and Kapitza had their eyes initially on P. A. M. Dirac, Van Vleck of Wisconsin, Falkenhagen in Cologne, a Russian named Gamow recommended by Lord Rutherford, and on an Indian called Raman. The first book to appear was Dirac's *Principles of Quantum Mechanics* in 1930. Sales were not sensational, but it was generally agreed that the book itself was. It was translated into many languages, including Russian. The pirated Russian edition carried a mysterious preface, warning scientists that the book did not always conform to the doctrines of dialectical materialism and should be handled with care.

Before anything could be done, however, John Johnson had to learn a new craft, that of mathematical printing which had been so long neglected in Oxford. He told Sisam that he proposed to make a fresh start, and assured him that he would go to endless pains to get it right. It was the kind of challenge he enjoyed, and he could be relied upon to do that. He bought in new types, studied the work of the German printers, and designed specimen pages which were circulated to mathematicians for comments. He received considerable help from Professor G. H. Hardy, then editor of the *Quarterly Journal of Mathematics*, which the Press took over in 1930, as well as from Fowler and from Dirac himself. In the end he felt he had produced a page of some magnificence—'to compel the admiration of the world'. Sisam agreed that a high standard had been reached, worthy of 'the recent renascence of mathematical studies in Oxford'.

In 1935 Kapitza settled permanently in Moscow, where he continued his researches into intense magnetic fields. Sir Ralph Fowler remained an energetic and alert editor of the series until his death in 1944. He became the great man in mathematical physics, as Sisam had predicted, not as a creative genius but as a great collaborator and co-ordinator and an inspiration to his colleagues. By the beginning of the war some seventeen monographs had been published under his editorship.

Sisam still found it an extraordinarily difficult field to understand. His intuition as a publisher deserted him when faced by a distinguished experimentalist, reputedly doing work of the greatest originality, for as a layman he had no way of knowing whether the man was articulate, or whether he could write. Some, it appeared, could not. But such judgements could be left to his editors, and once the decision had been made to invest in academic scientific books he went bravely ahead. Series on engineering, chemistry, and forestry were established. The scientific list was systematically built up until it became not merely reputable, but distinguished and advanced. Not until after the Second World War, however, was anybody with scientific training employed by the Press.

R

10. The Oxford History of England

ANOTHER major venture from Oxford in the inter-war years was The Oxford History of England. In the 1920s G. N. Clark was writing *The Seventeenth Century*, which was published in 1929. Initially it had not been intended to stand alone, but no satisfactory plan for a series ever matured. There were few historians prepared to take on a lengthy period in the history of Europe as a whole. G. N. Clark, Proctor from 1928 to 1930 and a Delegate in his own right from 1930 to 1936, began to reflect instead on the possibilities of a multi-volume history of England. The two existing series, published by Longmans and Methuens, were out of date, representing knowledge as it had been some twenty years before. Admittedly the work of all historians between the ages of 30 and 60 had been interrupted by the war, and abnormally little research had been done. But in Clark's view that retardation itself, along with the growth of research schools in universities, made the present time one of abnormally large output. The Press was ready and waiting for a major undertaking of this kind.

Though excellent in their way, the early Legacy books had reflected to some extent the retardation, and books such as Rostovtzeff's *Social and Economic History of the Roman Empire*, published in 1926, represented a return to normal. The prevailing opinion at the Press was that collaborative works were a confession of failure: the soundest principle was one man one book. The prevailing opinion in Cambridge was that this was sour grapes, and it is true that one of the objections to the Cambridge 'sausages' in Oxford was that they used up too many authors at once, authors who might have been better employed writing books of their own for Oxford.

Norrington assumed responsibility for the project, and after discussions with Clark early in 1929 was able to present a general plan. There would be up to fourteen volumes of about 200,000 words each, priced at 15s. a volume. He hoped to get six volumes out within five years, and that among them might be one or two best sellers. Clark was cautious, however, pointing out that there were no best sellers among historians except G. M. Trevelyan, and he was fully occupied with the reign of Queen Anne. They should choose young men and tell them not to hurry. There would be a particular emphasis throughout on social and economic history, and on literary and artistic developments, at the expense particularly of military and naval history, by then quite out of fashion. There would also be special attention to geography. A few names of possible authors were mentioned, but the first object was to get the approval of the Delegates. The news that Bells had had a similar idea and were capturing the best authors was disquieting, but later reports suggested that the competition need not be greatly feared. More awkward was the problem of putting the historian C. R. M. F. Cruttwell, Principal of Hertford and a Delegate since 1928, in the picture without at the same time allowing him to complain that he had not been consulted before. He was a sensitive, sometimes cantankerous man, and the problem was insuperable. 'I must say that it seems very strange that I should not have heard of the matter at an earlier stage', he wrote inevitably. It was necessary to call upon Chapman to disarm possible opposition from that quarter. He explained that the project was the outcome of many years of committees and negotiations, dating back to a time before Cruttwell became a Delegate. 'It seems a great opportunity for forestalling the Syndics,' he wrote, 'who seem to be getting to the end of their sausages and are likely to turn to monographs next. I have no doubt that we shall get better books on the one man one period system than if we handed out chapters.'

The Delegates responded cautiously, appointing a small committee consisting of the lawyer J. L. Brierley, Cruttwell, Collingwood, and Chapman to confer with Clark. Chapman reported that the view of the office was that this would not be a gold-mine, but that it would probably do quite well. The Press had tended, he thought, in recent years to produce books rather on the fringe than at the centre of historical studies. Certainly it was better than publishing monographs. Clark began to pick his team. Collingwood 'dramatically gave his adhesion'. Stenton of Reading, Jacob in Manchester, Veitch in Liverpool, Poole of St. John's, Woodward at All Souls, and Mackie in Glasgow expressed interest. Black in Aberdeen was a dark horse, but said to be promising; so too Williams in Edinburgh. Davies at Pasadena was doubtful whether he could take a wide sweep, but was willing to try. Cruttwell was now in favour of the project, and Chapman was prepared to describe it as 'one of the best and most promising enterprises of my time'.

In November 1929 the Delegates finally authorized Clark to go ahead and agreed that it should be called the 'Oxford' History of England. 'I regard it as equivalent to giving the book its blue,' he said. As the various contributors were assigned their tasks some other historians who had previously felt themselves to be too heavily committed began to be a little uneasy at being left out. Powicke, belatedly, agreed to join in. The plan was announced in the *Times Literary Supplement* in January 1930, but there were still gaps to be filled. The nineteenth century was treacherous territory, being too recent to allow for thorough scientific study, intruding into an author's own lifetime. Temperley had been invited as a matter of form, and had declined. Clark was tempted to ask Winston Churchill, and dissuaded by Norrington who explained that it would be necessary to offer rather special terms which would automatically price him out of the series. These 'advances of £5000 are payable to Winston and others because their books, which are really no longer than any one of our 15/- demys, are bumped out by every meretricious device known to publishers, and sold at two guineas, with a clear profit of about 30/-.'

For a while Clark became secretive: he had someone in mind for the job but was not immediately prepared to divulge the name. He had his eye on R. C. K. Ensor, a journalist, at one time a leader writer on the *Manchester Guardian* and more recently on the *Daily Chronicle*. The latter paper having merged to form the *News Chronicle*, Ensor was out of favour with the new proprietors. In 1930 he was in effect unemployed, living in High Wycombe, bird-watching and gardening. Though he had taken a double first at Balliol in the 1890s he had no academic reputation at all. Admitting that he was 'a long shot', Clark at last asked the Press whether anybody knew anything about him. It turned out that he had been an exact contemporary of Milford's at Winchester. He was very able, Milford reported, though considered in those days an extreme left-winger: 'but he has now, I gather, like so many of us, mellowed into pale pink.' Milford added that he had also written 'some rather jolly poems'. This was not very helpful, but it was decided to take the risk. It was an inspired choice. *England, 1870-1914* was published in 1936, acclaimed as a masterpiece, and immediately a success.

In March 1931 there was a plenary session in Oxford which all the contributors attended, at the Press's expense, except Davies in California. Norrington presided. The final plans were laid, questions of overlapping discussed, and Clark laid down his editorial guide rules. He was a model editor in every way, firm, tactful, always diligent. Each contributor had reason to be grateful for his advice. He also set an example, his volume on *The Later Stuarts* being the first to appear, in 1934. Norrington never achieved the original target, however, of publishing three volumes at a time in the autumn season. Interrupted by the war, the series was not finally completed until 1961. Even so, in the annals of the publishing of multi-volume works by different hands it was a not inconsiderable achievement. A supplementary volume, *English History 1914-1945* by A. J. P. Taylor, was published in 1965.

11. The Rumpus

THE Press rode out the Depression reasonably well. Necessary economy measures were taken: at Amen House three out of four subscriptions to the *Times Literary Supplement* were unkindly cut and the tea-break was abolished. The staff fell from 361 to 295 through natural causes. The old London bindery in Aldersgate was finally sold, and the Leipzig and Paris offices were closed. There were no cuts in salaries in London or Oxford, and in general Milford could claim that the business had come through without too great a strain. There had been losses, but no need whatsoever for panic measures, 'measures which, multiplied a million-fold, help to cause and accentuate these mysterious depressions'. Cash had been more plentiful during the slump when less business was being done, and there were no large capital outlays, such as those on Neasden and Jordan Hill.

The O.U.P. in New York suffered a much more bruising experience. In

1924–5 it made a profit of over £16,000, in 1925–6 of £8,000. This drop was ominous, and not fully understood. The next year there was a thumping loss of £19,255. By then Cumberlege had arrived in New York, accompanied by Chapman and Milford, to investigate the mystery of the Branch's declining fortunes. McIntosh, who had been with the business from the start, was now seventy-five and clearly too old to attempt the drastic measures called for. This did not explain the sudden change from profit to loss, however. Milford thought it was probably due to increased discounts to the trade, combined with 'non-buoyant sales'. It was not immediately seen to be part of a general depression; the profits of the previous year at first masked the true situation, for they had been generated almost entirely by a single best seller, H. Cushing's *William Osler*, a massive two-volume biography published by the Clarendon Press. Without it the crisis would have been plain sooner.

Cumberlege was left in charge, becoming Vice-President (Milford remained President) in September 1927. He took immediate action, reducing the staff by 20 per cent, and saving some £2,500 a year by moving to smaller and cheaper premises at 114 Fifth Avenue. He organized the office, developing departments for college and juvenile books. By 1928–9 he had reduced the loss to the manageable proportion of £4,000, sales were increasing, and there seemed no need for further alarm. Then, in October 1929, the slump hit Wall Street, and the work of reconstruction was undone. Even more draconian measures were needed, savage cuts in salaries and a ruthless examination of all expenditure, to keep the Branch in existence during several years of heavily falling sales. In 1930 the first edition of Morison and Commager's *Growth of the American Republic* was published, a portent of better days to come, but for the time being a deep depression hung over New York.

Depressions breed introspection, morbid symptoms of self-doubt. Sooner or later somebody will ask whether a business suffering from a slump is in fact being efficiently run. At the Press the question was asked by a new Delegate, Hugh Last, aged 38, who was appointed in 1932. An outspoken man, and much given to asking questions in the hope of provoking debate, he was in the process of acquiring an international reputation as an ancient historian. He became Camden Professor in 1936. His interests spread from Rome to the Near East, and to Egyptology, which brought him into touch with John Johnson. He was pleased to think of himself as an administrator, man of affairs, and a trenchant critic both of the new and of the established order. It is said that he once killed a proposal for an honour school in anthropology with the words 'an acquaintance with the habits of savages is not an education'. He was always rather exquisitely turned out. For five years as a Delegate and member of Finance Committee he managed to vex Milford and Chapman almost beyond endurance. 'I have often thought that my connivance at Last's appointment was the worst blunder of my life', Chapman told A. D. Lindsay, the Vice-Chancellor, in 1937.

As a self-appointed management consultant Last made recommendations about the organization of the Press several of which, though fiercely resisted at the time, were implemented years later, some through the Waldock Report, others as a result of the great inflation of the 1970s. But Last was a highly fallible individual, not a balanced committee of inquiry. The episode in the history of the Press that he created, moreover, was made unseemly by hints of departmental jealousy, personal animosities, strife between Secretary and Printer. For a generation or so it was agreed that it was best forgotten for the sake of the individuals involved, if not for the issues it raised. But it was essentially an ancient and familiar story. Last revived and personally encapsulated both sides in the old debate, simultaneously insisting like Bartholomew Price that the first concern of the officers of the Press should be business and commerce, and like Max Müller that its main object should be the endowment of research. His refusal to admit that there was any contradiction made it exasperatingly difficult to answer him.

Last's appointment coincided with another probe by Council into the affairs of the Press and the Delegates' responsibility to the University, which he interpreted as demonstrating a lack of confidence in the Board. He at once assumed a crisis and considered the possibility of the Delegates resigning as a body, so that 'the Vice-Chancellor could appoint a new board which did command confidence'. He urgently needed to see Chapman and wrote to him in this emergency, 'It is now a matter of days if not of hours. Oh, why, why this delay. However, let us keep our heads. Unfortunately Saturday is my day for shooting.'

The immediate crisis passed, but the question of whether the Delegates were in full and effective control of the Press had been raised and an answer had to be found. If they were not, Council would be right to intervene. Last himself had detected in the business 'certain signs of sprawling', which admittedly made the exercise of control more difficult. But also he had early premonitions that the Delegates and Finance Committee 'were being guided—with the greatest tact and gentleness, indeed, but still being guided—instead of being left to find their own way for themselves'. He allowed that it was right that the London Publisher should enjoy considerable freedom of action. Even so the independence of Amen House was the weakest point in the Delegates' case.

Chapman was not just aggravated by these observations but shocked and alarmed. The cure for sprawling was reorganization, which nobody wanted. The very existence of Amen House was being questioned and Chapman himself accused of manipulating the Delegates—which, it could be argued, made him the scapegoat, should one be needed.

Last was not without support of a kind from other Delegates. The veteran Bishop of Oxford, Thomas B. Strong, remarked on how the work of the Board had been reduced since he first joined it in 1904. Then they had met every Friday and actually discussed such matters as the price of books. Now they met four times a term, and so little was said that the meetings were unlike any others he had ever attended: business passed without discussion. G. N. Clark was also concerned about the welfare of the Press, casting a cool historian's eye over the peculiar combination of businesses for which the Delegates were responsible, which he recognized were the result of historical growth. 'I do not imagine that anyone, starting from scratch, would propose anything at all like it at the present time', he wrote. Nobody could disagree with that.

Chapman fell to brooding on this ugly turn of events. The more he thought about it the more convinced he became that John Johnson was the source of all the trouble. It was impossible to explain Last except as 'the *âme damnée* of Johnson'. He was the new broom to sweep clean in Johnson's interest. Johnson, he feared, had always resented his exclusion from the inner councils of Milford and himself, and felt like his predecessors that he was treated as an inferior. Chapman at the same time felt himself disregarded by Johnson, whom he unfairly accused of having taken control of all aspects of typographical design—Johnson in fact welcomed suggestions from the publisher—and, with more justice, of 'grasping at a tyranny over paper'—Johnson resented having to use inferior paper and believed that it was high time that the printers recovered the control over paper supplies that they had lost early in the eighteenth century. Chapman also suspected that he charged the publishing business more than he did his outside customers. Six months after Last became a Delegate Johnson, finding himself short of work, launched a surprise attack in Finance Committee on Chapman and his colleagues, charging them with lack of enterprise which threatened the ruin of the whole business. This was the beginning of what Last called a 'first class rumpus'. 'The sense we all had, that Johnson might at any moment "explode" at a meeting, has not seldom made me, for one, feel tongue-tied,' Chapman wrote.

In the quinquennial Report of 1930 the Press auditor had used a phrase that stuck in Last's mind—'when allowance is made for the fact that the Press is a University institution'. He was deeply suspicious. Why should allowance be made? The Press was a business, and should be conducted like any other business with maximum efficiency: the words clearly suggested an amateurish mishandling of an important University asset. No wonder its officers, with one exception, were gently pulling the wool over the Delegates' eyes. In any case the Delegates ought not to have to depend on the loyalty of their staff, he argued disturbingly: they should construct a machine which was proof against error.

'Every now and then', wrote the Fowlers, 'a word emerges from obscurity, or even from nothingness or a merely potential and not actual existence, into sudden popularity.' These were 'vogue words', and 'rationalization' at that time had recently joined the company. Last used it freely. He defined it as 'a systematic attack, with the help of outside advisers, on overhead expenses in every part of the business'. He had in mind the reorganization of the Lancashire cotton industry. For a start he personally would completely reorganize the education department under

Norrington, and transfer some of the other work done in the City to the less expensive site at Neasden. He further asserted that reading had been encouraged by the Depression and more books were being sold than ever before—but not by the O.U.P. It should publish more saleable and more topical books, like Gollancz and Collins. He himself suggested an Oxford Guide to the Washington Naval Agreements. But what was really needed was the appointment of a highly qualified, well-paid man who would anticipate public demand and have the right books ready at the right time. Sisam and Norrington shrugged their shoulders and went on with their work: they were not simply anticipating public demand but creating it. For Chapman it was almost more than he could bear.

Fortunately the financial results for 1933–4 seemed to show that the period of losses was over. Cumberlege's strenuous endeavours in New York were having their effect. On 1 January 1934 the Branch entered into an alliance with Longmans, which lasted for five years, but by then the corner had been turned. The Branch was in business as an original publisher, and new best sellers were on their way, including an expanded edition of Morison & Commager, and *The Odyssey of Homer* (1935) translated by T. E. Shaw, otherwise Lawrence of Arabia, which was a sensation. Cumberlege eventually prevailed upon the scholar Howard Lowry of Wooster College, of whom he had a high opinion, to join the business as General Editor and Manager of the Educational Department, a position he occupied between 1935 and 1941. He rapidly developed the list in American history and literature, and may be said to have completed the 'academicization' of the New York Branch.

In Britain the prospects were brighter too. Last appeared to be satisfied, and Chapman could hope that the matter was at an end. For the time being it was. There was a reconciliation of a kind between Sisam and Last. The Cambridge Ancient History was finished, and Last proposed to get the Oxford ancient historians to write for their own Press. As it happened, his contribution to the Cambridge history was to prove the culmination of his own career as a writer, and his energies henceforth were exclusively directed to teaching and University affairs, particularly those of the Press. These he found increasingly unsatisfactory.

Suddenly, in 1937, he took the unprecedented step of resigning in protest, leaving behind him a time-bomb in the form of a lengthy memorandum, called by Chapman the 'bowdlerized Phillipic', for it was a tempered version of a diatribe already delivered verbally to Finance Committee. Many of the allegations were wild: G. N. Clark thought his case weakened 'by the plain advertisement of his cantankerousness'. But it was never doubted for a moment that it had to be taken seriously, and that some steps would have to be taken to placate Last in order to prevent him making the whole issue public. From August 1937 to February 1938 an inordinate amount of time was given to considering and refuting his charges one by one.

In a covering letter Last expressed his personal feelings of friendship for all concerned. 'But commerce is commerce; and the interests of the University have an overriding claim.' He went on, in his curiously epicene style, 'I have nothing in my own action to regret—unless it be that by too great patience and the practice of some slight economy in forthrightness I have given the impression that ... I did not mean business.' Then he listed at length the abuses and failings he had discovered, the cure for everything being greater 'efficiency'. The charge of inefficiency appalled Milford, but Chapman, though equally outraged, found the whole concept of efficiency alien and dangerous. 'A business might well be efficient,' he wrote, 'the whole spirit and conduct of which might yet be quite different from what the O.U.P. ought to be.' He could hardly argue in favour of inefficiency. But he was very anxious that it should be understood that 'efficiency is one thing, and the *ethos* of a business is another'.

In the first place Last demanded that the Press should maximize its profits for the service of the University. At least £10,000 a year (in his speech he had said £20,000) should be set aside, for the publication of unremunerative works and the endowment of research. The Press indeed should endow research on the same sort of scale as the Carlsberg Brewery. This meant greater efficiency in all departments and better relations between them. Secondly, the Press like other firms should have turned the Depression to its advantage by making it 'the occasion for a thorough-going "rationalization" by outside experts'. London was still gravely vulnerable to depression, largely due to 'lack of vigilance and energy'. Thirdly, there were signs of rivalry, even of hostility, between departments within the Press. Finance Committee had decided as long ago as 1932 to concentrate elementary and secondary educational books in London, but still no action had been taken. Some unnamed officer had told him that it would upset 'the balance of power'. This he thought an insidious concept, indicating a failure to recognize that 'the Press is a single whole whose only purpose is to serve the University'. By its implied assent to the 'fatal doctrine' that the balance of power was more important than efficiency Finance Committee itself had demonstrated its general ineffectiveness. An outside expert should be appointed as Chairman. Being a Delegate, Last concluded, had been the most fruitless episode of his life.

Eventually Finance Committee expressed the view that in Last's memorandum there was a certain confusion of thought, and that in some respects it was founded on an inadequate or even erroneous view of the facts. Nevertheless it referred to certain fundamental questions which the Committee had felt for some time needed further exploration. So Last after all succeeded in creating a committee of inquiry, and Chapman and Milford, totally unaccustomed to criticism, found themselves held for questioning. They began to talk of 'impeachment'.

Milford took it particularly badly. There were sleepless nights and daily jottings to Chapman to relieve his feelings. He sat down to compose his defence, a deeply wounded man. After thirty-seven years of selfless devotion to duty, to have to defend himself against a charge of lack of energy and vigilance was intolerable. 'I'm afraid Milford is worrying,' Brierly, Chairman of Finance Committee, wrote to Chapman. 'I wish you could do something to set his mind at rest. I feel sure that the Committee does not want the "defence" that he says he has already partly written out.'

But Chapman was worrying too. He dashed off his 'First Impressions' to the newly appointed Vice-Chancellor, A. D. Lindsay. He had known Lindsay for years, but Lindsay had never been a Delegate and was quite without experience. The Press must certainly have seemed a bewildering institution, and like Last five years earlier he had stepped straight into a first-class rumpus. Chapman was frank to the point of total indiscretion. 'I have not complained, and do not now much complain, of the Printer's action in pointedly ignoring my existence,' he wrote. As for profitability, it had to be understood that 'the Press is not a commercial undertaking, and even its manufacturing departments are not conducted on lines of pure commerce.' Wolvercote was not for profit but for convenience, though as Milford said if it had not already existed it would not have been thought necessary to invent it. Nor essentially was the Printing House for profit. It would pay the Delegates to buy in the cheapest market. The Printer was there for 'the convenience and dignity . . . of the University at large and of education and learning. The reputation of the University, indeed of the country, is enhanced by the beauty, the dignity and the accuracy of Oxford printing.' Chapman was too moved, too incensed by the enormity of it all, to consider tactics. All he was doing was to plant in the Vice-Chancellor's mind a seed of suspicion that to some extent Last was right.

'Milford's whole interest . . . is not in money but in books,' he went recklessly on. (Ironically, Johnson would have agreed with him absolutely. He too deeply distrusted the profit motive. 'In any field,' he had written, 'profit comes most surely out of a disinterested quest in which eagerness for profit is secondary to the enthusiasm of the quest.') On the merging of the two educational departments, Chapman argued that it was not a question of balance of power but of 'equilibrium'—a subtle distinction, but one which to him clearly transcended considerations of administrative efficiency. If secondaries had gone to Amen House it would have taken away about a quarter of the business of the Clarendon Press. For Johnson, any scheme that weakened the publishing business—the 'post-office'—was attractive.

In due course Milford's uncalled-for 'Apologia' appeared, a long painstaking document. He was dealing with questions of 'deadly familiarity', and the exasperation of Lyttelton Gell is faithfully echoed in his comment to Chapman: 'I suppose all these able people dislike having to face the fact that the Press is a big business, run by professionals, and that an amateur board cannot do more than see that it gets good professionals, and then trust them.' To Finance Committee he expressed relief that there had been no 'thorough-going rationalization'. The Press had shown itself strong enough to withstand the slump and to continue its main function of publishing learned works. He confessed to some extravagance in his attempts to sell Clarendon Press books, but otherwise all necessary economies had been made. In Milford's recollection the annual payments to the University had been largely responsible for the enfeebled state of the Press when he had joined in 1900.

The idea of the 'outside expert' had been scouted not infrequently over the years too. Somebody in the City might have a ready answer to all the Press's problems. Chapman and Milford had been brought up by Cannan, however, and had long memories. Cannan had always said that bankers were incapable by training of understanding a publishing business, and Chapman's distrust of 'mere' businessmen with no academic connections was complete.

The minor and more precise forms of rationalization were equally abhorrent. 'Programmes' of capital expenditure tended to lead to expenditure for expenditure's sake: the word 'budgeting' was as repugnant to Chapman and Milford as 'rationalization' itself. Its effect on publishing policy could only be bad, for it would distract the editors from seeking out the best books of their kind in whatever field they might be. Sisam too was strongly against budgets, which he believed increased unnecessary expenditure. They were no more sympathetic to the idea of a more careful 'costing' of books. 'No system of costing was ever devised with the intention of reducing prices,' Chapman noted.

In the summer of 1937 Chapman visited A. D. Lindsay in Cumberland. He described the meeting in a thirty-one-page manuscript report to Milford, which like all Chapman's communications looks as though it had been written in a train. This one had, and is scarcely decipherable. Lindsay appears to have been not nearly so sympathetic as Chapman could have wished. He too was worried about divisions and frictions within the Press. Chapman had been altogether too frank in expressing his distrust of Johnson. Lindsay was irked by the 'balance of power' concept as well: 'odd that a harmless and almost conventional phrase should have upset them all', Milford commented. And Lindsay had strong views on the desirability of allocating fixed sums annually for the publication of Oxford-born works of learning, particularly in his own field of social studies. Chapman's visit evidently failed to allay the misgivings that had been forming in his mind.

When Finance Committee met again in September Chapman was in New York. There he received a letter from Lindsay informing him that 'all the members of the Committee agreed, as I knew they agreed, that you are too secretive'. They had begun to feel starved of information and craved detailed reports and estimates and memoranda, printed agendas, and printed minutes. Further, the Vice-Chancellor went on, there must be a clearer definition of the respective functions of Oxford and London, and an analysis should be made of all Amen House books—juvenile, general, musical, medical, educational, etc. The Committee wanted to see a budget each year showing how much had been put aside for unforeseen demands and for the publication of unremunerative books. Finally they would look into the possibility of appointing a non-resident Delegate 'from the City'. On his return from the Scillies towards the end of September Sisam reported 'a slight tinge of suspense in the air'. He wrote to the absent Chapman: 'I shall do my best to wear the mantle of discretion and responsibility—always irksome to me.'

Throughout Michaelmas term the two beleaguered equipollent officers battled to clear up misunderstandings which they had not thought to exist. The first difficulty was that they did not know whether they were still to be primarily concerned with answering Last's charges or whether the whole focus of debate had changed. It was obviously necessary for all concerned that the Delegates should not appear to have been guiltily galvanized into action they would not otherwise have contemplated. On the other hand Last had started so many hares that it was impossible both to answer him and to present the balanced account of the state of the Press that Finance Committee required. As Chapman pointed out, Last had appeared to be judging the Press by the standards of the 'get-rich-quick' publisher to whom a slow-selling book was a failure. The well-being of the Press depended to a considerable extent on the back-list, the vast accumulation of old titles selling by ordinary commercial standards in ridiculously small numbers, which still cumulatively supplied important revenue.

The attempt at a clearer definition of functions could only expose more of the anomalies that time had brought about. The separation of secondary and primary education departments, for instance, had much to do with the inseparability of Ely and L'Estrange, itself a historical accident of some thirty years' standing. The initiative of individuals made it almost impossible to define the respective functions of Oxford and London. The *Oxford History of England* was a Clarendon Press series because the idea for it had originated in Oxford: a seven-volume history of European civilization was a London publication because the idea had originated there. Given their origins the two works would eventually develop along different lines, but at the time of their inception the distinction was far from clear. *The Oxford Companion to English Literature* was Sisam's creature: *The Oxford Dictionary of Quotations* was a London book because Milford had had the idea and it was being compiled mostly by the editors at Amen House. It might be asked why A. S. Turberville's two-volume *Johnson's England* should like *Shakespeare's England* be Clarendon Press, whereas G. M. Young's two-volume *Early Victorian England* appeared as a London book. Was this a case of inter-departmental rivalry? Long ago London had staked its claim in the nineteenth century, and it was still respected, but who was to know that, and why should it be so? To those inside the Press it all seemed entirely natural: to a critic not imbued with the old traditions there might appear to be no logic in the arrangement. But neither Milford nor Chapman cared too much about the originating department, provided it was always understood that the Clarendon Press would retain its responsibility for academic publishing in the interest of the University and of scholarship generally. A little healthy competition could do no harm. 'Sisam *is* tenacious,' Chapman admitted to the Vice-Chancellor. 'As a departmental manager, or sub-manager, it is right that he should be so up to a point.'

In obedience to Finance Committee's request, Milford tried to divide his business into 'segregable categories', but having listed music, medicine, technical, juvenile and elementary, Bibles, Prayer Books, and hymn books, he still found himself with the peculiar jumble of his general list, of commission books, of British Academy and British Museum and the Carnegie Endowment and American University Press publications, the Chaucer Society, the E.E.T.S., and the productions of the American, Canadian, Indian, and South African branches. It was impossible to rationalize. Nobody had ever asked him to define his publishing policy. He would have considered it a singularly foolish request, and icily placed in the hands of his questioner a copy of the General Catalogue. It was also unfair to judge him by results. He reminded the Committee that the sales of Bibles had never reached anything like their pre-war volume, and that the competition had switched to the production of new Bibles, an extremely costly business. The Prayer Book trade had not recovered from the fiasco of 1927 when the revised Prayer Book, so long in preparation, had finally been rejected by Parliament. These were shocks to the system beyond his control. But it had always to be remembered too that the heaviest burden he had had to carry over the past ten years had been the sale of Clarendon Press books, the 'hidden subsidy', which incurred on average a deficit of £10,000 a year.

The Vice-Chancellor suspected that the main weakness of the Press was in its relation to the University. There was a general lack of communication, and a failure sufficiently to encourage and sponsor the young scholars on its doorstep. It was a complaint frequently to be heard in the future as it had been in the past. Chapman appreciated the problem, but still believed that the Press should aspire to publish the best work of mature scholars wherever they could be found. It must maintain the Oxford standard. Lindsay talked so much and so fast that Chapman often had difficulty in following him. After dining with him on one occasion he tried the next morning to write a summary of the discussion for Milford's benefit: 'He talked a great deal about lack of liaison both with individuals and (especially) with committees—especially Advanced Studies ... He "hankers very badly" after a budget—that we should say e.g. to Nuffield College (when it is in being) you can have £x this year for your researches. I said, But these committees, so far, are concerned only with dissertations. *Do* you want us to publish dissertations? He declared no, he doesn't, and was I thought very woolly about all these "bodies".' They were back to the question of the endowment of research, the abundant but unappetizing fruit of which Chapman now saw to be the thesis. His nightmare was that the Press might be turned into something like the H.M.S.O., obliged to publish whatever was put before it by the University. Cannan had not thought that

Oxford could produce enough books to ruin the Press: the time was not far off when it might well be able to do so.

In November 1937 Chapman hoped briefly that some conciliatory letters from Johnson had 'ingeminated Peace in our Time', but the impeachment proceedings dragged on until Finance Committee's report on Last's memorandum had been finally drafted, circulated, and approved in February 1938. A great deal of work had gone into it, the bulk of it by Chapman and Milford. They did not know what was in it, but through their memoranda, written as it seemed at the time in self-defence, they had effectively drafted the report themselves. The revelation of its contents, eagerly awaited, came as no surprise in the end. Milford's own words were faithfully reproduced to rebut Last's charges against the London business: with Chapman's help the Committee had come to the conclusion that 'it would be exceedingly difficult to obtain "experts" competent to deal with a Publishing business . . . and that proposals likely to be made by experts in "rationalization" in general might be largely inapplicable to the Press.' The diarchy had stated the case for preserving the *status quo* with overwhelming force.

The Vice-Chancellor's concern about the various 'bodies' was, however, noted in the report. The Delegates would have to be prepared for further demands on them in the coming years for the publication of learned works submitted by University Boards and Departments. It was time to start thinking how they were to cope with such demands without neglecting other claims on their resources. This was the one point in the report that seriously disturbed Chapman. It dangerously stressed the encouragement of largely immature local research, inevitably to the detriment of 'bigger things'. He admitted that the young were a problem, 'the most difficult of our tasks'. But professors and directors of studies were the worst possible judges of the work done by their underlings, and Chapman was by no means infatuated by the younger generation.

To many scholars the huge grey German dissertations that had nosed their way like tanks through the battlefields of learning before the war were further evidence of Germany's general superiority in every aspect of research. The Ph.D. degree had been introduced into British universities as a counter-attraction to the advanced degrees offered by the German universities, coveted by American graduates in particular. It was awarded solely on the basis of the thesis, which had to be in the view of the examiners an original contribution to scholarship and suitable for publication. Perhaps by definition, therefore, the Press was under an obligation to publish at least the theses written in Oxford. But as they proliferated the situation became increasingly threatening. A point would be reached when it could be argued that all the important original research in a particular subject was being done in the form of theses.

Chapman fought a long fight. In 1920 he had resisted a proposal from Professor Firth for a series of Oxford Historical and Literary Studies, of which he and Walter Raleigh would be editors. The Delegates had rejected it, according to Chapman, because it admitted the principle of the publication of degree dissertations as such, 'which the Delegates have always resisted both as vicious in itself and as entailing an unlimited liability (since what should be allowed in one faculty could not be refused in another).' The Delegates had rejected the principle: in practice they could not refuse to consider individual proposals put forward by the two professors and the series came into being after all.

In the 1930s the Delegates also reacted strongly, informing the University that in their experience good dissertations were not good books. If they were to be published, it should be the responsibility of the Faculties both to select and to finance them with the help of the Committee for Advanced Studies. The Oxford Historical Series, edited by G. N. Clark, C. R. M. F. Cruttwell, and Maurice Powicke, was the first of the series of Faculty Monographs, followed by English and Modern Languages. Some of the early dissertations turned out to be embarrassingly good: L. S. (now Dame Lucy) Sutherland's *A London Merchant*, J. E. A. Jolliffe's *Pre-Feudal England*, M. (now Sir Max) Beloff's *Public Order and Popular Disturbances*, or Enid Starkie's *Rimbaud in Abyssinia* could lay claim to being 'books'. But nobody was more unyielding than Sisam in upholding the principle that this was a contradiction in terms. They were given the bare 'Oxford University Press' imprint, which implied that the Delegates disowned them. 'They are segregated from our ordinary books,' he explained, 'so that any bookseller or member of the public knows he is not buying a full-dress Clarendon Press book.' It followed that if even Oxford theses could not attain to this status extraneous ones should be excluded altogether from the list. 'The dissertation is in itself always unprofitable,' Sisam went on. 'We here at Oxford can answer the argument which every writer of a dissertation takes—that his dissertation is at least a commercial proposition—by the argument that if it is so a commercial publisher will undertake it.' This argument held until the 1960s. When the commercial publishers did begin to show an interest, the Press had to change its tune. Victory in the 1930s went to Chapman and Sisam and the Delegates. For a time, however, under the Vice-Chancellorship of A. D. Lindsay, it had appeared that the principle laid down by Cannan in 1915 was threatened: the Delegates, he had insisted, 'are not and ought not to be representatives, but highly trained judges of books and administrators'. He meant that they should not represent a particular body, or department, or faculty.

By the spring of 1938 the rumpus had finally subsided. Chapman may have continued to brood over the injustice of a charge of secretiveness when his mistake had been candour, but he swore that he would bear no grudge against Johnson, who was devoting more and more time to his hobby. He collected ephemeral printing, or what many would call, as he himself admitted, 'indiscriminate rubbish'. He had built up probably the largest collection of jobbing and similar printing in the world: it consisted of beer-bottle labels and valentines, cigarette cards and posters, paper-bags and match-boxes—specimens of every kind, all carefully catalogued and classified. 'I keep every trade card of every traveller who comes within the gates,' he said, 'and treasure them in my archives. They are among the many gauges of our craft.' His extraordinary collection is now housed in the Bodleian Library.

12. After the Rumpus

WITH so much going on Chapman had little time for the day-to-day affairs of the Clarendon Press. These could safely be left to Sisam, Norrington, and a new recruit, John Mulgan. He was another New Zealander, a writer, and a young man of great promise. It was thought that a place would be found for him in New York when his apprenticeship was served, but by then he was reluctant to leave before Hitler had made up his mind. He left the Press for the army in 1939 and did not survive the war.

In the summer of 1937 Charles Williams met W. H. Auden in Oxford. 'He is an extraordinarily pleasant creature,' he told Milford. They had had an interesting talk, in the course of which Auden put forward a suggestion for a new Oxford Book of Verse. Characteristically Williams felt an inclination to dissuade him, not wishing business matters to mar an agreeable occasion. Auden had said that he thought Yeats's *Modern Verse* lacked authority: Williams replied that he was surprised that he allowed authority to any of the Oxford books of verse, to which Auden answered that the fifteenth-, sixteenth-, and seventeenth-century volumes were adequate and important collections. He proposed an Oxford Book of Light Verse. Williams 'murmured something to the effect that books of light verse were always very depressing when they were actually before one'. On the contrary, Auden insisted, light verse showed the difference between the sensibilities of various periods even better than the more solemn stuff. His book would be a contribution to criticism, as well as a collection of poems. Cornered, Williams was obliged to report the proposal to Milford and Norrington. He conceded that if Auden really became a figure there was a possibility that it might be quite a good investment.

Norrington was of the opinion that Auden had already become a figure and his name would sell a good many copies. The proposal was accepted by the Delegates at the first meeting of the new term, when Chapman was in America, and Mulgan wrote to inform Auden. 'Dear Whelgan,' Auden replied, explaining that his signature read like ULULGAU—'but all signatures do'. Apparently they did to him. On three separate occasions when dealing with Press editors he began his letters with this ploy, even when it might have been supposed that he would remember the name of the man writing to him. However, he was glad the Delegates had accepted, and he hoped to complete his selection by the end of December, when he was

Charles Williams, Editor

Sir Humphrey Milford, Publisher, 1913-45

leaving for China with Christopher Isherwood in search of a new war. That gave him three months. He accomplished the task after a fashion, but much checking and sorting had to be done by his friend Mrs. A. E. Dodds, wife of Professor E. R. Dodds to whom he dedicated the book.

By the end of March Mulgan was anxious to get the book into production, but Mrs. Dodds was experiencing difficulty in discovering Auden's sources, and when she did she often found quite different versions. Auden had disappeared without trace and there was no way of consulting him. So Mulgan went ahead, and Mrs. Dodds continued to correct errors on the proofs. At the end of July Auden returned. He suggested that her name should appear on the title-page; she declined the honour, but conscientiously read the proofs for him whilst he went 'café-crawling' in Belgium, evidently feeling no ties of paternity.

The book was published in October 1938, just a year after the proposal had been approved by the Delegates. It was then that it came to Chapman's attention for the first time. It was disconcerting that a book carrying the name 'Oxford' could slip through without his knowing anything about it from beginning to end. He was unprepared for the criticisms that began to reach him, concerning many inexplicable omissions and some poems that were thought to be highly objectionable. He himself had been shocked. 'When I had read the Dunbar I fairly placed the book on the top shelf and have not looked again.' At least this complaint could not have been levelled at Yeats, who had himself conscientiously bowdlerized with school libraries in mind. Sisam felt obliged to assume some sort of responsibility, but could not say that he had ever been consulted. Mulgan found himself being chided. He justified the use of 'Oxford' in the title by explaining that Auden was tied to Fabers and would not have felt free to do an anthology except in some recognized series. He had himself omitted some fifteen poems which he thought unsuitable. He agreed that it was a 'risky book', but his main argument in self-defence was that he did not expect it to have a long life. He wanted to assure Chapman that whatever trouble it was causing would soon blow over.

Sisam objected to Mulgan's general principle that the editor of an 'Oxford Book' should be solely responsible for its contents. 'We have a certain catholicity of standard,' he explained. Auden should never have been allowed to omit Austin Dobson simply because he did not like him. As for the dedication, he warned Mulgan to watch this 'silly and creeping evil'. Chapman gently impressed upon him the lesson to be learned. 'The general moral is, I think, that when trouble is foreseen (and it was easily foreseeable here?) it should be forestalled. Use your own judgement by all means; but if in doubt, make sure your superiors are embroiled.' The book was unfavourably reviewed in the *Winnipeg Tribune*, but it has sold steadily for forty years.

In 1936 Milford had been knighted. His list that year was not distinguished and contained perhaps his least inspired new series, The

S

Oxford Bookshelf. It was announced that books in the series would not be uniform in format or in price, and would thus avoid 'monotonous uniformity in their appearance'. They were in fact reprints of earlier Oxford reprints, distinguished only by a special binding and jacket. The first two volumes were Constance Holme's *The Lonely Plough* and *Crump Folk Going Home*, both of which had already sold some 30,000 copies as World's Classics. Angela Thirkell's *Three Houses* was included, the seventh impression of Rudolf Otto's *The Idea of the Holy*, and a reprint of Sir Arnold Wilson's *Walks and Talks*. It might appear that for the moment Amen House was resting on its laurels. Sir Arnold Wilson was a busy member of Parliament, who wrote a number of books including *Burial Reform and Funeral Costs*. Both *Walks and Talks* and its sequel, *Walks and Talks Abroad*, were popular, and the latter made its own small contribution to the complacency of the times. It was an account of a tour of Nazi Germany, which had given him much ground for hope: he was no belittler of Mussolini and Hitler, as *Punch* noted. 'Another war would destroy the white races', he wrote, 'and be the ruin of a racial policy.' Through Hitler the military tradition was being transmuted, turned to the arts of peace. When he saw his mistake, Wilson managed at the age of 55 to join the Royal Air Force. He was shot down in the first year of the war. His widow had been widowed before, when her first husband met just the same fate in the First World War. In 1947 she married her former husband's publisher and became Lady Milford. Milford's first wife had committed suicide in 1940.

'He was really very odd' is the final verdict of the oral tradition on many of the personalities who contributed to the history of the Press in the earlier years of the century. Milford became odder as he grew older. Chapman qualified perhaps from the start for this accolade, though he too grew odder as the years passed. He was a tall, shambling, awkward man, the reverse of nimble. His blacksmith-built bicycle became famous in Oxford, his mysteriously dogmatic hand-signals even more so. On turning into Walton Street on his daily journey to the Press he would immediately occupy the middle of the road, the right arm rigidly outstretched. The ultimate intention was clear, the exact timing difficult to ascertain for he still had a hundred yards to go. (Milford preferred being driven about London in a Studebaker, at a time when American cars in Britain were rare.) Much as he had once appreciated the old tobacco ceremonies of Bywater, the jars of different blends, the ritualistic filling and lighting of the pipe, Chapman's smoking habits were crude. He rolled his own cigarettes, thin as matchsticks, which either dropped ash as they drooped damply from his lower lip or went out. There were moments of joviality when he quipped amusingly with his staff, others when he was so much the absent-minded scholar that he was respectfully treated as non-existent. In warm weather he would roll his trousers up to his knees, as if about to go paddling. The only complaints from his staff concerned his handwriting and the habit of gnomic mystification that early association with Cannan had made irreversible. He is probably best remembered by a catchphrase—'in manus tuas'. Everybody who ever worked with him was familiar with the cryptogram, which usually meant simply that he wished a matter to be taken out of his own hands. The possibility that he himself believed he had already discussed it and made his intentions clear to the person concerned could not be ruled out, however. On one famous occasion he was visited by a man of eminence, who showed him a copy of his family Bible, an old Oxford Bible of some value showing signs of wear. Chapman assured him that he would get the Printer to attend to it: the binding and lettering could be made to look as good as new. He passed the precious volume to Johnson—'in manus tuas'. Some months later, the owner inquired politely when his family Bible might be restored to him. Chapman investigated. Johnson had pulped it. What else had he been supposed to do?

In 1939 the Press published the final part of W. E. Crum's *Coptic Dictionary*, the first part of which had been issued in 1929. It published H. W. Garrod's Oxford English Texts edition of Keats, and R. B. McKerrow's *Prolegomena for the Oxford Shakespeare*, as an introduction to the major old-spelling edition on which 'substantial progress' had already been made. It published Lord Hailey's *African Survey*, a work comparable in scope and authority with the History of the British Empire completed on the eve of the First World War. There was the second set of three volumes of Arnold Toynbee's *A Study of History*, concerned with the breakdown and disintegration of civilizations. The Delegates not without uneasiness agreed to publish *An Autobiography* by R. G. Collingwood, felt by some to be an alarmingly controversial if not defamatory little book, in which the crisis through which European civilization was passing appears first in the shape of an intellectual disease affecting academic life in Oxford. The philosophers of his youth, he wrote, 'were the propagandists of a coming Fascism. I know that Fascism means the end of clear thinking and the triumph of irrationalism. I know that all my life I have been engaged unawares in a political struggle, fighting against those things in the dark.'

In July 1939 the first of a new series of pamphlets, Oxford Pamphlets on World Affairs, were ominously beginning to appear. *The Prospects of Civilization* by Sir Alfred Zimmern and *Herr Hitler's Self-Disclosure in Mein Kampf* by R. C. K. Ensor were in the first batch. Sir Arthur Quiller-Couch, who had spent the last twenty years in Cambridge as Goldsmith Professor of English Literature, in an increasingly unsympathetic environment, composed his preface to the new edition of *The Oxford Book of English Verse*. An old man loyal to his old values, Q tried to rally his countrymen: 'Agincourt, Agincourt, know ye not Agincourt?' Writing in 1939, he confessed that he was 'at a loss what to do with a fashion of morose disparagement; of sneering at things long by catholic consent accounted beautiful; of scorning at "Man's unconquerable mind" and hanging up (without benefit of laundry) our common humanity as a rag on a clothes-line. Be it allowed that these present times are dark. Yet what are our poets of use—what are they *for*—if they cannot hearten the crew with auspices of daylight?'

PART VII

THE SECOND WORLD WAR

1. Pamphlets, Biggles, and the Home University Library

ON the outbreak of war a cable was sent to all branches instructing them to address future communications to Press Road, Neasden. Amen House was closing down for the duration. The first great Fire of London had demolished Warwick Square in 1666: Amen House, which arose from the ruins then, survived the great fire of December 1940 which destroyed Paternoster Row, and subsequent bombardments. When the staff returned nearly six years later there was a very different view to be seen from its windows. The buildings that had obscured St. Paul's Cathedral had disappeared, and it was a long time before the architects and planners could again conceal it by ingenious obtrusions of concrete and glass.

Some fifty refugees from London were billeted in an old farmhouse on the outskirts of Oxford, Southfield House. The numbers diminished, despite Milford's determination to keep all those he possibly could. E. C. Parnwell, almost fully trained as a fireman by September 1939, fretted because Sir Humphrey would not let him go. In November Cumberlege left, and there were recent recruits who joined up with the assurance that jobs would be waiting for them when they came back. Men with modest prospects returned as senior officers, ready to assume responsibilities never expected of them.

Chapman was fifty-eight. As he awaited the coming holocaust he could see little point in planning for the future. Sisam and Johnson, however, expected a long siege rather than sudden catastrophe: the prudent course was to lay in supplies. During 1939 they built up stocks of paper and other materials, some of which by careful hoarding could still be drawn on in an emergency in the leanest days of 1944. But the Government requisitioned the supplies from the Wolvercote Mill, and it was soon clear that paper, perhaps even more than manpower, was going to be the main problem in the years ahead. At the end of 1939 Sisam wrote, 'In this respect we have reached much about the condition of 1917 in the last war. But paper is quite exceptional. Other things are merely dearer.'

Shortly after Munich G. N. Clark, recalling *Why we are at War* of 1914, had suggested to Norrington that the Press might bring out a series of brief essays on the general theme of 'why we are about to be at war again'. The 'Statements' (the provisional title for the series) were to enlighten the public and expose the mendacity of Nazi propaganda. Norrington began collecting authors in May 1939. He also got in touch with the Foreign Office, which welcomed the scheme and proposed that the pamphlets should be translated into several European languages for propaganda purposes. The Foreign Secretary, Lord Halifax, gave warm encouragement. The Delegates in turn gave the project their approval but, as Norrington recalls, 'bade me not lose more than £1000 if I could help. Well, we published at 3*d*., 50% discount, on sale or return, so we can't really have made anything out of the enterprise. On the other hand the length was only 32 pp., we paid the authors only £12 down, no royalty, there was no general editor to pay, and we did sell about six million in the end. Anyway, we kept no careful accounts, and the Delegates never inquired. I had in effect a free hand.'

Oxford Pamphlets on World Affairs became almost as much a part of the wartime scene as gas-masks and ration books. At the outset booksellers showed a natural reluctance to stock them, the return on 3*d*. books being no great incentive; but the readiness of the public to buy them soon overcame it. The Foreign Office ordered 70,000 copies in English of the first seven pamphlets and 100,000 in French, German, Dutch, Spanish, and Italian. Some thirty-five titles had appeared when Norrington, with the Government's sanction, set out on an ill-timed mission to the Continent in April 1940. He planned to go from Holland to Denmark and the other Scandinavian countries. Hitler invaded Denmark on the day he was to fly to Copenhagen, necessitating a change of plan. He went from Holland through Belgium to Paris, with a sense of Europe disintegrating about him, promoting his pamphlets as best he could in a distracted city.

The Pamphlets continued to appear throughout the war. By 1945 over seventy titles had been published in Oxford, and the Indian, Canadian, and American branches had produced series of their own. Extra paper, outside the ration, was allowed for those required by the Government for distribution on the Continent by the Ministry of Information. In general the pamphlets were more informational, less controversial or meditative, than those of 1914. There was no Sir William Sanday to reflect on the deeper meaning of the war; nor was there the same necessity to explain why the country was at war in the first place. Six lectures given at the Sheldonian Theatre and published as *The Background and Issues of the War* early in 1940 did carry some echoes of the earlier conflict and of *Why we are at War*. H. A. L. Fisher inveighed once more against the old villain, Heinrich von Treitschke; R. C. K. Ensor wrote on Hitler; Harold Nicolson on the diplomatic background; A. D. Lindsay on wars to end wars; and Gilbert Murray on the League of Nations in which he had so fervently believed. He felt, he said, like a Greek magistrate, there to 'stand his trial for having "given false advice to the people"'.

Difficulties of all kinds began immediately, but during 1940 and 1941 the war made no obvious impact on the publishing programme of the Press. The demands of the Government on the Printer for war work had only just begun to take their toll. The new edition of Liddell & Scott, which had been in preparation since before the first war, and which had been appearing in fascicles since 1925, was at last completed, and the whole work appeared in two large volumes in 1940. In the same year, Collingwood's *Essay on Metaphysics*, E. E. Evans-Pritchard's *The Nuer*, Gilbert Murray's *Aeschylus*, and Lord David Cecil's *Oxford Book of Christian Verse* were published. The various volumes of Oxford 'Garlands' were recommended by Leonard in the *Periodical*, which had recently reached its two-hundredth number under his editorship, because there was nothing in the whole series 'of the ultra-modern type which may perplex or repel'. Biggles dominated the juvenile list: *Biggles Goes to War* and *Biggles Defies the Swastika* began the long saga that took him through Africa, Borneo, and the South Seas. His creator, Captain W. E. Johns, had been deftly trapped by an enterprising member of the department into turning out two or three books a year without benefit of royalty. They continued to sell in huge quantities, but were bought by Hodder & Stoughton after the war, when the Oxford juvenile list was refurbished. Oxford children's books then came to epitomize 'good taste', and won many prizes. The haphazard and robust concoctions of Ely and L'Estrange were convicted of infantilism and allowed to fade away. In 1941 *The Oxford Dictionary of Quotations* appeared, Milford's creation on which many had laboured: it sold 20,000 copies in two months, and was quickly followed by a second edition. The writer most frequently quoted was Browning.

In the same year Milford assumed a new burden by acquiring the Home University Library. He had been an under-bidder in 1928, when Thornton Butterworth had taken it over from Williams & Norgate. Chapman had been sceptical then, though he had been prepared to pay £10,000 'or a little more' for the series. Milford did not venture the 'little more' and it went for £10,700. When Thornton Butterworth's offices were destroyed in the blitz most of the business was taken over by Eyre & Spottiswoode, but Milford picked up the H.U.L. for a mere £4,750. He could point out convincingly enough that the series carried a great deal of dead stock. It had been in existence for thirty years; by 1941 there were 191 titles in print. It would be difficult to infuse new life into a series already showing signs of middle age. There were some excellent titles which would endure: Bertrand Russell's *Problems of Philosophy*, Geldart's *Elements of English Law*, Fisher's *Napoleon*, Isaiah Berlin's *Karl Marx*, Trevelyan's *English Revolution*. But there were also many in a condition of some decrepitude, selling under 100 copies a year, and the three general editors—Gilbert Murray, Julian Huxley, and H. A. L. Fisher—seemed to have run out of ideas. G. N. Clark was soon substituted for Fisher. But it was not the most opportune time to be assuming so considerable a responsibility. There was hardly enough staff left to cope with the list as it was, and for the next five years it would become increasingly difficult both to keep books in print and to produce new ones.

Sisam was dissatisfied with the arrangement. In a memorandum to Milford headed 'Destruction' he wrote: 'I am inclined to think that firms like Longmans, who lose their stock and reprint only what is worth while, will find an unexpected gold-mine in the reduced overhead on poor lines: for I reckon every title with us must cost a considerable sum, as well as the labour of keeping up a large number of books of account and records, which we can ill afford in war-time.'

He could not feel hospitable towards the Home University Library. Moreover the purchase had brought Milford right into the middle of the Clarendon Press field of publishing. Earlier attempts to distinguish the activities of the two departments by subject were obscured. The World's Manuals, almost identical in scope and content, had always been Clarendon Press books. His latest acquisition led Milford towards the doctrine that he might publish in every field where there was a general sale. If this were allowed, the Clarendon Press would be deprived of all profitable items and become financially the most insignificant department of the University Press as a whole. By the end of the war Sisam believed that this had happened. London had not only taken over all new subjects, which tended to be too controversial for the Delegates, but had gradually moved into the Delegates' old fields if the books had any general interest. Sisam maintained that as long ago as 1940 there had been 'some avowal of the doctrine that the Delegates had better restrict their publishing to Greek and such things which only specialists read, leaving the rest to London'. When Cumberlege succeeded Milford in 1945 another attempt was made to define publishing fields and to adjust the balance. In the last years of the war, with the virtual suspension of learned publishing, Sisam could do little but watch and occasionally complain about Milford's encroachments. Milford, however, could claim that he was only doing what he had always done—making what profits he could to subsidize the learned works that were waiting to be published.

The Home University Library itself survived and prospered until the 1960s, by which time both in appearance and purpose it had come to seem antiquated, smacking too much of the old Mechanics' Institutes. It was replaced by the Oxford Paperback University Series (OPUS).

2. Sisam Calling

JOHNSON's sense of being under siege became extremely localized. His territory was the printing works in Walton Street, which he had every intention of defending with his life if necessary. The worst danger was from fire. The Press fire brigade was a proud body of men, never seriously tested but conscious of a long tradition of preparedness going back to 1885. But if the Press caught fire Johnson was determined to be there in person to put the fire out. He could not be persuaded to leave the premises at night, sleeping if he slept at all on a mean cot ready for any emergency. A five-and-a-half-hour air-raid alert one night found him in the highest possible spirits. The *Clarendonian*, the organ of the craftsmen of the Press, reported this enjoyable occasion: 'yarns were spun', and refreshments were provided by the Printer, who it was feared would become a poor man if there were many such alarms. Highly confidential papers, mostly Admiralty reports, were being printed (the proofs read by the graduate readers who scrupulously applied Hart's Rules to the puzzlement of Admiralty officials, and generally sought to maintain the standard that Archbishop Laud would have expected of them). The possibility that the Press might consequently become a target for German bombers was in part responsible for Johnson's fanatical vigilance.

Sisam was more than ready for the bombers too. Their failure to turn up was a disappointment, as he often confessed in his letters to America during the early part of the war. In November 1939 he was assuring an author at the University of Michigan that he 'need not think of us going to bed every evening harassed with doubts and anxieties. On the contrary I find people now a little disappointed that air-raids do not come to anything.' He added that he had just heard that it was impossible to get accommodation near the Firth of Forth, 'owing to the rush of visitors to see the air-raids in that favoured area!!' In his domestic correspondence he explained to authors, with unflagging patience if inner weariness, the basic facts of war-time life— shortages, rising costs, inevitable delays. In many hundreds of letters written to American acquaintances, or even strangers, he proselytized, preached, and exhorted, and in effect wrote his own history of the war. It was said that his letters had a wide circulation on the American campuses.

In 1942 he told Harold Butler, then Warden of Nuffield College and about to leave on an important mission to the United States, that he had long made it his practice to write at least one letter a week to American correspondents about ordinary life in Britain. He was convinced that they had very little idea of what was going on. Amongst those with whom he was in touch, he mentioned David H. Stevens and John Marshall at the Rockefeller Foundation, and Professor C. W. de Kiewiet, a South African at Cornell. Marshall was Sisam's own best informant, for he reciprocated to the full Sisam's belief in the importance of disseminating news. The first of his regular and copious reports on the state of the nation was welcomed as an invaluable supplement to the broadcasts from America by Raymond Gram Swing, in whom Sisam had some grudging confidence. In general he did not trust the media. He preferred to set up his own network of communications.

'In such a war as this business letters can excusably, I think, become a little emotional as well,' de Kiewiet had written. The correspondence that began with the arrangements for publishing his *History of South Africa* in

1940 continued throughout the war. Sisam's bulletins to him have a special quality. The New Zealander had discovered in the South African a 'true patriot', and he wrote as a comrade in arms. 'Now that we are fighting single-handed (at least in England), the country continues to be calm and steady,' he wrote in August 1940. 'Given help from the factories of America, I hope we shall put up a good fight. Anyhow, we are in good heart, not likely, I think, to be panicked.' And later he was writing, 'We are now, I think, very near a big attack, but the country is in excellent heart . . . Anyhow, you may be sure that the Press will continue its work until it is stopped by force, and as far as I know that is the disposition of everybody in the country.'

The Battle of Britain began. Sisam heard the sound of distant bombs in the night: 'I write in the middle of great air-raids: no doubt the German communiqués are telling you that England has been wiped out! But we are doing very nicely so far . . . The people here are standing up to it with complete coolness, and foolish as it may be, most of us feel a little disappointed when nothing happens near us.'

Disasters did nothing to diminish his buoyancy. Only when the worst was over did his spirits begin to flag, and by then the day-to-day running-down of the Press was cause enough for dejection. In the winter of 1944 he wrote to de Kiewiet, 'I should guess that national efficiency was falling now . . . owing to the amount of dislocation and wear and tear, human and material.' He even complained on behalf of his fellow citizens of the poor diet. It was remarkable that the Government had not 'diverted to heavy workers certain quantities of essential commodities — bacon for instance'. It was a cold and foggy January, hard to believe then that four winters before he could have written to another American friend, 'In some ways you would enjoy the quiet of war conditions, and the release from evening engagements which a very thorough black-out gives.'

The coming of spring and the opening of the second front could not revive the old defiant optimism, which obviously prospered best when backs were to the wall. To Marshall he attributed the apparent lack of jubilation in the land to the fact that the British, unlike the Germans, hated war just as much when they were winning as when they were losing. The flying bombs were described first as 'a nuisance', later as a fearful waste of time and nervous energy. People would rather be aimed at by German bombers, he thought, than take their chance against these aimless missiles. In the summer of 1944 he described the mood to Marshall as 'confidently unoptimistic'. He added, 'I believe too that joy has been more thoroughly killed here than in 1918.'

Sisam's personal newsletters from the Press during the war, which might appear not strictly to concern business, would fill several volumes. In Sisam's mind they were business, essential business, for they gave notice of the national intention to survive, and eventually to win.

By 1942 Chapman was unable to carry on. The war had brought no sense of relief or rejuvenation, as it had to so many: he had watched and feared its stealthy approach for twenty years. He felt as Cannan had felt, and could not bear to watch the young men go. He could not bear to see the Press he had helped to rescue in 1919 brought again almost to its knees. He retired, knowing at least that the flag he had not the heart to show would be kept flying by a man who still relished the fight. Sisam never wanted to be Secretary, but he had been acting in that capacity for so long by 1942 that he scarcely noticed the transition. Chapman died in 1960 at the age of 79. During the latter part of the war he devoted himself to completing his edition of Dr. Johnson's letters.

3. Rationing

THE *Clarendonian*, which had appeared regularly since 1919, disappeared after a final wartime issue in January 1942. It then reported that 209 men and women from the printing business had left for war service. The Piscatorial Society still flourished, but the entire first and second XI football teams had joined up. In the Clarendon Press Institute, 90 service men had been billeted just after the dance floor had been planed and polished, and they had been followed by evacuees from London: 'the floor can hardly have been improved thereby'. New books by Ruby M. Ayres, A. J. Cronin, Ethel M. Dell, and Daphne du Maurier had been added to the library, as well as the latest crop of World's Classics presented by Milford. The reading-room had been improved by Johnson's gift of a magnificent settee and a chair—'much appreciated by our retired members . . . who spend many hours there'. The editor reported that the weeping willow in the quad, over 110 years old, had been sadly shaken by the wind and weather, 'and now a stump and one branch are all that remain. But still there is that branch, which in spring will delight us with its tender green, against the more subtle tones of the copper beech.'

The next *Clarendonian* was 'A Victory News Sheet' early in 1946. In the end 254 people had gone from the Printer's staff, and 18 had died. The O.U.P. comforts fund had raised enough money to send £2 to each serving member at Christmas, 1944. There seemed little else to report, except that the canteen, one of Johnson's wartime innovations of which he was proud, served the best tenpenny dinner in town.

Major John Mulgan, bound for Egypt in 1942, reported for the gratification of Norrington that several complete sets of Oxford Pamphlets had to be included by War Office order in the library of every troopship. Sisam sent him a copy of *The Legacy of Egypt* that had just come out. 'It is an amazingly dry book, like the sands,' he wrote, 'but it may come in for some odd use—killing flies or throwing at a dog—and it is really much lighter than the book we have just brought to advance copy—Beazley's *Attic Greek Vases* in 1200 pages, without a paragraph of open prose, and about 6 in. through!'

Sir John Beazley's great work had been in preparation since 1912, when the Delegates had voted £100 towards the purchase of drawings. It had also been long in the press. To have brought it to completion at all was a notable achievement. Only 300 copies were printed. In 1963 a greatly enlarged second edition was published in three volumes. The appearance of the first edition, however, marked the end of the period which could lay any claim to normality. Few comparable extravagances could be allowed again for many years. Sisam's policy was to concentrate on keeping the learned journals going, as the best contribution to scholarship that could be made under the circumstances. Major works already completed, like *The Oxford Classical Dictionary*, were put aside until after the war, and the learned Clarendon Press book became a rarity.

The main task for Sisam and Milford was to determine the allocation of their dwindling resources. For Milford there was some relief in that until 1943 at least he could still publish new books on current affairs which seemed to be in the national interest and would also sell. He published *The Speeches of Adolf Hitler*, kept up a 'World To-Day Series', and issued a series of pamphlets called 'America Faces the War'. But most of his paper ration necessarily went on Bibles, Prayer Books, and hymnals, with only a little left over for reprints of the standard classics. Indeed it seemed that all of it could have been spent on supplying the popular demand for the five-volume World's Classics edition of *War and Peace*. Not to be able to supply his customers was for Milford a deeply depressing experience.

Sisam was the more temperamentally adjusted to rationing, in which he saw a rough egalitarian justice. It was like old times at the Ministry of Food too, and there was virtue in thrift. Each quarter he issued to the trade a fixed number of copies of the dictionaries, books of verse, companions, and other books in great demand. For 1942 he allowed 1,000 copies of Harvey's *Companion to English Literature*: in the last month before rationing was introduced it had sold 750 copies. More specialized works for which at the best of times the market had been small were also supplied in fixed quantities, perhaps no more than 50 copies a year. A situation that caused Milford to feel helpless and frustrated aroused in Sisam a powerful sense of responsibility.

In the summer of 1942 he estimated that the Press was selling 50 per cent more books than it was able to produce. It was in fact possible to maintain this ratio throughout the war. In 1939 there had been some five million books in stock. In the end the stocks appeared to have been catastrophically reduced, but there were still two and a half million books left. Unfortunately they were not the books most wanted. But they had survived, despite Sisam's ruthless abandonment of the old tradition that allowed books to live out their natural lives. He had been putting books out of print at a rate undreamed of at any time in the Press's history.

He was in fact pulping unwanted stock and recovering the paper. But binding materials were also scarce, and the girls traditionally employed in the bindery had been enticed away into war work. Even if he decided to keep the sheets it was not always possible to bind them, and many titles remained 'out of stock', if not out of print. In a memorandum on the shortage of school-books written for the Board of Education, Sisam explained the binding problems and emphasized that paper covers were not a solution. Their retention on the continent was, in his view, as much a survival as peasant agriculture: they depended on facilities for binding by hand, and the machine-bound book was much more economical. In a sense he was right. The 'paperback revolution' when it came was a revolution in marketing techniques.

In 1943 a discovery was made that radically affected publishing policy: people were no longer interested in books about the war or anything related to it. It had seemed almost a patriotic duty to be reasonably well-informed on current affairs, and the publishers had maintained a massive output of informative works on Anglo-American relations, Anglo-Russian relations, Japan, the fall of France, on what might or might not be going on inside Germany. The intelligence that the mood had changed was brought back to Oxford by a traveller who had totally failed to interest the buyer at Boots in *A Little History of the United States*. Though this particular work seemed harmless enough, it had at once been categorized as 'topical', and therefore unsaleable. Having canvassed branches throughout the country, Boots had concluded that the great majority of the reading public was 'only too anxious to get books which leave the war severely alone'. It had decided of a sudden that it preferred entertainment. The Times Book Club confirmed, adding that it was 'painfully difficult to sell any books on Poland and Czechoslovakia'. Much the same had happened in the First World War.

Given his own insatiable appetite for news and information, Sisam could not have been expected to know that it had happened again. But once the fact had been brought to his attention he reacted promptly. He decreed an end to ephemeral books. The energies and resources of the Press were to be devoted to works of more permanent value: money should be invested in long-term projects which would bring in revenue in the future. Milford also took heed. 'I have always feared saturation for these topical books,' he wrote, 'but had hardly expected it to be reached as soon as this. The more paper that I can devote to reprinting World's Classics etc., the better I shall personally be pleased.'

In 1943 a former Inspector of Elementary Schools, Miss Laura Salt, joined the Press to help Norrington with his school-books. There was not much to be done immediately, so in accordance with the policy of planning for the future Miss Salt was invited to pullulate freely. After vacant despair and a few false starts an idea began to form. It was for a multi-volume encyclopedia for children, each volume being devoted to a particular subject—'mankind', 'the universe', 'engineering'. By 1944 the plan was far enough advanced to be presented to Sisam, who devoted an hour and a half to discussing it with her. Miss Salt left him feeling that she had never before been so intensively instructed in wisdom. The first of the thirteen volumes of the *Oxford Junior Encyclopaedia* began to appear in 1948. The articles were written by experts, after experience had taught that those who specialized in writing for children usually got the facts wrong.

Meanwhile Norrington started a new series of Oxford Pamphlets on Home Affairs. The Pamphlets were clearly an exception to the rule against topical books, having achieved a semi-official status. They kept Norrington fully employed, allowing a more creative outlet for his energies than any available to Sisam and Milford. Before the invasion of Europe he also got Ensor to write a history of the war so far. It was to be an instant antidote for minds poisoned by years of German propaganda, the moment the way was clear. A large consignment reached France on D-Day plus 4, and the advancing armies were never far ahead of either the Oxford Pamphlets or Ensor's unfolding history.

4. Refugee Scholars

IN 1944, apart from the journals and University publications, the Clarendon Press managed to produce nine new books. They were all, as Sisam had resolved, of the enduring kind. Among them were the second volume of de Selincourt's posthumous Oxford English Text edition of Wordsworth's *Poems*, C. M. Bowra's *Sophoclean Tragedy*, the first volume of A. W. Gomme's *Historical Commentary* on Thucydides, and Paul Jacobsthal's *Early Celtic Art*. The last, in two volumes, was priced at 10 guineas: it had cost the Delegates £2,000 to produce, and they expected to lose £1,000.

Jacobsthal, formerly Professor of Classical Archaeology at Marburg, had found shelter in Christ Church, but he was one of the many distinguished refugee scholars from the Continent for whom Sisam on behalf of the University assumed a kind of responsibility. Sisam's efforts before the war to prepare for the exodus from Nazi Germany had met with little success. He complained at times that he got little help from the University, and less from the Society for the Protection of Science and Learning, which was usually out of funds. An attempt to persuade the University to apply to the Government for £5,000 a year for ten years while there was still time was thwarted by the outbreak of war, when charity of all kinds was abruptly suspended.

The colleges did what they could to help, hoping that the refugees would reciprocate by taking on some of the work of the absent dons. This was not always possible, either because their English was inadequate or because their subjects were too recondite. The special contribution of the Press was that it could not only offer some financial support but could encourage a scholar to continue, in a time of catastrophic discontinuity, his life's work. Great discretion was needed. The work of British scholars had been violently interrupted too: that enemy aliens should be so privileged was not an obvious justice.

In his campaign to secure funds for the refugees, therefore, Sisam was at pains to stress that he was concerned only with scholarship, not individuals. He was not prepared to help anybody who was not a first-class scholar, and saw no case for helping a first-class scholar who was not content with a bare subsistence allowance for which he was willing to work hard. And Sisam in truth was not in a particularly compassionate frame of mind. 'Probably neither you nor I have any natural affection for aliens,' he wrote to the Warden of All Souls, W. G. S. Adams, 'but we can't stand by and see good scholars starve.' To qualify for Sisam's benevolence the refugees had to be exemplary both in conduct and attainment. They were to remember that asylum itself was their greatest privilege. 'I cannot stand the refugees who are always grumbling about their hard lot,' he said.

It was necessary therefore to present all his candidates as exceptional, as truly great and innocent men whose contribution to British scholarship would be the one benign consequence of Hitler's barbarism. The model was Paul Maas, formerly Professor at Königsberg, who had already experienced the concentration camps. A Greek textual scholar of the calibre of Wilamowitz, he could be looked after indefinitely by the Press, for he was 'incredibly frugal'—as well as incredibly helpful. He insisted that in wartime Oxford he was not entitled to more than £100 a year, though Balliol and the Press between them were prepared to double his allowance. He paid £60 a year for a miserable room with breakfast, and worked fourteen hours a day. Almost equally exemplary was another classical scholar, Rudolf Pfeiffer, from Munich. With such men Sisam became very personally involved. Greatly learned, innocent, industrious, untouched by avarice, they represented his idea of what a Clarendon Press author should be.

In May 1940 Sisam wrote the first of several informal letters to David H. Stevens at the Rockefeller Foundation about the first-class refugee scholars in Oxford who needed help. He explained that the Press had done all that it could: 'We have taken in hand several of them, but our business is primarily to publish the work that scholars . . . produce, not to provide funds for the preparation of learned and unremunerative work. . . . This is a real social problem at the moment.' He also wrote to Adams at All Souls, who was active in the cause. He mentioned the help already given by the Press to various scholars: F. Schulz, formerly Professor of Roman Law in Berlin, had been taken under its wing together with Maas: the immediate position of others had been eased by paying over £1,000 for contributions to *The Oxford Classical Dictionary*, which he was then unable to print. The Press was committed to publishing and paying royalties on a book on Byzantine music by Egon Wellesz from Vienna, on the Greek law of Sale by Fritz Pringsheim of Freiburg, an edition of Callimachus by Pfeiffer, as well as

Jacobsthal's *Early Celtic Art*. But this was not nearly enough. 'It is hard to realise', he wrote, 'how much learning and teaching in England and America depended on the production of certain basic reference books on the Continent. . . . Many of the men capable of producing these books are refugees; and to direct their ability into the right channels is something more than a necessary service to them: it would help to maintain the continuity of learning in all countries. At the Press we can see that this war has shaken that continuity in Europe as it has not been shaken for many centuries. There are few good scholars left free to work, and it is essential that those who are free should somehow be enabled to work.'

Adams made a further approach to the Rockefeller Foundation through different channels. Unfortunately this did not immediately help and led to administrative confusion and delay. Sisam's proposals and the detailed memoranda that accompanied them got directed to the Foundation's 'program in the Social Sciences'. Not until April 1941 was it realized that it more properly came under 'Humanities', and thus fell in the province of Sisam's friends, Marshall and Stevens. On 19 May, a year after his first overtures, Sisam learned by cable that a grant to the Delegates of $10,000 had been approved. It was for one year only. For what he had in mind, and reckoning on a minimum subsistence allowance of £100 a year for a single man, this sum of about £2,500 was more than enough. 'To be able to look one more year ahead is a real help to a scholar contemplating a great work,' Sisam wrote in his moment of triumph to the Vice-Chancellor. Milford, on learning the news, sent a message from Southfield House: 'Congratulations: a splendid combination of business and philanthropy. You must have been most persuasive.'

The Rockefeller grants were renewed each year. Sisam reported regularly to Stevens and Marshall, writing brief character sketches of the scholars he had chosen to support, describing the books they were planning to write, and their economic and domestic backgrounds. 'The modesty of their requests often bears no relation to the importance of the work, for they have long been compelled to work on small margins,' he wrote to Stevens. In 1944 the case for the fourth grant to the Clarendon Press was so clear, Marshall told Sisam, that the Trustees had agreed to it without the slightest hesitation.

The source of the funds that Sisam administered was kept secret. This was stipulated by the Foundation, and it was also essential from Sisam's point of view if he were not to be plagued by supplicants. It worked well. There were few begging letters, and the scholars who benefited from the grants were all selected by the Press. Most of them were classicists, partly for historical reasons, partly because they appeared to be the most needy, and the least able to adapt themselves to other occupations. It was assumed that the scientists could look after themselves, though Sisam told Fowler in Cambridge that if there were any promising mathematicians or physicists in danger of starving he would be in a position to help. The young and able-bodied were not eligible for Sisam's bounty.

There were two eminent Roman lawyers in Oxford, F. de Zulueta and H. F. Jolowicz. Early in 1939 it was learned that their equally eminent colleague in Berlin, Fritz Schulz, was in trouble. Sisam wrote inviting him to Oxford, thereby enabling him to get a visa from the British consulate and apply for a passport. He eventually arrived in England from Holland in 1940, having acquired an entry permit only with great difficulty: he was over sixty, too old to be allowed into the country without a supposedly permanent guarantee that he would be provided for. On arriving in England he was interned. Sisam was indignant: was it to be impossible 'to import a senior man'? He secured his release by offering £100 a year for two years while he wrote a book on Roman law: Balliol contributed £100 for one year. This was not enough. 'There is not much point in inviting distinguished professors here as refugees if they are to be on a semi-starvation basis,' wrote Sisam, 'nor will it do the University any credit.' However Schulz was his responsibility, and he had to be put to work in the hope that he might eventually be able to earn his keep. A comprehensive Oxford History of Legal Science in three volumes, edited by Zulueta and Kantorowicz, had been ambitiously projected in 1938: the scheme foundered during the war, but Schulz was invited to contribute to what was to have been the first volume of a collaborative work. His chapter became a book in itself, and it occupied him until 1945. It was constantly revised, de Zulueta translated and edited it, and Schulz finally delivered the manuscript on 11 February 1945, the day the Russians took Bunzlau in Silesia, 'where I was born and educated. Omen accipio.'

Without the Rockefeller money it would have been impossible to continue to support Schulz year after year. He was among the first recipients of a grant of £200 from the 'anonymous benefactor' in 1941. Sisam's report on him to the Foundation read: 'A good scholar, very hard working. A leading Democrat in Berlin, and first forbidden to lecture on that ground. Has a wife and daughter.... An economical household, and all show the best spirit.' They occupied the small house at 5 Tackley Place where Paul Maas had his humble room.

Some of the refugee scholars eventually made their way to America, but throughout the war there were usually twenty or more of them living in Oxford, working to some extent under Sisam's supervision. Once a book had been accepted in principle by the Delegates, the author became in his view one of the family, entitled to certain privileges and help in emergencies. Unworldly men from the start, some of them felt permanently lost in the new environment, though perhaps this was a condition of mind to which they were not unaccustomed. Sisam's fatherly attention was often needed. Accusations or at least rumours of spying were not unknown, and he might have to vouch for the victim's character if the authorities followed them up. When Schulz broke a tooth, he had to arrange the dental appointment and pay the bill. He compelled Maas to see a doctor, for he suffered from acute cardiac spasms which, alarming to witnesses, he himself lightly dismissed. The doctor reported to Sisam that the condition could be serious if Maas

G. F. J. Cumberlege, Publisher, 1945–56

Kenneth Sisam, Secretary, 1942–6

C. H. Roberts, A. L. P. Norrington, C. Batey

were not persuaded to take the treatment prescribed: he regarded visits to the doctor and the medicines themselves as an extravagance. Sisam urged the doctor to insist that he kept his appointments: 'Send all fees to the Press,' he wrote. 'We shan't begrudge anything that is for his good.' At another time he was supporting Maas's appeal to the officer in charge of aliens for permission to ride a bicycle within and outside the city limits. It was necessary for the Professor in the course of his work, he explained, to visit both himself and Professor Gilbert Murray out at Boar's Hill. Pringsheim, who had brought with him a wife and five children, was forced to appeal for help when one of his sons had appendicitis. Sisam reviewed the case, decided that it qualified as a 'real emergency', and sent a cheque to cover the operation and hospital fees.

Once having delivered his manuscript, Schulz had every intention of seeing it through the press in traditional fashion. He looked forward to a close daily association with the compositor and everybody else concerned. It was not easy to explain to him that times had changed. 'You must bear in mind that in these modern organizations there is no provision for the author sitting in,' Sisam wrote. In fact, he added, under the security regulations he would not be allowed in the printing works at all. It seemed to Schulz a cruel and curious thing to deprive an author of access to his own book. When the proofs began he had again to be warned off: 'Whatever you do,' Sisam told him, 'you must not think that we are working in the old days when sheets could be taken in and out by the author.' The *History of Roman Legal Science* was safely published in 1946. It was a work of advanced scholarship, acclaimed as one of the most important books on Roman law to appear in this century. But Sisam had once hoped for a money-making textbook for students. Schulz went on to write another large volume, and remained impoverished.

Amongst the other scholars to receive help were Arnoldo Momigliano, who had been Professor of Greek History in Rome; Martin Wolff, who wrote a major work on international law; W. von Leyden, who worked on Locke's papers; and Joseph Schacht, the great authority on Islamic law. After the war some were able to resume their careers, others had forged new ones. Some were too old and continued to need all the support they could find. They nearly all produced in the end major works of scholarship for the Press, though their immense diligence did not lead to quick results. Pfeiffer's edition of Callimachus, which he had been planning from the start of his career, was published in 1949, the first volume of his *History of Classical Scholarship* in 1968, the second in 1976. Maas's book on *Textual Criticism* was translated from the German and published in 1958, but his main contribution was as an adviser and consultant. One of the first of the refugees, who reached Oxford via Cambridge in 1934, was Edouard Fraenkel. As Corpus Christi Professor of Latin Languages and Literature, he never needed financial support, but he relied upon Sisam for advice and encouragement. In 1935, Hugh Last had reported that he was working on a book on Horace. In 1941 Sisam noted that he was doing an edition with

T

commentary of the *Agamemnon* of Aeschylus which threatened to be vast. In 1950 the latter appeared in three volumes, the commentary filling 800 pages. The gigantic scale evoked some adverse criticism, but as the work of 'one of the most distinguished of living scholars' it really defied normal judgement and its publication could only be described as an important event. The book on Horace was published in 1957.

The unhappy Pringsheim was left with a manuscript of 300,000 words on the Greek law of sale. The Delegates had agreed in 1942 to publish after the war a 70,000-word monograph on the subject—though Zulueta had once expressed a doubt whether the subject could be said to exist. The work, delivered into Sisam's hands in 1945, was not only much too long: it was painfully clear that he should never have attempted to write it in English in the first place. For two more years he struggled to shape a short essay out of his material, but the words would not go away and the problem remained insoluble.

Sisam chose not to mention this episode when he wrote to David Stevens in October 1946: 'I can make a final report of these four grants in brief terms:— they fulfilled their purpose of encouraging refugee scholars to continue their learned work at a time when, without this encouragement, they might have despaired; they solved a number of human problems; and they have left no problems behind.' This was not entirely so. When Sisam retired in 1948 he still had plenty of problems to bequeath to his successors.

EPILOGUE

1. Little Pressites

IN order to return to normal after the war, it seemed to Sisam that ideally the Press should stop selling books altogether for two years. Then if there were a government grant several times greater than that to the University he could set about repairing the damage. But the shortages of paper, of staff, of new machinery, of all basic materials continued. It was a time of extraordinary frustration. For six years the words 'after the war' had defined the promised land; now land had been reached and every promise was unfulfilled. Sisam had always intended to retire at sixty to the Isles of Scilly—to which in fact he retired each summer in peacetime, believing firmly, like Lyttelton Gell, that it was essential to have six weeks away each year without Press business constantly following him about. But like Cannan he could not leave when the Press was so clearly in the lurch, though there were at least inklings, denied to Chapman in 1919, of prosperity ahead. At the end of 1945 the second volume in the Oxford History of English Literature, on the fifteenth century by Sir Edmund Chambers, was published. The period covered was not one of the most popular, but within a few months 7,000 copies had been sold in the United Kingdom alone. The market was there, if Sisam could only supply it.

In 1946 John Johnson retired and was succeeded by Charles Batey, who had been Assistant Printer for seventeen years. Batey's task was not only to reorganize the printing works as soon as it was possible to do so, but to humanize them. He had already seen scope for improving relations between management and labour, or at least for mitigating the severity of Johnson's rule. During his twelve years as Printer, his 'sense of the importance of human relationships', as it was delicately put in a tribute to him on retirement, bore fruit in the establishment of a Joint Works Council, of a Press Housing Society, and the introduction of an incentive scheme. It was a relief to the publishing department to be able to rely on his neighbourly understanding. One of his triumphs as a printer was the Order of Service for Her Majesty's Coronation in 1953.

As Sisam grappled with the problems of reconstruction he became aware of a stabbing pain, as of a knife entering the back. Ingratitude was abroad. Dons returning to Oxford after the war appeared not to appreciate the plight he was in. The Press was blamed for the non-availability of necessary textbooks; it was also blamed for the availability of books by authors who had no connection with the University, and for various luxuries like the World's Classics and Standard Authors made available by Amen House.

The books the Press did actually publish, it was said, had no more to do with the University than the motor cars and marmalade for which the city was also renowned.

In February 1946 an article appeared in the *Oxford Magazine*. The writer recalled how as a serviceman on leave in Calcutta he had stumbled upon the O.U.P. office and showrooms there, and discovered in this outpost of the civilization he had been defending a heart-warming, even heart-rending, display of Oxford books. Back in utility Oxford all this seemed like a dream. The books he needed as a history tutor were not to be found. What, he began to wonder, was the Press doing in India? In less than a hundred years it had grown into a vast multinational business, and its relationship to 'the modest printing press set up in the vaults of the Sheldonian Theatre less than a dozen generations ago' escaped him. The writer concluded that 'if the University really wants its own press it must either bring the O.U.P. to heel or found anew a more amenable press, leaving the O.U.P. to adventure as business blows across the seven seas'.

So began the campaign of the 'Little Pressites', as Geoffrey Cumberlege called them. They continued to harass Sisam until his retirement, levelling as it seemed outrageous and uninformed charges against him. In a reply to the *Magazine* he tried to make clear the extent to which the Press had suffered. Before the war there had been some 5,000 Clarendon Press titles available, from stock built up over the generations. Half of these had vanished from the list. It had been estimated that in the bombing of Leipzig two and a half million books had been destroyed: that was roughly equivalent to the reduction of Clarendon Press stocks. Sisam had rationed the sale of books in general demand since 1941, in order to concentrate his scarce resources on supplying the needs of universities and schools. He had done his best, but with the continuing shortages he could do no more.

The original writer, G. D. Ramsay, was far from satisfied. What was the use of a university press if it could not come to the rescue of its teaching faculties in their hour of need? Those books in Calcutta carrying Milford's imprint were surely using up resources which could have been diverted to meet local needs. Were the Delegates in any real control at all? If not, in what sense could it be called 'The University Press'?

Others joined in, among them Hugh Last, who had something to say about the need for bringing in outside experts. Breaches were opening in the walls allegedly built up about the Press by Charles Cannan, but for the time being there was nothing but a heavy silence from within. The Delegates considered what action should be taken, if any. It was undeniably true that only a dozen generations ago it had all been different, but the notion of a great leap backwards into the dark was difficult to contemplate. There was an element of truth too in the charge that the needs of the University were not uppermost in the calculations of one of its own departments. National policy dictated that priority should be given to exports, whilst the country stayed on short rations. So extra allocations of paper were allowed for books of no conceivable use to the teaching faculties. A. S. Hornby's

Advanced Learner's Dictionary, a proof of which had been smuggled out of Japan by diplomatic bag just before Pearl Harbor, was at last printed, and it became the biggest seller of all Oxford books after the Bible. It was perhaps prudent not to advertise such matters to Oxford dons deprived of Aristotle's *Politics*, Rousseau's *Social Contract*, and other essential tools. On the other hand there was no truth whatsoever in allegations that any member of the University below the rank of Head of House or Professor who presumed to offer a book to the Press would be turned away with a sneer. This was particularly unjust at a time when Sisam was recruiting new editors only too eager to discover young talent in the University.

Eventually, in response to a suggestion from Hugh Last, the Delegates agreed that a public meeting should be held at which grievances could be ventilated, and the impression that the Press only wanted to make a mystery of itself could be dispelled. They did so in June, with the balm of a Long Vacation imminent, but the meeting finally took place on 18 November at All Souls, with Sir Henry Tizard, President of Magdalen, in the chair, and with W. D. Ross, Provost of Oriel, Chairman of Finance Committee and a former Vice-Chancellor, as the Delegates' spokesman. Taking the line that information rather than controversy was what was wanted, Ross gave a succinct account of the history and structure of the Press, of its finances, of the functions of its various departments and branches. He also recalled that long before he was either a Delegate, or a Professor, or the Head of a House, he had himself as a young author received the greatest possible encouragement from the officials of the Press. He refused to believe that the attitude to young authors had changed.

Some of the arguments of the Little Pressites were substantially weakened by errors of fact. It had been stated that in the years 1933 to 1935, of the learned books reviewed in the *Magazine* only a very small proportion had been published by the Press. This turned out to be a misprint for 1943 to 1945, when for reasons fully explained already the Press was scarcely able to publish any books at all. It had also been said that about half the books needed by the various faculties and published by the Press were not available. Sisam calculated that of 45 Oxford books specifically listed 39 had in spite of everything been kept in print. Four were books which could not be reprinted for lack of new editions, and one 'was a book of a kind where we sometimes have to tell the Faculty that the demand does not warrant it'. He was referring to Becker's edition of Aristotle's *Politics* published in 1837, of which no copy had been sold in England in any of the three years before the war.

Hugh Last spoke at length, covering ground familiar enough to Ross and Sisam but new to many of his listeners. G. D. Ramsay, 'speaking as a very simple person', again wondered what the value to the University of a world-wide business centred at Amen House really was. There still seemed a case for having just a small press in Oxford that the University could call its own. Specific instances of faulty liaison between the Faculties and the Press interrupted the debate on principles, and when the lateness of the hour brought the meeting to an end many questions remained unanswered or unasked. The President of Magdalen thought that he spoke for a majority when he confessed to 'an uneasy mind'. He began his summing-up with a gibe Sisam was unlikely to appreciate: 'I hope the Delegates who are responsible for this very big business are happy that some of the Shareholders, if I may call them that, are taking a great interest in it.' It seemed to the representatives of the Press that there was something a little authoritarian, ironic, even menacing in Tizard's manner, though his large responsibility for the development of nuclear weapons may have affected judgement. The method of appointing the Delegates struck him as most curious. He could not think of any other large private company run in such an extraordinary fashion. It was interesting, he observed, that it worked as well as it did under a constitution by which the Board of Directors, half of whom held office until the age of 75, were appointed by a temporary Chairman of the Board (himself appointed for qualities other than those of business acumen) and two temporary directors. He was not convinced that it could not be made to work better under some other arrangement. It was just possible that the profits might go up and that the Press would then be able to give even greater service to the cause of learning. He hoped that the Vice-Chancellor and Delegates would consider that possibility.

The Press escaped further public inquisition for another twenty years, but this encounter with the Little Pressites left its scars. The knowledge that there existed in the University a party antagonistic to it was disturbing, and perhaps contributed to the secretiveness with which the Press was so often charged. For Sisam as he approached the end of his publishing career it was saddening as well.

2. Global Strategy

GEOFFREY ('JOCK') CUMBERLEGE succeeded Milford as Publisher in 1945. Although he had himself once asked what the Press was doing in India, he had since had the opportunity to find out. He was now convinced that the revival and future development of the Press would depend upon sales, as soon as there was anything to sell, and like Henry Frowde he was a believer in the man on the spot. The occasional representative, visiting an area once every two years or so, made a visible but sporadic difference to sales abroad; a permanent representative could sustain and supply the demand for Oxford books. He did not underestimate the seriousness of bickerings at the centre. Such tea-cup storms could rock the boat he had in the past personally navigated across treacherous seas. But with E. C. Parnwell's enthusiastic support he was ready to embark on a new phase of expansion, carrying on from where Milford had left off before the First World War. As the old Empire dissolved, the Overseas Education Department set out to build a new one.

Cumberlege's staff problems were the opposite of those experienced in other parts of the business. In Oxford the Printer found that he could not get men unless he could provide houses, and for the time being the universal shortage of materials made that impossible. Back at Amen House, scarcely a day passed without somebody turning up in a demob suit hoping to be recognized as that promising young man who had been summarily called away six years before. Or he might in fact be still dressed as a lieutenant-colonel, ready to resume a humble pre-war occupation on a paltry pre-war salary. Over a hundred jobs had to be found, rather than filled. But on the assumption that there was light at the end of the tunnel, the home sales and publicity departments could be built up.

Redman, Glover, Billings, Barrett, Tolleday, Holman, Pack, Rayner: these were the names of the almost legendary first generation of O.U.P. travellers who in the days of Frowde and Milford had helped to forge links of confidence with booksellers throughout the country. Rayner was known to have had a horse-conveyance of his own. The others, commonly referred to as 'bagmen', travelled by train, hiring porters with trolleys at the railway stations to carry their samples to the bookshops. The early Bible salesmen from New York travelled the States in similar fashion, but their journeys lasted up to three months. At each stop they made for the main hotel and set up a display. They were even more distinguished figures than their frock-coated, silk-hatted British counterparts, their sacred wares lending them an odour of sanctity. They were known to the booksellers as 'Preacher' or 'Bishop'.

In 1939 all the British travellers had joined up, with the exception of two who had served in the First World War. By 1946 they were back on the road again, a team of ten dividing the country between them, now equipped with motor cars. 'Out of stock' and 'binding no date' were too often the messages they carried to the booksellers, but gradually the tidings changed to 'now available again'. Until his retirement in 1956 they were briefed by Gerard Hopkins, who witnessed a notable change in the concept of 'publicity' after the war. Milford had economized on advertising, and regarded modern methods of publicity as not a little vulgar. 'The fact that the Oxford Publicity Machine is today in its smoothness and power ... a Rolls-Royce among bubble cars, is mainly due to Gerard Hopkins', the *Bookseller* wrote in 1957. New models of even more sophisticated design were subsequently introduced.

Whilst the propriety of the O.U.P.'s very existence overseas was being debated in Oxford, Cumberlege dispatched a man to South America to investigate the prospects there. Turkey, the Near East, and Persia were already under Parnwell's surveillance. In 1946 the South African Branch was opened with the appointment of Leo Marquard as educational manager in Cape Town, empowered to publish books locally in English, Afrikaans, and the Bantu languages. A branch had existed there since 1915, but the meaning of the word had changed. Branches which only sold and did not publish books came to be known as 'offices'. Overseas Education emerged as a 'self-eliminating' department, and could trace its dis-appearance through various stages. First a representative was sent out to travel an area and survey the prospects: if these looked promising he would open an office. By the time the office had acquired a warehouse and started publishing books of its own choice locally, it had become a branch. The process might take several years. But once it was complete, O.E.'s responsibility was at an end. As a member of the department put it with a felicitous mixture of metaphors, 'the O.E. hand that rocked the cradle waves goodbye, and another fledgling has left the nest'.

When Parnwell started in 1926, only the American, Canadian, and Indian Branches could be said to exist according to the later definition. India had been a branch more or less from the start in 1912, when local publishing appeared to be forced upon it if it were to survive at all. After Independence educational publishing in the Indian languages ceased to be rewarding, but under the very individual guidance of R. E. Hawkins it developed a small but distinguished general list of its own. Succumbing to an irresistible urge to see India, brought on at an early age by photographs of Gandhi's demonstrations in the illustrated magazines, Hawkins had joined the Press in Bombay in 1930. He was general manager from 1937 until retirement in 1970, when some 215 people were employed in Bombay, Calcutta, and Madras—three of them English. Among the authors he found, befriended, and encouraged were Verrier Elwin, the anthropologist; K. P. S. Menon, India's ambassador in Moscow and Peking; Minoo Masani, whose *Our India* was a best seller; and Jim Corbett, whose *Man-Eaters of Kumaon* became a World's Classic. Hawkins's interest in ornithology was responsible for a surprising number of bird books. He took a jealous pride in his own publications, but with the spread of education and the opening of new universities he could also fulfil the primary function of the Branch. He returned to the mother country every two years, never following the same route twice. The only occasion when he chose to come direct he travelled by bus. His approach could often be charted, however, for in the course of his eccentric journeyings reports of sightings by those who had run into him unexpectedly, though without surprise, would reach Amen House from far and wide.

In the first decade after the war, offices which were to turn into branches opened in New Zealand early in 1947; in Nigeria with one man in 1949 (it became a branch ten years later); in Pakistan in 1952; in East Africa in 1954 (a branch in 1963); and in the Gold Coast and Singapore in 1955, the latter being subsumed in the East Asian Branch in Kuala Lumpur in 1957 and the former not quite making the grade. It had long been tacitly accepted that they could not hope to survive on Clarendon Press books alone. But increasingly the Clarendon Press depended for survival on the export market, especially when the home market was weak, as it not infrequently was. By 1967 exports of nine million books accounted for 55 per cent of sales. When New York and branch publications were included, sales overseas amounted to almost 75 per cent of the total turnover in books.

In 1950 the New York Branch was incorporated separately under American law as a private company and ceased to be a branch at all. Rather than discard the familiar initials, N.Y.B., it came to be called the New York Business. All the shares were owned by the Delegates, and the Secretary was *ex officio* Chairman of the Board. With the change of status and the new independence it appeared to imply, Oxford New York hoped to broaden its activities by publishing learned works, perhaps with a distinctive imprint. It would thereby acquire a special standing in American academic circles, it was thought, and show that it was a genuine projection of the Press in Oxford, not merely a selling agency. The time was not perhaps quite ripe. Some scholarly works had been published, but in Oxford it seemed that a further move in this direction might prove to be contrary to the interests of the Clarendon Press. It was pointed out that the principal effect of the change was not emancipation from Amen House but closer control by the Delegates. As the Clarendon Press was an international institution for publishing learned books, it would be confusing if important works of scholarship were to appear under any other Oxford imprint. Moreover it was believed, particularly by Sisam, that Clarendon Press traditions could not simply be adopted: they had to be bred by long and intimate association with the parent body. Nobody in New York had that experience. As he pondered the issue in retirement in the Scillies in 1950 the only way of humouring this new pretension that Sisam could see was by establishing, some time in the future, a Clarendon Press department in New York, run by a real Clarendon Press person who might be seconded for a year or two, before being relieved by an equally authentic Oxford man. He was ready enough to believe that soon the chief source of learned books would be the United States. But equally the chief outlet had by no accident of history become the Clarendon Press. Oxford University Press New York Inc. was still in illegitimate infancy. It was after all younger than he was, but times would change.

3. A Benign Era

Sisam retired at the age of 61 in 1948 with a great sigh of relief. His spirits improved as the day of release came closer, though his prognosis for the future was never sanguine after 1944. The final hurdle, for him and probably the country, was the winter of 1947–8. 'Most people here are puzzled to be working so hard and apparently making nothing but leeway,' he wrote to Stevens in November 1947. 'However, if we get past the tail end of the winter—February, March, and even April—without some kind of crash, we shall probably pull through.' The most rewarding work in the last two years before retirement had been the training of the new men who had joined on leaving the services. By the summer of 1948 he was confident that the job had been done, and his last letters as Secretary frequently referred with pride to the 'fine team' he was leaving behind. In the team itself he inspired complete devotion. To the New Zealander D. M. Davin, who became Assistant Secretary, and P. J. Spicer, Junior Assistant Secretary, his judgement appeared infallible, his experience inexhaustible, his greatness unquestionable. Both continued to seek regular transfusions of his wisdom by spending holidays in the Scillies. For thirty years D. M. Davin, as Assistant Secretary and Academic Publisher, imparted the Sisam ethos. Though very different in their social habits, as publishers they thought with one mind, and were as akin to each other as Cannan and Milford.

To some of his contemporaries, on the other hand, who had worked with him during and before the war, Sisam seemed a hard man. His many acts of generosity were seen as exceptions to a general rule of sternness bordering on parsimony. It was even said that he actually enjoyed rationing. He was certainly unyielding, often stubborn, and on the rare occasions when he was persuaded to change his mind there was a rumbling and creaking of machinery unaccustomed to shifts of gear. He was, of course, essentially a scholar. Eugene Vinaver, whose great edition of Malory Sisam piloted through many shoals, wrote to the Press on his death in 1971, after supplementing *The Times* obituary notice: 'For many years I have felt strongly that much less than justice had been done to Sisam the scholar and the model of scholarship. Everyone knows what a terrible mistake Oxford made when they by-passed him for the Chair of Anglo-Saxon. . . . But Oxford seldom recognizes its mistakes, and to say with the rest of the world that Sisam was a king among medievalists would have been an admission of an unforgivable error. And so they found it convenient to classify him as a very able publisher. But you have only to talk for five minutes to any American Old English specialist to discover whom *they* regard as the leading person in that field. They and everybody else.' After his retirement the Press published Sisam's *Studies in the History of Old English Literature* (1953) and *The Structure of Beowulf* (1965). The new Secretary was A. L. P. Norrington.

Paper rationing ceased in 1949 and that was a major irritant gone. While it lasted it was impossible to replenish stocks or to pursue any rational policy. Books in great demand could not be reprinted in anything like sufficient quantities. The machines had to be stopped in their tracks, which was wasteful: designed for long runs they were not suited to the short sprint. With the restrictions lifted the machine rooms came under heavy pressure. Impossible demands were made. In 1949, 1,500,000 books were printed; the last time the Press had exceeded a million copies had been in 1939, and only once in its history, in 1925, had it exceeded this figure. It was still not enough, but by 1950 it was estimated that stocks were more or less restored to the level they had been at early in 1943, when the rot set in. Old Clarendon Press favourites were returning to the list in strength. Cowley's *Samaritan Liturgy* was available again, thirteen volumes of the Sacred Books of the East were reprinted, Hooker's *Complete Works* in the seventh edition of 1883–8, three titles from the Tudor and Stuart Library, Scheller's Latin Dictionary of 1835, Plato's *Republic* in Jowett and Campbell's edition of 1894, Thomas Hodgkin's *Italy and her Invaders* (1892–9), and Falconer Madan's *Oxford Books, '1468'–1680*. The old considerably outnumbered the new books announced, but among the latter were two volumes of Ben Jonson (with only one left to come), J. Z. Young's *The Life of Vertebrates*, R. A. Knox's *Enthusiasm*, and two volumes of Marlowe edited by W. W. Greg. The demand for learned books was extraordinary. Clarendon Press titles were selling in quantities that tested credulity: 'The unsaleable books continue to do better than the saleable,' wrote Norrington.

The demand for dictionaries could still hardly be met without seriously interrupting the supply of other books. In 1950 a reprint of 20,000 copies of the *Shorter Oxford English Dictionary* was completed—no more than 5,000 had ever been printed at one time before. Within a year half had gone. Norrington had intended it as 'a major flushing operation, cleaning up all back orders', and assumed that sales would eventually settle down to normal at 1,500 copies a year. But it looked as if the 'normal' sale was going to be about 5,000 a year. A reprint of the *D.N.B.* had been ordered in 1948. Sisam had decided on 1,500 sets, which seemed at the time a vast quantity. Four years later when the 30,000 pages were finally off machine and the first sets bound it already seemed too few. Demand could only be surmised, when for so many years it had been impossible to supply it. Nobody knew what was normal. Contrary to expectations, it was not something that was going to be returned to, and as a guide to the future 1939 was no use at all. It was also becoming clear that it was no longer a matter of filling the immense void created by the war; the world market for books had acquired quite new dimensions, as indeed had the world's population. It was certainly a problem the Press had never had to face before, an excess of vent.

In 1951, just when it seemed that recovery was all but complete, the Press found itself reeling again under the impact of sudden inflation, described as 'galloping'. The Korean war had begun. Within little more than a year there was a 40 per cent rise in production costs, mostly of paper and binding. In spite of ever-increasing sales, a grave cash crisis developed.

Norrington anxiously awaited publication of *The Oxford Atlas*, expected to be the big seller of the year. It was the first product of the Cartographic Department established by one of the new editorial team, David Bickmore. He had been acting as Norrington's assistant on school-books, but having worked with Bartholomews of Edinburgh before the war, and served in a Field Survey Company during it, maps were his obvious occupation. There were a number of 'Oxford' atlases in existence with little right to the name, for they were edited and produced by Bartholomews. Norrington suggested a revision of the world atlas. It turned out to be more than a revision. *The Oxford Atlas*, of which 50,000 copies were printed, was a success and heralded a profusion of atlases from the new department—Concise, Shorter, and Little Atlases, regional and economic atlases, and an *Atlas of*

Britain and Northern Ireland which was perhaps a little too extravagant in conception.

Inflation stopped as suddenly as it had begun in July 1952, after fifteen alarming months, and by 1953 the cash was beginning to flow back in. The Press could at last enter what has been described as the most benign era in the history of the industrial economy.

In that year student enrolment in American universities reached $2\frac{1}{2}$ million; by 1960 it was 4 million and still climbing steeply. The British in 1953 were acclaiming a new Elizabethan age, but aware of a certain hollowness in the aspiration. The country had too clearly fallen behind both former enemies and allies in terms of economic growth. Since the nineteenth century a connection between the universities and the gross national product had been discerned, and it was the endowment of many of the provincial universities by industrial magnates with specific interests—from metallurgy in Sheffield to biscuits in Reading—that made necessary the restatement of the traditional and antithetical idea of a university as understood by Pattison or Newman. Those who believed in the utility of the higher education had argued that in the face of German, French, and American competition prosperity depended on mobilizing and training the national intelligence. They came into their own again in the 1950s. C. P. Snow's *Two Cultures*, which prompted much debate, not only deplored the neglect of science and technology in the older universities but the inadequate output of graduates of all kinds. So Britain followed the American lead in giving a new priority to the higher education, political egalitarianism adding its weight to economic considerations. In the 1960s the achievements of the 1950s came to appear negligible as more and more public money was made available for educational purposes, which included the purchase of books.

University presses ought to have been in a privileged position to exploit the hectic development on their doorsteps, but the commercial publishers were quicker off the mark, some too quick. Quality paperbacks had already almost swamped the American market when Oxford New York cautiously put out its first three Galaxy Books in 1956. The college sale on which the new series would depend could not be easily predicted, but the timing of the experiment turned out to be well judged. The colleges were beginning to use paperbacks on a massive scale. Soon it was to be taken for granted that students would buy only paperbacks, that they would insist on doing so even if a hardback edition were available at the same price. Galaxy Books could draw on titles published by any department of the Press, but when Galaxy Book 100, *Modern American Fiction*, appeared in 1963 the top three best sellers were all books originally published by N.Y.B.: *The Power Elite* by C. Wright Mills, *The Strange Career of Jim Crow* by C. Vann Woodward, and *Man, Culture, and Society* by Harry L. Shapiro. In the General Catalogue of 1973 all the books listed under 'Sociology' were of American origin.

The paperback revolution in America became increasingly bloody, with publishers competing for authors with heedless savagery, advances reaching grotesque proportions, and the whole apparatus of production and distribution almost breaking down under the strain. But Oxford New York avoided over-production, did not speculate too much on marginal titles, kept the college market clearly in its sights, and enjoyed the advantage of Oxford's immense back list. In 1962 Arnold Toynbee's *A Study of History* began to appear as a paperback. In that year the fifth edition of Morison and Commager was published, now in two volumes and almost 2,000 pages, the most successful college textbook ever published by the Press in New York. A gratifying flow of best-selling trade books continued to distinguish the general list—Edmund Wilson's *The Scrolls from the Dead Sea, Atomic Quest* by A. H. Compton whom Sisam had once ruled out as a contributor to the International Monographs on Physics because he understood him to be inarticulate, the works of Wright Mills, *James Joyce* by Richard Ellmann, and several others. But there was no longer any question of being dependent on them. American history and literature became the province of N.Y.B., which could at last with an easy conscience become an academic publisher as well. But it was the college department that truly prospered, numbering its clients by the million. Even the Bible entered college classrooms in the new Oxford Annotated Revised Standard Version.

Educational publishing required a degree of specialization, and with the suspected demise of the general reader Amen House's long tradition of general publishing for the incurious lover of literature was imperilled. Competition from the commercial publishers was also disturbing, for it was flaring up at all levels. The Press could only speculate on the significance of Nelson's Medieval Texts which began in 1949, a series that by all the laws of history should have carried the Clarendon Press imprint. Such books Oxford would once have published as unremunerative, in the knowledge that if it did not, and Cambridge also declined, the books were unlikely to be published at all. Nelsons had discovered no secret formula to make them profitable. The Managing Director, H. P. Morrison, happened to be a dedicated scholar himself. Under new management and in more straitened times the series was recognized as anomalous and the Press gladly took possession. This was competition of an unusual kind. But the commercial publishers were hiring leading academics to edit series for them and tout for authors. Rival 'Histories of England' multiplied. Hutchinson's University Library, apparently gaining momentum in the early 1950s, was spreading confusion in the public mind as to what H.U.L. stood for. And, as Norrington wrote to Sisam in 1952, 'These high-class Pelicans are a real nuisance.' They were not only a nuisance but puzzling, for they seemed to prove despite all other evidence to the contrary that the general reader had not after all passed away. Moreover Oxford's strength in reference books and other 'popular' lines was being directly tested by Penguins. The price of Oxford books was about double the pre-war price, it could be pointed out, whereas Penguins had gone up from 6*d.* to 2*s.* 6*d.* But this argument carried little weight. Penguins and Pelicans were still cheap, whilst Oxford was in danger of getting a reputation for publishing only books that cost over £1. In 1960 a dozen Oxford Paperbacks appeared, six Clarendon Press and six Amen House titles. The first on the list was *The Roman Revolution* by Ronald Syme, originally published in 1939. It cost 15s. Overseas Education was also meeting increasingly fierce competition. It had long been accustomed to running neck and neck with Longmans, but Macmillans, Nelsons, and many other publishers were now participating, especially in the scramble for Africa.

One inevitable consequence of the education boom was more theses, the proliferation of which had already caused so much concern before the war. The peculiarly pernicious doctrine of 'publish or perish' harrowed the academic community in America, and to a considerable extent elsewhere. At the same time there was still nothing quite like the Clarendon Press imprint, it seemed to many aspiring academics, to guarantee rapid promotion: loyalty to their own university presses rarely deterred them from trying Oxford first. Amen House, the New York Business, and the branches dutifully passed on all the dissertations that came their way to Oxford, where they became and remained a serious problem. Sisam had insisted that to give the Clarendon Press imprint to dissertations was nothing short of 'passing off'. A long dispute with A. D. Lindsay had ended with a peremptory request that Sisam should never again, at least in Lindsay's hearing, say that by definition a thesis was not a book. Despite Sisam's and Chapman's sensibilities, the Delegates had long since recognized an obligation to publish the best of Oxford theses in the various series of faculty monographs, without, however, accepting full responsibility for them. They were published with the help of subsidies from the Board for Advanced Studies, and no royalty was paid. The final concession of defeat came in 1965, when the Oxford Historical Series became the Oxford Historical Monographs, the Press assuming full financial responsibility, paying a royalty as for any other book if sales seemed likely to justify one, and the word limit being lifted. The other faculty monographs were similarly freed of the stigma hitherto attached to them.

The rule against alien theses also had to be relaxed. The Press was forced to accommodate itself to the times when the commercial publishers discovered that, while the pedagogues were in the ascendancy and the libraries were taking a handsome share of university budgets, there was money to be made in academic publishing. It was in any case true that much original research was being done, and indeed major contributions to scholarship were being made, by the thesis writers. The Press was in danger of losing authors, of acquiring a reputation for arrogant elitism, even of not making its proper contribution to learning—though the object was to maintain standards. But it gave way grudgingly. The triumph of the thesis seemed to make a mockery of the old debate about teaching and research. The Ph.D. student did his research in the adolescence of his academic career, and as likely as not then vanished into the teaching fraternity never to be heard of again. Mature and articulate scholars remained as scarce as ever. The requirements of academic advancement forced many a good teacher to put pen to paper, even if every word he wrote were an affront to literature. The learned corrector at the University Press, who had served under and survived John Johnson, wrote of the theses of the 1950s, 'I was appalled by the slovenly writing and punctuation. . . . The new set of research students had never been drilled in linguistic accuracy—or indeed in exactitude of any kind.'

In 1954 Norrington was enticed away from the Press after thirty-one years to become President of Trinity College, Oxford. His successor, C. H. Roberts, Fellow of St. John's, classicist and papyrologist, had been a Delegate for eight years. His *Greek Literary Hands 350 B.C.–A.D. 400* was published in 1955, and he was one of the general editors of the Oxford Palaeographical Handbooks. During his twenty years as Secretary he saw the Press go through its most explosive period since the beginning of the century, and enter one of universal inflation and forecasts of doom. In the transition from one to another the Delegates recognized that their Secretary could no longer be expected to attend to the daily running of the Clarendon Press as well as oversee the business as a whole. He was set free to concentrate on his global responsibilities in 1970 in a transformation of the Secretarial office comparable with that of 1873 when Bartholomew Price had been put in charge of all the businesses. The diarchal constitution of the inter-war years had never been officially sanctioned.

In 1956 Geoffrey Cumberlege retired as London Publisher, only to be immediately recalled to duty in his old capacity as trouble-shooter. He reappeared as Vice-President in New York during a period of uneasy interregnum. His successor at Amen House was John (now Sir John) Brown, who like Cumberlege and Norrington had served his apprenticeship in India, joining Hawkins in Bombay in 1937. He was taken prisoner by the Japanese late in 1942, and eventually returned to Amen House as sales manager.

The tradition that London books carried the name of the London Publisher in their imprints, which went back to Macmillan, ended with the retirement of Cumberlege. It had become confusing, perhaps even provocative, lending weight to the view that the Delegates lacked control over an important part of their business. Milford had been able to stamp a certain authority on his publications by lending his name to them for so long, but there was no obvious justification for continuing the practice. As it was permissible for Amen House to publish works of a controversial nature it could also be argued that the Delegates, and the University itself, were sheltering a little cravenly behind their London agent.

Papyrology was the poorer for the defection of Colin Roberts—as no doubt it had been when John Johnson left the field—but he was drawn to the Press not only by the challenge of big business, an inclination towards which he had hitherto concealed from his colleagues, but by a deep and abiding interest in the Clarendon Press and the books it produced. He quickly entered into the spirit of the place by adopting a style of calligraphy not unlike that of Chapman when writing on trains. It was impossible to remain long in the Secretary's office without being steeped in tradition. Publication of the *Patristic Greek Lexicon* was an early and instructive experience. The project went back to 1906, when some eighty clergymen and others interested in patristic studies had started gathering materials. The involvement of T. B. Strong and William Sanday led to its acceptance in principle by the Delegates, though it was not to be published until after the revised Liddell & Scott, to which it would be a supplement. In 1918 specimen pages were set up, and again in 1930. In 1933 Chapman reported that the Lexicon was 'moving very slowly and liable to collapse', and a few years later Sisam was writing, 'the prospects are that it will not come in our time'. Milford, having met one of the more elderly contributors, felt confident that he would not live to finish 'his awful work'. But the slips were accumulating, and committees were regularly formed to sift through and revise the very uneven materials. Errors multiplied and the confusion grew worse. During the Second World War, however, with the revised Liddell & Scott published, Paul Maas brought his great learning to bear, other scholars advised and contributed, a new editor was appointed, and by 1946 the writing of the articles had begun in earnest. In 1950 bits of copy in an appalling state began to reach the Press. In 1956 Colin Roberts, himself a member of the sponsoring committee, still doubted whether the enterprise could ever be completed. Even so, in his capacity as a publisher, he felt it prudent to advise the editor and his assistants against reckless haste, for it would not do after so many years to publish anything far short of perfect. The Revd. Professor G. W. H. Lampe, then at Birmingham, eventually achieved what had appeared impossible, and called upon the Printer to do the same. As 'a very large work', Lampe wrote, 'consisting in the main of Greek citations and written in long-hand by different hands of various nationalities, repeatedly revised and corrected by yet other hands, [it] confronted the printer with what might seem to be an almost impossible task. The skill and care with which these difficulties have been overcome has been matched by the extraordinary vigilance and accuracy of the Press reader of page proofs, who has eliminated a great number of minor errors and inconsistencies.' The Lexicon appeared in five fascicles during the 1960s and, when complete in 1968, it made a volume of 1,616 pages.

Other ancient monuments of scholarship that engaged Colin Roberts's attention were the great series of *Codices Latini Antiquiores*, 'A Palaeographical Guide to Latin Manuscripts prior to the Ninth Century' edited by E. A. Lowe; *Early Muslim Architecture* by K. A. C. Creswell; and the second edition of Sir John Beazley's *Attic Red-Figure Vase-Painters*, which had to be hurried through the press in order to overtake the author, whose discoveries grew no less frequent with age. A most singular link with the past was Sir Harold Hartley who in 1968 delivered the copy for *Studies in the History of Chemistry*. It had been accepted by the Delegates in 1901, subject to approval of the finished manuscript. It was published seventy years later.

Eras could not be allowed to elapse without an Oxford Bible making news. The Authorized Version still held its own, but with each generation its language became more remote, less comprehensible. Chaplains, pastors, and teachers were finding that they had to translate it themselves into modern English as they went along in order to get the message across. At the first post-war Assembly of the Church of Scotland in 1946, a new translation 'in the language of the present day' was proposed. Anglicans, Methodists, Baptists, and Congregationalists welcomed the idea, and the Roman Catholics were represented by 'observers' later on. The two University Presses (Oxford and Cambridge) were brought in at an early stage, and by the time the Old Testament was published in 1970 they had invested about £1 million in the New English Bible.

The Joint Committee on the New Translation of the Bible began to meet regularly in 1948. Three translation panels were set up, responsible for the Old and New Testaments and the Apocrypha. Dr. C. H. Dodd was Director of the project throughout, and in 1965 Professor G. R. Driver was appointed Joint Director. It was emphasized from the start that this was to be a wholly new translation in both its scholarship and its presentation. A literary panel was formed to ponder the problems of style. Each book was entrusted to an individual scholar, who submitted a draft translation to be mauled by the translation panel. When fully amended, it was examined by the literary panel for elegance and lucidity. It was then returned to the original panel for a final check to ensure that the stylists had not changed the meaning. The New English Bible had somehow to be contemporary without falling into profanity. The literary panel hoped to combine plainness with dignity.

After fifteen years the New Testament was to be published on 14 March 1961. For nearly six months Neasden had been preparing for simultaneous publication all over the world. The last consignments to distant branches had gone out the previous December. At home publicity built up to an extraordinary degree. Public excitement was perhaps less spontaneous than eighty years earlier, but the media were alert to a great event. As the clocks of Neasden struck midnight to herald publication day the warehouse did not throw open its doors, no traffic jams built up on the North Circular. Even so, as the Neasden Manager recorded, 'publication day was almost a nightmare and one of mad excitement'. The nightmare grew worse. By 22 March the warehouse was out of stock.

It was as if the two Presses were determined not to repeat the mistake they had made with the Revised Version. The New English Bible was published first in two editions, a Library edition printed in Cambridge, and a Popular edition, smaller and cheaper, printed in Oxford. In January it was realized that the former was likely to run out before publication, and as the day approached deliveries became increasingly intermittent. When the Popular edition ran out too there was an awful hiatus which lasted throughout April. In an age of advanced technology, organized labour, and more refined management techniques it was impossible to respond

U

instantly, as Horace Hart could and would have done. Moreover an immediate supply of raw materials could not be depended upon. By the end of the year there was a shortage of goats, and the morocco-bound edition was not available.

So Frowde's record of a million copies in a day remained intact. Nevertheless the Bible was again big business and, when the Old Testament was published in 1970, some seven million copies of the New Testament had been printed. The New English Bible was accepted to be read in churches, and was much used in schools. The criticism was as foreseen. The translators had achieved plainness but too often lost their dignity. Modern English could not easily be made to soar, and passages which in the Authorized Version reverberated as if with the authentic voice of truth disintegrated into bathos and banality. Holy writ it was not, to some. Few were in a position to question its scholarship.

The New York Business was responsible for manufacturing the American edition of the complete Bible in 1970 on behalf of both Oxford and Cambridge. By the end of the year a million copies had been printed. The Bible business in the United States was thriving more than ever. Between the appearance of the New Testament and the complete New English Bible the Press had also published The New Scofield Reference Bible (1967), and The Oxford Annotated Bible (1965) using the Revised Standard Version, and was able to cater for all denominations.

During the post-war boom, which lasted for nearly twenty years, the Press had opportunities to contract but was in a mood to expand. It could have closed down the Paper-Mill in 1954 when the machine installed in 1899 was coming to the end of its natural life. Instead it was decided to install a new machine at a cost of about £1,000,000, including the building to house it. Paper was still in short supply. When the new Mill went into production in 1957 the economic situation was changing and imports from Scandinavia were soon to deprive the Mill of its share in the general prosperity.

At Neasden a seven-storey office and computer building opened in 1965. The computer itself was a startling innovation. It was held to be in advance of its time, but to those accustomed to getting information from genial men with ledgers it seemed remote if not hostile. In 1962 the first rumours were heard of a threat to Amen House. The Old Bailey extension was moving in its direction, and demolition was to be its destiny. The destiny of those who worked there remained uncertain for a long time. Some moved to Neasden, and the possibility of banishment to that remote suburb troubled all those who remained. Not only was it remote: the new office block singularly lacked the elegance and atmosphere of the seventeenth-century mansion to which they were accustomed. A move was bound to be painful, but when it came at last in 1966 it was to Ely House in Dover Street, one of the finest surviving eighteenth-century mansions in central London. It had been built as the town house of the Bishop of Ely by Sir Robert Taylor, architect of the Bank of England and founder by bequest of the Taylorian Institute in Oxford. Though the departure from Amen House was sorrowful it involved no loss of architectural status. After ten years, when it was time to move on, the London business had made itself very much at home there.

In Oxford both the Printer and the publishing staff needed more space. Nothing much had been done in Walton Street since the mid 1920s. By 1966 it seemed clear that the architect had made a mistake in adopting the quadrangular plan. What little sense it had originally made had been lost with the unification of the Bible and Learned Presses. An extension west into Jericho was approved and the Printer acquired another 100,000 square feet of floor space. The upper floors of the south wing were converted into offices for the publishing business. Later the upper floor of the north wing, where the Printer's readers once sat, was occupied by the academic publishing staff as well.

There was still not room for everybody, and the Press spilled out into other habitations. The Cartographic Department occupied 37A St. Giles'. In a couple of semi-detached Victorian 'villas' round the corner in Walton Crescent were two other important satellites: at No. 41, Miss Laura Salt worked on *The Oxford Junior Encyclopaedia* and other children's reference books, and at No. 40 nothing less than a new 'Scriptorium' had been created. R. W. Burchfield, a New Zealander, was editing the *O.E.D. Supplement*. From there too came new editions of *C.O.D.*, *P.O.D.*, and *L.O.D.*, not to mention the *Oxford Illustrated Dictionary* and *The Oxford Dictionary of English Etymology*. The plates of *S.O.E.D.* being at last worn out the entire work had to be reset: all the proofs were corrected by Mrs. Jessie Coulson, who had worked on the original edition. She also compiled the *Little Oxford Dictionary*, and translated the Russian novelists in her spare time.

The Supplement itself was to be in four large volumes. Burchfield had been recruiting outside readers and appealing to the public at large through the *Periodical*. He had built up a staff of eighteen in Walton Crescent, and it was well known that there remained a team in Oxford monitoring and hoarding the language from wherever in the world English was spoken or written. Many had been playing havoc with it since Murray's day, not least James Joyce, and those who aped him. It was very much alive but living perhaps too riotously and many words were destined for an untimely end. They would find their resting-place in the Supplement, with the help of which future generations might be able to grapple with the English of the twentieth century.

By 1967—in which year the most fashionable word was *psychedelic*—copy for the first volume of the Supplement, A–Gyver, was reaching the Printer. It was eventually published, 1,356 pages, in 1972. The previous year the entire *O.E.D.* had been published in a 'compact' edition, the text reproduced micrographically, so that the thirteen volumes appeared as two: a reading glass was supplied. The *Compact* won the Carey-Thomas

Award for the best example of creative publishing of the year. Later the same technique was applied to the *D.N.B.*

Meanwhile work was continuing on the *Oxford Russian–English Dictionary*, the *English–Arabic Dictionary*, and on the *Oxford Latin Dictionary*, the first fascicle of which, A–B, was published in 1968. This ambitious project had been conceived by Sisam in 1929, the intention being to produce the first genuinely original Latin–English dictionary, based on a fresh and thorough reading of all the sources. Previous dictionaries, including Lewis & Short, had been largely translated or adapted from continental dictionaries, themselves in part derivative. The new Dictionary was to be completed in eight fascicles: not surprisingly, it was slow work. At a time when some major publishing projects, which turned into small 'industries', appeared to be sponsored by academic bodies in order to keep expensively qualified scholars employed and to consume available funds, the Press persevered with its old commitments, still without endowment and still with little prospect of immediate reward.

Some of the multi-volume 'Series' proceeded haltingly; the Oxford Histories of Modern Europe, of English Literature, of English Art, of Music, made progress of a sort, and major works of scholarship appeared, but scholars were no less prone to distraction, misadventure, or sloth than they had always been and the end could rarely be said to be in sight. Titles appeared on the Clarendon Press list which suggested that the distinction between London and Oxford was becoming ever more blurred: Winifred Gérin's biographies of the Brontës, Peter and Iona Opie's *Lore and Language of School Children*, might once have been classed as 'general' books. In London, the Oxford Standard Authors and a new series of Oxford English Novels appeared as Oxford Paperbacks, but irrespective of the publishing department from which they originated Oxford Paperbacks seemed to be bought by the same breed of student purchaser. This drawing together of the two businesses was perceptible in the 1960s, though the Oxford English Texts, Classical Texts, Medieval, and Early Christian Texts were still easily identifiable as Clarendon Press books. Equally nobody could mistake the Clarendon Dickens, with its massive scholarly apparatus, for the Oxford Illustrated Dickens, the standard London edition.

By 1967 Overseas Education had been superseded by E.L.T. (English Language Teaching) and T.B.D. (Tutorial Books Department). The former continued to extend the old O.E. list of dictionaries, general adult courses in English, and specially prepared courses for particular areas overseas. New linguistic skills were acquired, and more experimental projects pursued with audio-visual and other advanced techniques. Textbooks had a way of going out of date more rapidly than formerly—partly as a result of competition— and some that had for long appeared quite harmless might suddenly display symptoms of a malign neo-colonialism which had to be treated immediately. The European market became increasingly important, but for two decades the demand for school-books made Africa the most coveted market. The New Oxford English Course, variously adapted, sold in large quantities. The emergence of state monopoly publishing houses, and the adoption of the Protocol to the Berne Copyright Convention, under which the developing nations could relax their copyright laws to allow publication without permission of works for educational purposes, appeared to bode ill. But the principle was that quality would count in the end. It could be pointed out that the fastest growing and most important market for British books was the country which also had the most developed publishing industry, the United States. The Oxford Library of African Literature and Oxford Studies in African Affairs were scholarly and unremunerative Clarendon Press series which reflected the interest in Africa. A part of E.L.T. removed to Colchester and established a language laboratory.

The market for academic books remained buoyant until the end of the 1960s. It was possible to reprint the old slow-selling Clarendon Press books and to sell them swiftly to the new libraries, as the numerous reprint houses which flourished during the period had shown. The series of 'Oxford Reprints' was launched in the mid 1960s to meet this demand and to counter the activities of the upstarts. In 1969 the 'Reprints' included Wright's *Dialect Dictionary* (at £50), Simpson's *Shakespearian Punctuation* (1911), A. C. Clark's *Descent of Manuscripts* (1918), seven books on Africa by R. S. Rattray published between 1913 and 1932, two books by Charles Williams, and Jacobsthal's *Early Celtic Art*. All appeared to pinpoint some significant moment in the history of the modern Press.

4. The Waldock Report

DURING the years of prosperity the Press expanded everywhere and more rapidly than ever before, often as a result of individual initiatives, particularly by branch managers, and of the strengthening of what Gell had been first to call 'middle management'. But the vastness and complexity of the enterprise was troubling even when business was good. There was a danger of fragmentation, of galloping autonomy, of things slipping out of control. The centre might not hold. Rationalization of some sort would perhaps after all be necessary if the senior officers were themselves to remain rational. Consultants and analysts were summoned, though the patient in most respects appeared to be in rude health.

Organization and reorganization committees sat, and planners moved in upon the Clarendon Press itself. The filing system, invented by the supreme rationalist Cannan in 1902, was rationalized. The main office was partitioned off, and what had always been called, and still was called, the 'office' finally lost its singularity. The fire no longer burned in the grate and the smell of printer's ink was kept at a distance. Major changes appeared to be afoot, and the words of Chapman echoed inevitably across the decades: 'Efficiency is one thing, and the *ethos* of a business is another.' Departments of the Press were jealous of their individuality, which might be threatened by change of any kind.

The University itself appeared to be passing through another crisis of doubt, ready to deliver itself up and stretch out on the analyst's couch. The Commission of Inquiry into the University conducted by Lord Franks began its work during the period of affluence, but by 1967 the time had perhaps come for cautious retrenchment. There were signs of a creeping inflation. That year began the most comprehensive inquiry into the Press ever attempted, with the appointment of a Committee under the chairmanship of Professor Sir Humphrey Waldock, an international lawyer, 'to investigate the function, organization, and operations of the University Press and its relationship to the University'. The Committee of five included a former Secretary to the Syndics of the Cambridge University Press and the Senior Managing Director of Lazard Brothers & Co. Ltd., merchant bankers. The Waldock Report, a document of 184 pages, was eventually published in 1970. It was itself a product of the Franks Report, published in 1966, a work of 946 pages in two volumes printed at the Press and at the Delegates' expense. The Franks Commission had found it impossible to bring the Press within its terms of reference, but had recommended a full inquiry into it. Both reports were, in the view of D. M. Davin, 'symptoms of a penitential navel-gazing, hair-shirt, apologetic, prostrate defeatism that was rife in Oxford just when it should have been either fierce in counter-attack or keeping its head down'.

The work of the Committee was endured without that profound sense of injustice, wringing of hands, and outraged dignity with which Chapman and Milford had faced a much less stringent inquisition. At least nobody was being accused of lack of vigilance, and there was no talk of impeachment. But it took up a lot of time. Evidence was sought from other university presses, from commercial publishers, from all the University faculties, from business men, even authors, but the only people who could supply the essential information about the history and functions of the Press were those in charge of it. Inevitably the preparation and the writing of the Report depended on their co-operation, and their willingness to interpret and explain facts which did not speak for themselves.

Meanwhile the economic climate worsened and there were symptoms of crisis. In 1968 students rioted in France and the United States, starting an epidemic of unrest. Far from contributing to productivity students seemed bent on destroying the liberal society that had spawned them. Public opinion turned sullen towards the spoilt children of the age, and governments frowned nervously on their tantrums. If expenditure had to be cut the universities would be among the first to feel the pinch. Inflation was no longer creeping but had broken into a brisk trot.

It always seemed impossible to Gell to make the Delegates realize how big the business was. By 1970 the Delegates had a shrewd idea of its immensity, but the first assumption of the Committee was that nobody else had. Its size had to be stressed from the start. It was publishing some 850 new titles a year; the current catalogue listed about 17,000 items; Neasden carried some 3 million volumes; it distributed 17 million books annually; the turnover of the Press as a whole was well in excess of £10 million per annum. 'Owing to the reticence which surrounds its affairs', its true nature and magnitude were, in the opinion of the Committee, 'very imperfectly known to anyone in the University outside the Delegates.' Yet the Press was comparable in importance to the University itself and, 'inasmuch as the products of the Press come into the hands of literally millions of people who may otherwise have little or no knowledge of or connection with Oxford, the international reputation of the University in practice resides to a very considerable degree in the hands of the officers of the Press'.

How far, if at all, should growth continue? There were clearly three choices: the Press could be stabilized at its present size; it could contract; or it could continue to expand and diversify. The Waldock Report came down firmly in favour of the last course. It did so partly because the Committee accepted that any business had to grow if it were not to stagnate. More particularly it was concerned with the mergers and take-overs which had recently caused many small publishing businesses to disappear or to be absorbed in large conglomerates. To maintain its relative position in British publishing the Press was compelled to go on getting bigger. Moreover it was in the interests of both Oxford and the country that it should continue to expand its activities overseas, 'not simply because of the possible financial rewards but because of the benefit to the spread of British culture and influence'. The possibility of standing still was not seriously considered, and the idea of contraction was summarily dismissed. The Committee had been told by the President of the Publishers Association that 'any suggestion that Oxford should withdraw from general book publishing or from publishing overseas, would be calamitous and contrary to the national interest'.

To many members of the O.U.P., especially those remote from Oxford, the Committee's long deliberations on the constitutional relationship between the Press and the University seemed esoteric. A powerful recommendation to contract, or retrench, supported by Little Pressites in Congregation, might have made them seem less so, but on most major issues of policy the Committee appeared only to be endorsing what had already been done and could not be undone. It accepted of necessity the historical accidents and bouts of individual initiative that had created the modern Press. The Music Department had grown into the second largest music publisher in the country, and it was too late to ask how or why. Children's books on the other hand might be a little questionable, not the most obviously appropriate way of engaging the energies of a university press. Being assured that they were the very best of their kind, and that imaginative literature for children was not without a fundamental place in education, the Committee conceded the Department's right to exist. It also endorsed the reasoning behind the Delegates' decision to expand and modernize the printing works at a time when the University Printer was doing less than half of the printing required by the home publishing departments, and to re-equip the Mill at Wolvercote in 1954 even though by the late 1960s what had been a seller's market had become a highly competitive buyer's market and the Mill had fallen upon hard times. It sanctioned the existence of the New York Business, which 'more than any other section, exemplifies the paradox of O.U.P.'s publishing'. Like the smallest of the overseas branches, its declared primary function was the stocking and sale of Oxford and London books. The Cambridge University Press had demonstrated that in order to fulfil a function of that kind it was not necessary to grow into a large indigenous publishing house. However, given the original decision to allow branches to publish on their own account, it was easy for the Committee to see how it had happened. And finally it stressed once again the importance to the Press of maintaining the 'image' of a 'non-profit-distributing' business. Any resumption of payments to the University would restrict its ability to finance itself, and lead in the end to periodic demands on the University for support 'of a quite unwelcome size'. Or else there would soon be fewer unremunerative books, which would be even more damaging to the reputation of the Press.

The relationship between Oxford and London had always been obscure to the uninitiated. But in 1970 it seemed that a once clear demarcation of boundaries was being eroded by a change in the habits of the book-buying public. The Report summarized the dilemma as explained to them by the Secretary. There was 'a demand for books at what may perhaps be termed a "popular learned" level (and of this college textbooks form a particular genre), while at the same time the rewards of "general trade publishing" may be declining. In the past the London Publisher could aim at a particular kind of "generally cultivated reader", who could be presumed to have a wide if perhaps somewhat amateurish knowledge of, and interest in, many subjects. It seems that such readers are becoming rarer, and the buyer of books today is likely to be at once more professional in his attitude to what he reads—often in the sense that he is or has been a student of the subject at degree level—and at the same time to lack the kind of general cultural background which could formerly be taken for granted.' So the old categories were less easy to apply. General books were becoming more academic, or being made more academic in appearance by the need for explanatory notes; academic books, on the other hand, might be prescribed for study in universities, and so achieve a sale hitherto expected only from general books. 'In the long run, then, the distinction between "learned" and "general" books may become very blurred or even disappear altogether.' The Report made no recommendation on this complex issue. In fact the monographs issuing from the Clarendon Press were, inevitably, becoming ever more specialized.

The Report did in the end make thirty-eight 'recommendations'. These were not intended as criticisms of the management but rather as 'proposals for continuing a process of modernization and rationalization of the Press already in progress'. It was indeed in a state of flux, and by 1970 it was exceedingly difficult for either the Committee or the Press itself to determine which changes would have occurred anyway, and which had been initiated, stimulated, or hastened by the inquiry.

The most important recommendations concerned the Delegacy, Finance Committee, and relations with the University. The number of Delegates was increased from ten to fifteen—three to be appointed by Council and twelve by the General Board of Faculties. They were to hold office for six years (later reduced to five years, but with the possibility of re-election for a further term), and the concept of perpetuity was to be abandoned. The Perpetual Delegates at the time were Professors G. E. Blackman and Sir John Hicks, Sir Maurice Bowra, Dame Helen Gardner, and Dr. J. H. C. Thompson, Chairman of Finance Committee. The full Board, including the four *ex officio* Delegates (the University 'Assessor' now counting as one), would thus consist of nineteen members. It seemed to the Committee that the activities of the Press had become far too large and complex for the Delegates to exercise full control. Their work was thought to be largely confined to selecting Clarendon Press titles for publication, and in practice responsibility for the business as a whole had devolved almost entirely on Finance Committee, described as the equivalent of a Board of Directors. As such it needed strengthening. It was recommended that six members should be appointed by the Delegates from among themselves, that five executive officers of the Press should become full members (hitherto some had always been 'in attendance', including the Secretary), and that an outside member with a wide knowledge of business and finance should be appointed. For the first time since Bartholomew Price, the chairman was to be remunerated. Within the Press a new post was to be created, that of 'Assistant Secretary (Finance)'.

Something had to be done about the 'extreme reticence' of the Press. A start could be made by publishing a rather fuller report of its activities, and by shedding some of the secrecy that had always shrouded its finances. This had been justified in the past on the ground that it was unwise to give away information to competitors. The Committee had a suspicion that fear of provoking interference from the University had also contributed to it. A more intimate and candid relationship was recommended, even to the extent of exposing to Congregation an abstract of the accounts more revealing than business prudence had previously allowed. Information must be made to flow in all directions. To this end the Faculties were invited to appoint liaison officers, with no clearly defined functions, but presumably to act rather as lock-keepers and to control the flow.

The Clarendon Press naturally came under the closest scrutiny, as the department most closely related to the University. One recommendation was that a system of forward budgeting should be applied, and a method of accounting that treated as a cost any losses deliberately incurred on unremunerative books. This led to a sophisticated elaboration of the form devised by William Markby in 1892 and long forgotten. The paperwork had to be done in the office, however, and not by individual Delegates.

The office itself had seemed to the Committee to be pitifully under-manned. The work, if not beyond the strength of the existing staff, imposed demands that could ultimately impair efficiency, allowing an editor too little time to foster the illusion comforting to authors that a particular book is the editor's exclusive concern. It would be a fitting contribution to learning, the Report suggested, if the Clarendon Press were more generously staffed. A staff of three to cover the whole area of science publishing was clearly inadequate. This was a major issue. The sales value of all scientific publications in 1967 was barely half that of the sales of children's books, and the Press failed 'to reflect at all correctly the image of the present-day University', in which two out of every five members of the academic community were scientists. In fact, plans already existed to increase the staff as quickly as the Printer's extension made new office space available, and the development of scientific publishing was being given first priority.

The actual effects of the Report were hard to calculate. To some extent it prevailed over better judgement, urging acceleration when prudence dictated application of the brakes. Virtually all the recommendations were adopted, or had already been adopted by the time it was published. A concerted attempt had been made to modernize and rationalize the Press, to apply 'Commercial Standards'—and there was certainly more financial expertise available than ever before. The Press changed, but so too did everything else in the three years spent planning for a future that never came. The year the Report was finally made public, the profits of the Press as a whole fell by 75 per cent. It was committed to a policy of expansion when the market was contracting in convulsive spasms: student enrolments were dropping, educational budgets being slashed, and inflation galloping. Spokesmen, tired of referring to the worst crisis since the war, or since the Great Depression, were searching for more lurid parallels in the collapse of the Weimar Republic, the Black Death, or in the Roman Empire of the third century when inflation had last afflicted a whole civilization. The Chief Rabbi announced it to be the worst crisis since the Flood. The modern Press could now count its crises in twenty-five-year cycles. The last two had left those who had to sit them out with little room to manœuvre; but patience and courage had been rewarded. This time it was by no means certain that they would be, and a vast paraphernalia of administrative techniques was brought into play as the experts within and corporate planners from without battled to hold the dikes through which cash flowed and did not flow back. No one man could take the place of all the committees necessary to reorganize the Press and ensure survival. Editors, who believed themselves to be in the front line, winced and flinched from the artillery barrage that went over their heads, from a new terminology and a new proliferation of forms. Unremunerative books were still accepted by the Delegates, but in a spirit of hopeful defiance. And for a time the numbers were limited by budgetary considerations. The price of books brought another change in the habits of the book-buying public: it made determined efforts to give the habit up, rather than see the children starve. Librarians who would once have bought six copies of a book made do with one.

The Waldock Report was only a start, as it turned out, and there was still much to be done. The Press had entered a new era. And inevitably to some of those who joined it in those difficult years it seemed that in the pre-Waldock age it must have been in a state of medieval muddle, at its lowest ebb, with doddering Perpetual Delegates sipping tea whilst the federation of businesses stumbled in the dark, lacking management structures, decision-making machinery, information-flow; with uninstructed middle-management attitudes, and no forward planning or administrative disciplines. A sorry business it must have been. The reaction was traditional enough. Breaks in continuity give rise to such imaginings. It may even have been thought that the dead-lift which heaved the Press into modern times would never need to be done again. But as new departments multiplied, and the new recruits braced themselves for the new era, one imponderable question remained unanswered. How, in the past, had so much been achieved by so few? The ghost of C. E. Doble, self-effacing as the man himself, stalked only at night.

5. Reorganization: Relocation

THE business righted itself in the end, emerging from the nadir of 1974–5 during which it dipped deeply into the ancestral hoards (if only in the form of an overdraft, for the ancestral credit was still good) into the brave new world fashioned for it by the planners and a crumbling economy. The major transformation of the Press in the 1970s was not attributable, however, either to the Waldock Report or to the economic crisis. In 1968 the Delegates had approved the creation of a Joint Management Committee consisting of senior officers from the home departments to consider problems of common interest. It was to meet monthly, alternately in London and Oxford, and a representative from New York was to attend at least once a quarter. The Delegates had told the Committee of Inquiry that 'greater unification' of the business would be beneficial, and this was the first step towards realizing that aim. The Committee, pursuing this concept to its logical conclusion, considered the next step. It was neither possible nor desirable to move the Clarendon Press to London. The alternative would mean abandoning a policy boldly and profitably pursued for over a hundred years. The Committee was gravely apprehensive about the 'dangers attendant upon a move away from the capital'. It was true that other publishers were leaving, as the book printers had done in the previous century. Macmillans, through whom the O.U.P. had made its first appearance on the metropolitan scene, was gone to Basingstoke. And there were obvious advantages of organizational convenience in having both publishing departments under one roof. On the other hand, as the Committee pointed out, there were less tangible considerations, such as the need to preserve that 'vital spirit of initiative' which had characterized the London Business and done so much to make the Press what it was. Moreover a close involvement in the world of general publishing was a source of strength, which might be lost in Oxford's cloisters, and although those in London retained a sense of being 'different' from other publishers, rivalry induced a healthy commercial spirit. Ely House itself was admittedly a problem. It was a London residence of which any bishop might be proud, and it made a handsome shop front, but it was strange accommodation from which to administer effectively a large modern business. From a utilitarian point of view it was not much of an improvement on Amen Corner. For that reason a move to more conventional premises might eventually be necessary. But the Waldock Committee could not bring itself to recommend a move to Oxford. Frowde, Milford, Cumberlege, and Brown had represented Oxford to the world at large, which knew little or nothing of that shadowy eminence, the Secretary, let alone the Delegates. A return to Oxford might be a return to obscurity.

But powerful centripetal forces were at work. The administrative pressures on the Secretary had been relieved by the appointment of the Oxford Publisher, and also of a Finance Director as the 'Assistant Secretary (Finance)' came to be called. In 1974, C. H. Roberts retired and was succeeded by G. B. Richardson, an economist and Fellow of St. John's and a Delegate since 1971. There was by now something archaic about the very title of 'Secretary' standing alone: 'Secretary and Chief Executive' seemed more appropriate to the times, and a more accurate description of the role.

It had once been said that Frowde had a far heavier burden to carry than was wholesome. By the 1970s the three responsibilities of the London Publisher—London publishing, distribution, and supervision of the branches—had all become vastly more complex. As they were divided into three parts already it was logical to reorganize them along existing lines and to create three separate divisions. The Waldock Report had mooted the possibility of a 'Branch' department in London. This became the International Division based in Oxford. At the same time a U.K. Publishing Services Division was created, responsible for distribution, sales, and production. London's publishing activities were conducted by the General Division. Meanwhile the Clarendon Press became the Academic Division, which included scientific and medical books, college textbooks, and reference books, but not school-books. They were the concern of the new Education Division, which also absorbed into itself the progeny of Overseas Education. The Music Department and Children's Books were part of the General Division, but the former defied assimilation to the extent of remaining in London.

The next step, from which the Committee of Inquiry had flinched, was finally announced in 1973. The case for establishing a single publishing organization in one place appeared overwhelming. The Press had sprawled enough. In 1922 Finance Committee had expressed concern about the emotional problems to which the move from Amen Corner to Amen House might give rise. In 1970 the Waldock Report had warned of damage to morale if the next move were carried out. In 1977 the traumatic consequences of impending deportation to the provinces had to be faced. Many valued members of the Press in London chose not to make the change.

A second south wing went up in Walton Street, so that all could be joined together on the site that had once been the Printer's sole preserve. Vivian Ridler, who as Printer to the University had for twenty years maintained the standards to which Hart had aspired, found a whole new office block arising on top of the machine rooms of the old Bible Press. The move was scheduled for 1976; in November of that year the 'Roberts' Building was opened, and the migrants moved in. The London Business to all intents and purposes ceased to exist. The Clarendon Press had quietly disappeared too: it remained only as an imprint. The five new divisions between them employed as many people as the two manufacturing departments put together.

The second volume of the *O.E.D. Supplement* took the language from H and 'the screaming habdabs' to 'nyumyum', *rare*, for 'yum-yum'. Soon a man on a ladder was observed above the portals in Walton Street and the words 'Oxford University Press' were inscribed in letters of bronze for all to see. After 150 years of daunting anonymity if had finally put aside its reticence.

X

INDEX

The O.U.P. at large

- • Branch
- ▲ Office
- ○ Closed

Toronto
New York
San Francisco
Mexico City
Buenos Aires

Glasgow
Belfast
Accra